WEST AFRICAN COMBS

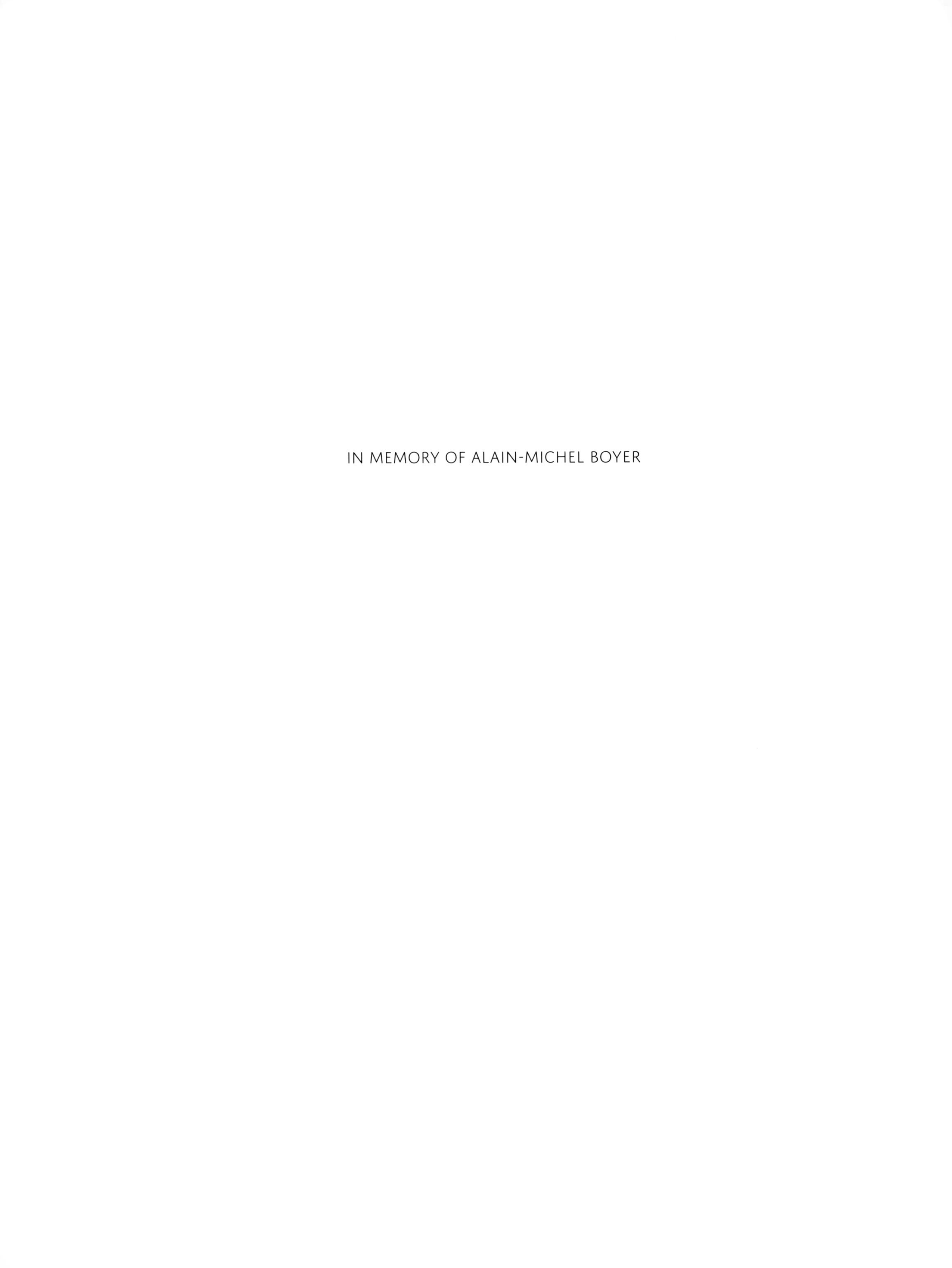

IN MEMORY OF ALAIN-MICHEL BOYER

WEST AFRICAN COMBS

MINA & SAMIR BORRO COLLECTION

EDITED BY NAJWA BORRO, SARAH BOUKAMEL,
FAOUZI BORRO, AND VALENTINE PLISNIER

WITH AN ESSAY BY ALAIN-MICHEL BOYER

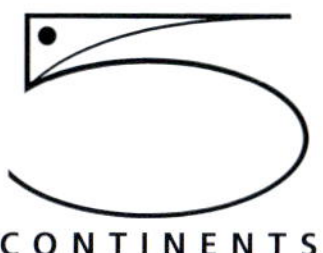

CONTINENTS

Contents

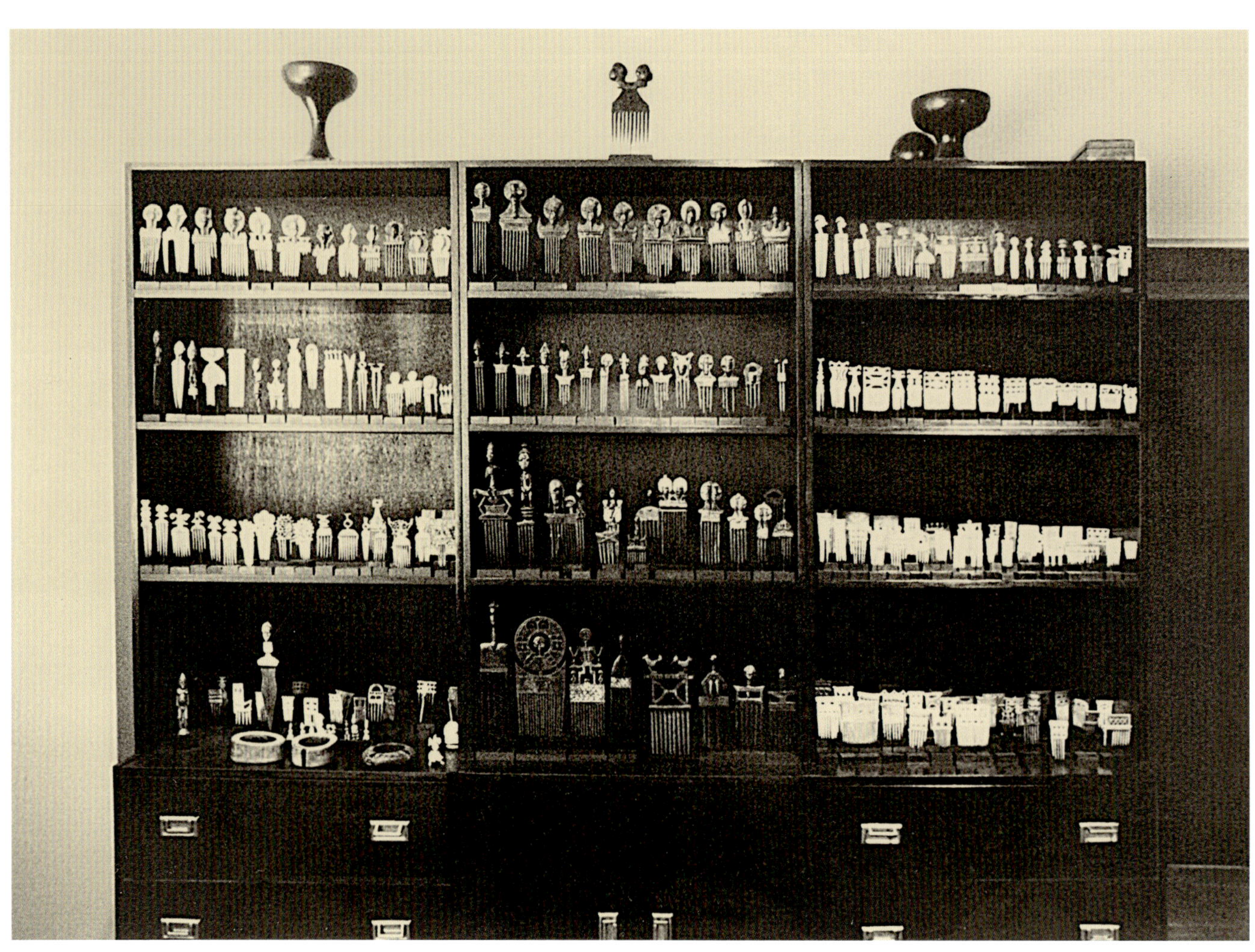

Foreword

François Neyt

Was it our first meeting? I don't know. It was a day of rejoicing in an idyllic setting: Nathalie and Guy Porré were celebrating their wedding. Around the table sat Samir and Mina Borro, Colette Delbecque, a lifelong friend, and myself. Colette and I had just finished a book on the Songye, a people living in the heart of the African continent and whose sense of the sacred was to be highlighted later in the Palatine Chapel in Naples. Three of us were born and grew up in Africa: Samir in Abidjan, Mina in Casablanca, and myself in Likasi, in Congo. Our identities had been profoundly shaped by the traditions of Africa, its exuberant nature, its smells, its sounds, its colours, the temperaments of the men and women we met. Yes, we had a passion for Africa, a shared fascination.

When I was a teenager I felt God calling, urging me to enter into the mystery of His creation. I became a Benedictine monk and submitted my PhD thesis at the Catholic University of Louvain, in 1969. After this, I initially returned to Africa to teach in Lubumbashi. I was later offered the Chair in African Arts and Culture. Preparing the courses was hard work, and I felt the need to get out, to meet and become acquainted with this population, in all its myriad aspects. I tried to get to grips with their mindset and slowly came to understand the spiritual nature of their masks, effigies, and celebrations. Intrigued by ancestor statues, I travelled across Hemba territory and, thanks to some photos I was given, I met some people in Kongolo who collected statues. They pointed me in the right direction and put me in touch with local village chiefs. The result was my first important publication on African art: *La grande statuaire hemba du Zaïre*, published in 1977.

I returned to Belgium and was elected my monastery's superior. The Catholic University of Louvain offered me the Chair in African Art as the successor of professor Albert Maesen of Tervuren Museum. Twenty years later, I moved to Paris and continued my research, combining my spiritual vocation with my interest in sculpture. After organising the *Fleuve Congo* exhibition at the Musée du quai Branly in 2010, I was asked to write a book on Ivory Coast. At this point I pinned down three topics to examine: exploring Baule lagoons, forests, towns, and villages; witnessing the Akan Yam Festival, the performers all bedecked in gold; and attending weddings and baptisms. All these things are a source of life and they transformed me. On my return to Brussels, I had occasion to reinforce my friendship with Mina and Samir Borro. My work on *Trésors de Côte d'Ivoire*, published in 2014, which I have often compared to an initiatory adventure, went well beyond straightforward scientific research. I wrote in that book's introduction that 'the art in Ivory Coast, more than elsewhere [...], was for me an apprenticeship in the beautiful and the sublime, the fearsome and the unknown. Every certainty melted away before a fresh discovery: it was a real initiatory journey, an encouragement to remain humble and to forge ahead ever further. Such are the requirements in the quest for beauty, such too are the discoveries of meaning, goodness, and what permeates the human.' During the course of long and regular work meetings over several years, generally on Saturdays, Samir and Mina Borro shared their knowledge with me, giving me access to their

Mina and Samir Borro's comb collection in their New York flat, 1981

work and their records. Through their discernment and the variety in their collection, which consists of unique pieces or categories assembled over decades – categories that often made it possible to appreciate the distinctiveness of each individual object – I discovered the incomparable beauty of numerous West African masterpieces. Samir described to me the meaning underlying a stunning Ndoma portrait-mask; he showed me sculptures of mystical spouses I knew nothing about and figurines of spirits of nature. Later, he revealed to me statues covered in gold leaf, drum-shaped Akan ornaments, portraits of the Attie queen, Koulango figurines, a gold Akan crown from Ghana, and many other wonders. Not to be outdone, Mina took me to see their collection of Senufo works and was especially proud to show me a huge anthropo-zoomorphic mask combining a crocodile's jaws and body, long multicoloured horns, and birds' beaks. I bade them goodbye with all those marvellous works and astonishing forms fresh in my mind's eye. Both friends became figures I knew I could always turn to: Mina because of her courage and her noble, pugnacious character; Samir for his determination, enthusiasm, and astonishing perspicacity. Both have an unrivalled knowledge of these peoples and, with their typical generosity and humility, they have always been delighted to share it with art lovers, collectors, curators, and friends in all walks of life. Thus, Jacques Kerchache, whose vision of art and approach to creating a collection they felt particularly close to, wrote in their visitors' book, thirty years after first meeting them in Abidjan, that all those years of friendship, enthusiasm, love, 'emotions, [...] suffering and happiness, [...] risks, adventures, [...], misgivings, [...] and apprenticeship [made it possible] to show and demonstrate that all the world's masterpieces are created free and equal'.

Mina and Samir Borro in Paris, 1979

Imbued as they are with modesty and goodwill, Samir and Mina are discreet people motivated by an insatiable curiosity and filled by unlimited cordiality. Their story springs from a profound joy expressed in their enduring happiness and in the family they have built. Their collection is a treasure trove that has been an invaluable and ever-accessible resource for research projects and exhibitions alike. It showcases several masterpieces, to be sure, but it also contains numerous examples of various categories of object painstakingly chosen over a period of more than sixty years, such as the most extraordinary West African combs, pulleys, and music hammers, among others.

Comb
Baule, Akan, Ivory Coast
Ivory, red pigments
13 × 4.5 cm

Provenance
Charles Ratton, 1979

Publication
Antoine Ferrari de la Salle, *Le Taureau qui aime les masques d'hommes. Regards sur Samir Borro*, Oser Dire Éditions, Bruxelles, Beyrouth, 2018, p. 75

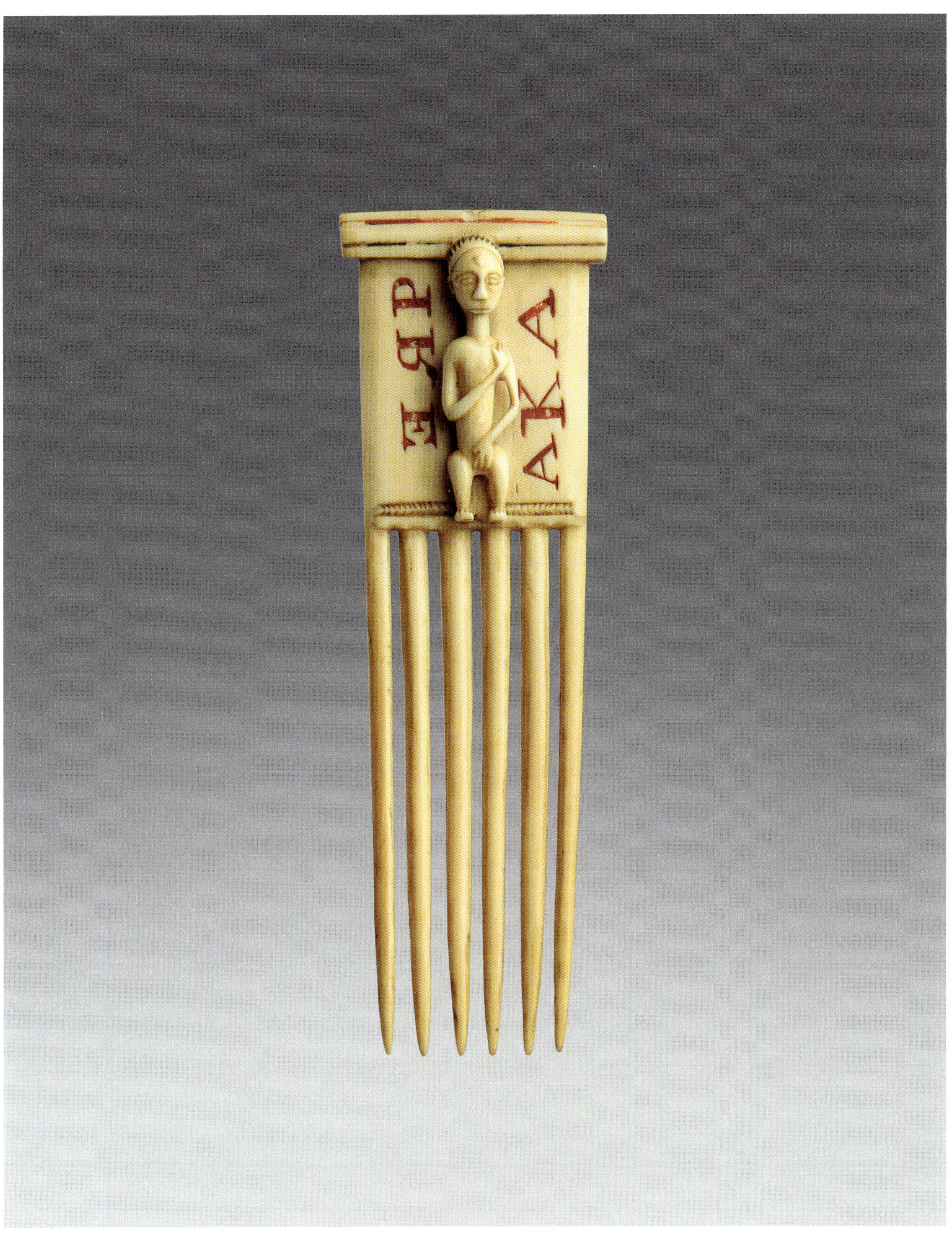

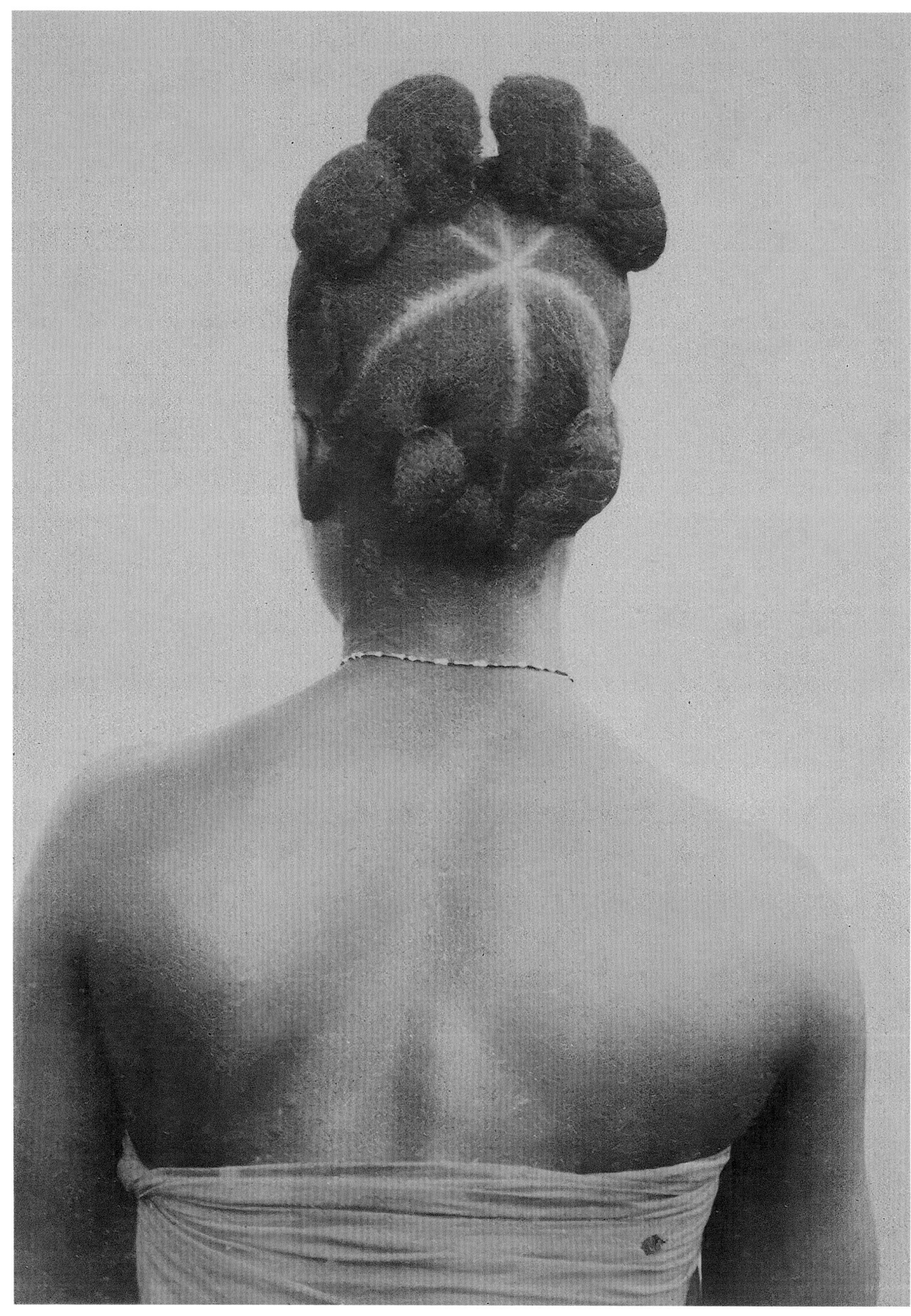

Introduction: From Ordinary Combs to the Ornamental Combs of West Africa

Valentine Plisnier and Najwa Borro

In 1999, the exhibition titled Hair in *African Art and Culture* at the Museum for African Art, in New York, explored the cultural, social, spiritual, and aesthetic importance of hair and hairstyles in certain African societies. It illustrated how hair could become a marker of identity, social status, power, and even spirituality. Discussing the handling of hair obviously includes considering the tools used in giving it shape, and combs are among the most fundamental, from both a practical and symbolic point of view.

In 2013, the exhibition titled *Origins of the Afro Comb: 6000 Years of Culture, Politics and Identity*, held at the Fitzwilliam Museum in Cambridge (UK), reviewed a history stretching over thousands of years. Whether signs of rank or part of a dowry, some of these objects go beyond their primary function – to comb hair – and become miniature sculptures matching the aesthetic aspirations of the greatest African statues. This book aims to show how everyday objects can be carved and modelled by skilled craftsmen into fine articles of hair adornment. Their efforts turn these works into nothing short of masterpieces. This is what attracted the discriminating eyes of the Belgian collectors Mina and Samir Borro and led them to begin collecting old West African ornamental combs. This couple, hailing from the Ivory Coast, have now amassed more than one hundred combs from Ivory Coast, Ghana, and Nigeria. The wonderful carving of these pieces is presented here, accompanied by a text by the field anthropologist and professor emeritus Alain-Michel Boyer. It is the last work he completed before his death on 27 March 2025. We take this opportunity to pay tribute to him.

Carved in wood, ivory, bone, or horn, and sometimes coated with gold leaf, these pieces are decorated with human or animal figures or abstract geometric patterns. Together, they make up a collection unparalleled in the world and reveal the talent of sculptors who contributed to the embellishment of skilfully and patiently constructed coiffures, boosting the impact of a person's appearance. Two peripheral works, a Guro mask and a Baule music hammer featuring a comb and a hairpin close the book.

This collection makes use of the full range of different combs presented to refute all simplistic notions regarding African beauty. We hope that this book will help change attitudes in this field and accord hairstyles and the combs that adorn them the status of true art.

Akan headdress, Ghana, 1888–1895
Friedrich August Louis Ramseyer
QD-30.024.0073

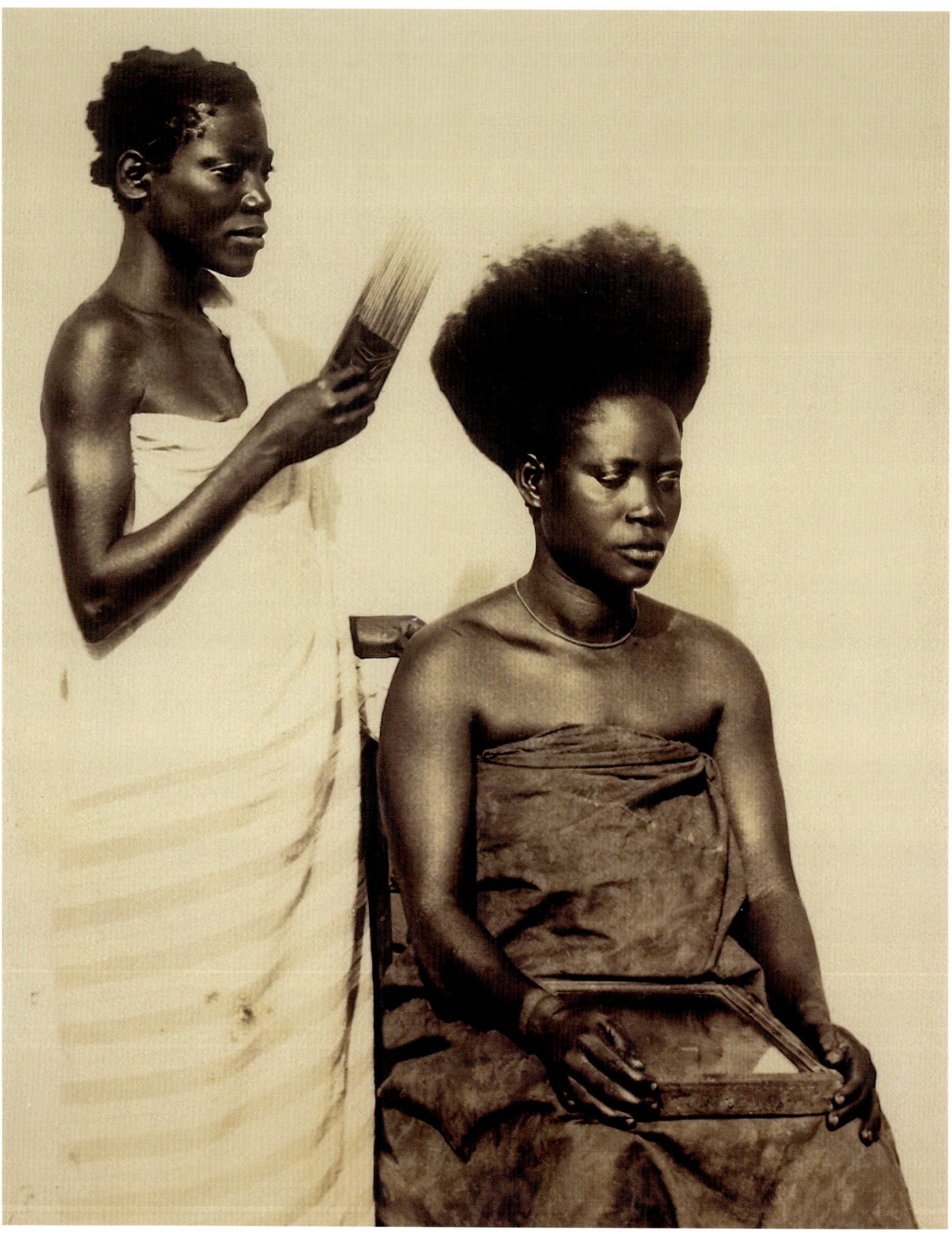

Hair Ornaments: Exalted Presences

Alain-Michel Boyer

I want to know my hair again, the way I knew it before I knew that my hair is me, before I lost the right to me, before I knew that the burden of beauty – or lack of it – for an entire race of people could be tied up with my hair and me.

Paulette M. Caldwell
A Hair Piece (1991)

À l'ombre de ta chevelure, s'éclaire mon angoisse
aux soleils prochains de tes yeux.

Léopold Sédar Senghor
« Femme noire »
Chants d'ombre (1945)

Hairdressing session, Ghana, 1888–1895
Friedrich August Louis Ramseyer
QD-30.041.0051

Introduction: An Art of the Conspicuous

Do African artists only sculpt gods and spirits, fashioning statues and masks made in order to worship mysterious creatures from the afterlife that haunt mortals? In fact, there are many extraordinarily inventive creations that exalt pure beauty, with no sacred purpose or desire for talismanic protection. These graceful, audacious works have raised bodily adornment to the rank of a fine art.

Rooted in the most down-to-earth everyday existence, they have no magical or religious significance and can therefore be seen by everyone, without exception, unlike the forbidden effigies that are strictly prohibited but paradoxically valued by collectors and put on exhibition by the most prestigious Western museums, from the Metropolitan Museum of Art in New York to the British Museum in London. By contrast, in the villages of Ivory Coast and Nigeria, many of these masks – except those used in so-called 'entertainment' dances – are carefully hidden from part of the population (women and children) because they belong to secret cults, such as male brotherhoods. These cannot be witnessed by wives and teenage girls because seeing them could make them sterile.

But even the statues are not readily visible in the villages. They are hidden away inside the house, in a room, at the bedside, often wrapped in a cloth, and brought out

Young Akan women getting their hair styled
Ghana, 1888–1895
Friedrich August Louis Ramseyer
QD-30.042.0024

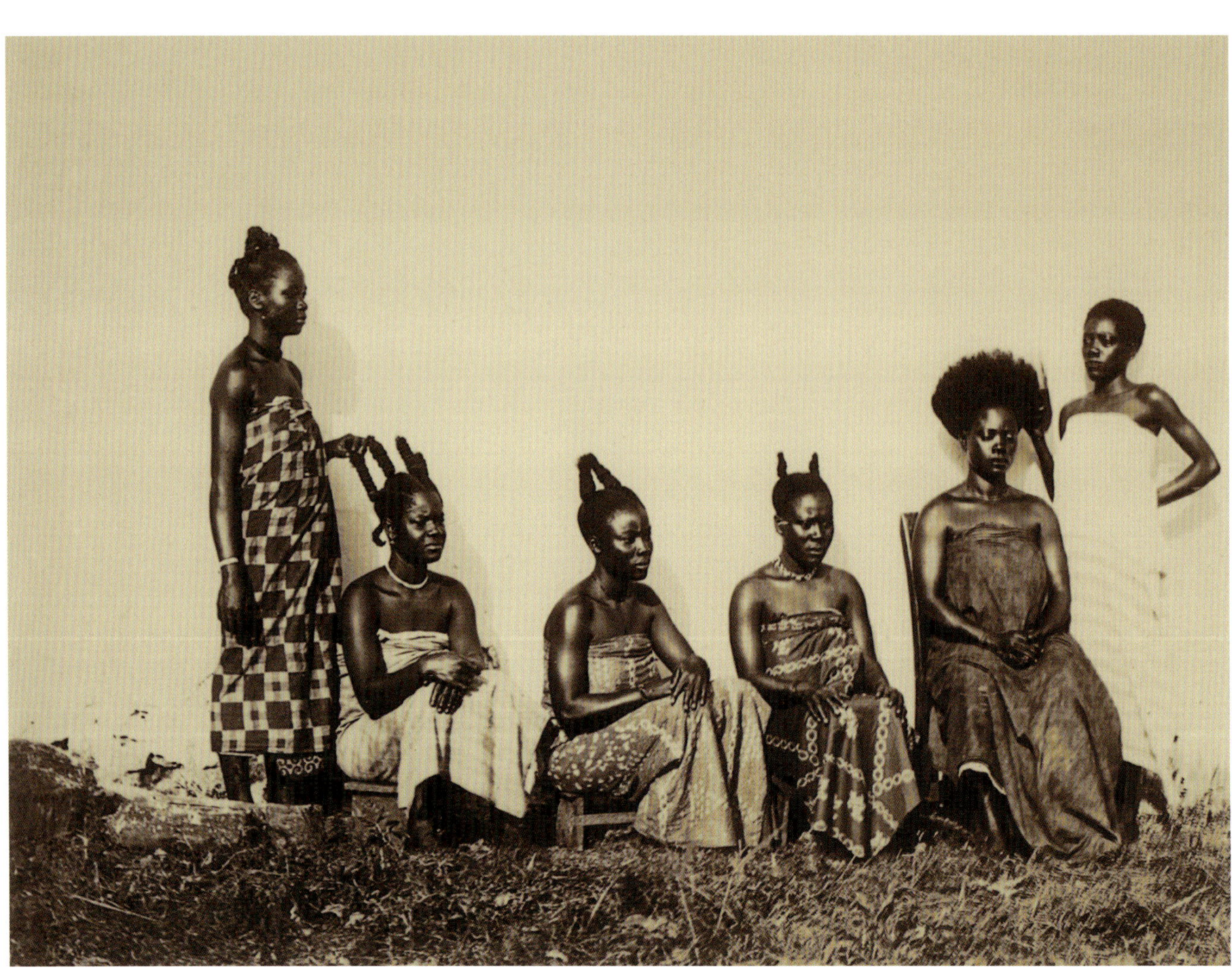

into the courtyard in front of the threshold on special occasions – when making an offering or an animal sacrifice – because they are associated with discreet and entirely private, even intimate, celebrations (for example, among the Attie and Baule are statues of mystical spouses, which concern personal worship). The first Western travellers to Africa never mentioned these statues or sacred masks – they had never seen them, having never been allowed to witness nocturnal ceremonies – and the few times they expressed an interest in aesthetic matters, they confined themselves to the only objects that caught their attention: decorations and jewellery.

Far away from these *invisible* arts – these statues and masks hidden away with infinite precaution, always inaccessible, even non-existent to the passing traveller who might wander around the huts of a village today – there are objects that can, or could, be scrutinised at any time. These include oracles, loom ornaments, bracelets and, in Central Africa,[1] decorated shields and harps with a small carved head adorning the top.

Other creations, such as the hair ornaments shown in this book, are even more *conspicuous*. They are conspicuous precisely in order to celebrate the poise, refinement, and elegance that women, and men too, like to flaunt, and because they highlight an aesthetic sensibility that puts a premium on display, adorning skilfully created hairstyles, which they extend, enlarge, and metamorphose. They were the most immediately visible and also the easiest to reproduce for a talented sculptor, who could exploit the full range of innovative techniques, since their form was not determined by ceremonial and ritual conventions. Indeed, artists would make a point of upstaging standard designs.

Worn by the African men and women of the past, just as Western women would prepare for an evening out by adorning their hair with tiaras or headbands studded with precious stones or cloth flowers, these ornaments exude a magnetic fascination and reflect the glory of the local monarchies (Ashanti in Ghana, Bouna and Gyaman in eastern Ivory Coast, and Benin in Nigeria), whose splendour equalled the pomp and pageantry of the European courts.[2]

Of course, European women sometimes used small tortoiseshell combs to hold their long hair in place, but they remained inconspicuous. And as Japanese *ukiyo-e* prints by Utamaro show, high-ranking *oiran* courtesans in the late eighteenth and early nineteenth centuries slipped tortoiseshell combs (*kushi*), multi-pronged pins (*kanzashi*), and flat chopsticks (*kogai*) into their luxuriant coiffures. But these objects, arranged in a fan-like display, were never decorated, and the aim of these engravings, which were mostly produced for publicity purposes, was to show off the courtesan as a commodity.

These African ornaments, treated with the same concern for technical and formal beauty, were never mere accessories, because they were considered to be real works of art in their own right.

In Africa, an ingrained taste and an insatiable desire to decorate has led even the most 'banal' utensils – spoons, locks, walking sticks, fly-swat handles, and so on – to be totally transformed. More than half a century ago, it was hard for artists to resist the desire to transfigure seemingly humble objects by decorating them. In reaching for a very high degree of perfection, all these creations are evidence of the astonishing skill and great inventiveness that has been applied and are a testament to the sheer virtuosity of sculptors whose creativity always strove to astonish. Consequently, these peoples had very little use for 'ordinary' combs, reduced to their purely utilitarian function, as they exist in the West. Following a process often typical of this continent, the original object, sometimes copied from Western models, was adopted and adapted for local use. And above all, the urge to develop a style and artistic self-indulgence led to it being topped with a decorative motif, turning it into a pure creation – as if, through this need to exalt the object, refinement and elegance were added to counter a certain disdain for its mundane function. In the past, the introduction of a utilitarian object was always accompanied in Africa by an increase in refinement and decoration, an unabated emphasis on style and a quest for perfection.

So the virtues of a comb, its quality, its suitability, also stem from its aesthetics. The more strikingly elegant it is, the more the hairdresser will like it, and the better it will 'work', as they say in Ivory Coast and Burkina Faso. This correlation between artistic value, emotional charge, and 'functional appropriateness' is specific to African art. The purpose of embellishment is not so much to act as a substitute for practical effectiveness, but rather to adorn and brighten everyday life.

The Hair

As a matter of fact, these objects are by nature multi-purpose. They were obviously originally used as normal combs – utilitarian articles. The Baule of central Ivory Coast, who created many of the pieces shown here, even have two names for combs: *saka* and *kwèkwè*.

This book includes numerous photos of combs. Their patina, their scratches, the damage some have sustained, the loss of one, two, or three teeth, bear witness to their tireless use. Without unwelcome repair, they appear all the more real, retaining all the expressive power that decay and mutilation have endowed them with.

But how strange these combs look! Usually with few but incredibly long teeth and tapering handles, they look like miniature sculptures designed to be lodged in soft ground. Actually, they can still be found for sale in large quantities in African markets: whether made of wood – with no extra decoration, or even carved markings – or more frequently thermoplastic. If they are still in common use, it is because of the specific nature that generally characterises African hair.

Its curls are always small but very tight and well defined, and they also have the peculiarity of interweaving endlessly with the adjoining hair.

This kind of hair tends to be at its very worst around dawn, when an African gets out of bed after a night's sleep. Tossing and turning has prompted the formation of knots; the hair has become tangled and the frizz seems to be accentuated, creating a bushier, airier, more vaporous effect, like a sort of cloud looming over the face. At this point, many women find that their wild, shaggy hair gives them an 'unkempt', 'dishevelled' appearance and that the whole towering mass is hopelessly 'unmanageable', as some women in the Ivory Coast put it. For this reason it was common in West Africa in the past to turn to a neck support to minimise the disarray caused to particularly elaborate hairstyles overnight. It has now completely disappeared in this region, owing to the obvious discomfort of sleeping a whole night resting one's head on such a hard, stiff object, a habit that must be acquired at a very young age. However, headrests

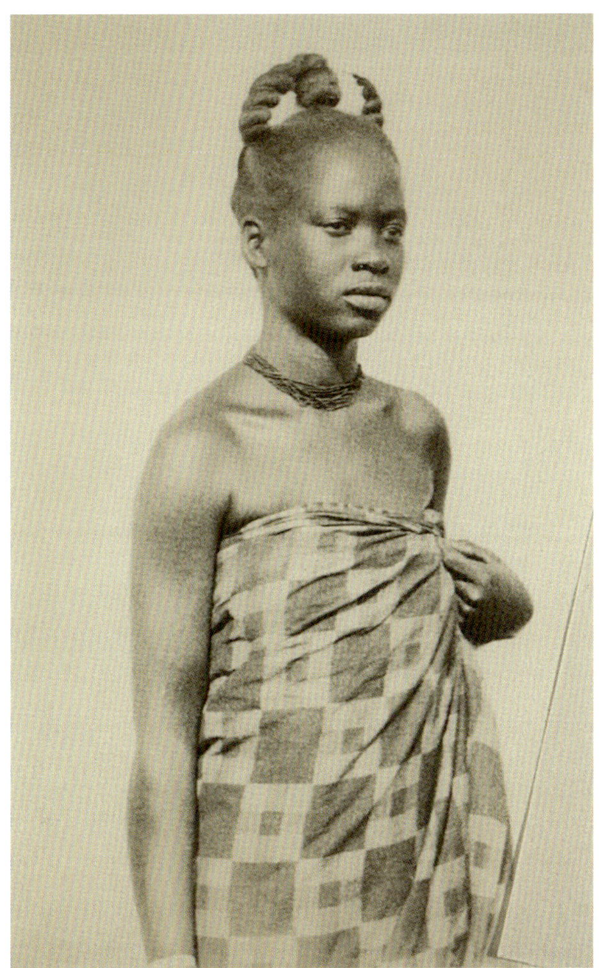

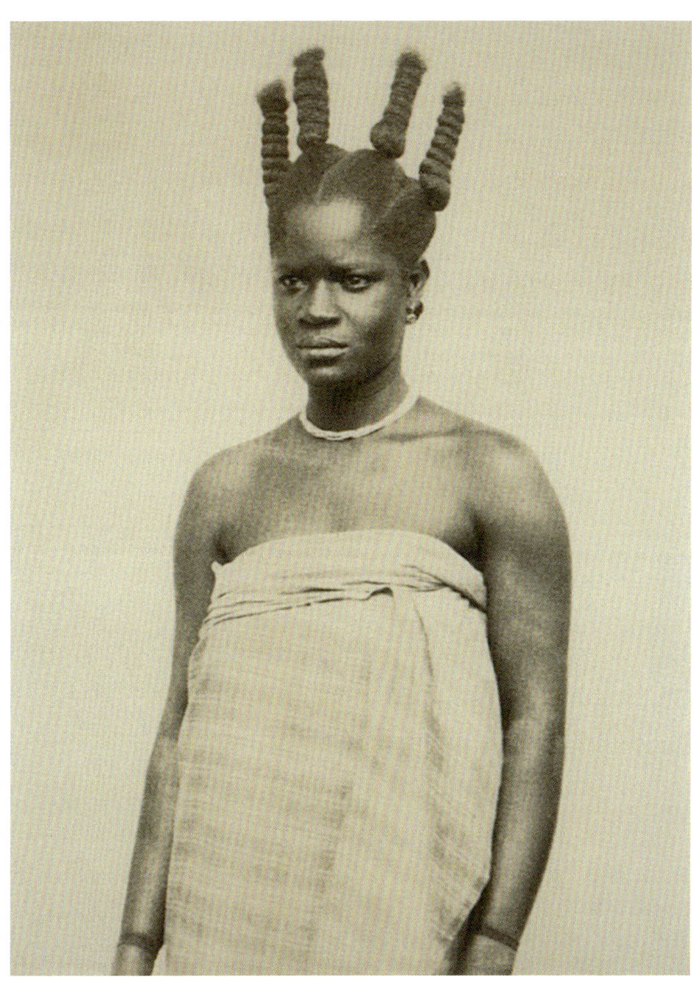

Young Akan women, Ghana, 1888–1895
Friedrich August Louis Ramseyer
QD-30.041.0054
QD-30.041.0055

like this are still commonly used among the peoples of the Omo Valley, in the south of Ethiopia, and in Kenya and South Sudan; not only by women, but also by men, especially the elderly, who have no trouble adapting to it and also use it as a stool.[3]

Untangling hair is no easy task, because the strands fold back on themselves so many times. This type of hair is highly sensitive to static electricity and becomes dry and fragile, leading to split ends and a tendency to break when a comb is passed through it. The narrowing at the curves due to differences in diameter along the hair shafts, which follow variously curled spiralling paths, with twists in different directions, constitute areas of fragility and potential breakage.

Hence the vital role of these combs: the long, wide, relatively strong teeth, spaced far enough apart, make it easier to untangle the hair than using a brush. The handle of the comb, carved into the shape of a human face or body, is made to fit the shape of the hand and make it easier to grip – which explains why they are so smooth and shiny, and accounts for their glossy, polished patina. The teeth have rounded tips so as not to damage the scalp and are few – never more than ten and sometimes just two or three – thus making styling easier. The most common number is seven (especially among the Akan), no doubt because of its symbolic importance in Africa, but also in many other cultures, recurring in Sumer, ancient Greece, the Bible, and Islam. The number seven always carries with it the idea of perfection, of a transformation leading to renewal. It announces a sense of completion, implying a change, a desired end, and always possesses a certain power in itself.

Owing to the poor distribution of sebum throughout the strand, this type of hair is dry by nature and needs to be carefully looked after and moderately moisturised to make it more elastic. Shea oil is applied in an infinitely meticulous and extremely delicate ritual: it begins by gently separating the mass of hair into different types, depending on density and texture, so that each can be untangled separately, section by section; once the knots have been removed, temporary braids are used to hold each section in place; one or more of these combs are inserted 'provisionally' into the hair that has just been smoothed out, to hold it in place while the hairdresser continues her work with another comb, sliding it along the ends and gradually working down towards the roots to prevent knots from forming, sometimes gently using her fingers to avoid 'snapping the hair', as some hairdressers put it. It is important always to comb slowly from the ends down to the roots, never the other way round. At this point the strands are finally free and are ready to build a new coiffure. And this is when real metamorphoses take place, in every possible way. The procedure goes way beyond mere embellishment; the tool, the comb, the entire person are turned into adornment, and the simple ornament into a work of art.

Metamorphoses: From Comb to Artwork

The first phase of the metamorphosis is the appearance of the man or woman having his or her hair done. Such an intimately personal *composition* is always a genuine creation, an architectural monument which, in Africa, can in some cases take half a day to complete – especially at the hands of a true artist who, with skill and dexterity, manages to achieve a high level of aesthetic expression. The whole agglomeration of strands of hair becomes a kind of material to be sculpted, modelled, and embellished, leading to an almost infinite range of variations. Those who have had the patience to witness such

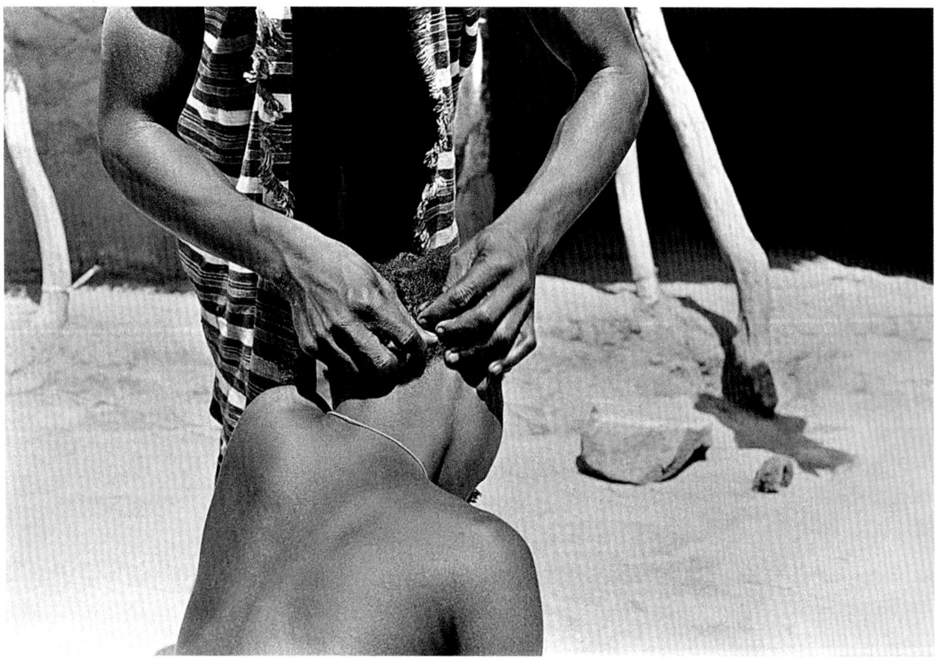

Hairdressing session
Baule village, Ivory Coast, 1934
CC by Hans Himmelheber
Inv. FHH 76-8, Museum Rietberg, Zürich
www.africa-art-archive.ch

Hairdressing session
Baule village, Ivory Coast, 1935
CC by Hans Himmelheber
Inv. FHH 97-33, Rietberg Museum, Zurich

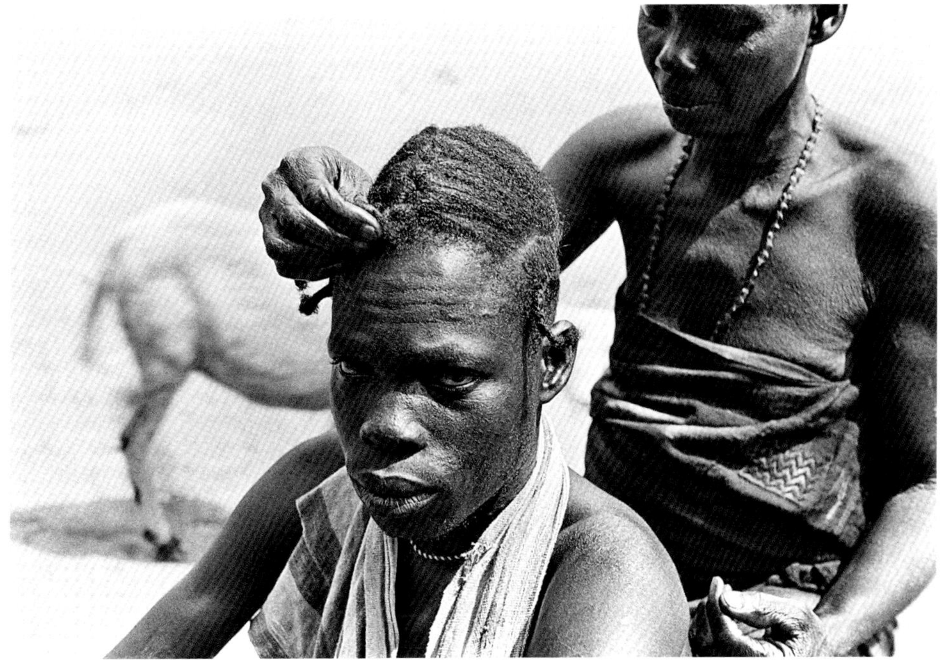

performances cannot help thinking that the hairdresser sees the pile of hair as a material in its natural state, to be manipulated, shaped, and moulded. Equanimity, impassiveness, and endurance are required both by those one feels it appropriate to call 'patients' and by the experts in this science of hair scaffolding, which involves emblematically *recomposing* the body by rectifying what crowns it. Knowing I was interested in the work of the area's wood carvers, Akissi, a hairdresser in the Baule village of Beoumi, told me one day almost half a century ago: 'You see, I'm a sculptor too; hair is the material I sculpt and it's even trickier than wood.'

It is essential that the meticulously arranged hairstyle meet the requirements of excellence and harmony, for parading endlessly novel creations in the art of hairdressing used to act as a clear indication of a person's identity and position in society. Elaborate hairstyles were precisely categorised within societies; depending on their size, shape, and complexity, one could to a certain extent gauge a person's status, ethnic origin, and, above all, marital status.

Social intervention to repair the disorder of nature is a major requirement in Africa, where physical beauty, embellishment, finery, and especially the extreme cleanliness of the body are of paramount importance – even in villages where one has to travel a fair distance to fetch water. Just as men clear, tidy, and manage the forest or savannah – every village being a space reclaimed from the wild – so every person is duty bound to aim for an ideal physical appearance. A neglected head of hair is a sign of mental disorder or loss of status – literally. This is made perfectly clear in African myths of origin or tales: long or badly combed hair that is spiky or untidy, dirty or matted, is always a sign of deviance, abnormality, or even madness in these stories. This is even truer in everyday life. An unusually hirsute, dishevelled, or excessively scruffy individual, whether male or female, is often looked upon as a madman and despised. An unkempt head of hair alone is thought by association and a supposed link between the visual and the olfactory to mean that the individual in question should be rightly regarded as nauseating, unclean, and repulsive. Sporting a well-groomed head of hair is therefore a fundamental act of socialisation, enabling individuals to communicate information about themselves, their standing, and their cultural identity.

The second stage in this metamorphosis is the comb, whose original purpose was to hold the hairstyle in place, accentuating the verticality of the piled-up hair, extending and lengthening it even further and swelling it. Why not keep this same comb permanently as a feature, a statement, and use the hair as a kind of plinth? What better medium than the human body to showcase a work of art? A fine head of hair offers ideal possibilities for display, more than the ears, neck, or nose. It is easy to understand how this taste for exploiting this article might have emerged. Other peoples put feathers, charms, and gold clasps in their hair, so what could be more natural than to leave the object that was used to perfect a hairstyle where it was? In any case, when special ceremonies required it, hair used to be adorned with brooches, pins, animal horns, gold plates, and shells in Africa too, particularly among the Ashanti, Attie, and Agni. Like these adornments, a comb would be slipped deep into the body of the hair, inserted over a bun or a cluster of plaits, or perched at the top of the head, upright or tilted, almost everywhere in Africa. Indeed, a photograph dating from the first half of the twentieth century shows a young man in Guinea-Bissau wearing a comb set horizontally into his hair at his left temple, with the other end partly covering his eyebrow. Another very old photograph depicts a middle-aged man in the Congo basin wearing an almost identical comb at a slight angle in his forelock and at the same time sporting a string of beads in the middle of his forehead and the claw of a big cat on his upper lip. More recently, between 2005 and 2010, I even saw young girls tucking ballpoint pens into their hair in South Sudan and among the Mursi, Turkana, and Dassanetch in the Omo Valley in southern Ethiopia. But in the same regions, it is mainly the elderly, both men and women, who like to accumulate objects in this way. These certainly include combs, but also feathers (in large numbers), two or three watch straps, small mirrors, padlocks, keys, bottle caps attached to a piece of string, etc. – all hanging from their hair gathered in little tufts. When you do not own a fancy object, or not any longer, you make do with something whose value is enhanced by its Western provenance.

It is important to have evidence from the past. For example, as regards West Africa, in 1900 the captain of engineers Robert Wallace Crosson-Duplessis (who helped build the port of Abidjan in 1898 and was subsequently head of the Abidjan-Niger Railway Company) described in an article in the *Bulletin du Comité de l'Afrique française*[4] how, at the end of the nineteenth century, the Attie often adorned their hair with combs throughout the day. Made of wood with carved patterns, these objects were used as decorations for plaits and braids and to keep the hair in place, as well as to comb it, obviously.

Aside from the accounts of travellers and settlers, what really provides valuable information are works of art from the late nineteenth and early twentieth centuries. In the absence of photographs, of which there are very few in any case, the only means of learning about the hairstyles of yesteryear are the statues and ancient masks in museums and private collections. Now, some of these masks in the Ivory Coast – for instance, those of the Yohoure, the Guro, and the Baule (including their *ndoma* portrait masks)

Young women styling their hair, Ghana, 1904
Max Otto Schultze
D-30.24.017

– clearly have 'strange' rectangular accessories at the top that, even today, are often interpreted as 'erect horns' [*sic*], 'curious bovine horns', or simple 'embellishments', 'baubles', or even 'kinds of rakes'! These curious projections on ancient objects are in fact combs.[5]

The third and final stage in this metamorphosis was a subtle and spontaneous shift in the way sculpture influenced the manufacture of the combs used in these hairstyles, by adding carved faces, animals, narrative scenes, and sometimes entire figures. These were in effect miniatures copying the style found in large statues.

Far from being minor works, these technically highly accomplished carvings actually represent a fully realised creative ambition. Indeed, the history of art confirms that small sculptures, such as the ivories of the Middle Ages and the porcelain designs of the Age of Enlightenment, require an even greater degree of skill. Besides, was not the competition organised in Florence in 1425 to choose the bronze decorations for the small panels on the north door of the baptistery, opposite the cathedral, one of the founding acts of the Renaissance?

Paradoxically, the smaller the object, the greater the work required: the wood or ivory has to be carefully shaped, the details more meticulously incised and engraved, and a new equilibrium established. No error or technical slip is sanctioned, for on

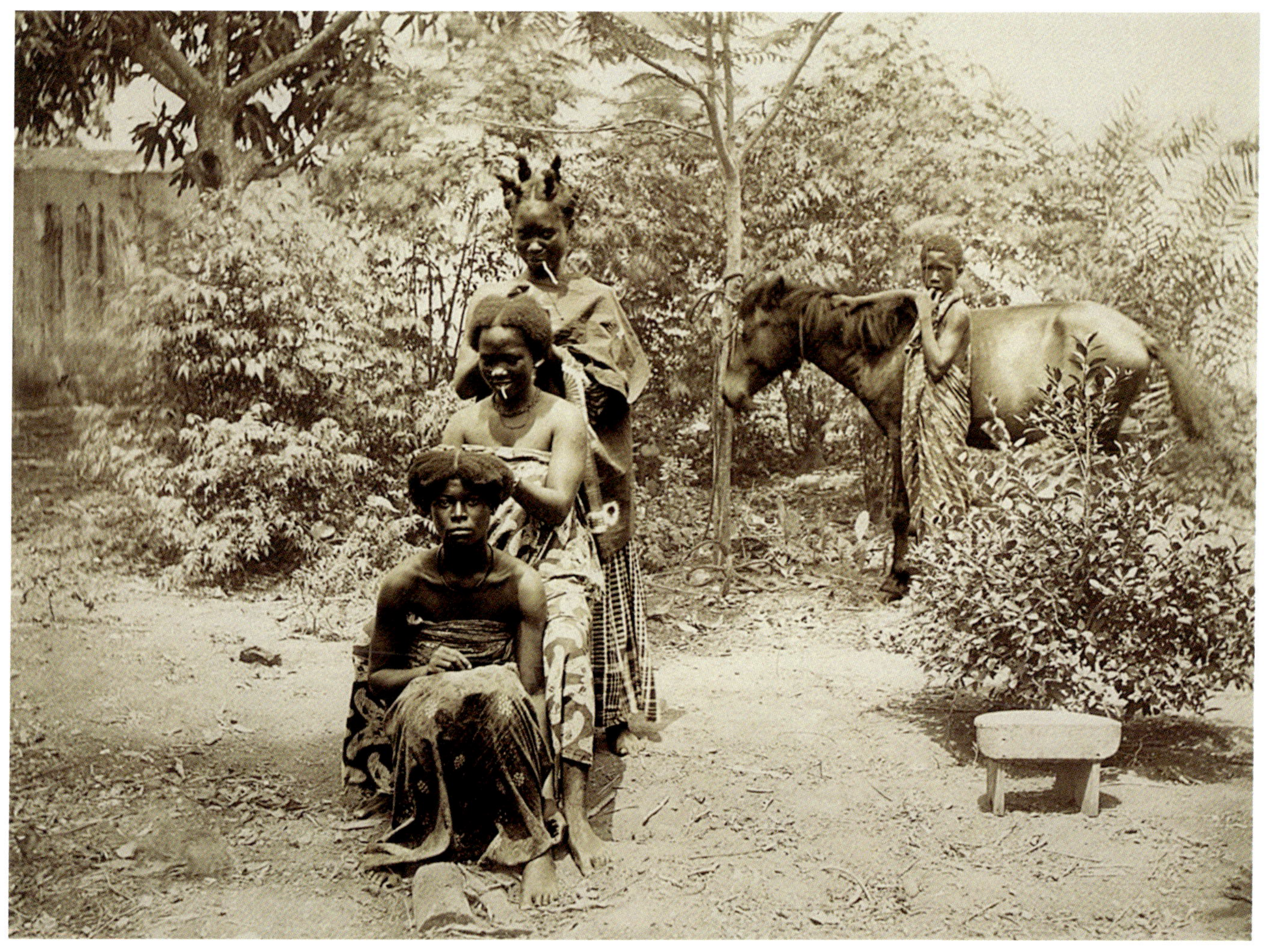

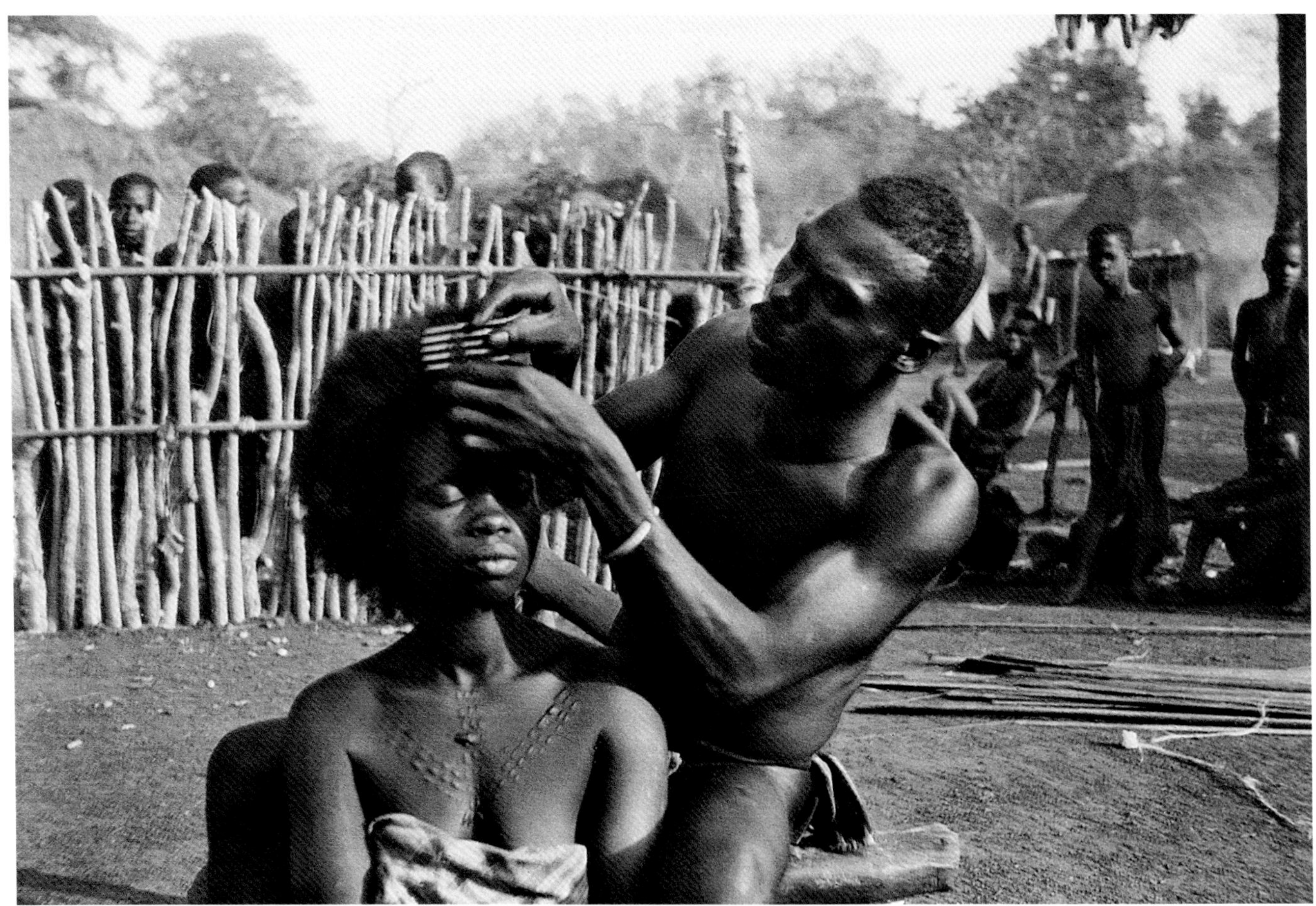

Hairdressing session
Baule village, Ivory Coast, 1934
CC by Hans Himmelheber
Inv. FHH 76-8, Museum Rietberg, Zürich
www.africa-art-archive.ch

such a small scale, every defect is immediately visible; it stands out and cannot fail to strike the viewer. It is important for the eyes and fingers of the men or women who hold the piece in their hands to be able to move smoothly from the round to the high relief, from the bas-relief to the almost flat modelling of the engraving. One must be free to take delight in these examples of condensed grace through the senses of both sight and touch.

The Art of Pomp for Men and Women

Thanks to its considerable visual impact, this ornament enhanced the coiffure, extending it and attracting the eye in lieu of a crest. It also played an active role for both men and women, to some extent similar to that of a village chief's sceptre or the ornate cane of a religious leader. It had a number of advantages: it was instrumental in creating a sense of identity, and was not just a piece of frippery or a bauble, a superfluous finishing touch, hastily and casually added on in order to enchant the onlooker. Coiffure and ornament complemented and completed each other.

A permanent mark of the ephemeral body, this combination's primary purpose was to set the wearer apart, to enhance his or her prestige, to inspire respect and admiration. We all know that a single piece of well-chosen jewellery worn in a public context is able to affect the way one presents oneself through bearing, poise, and composure, as well as to change the awareness of both the person donning it and the person looking at it.

As the final touch to someone's attire, an ornament of this kind would be like putting the icing on the cake. Since it played such an important role in building an identity, this accessory was never a pure whim. Dependent for its effect on others' eyes, it became a focus of attention and validation. Both men and women would take the opportunity to make it a luxury item, an emblem of their prominence. As an attribute of dignity, a sign of assertiveness and self-assurance, it was, in every sense of the word, a sign of distinction, going hand in hand with the concepts of pomp and charisma and worn only on special occasions, festivals, and ceremonial events.

The second advantage is that, by acting on the body it adorns, any ornament requires appropriate behaviour. Does not every piece of jewellery make one more self-confident? This seems to corroborate the idea that if one is partly what one wears, it is because one wears it that one becomes what one is. The function of an ornament is thus never simply to decorate; it can promote. But in Africa, wearing a comb like this had a clearer, more obvious, if little-known, role. It acted as a straightforward declaration that the woman – and it applied much more to women than to men – could not on that particular day, under any circumstances, carry out the task incumbent on wives and young girls in the villages: to fetch water from the river or the well, in a jug – or *canari*, in African French.

Now, putting an elaborate comb precisely where a jug or parcel would normally be was tantamount to proclaiming – without blurting it out, but by using a visual signal, which was actually more effective, more direct, and more enduring – 'I'm not working today; I'm on parade, so you can count me out. There's no way I can put a weight on my head.' Perched up high and carried haughtily, this adornment challenged the way women were conventionally thought of, especially in the villages. It was a way to categorically reject all stereotypes and disavow all clichés. By taking the place of a parcel, a sign of labour, it also magnificently underlined – in the same way as the ewer they would normally have borne – the typical carriage of African women: always upright, slender, with controlled tension, while holding the head in a confident, vertical, even majestic manner.

This adornment had a third role, at least in the kingdoms of Ashanti and Gyaman in Benin, and in the chiefdoms: to proclaim one's social status instantly and to signal community membership, cultural importance, and one's place in the village or capital much more effectively than other body ornaments or clothing. Having no functional purpose and being particularly prized for its elegance, this badge of rank was the exclusive property of well-to-do women, wealthy men, and dignitaries. Personages who were greatly esteemed wanted in this way to declare both their sense of personal taste and their status, especially as the personal nature of the object was reflected in the way it was embellished.

This art was not aimed at women alone. Men in Ghana and the Ivory Coast, especially the Ashanti and Attie, once wore hairpins on the tops of their heads, but on special occasions, such as festivals and major ceremonies, they might don decorated combs too. Nevertheless, the sculptors were always men, for it has to be said (and perhaps this will change one day) that carving, chiselling, cutting, and incising wood, ivory, and bone is the exclusive preserve of men.

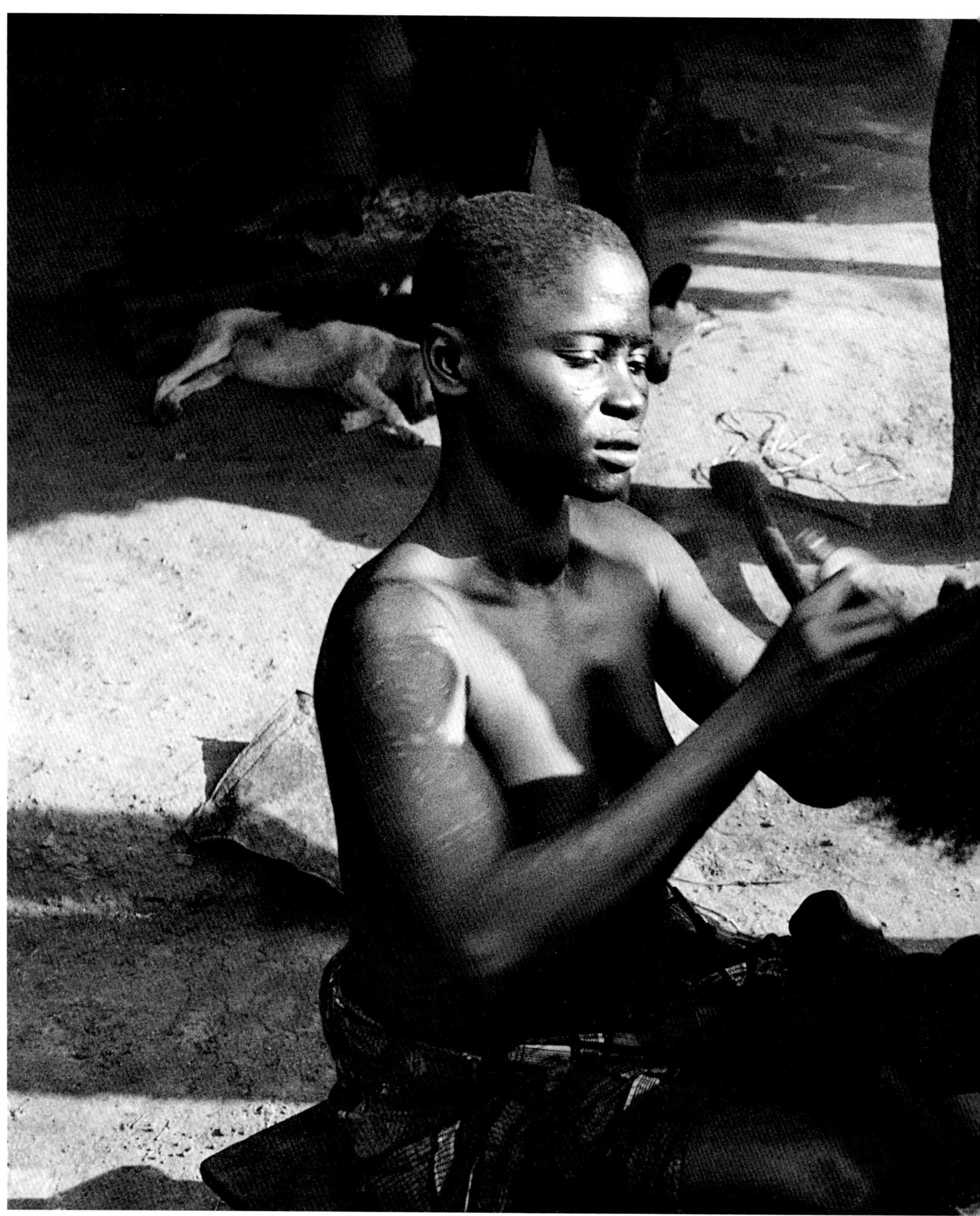

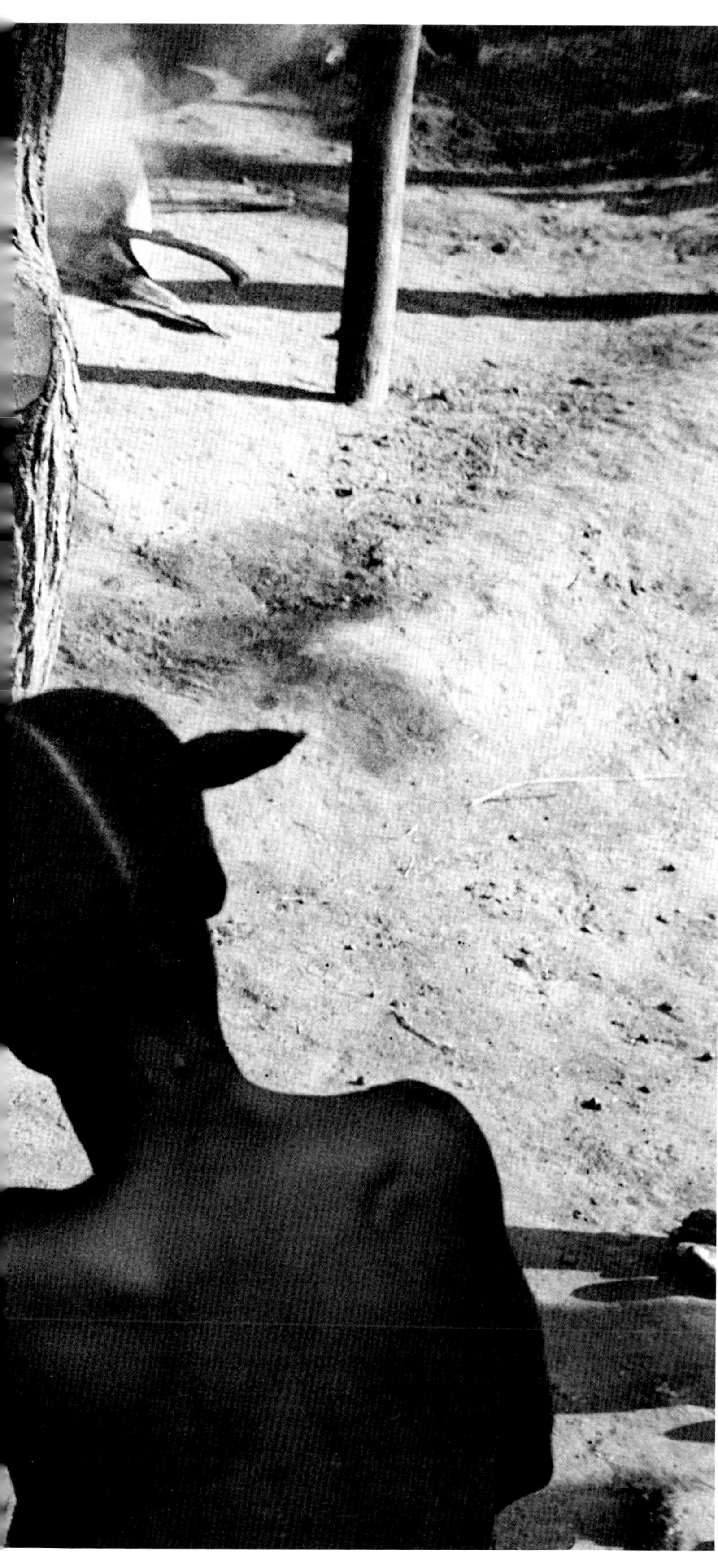

Hairdressing session
Baule village, Ivory Coast, 1935
CC by Hans Himmelheber,
Inv. FHH 125-14, Museum Rietberg, Zürich
www.africa-art-archive.ch

Sensually Experienced Form: Materials and Patina

It goes without saying that a decorated comb is an object that can be used as well as looked at or admired even. It attracts through its welcoming texture, the unexpected marks and scratches on its surface, and the sounds it can make. The line of the nose, forehead, and shoulders of the figure, the worn features of the ornamental face or rosettes are all elements that exude an irresistible sensuality. In Africa, anything that is harmonious, pleasing to the eye, or enjoyable to handle is close to an ideal.

Furthermore, in order for a comb to be effective it should not only be pretty, but also pleasant to hold. This is another invaluable aspect of this type of work. It restores to sculpture in the round its double nature: both visible and sensually tactile, conspicuous and carnal, so that the owner of such an article is no longer a passive spectator, but has the pleasure of experiencing the object by living with it.

What lover of Italian Renaissance sculpture hasn't dreamt one day of being able to caress a marble by Michelangelo: his *David* (safe behind metal barriers), his *Bacchus* (under electronic surveillance), or his *Pietà* (locked away in a reinforced glass case)?

Here's the thing: the great attraction of these combs is to be both visible and sensually tangible, intelligible to the eye as well as to the touch, conspicuous and carnal. These African ornaments were never made to be inaccessible, to be contemplated and admired passively from a distance. In dovetailing two facets so perfectly, the combs are also intended to titillate the skin through a tactile experience of the form, adapting effortlessly to the hand and free of any roughness, so smooth as to feel totally at home there, thanks to the harmony of flowing swells and undulating lines – even if it means that after long contact, these objects forever bear the intimate marks of their successive owners.

Indeed, combs are also transformed by use. These objects, which have been endlessly brushed, caressed, and coaxed, have retained a magnificent patina, with variations in colour and texture resulting from years of handling. The patina plays a more important role in the appeal of these works than it does in others that have been handled less or not at all. It may be very dark or, on the contrary, have left all its original sheen on the edges. Glowing on the reliefs and veins, and highlighting surface wear, it gives the combs an extra sparkle, bringing out the full potential of the material, which can acquire a satin lustre, or enable the wood or ivory to retain all their original freshness. In spite of breaks and cracks or corrosion, if they are made of metal, these combs are also beguiling, for the 'mutilations' themselves 'create a style', since 'time is as visible in them as art', to quote André Malraux in *Les Voix du silence*.

In short, not the eye alone, but the finger too is able to follow the uninterrupted outlines, where all sense of solemn remoteness is erased, and to sense that the object's purpose has been surmounted as if in a game and, through the greatest technical skill, treated as part of the decoration, displaying a marvellous sense of life. The ornamental purpose is fully incorporated in the concept and not superimposed on a work that is in no way inferior to the most successful 'proper' sculptures. For the sculptor is not content to simply add a head or a body to a comb: a head or a body merges seamlessly with its support, a fully achieved being, with a taut harmony that combines shapes, swells and hollows, straight lines and circles, so that the volumes interpenetrate, as if mindful of a common mould. In short, this is an intimate, highly personal and even personalised art form because the decoration acts symbolically to associate the object

Akan headdresses, Ghana, 1888–1895
Friedrich August Louis Ramseyer
QD-30.042.0100
QD-30.016.0027

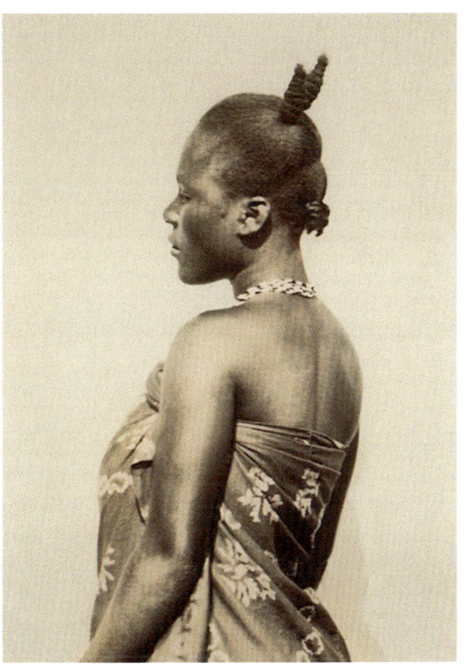

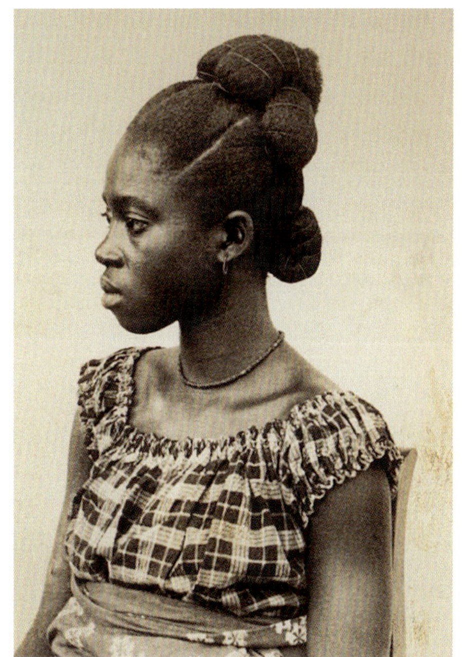

more closely with the man or woman who touches it, as if to mark him or her with a sign; indeed, to distinguish them.

Certain materials have always been favoured: wood, elephant, warthog, or hippopotamus ivory, as well as bone or horn on certain occasions.

In the first instance, it is obviously essential to choose a tough, hard wood. Not the kind of wood used for masks, especially the bulky helmets that require a soft, light wood such as kapok (*Ceiba pentandra*, or *gnin* in the Baule language). As Baule carvers say, '*Waka o ti kpa treman wu*' (some woods are more woody than others) or '*Waka ngba ityakum*' (not all woods are the same, they have different types of vigour). Before cutting a tree, even if it is intended for an object that is not sacred, it is appropriate to pour a libation and make an offering (for instance an egg, the symbol of future germination) and then say a few words extolling the spirit within the tree.

Looking at the Baule ornaments in Mina and Samir Borro's collection, it is clear that these works were mainly carved from a hard, fine-fibred wood with a tight, dense grain, known locally as *orovia* – or, depending on the dialect, *movingi* (*Distemonanthus benthamianus*, in the family Caesalpinaceae). The Baule have also used *bable ngole*, also known as *sunsu* (*Diospyros mespiliformis*, in the family Ebenaceae), but there is actually quite a wide choice, depending on regional traditions, availability, and the preferences of the sculptor. It is also worth mentioning *sewe* (*Holarrhena floribunda*, in the family Apocynaceae), and *soka*, or 'coral tree' (*Erythrina senegalensis*, in the family Papilionaceae). The Guro's favourite hardwood for making combs has always been *iroko*, known locally as *gore* (*Milicia excelsa*), while the Ashanti in Ghana prefer *twafo yeden* (Harrisonia occidentalis) or *tweneboa* (*Cordia millenii*).

Depending on the object's stage of advancement, the sculptor would use a number of instruments that have always inspired the intelligence of the hands. They are clearly distinguished among the Ashanti of Ghana: axe (*akuma*), adze (*soso*), mallet (*peewa*), penknife (*asekamma*), large knife (*nkrante*), scraper (*nwanee*), and a tool called a *fitii*, for drilling.

Once the carving had been completed, first with an adze and then with a knife, the object was meticulously polished to a smooth, shiny finish with the rough leaves of a ficus tree, *Ficus exasperata Vahl* (*yengle nya* in Baule, *kyokanola* in Guro), which were widely used in West Africa in the past, then dyed with traditional pigments: black from the vine *ndwin* (of the genus *Cissus*), in the Baule language, whose leaves produce a very dark paste when crushed in a mortar with a little water mixed with soot. The object was then immersed in a mud bath for a long time. The ochre tones that appear on some pieces, giving them a light lustre, were achieved using the crushed seeds of a fruit, the achiote (*Bixa orellana*, in the family Bixaceae), *dieka* in Baule and *nyo* in Guro, mixed with egg, which is exactly the same as the tempera technique used in the Italian Renaissance.

Adding round-headed brass nails, known as carpet tacks [Figs. 26, 35, 40, 62] constituted an exceptional decoration for some head ornaments, although they were more common in the more precious masks, except among the Yohoure. Why choose brass over gold? Well, when carefully polished with lime juice, it is extraordinarily bright and gleams brighter than gold in the sun.

Like the wooden objects, the ivory ornaments in the collection display clean, delicate, and precise carving that is at once energetic and supple, firm and soft, in a style reminiscent of that found among Attie goldsmiths in particular [Figs. 44, 45, 46, 47, 48, 49, 50, 51, 52, 53, 54, 55], but is also present among the Baule [Figs. 97, 98, 99].

Employing an illuminator's skills, the dense material is always handled with brief strokes, broad, sure effects, and multiple angles, taking care to exploit the play of reflections. For their allure relies on the subtlety of the modelling and the extraordinary play of light and shadow that depends on the height or position of the sun. Furthermore, while displaying no defects or flamboyance, these handsome pieces denote a taste for luxury and a great understanding of the material, thanks to which the functional aspect becomes an integral part of the object as a whole.

Ivory [Figs. 100, 101], horn [Figs. 67, 68, 90, 92, 95], and bone have always attracted African sculptors, and there are many cane and sceptre knobs made of these materials to be found in this region along the Gulf of Guinea, particularly among the so-called 'lagoon peoples': the Abidji, the Odiukru, the Alladian, the Ehotile, and the Tchaman (or Ebrie). Ivory from Ghana, Liberia, and Ivory Coast used to be abundant, as suggested by the name *Côte des Dents* (Coast of Teeth), which can be found on ancient maps and in the accounts of early travellers and was the original name for the present-day coast of Guinea. This ivory was veined like wood and opaque, or, conversely, slightly translucent with uneven natural shades. It was very solid and had the advantage over ivories from other parts of Africa of taking on orange or pink tones under the effects of light, producing contrasts in colour and acquiring a milky appearance or otherwise a warm russet patina. But whatever the material, one cannot help admiring the prowess of the sculptors, who succeeded in drawing together, in a single piece of wood, ivory, bone, or horn, such apparently diverse elements, creating the most varied forms and combining them in a single harmonious whole by constantly inventing new designs.

An Unsung Art, a Vanished Art

Yet this art, an invigorating alternative to other works that are typically preferred, long remained unknown – at least in this region. While combs from the Democratic Republic of Congo were exhibited and celebrated at major auctions, in West Africa they were more often than not ignored and forgotten. Not hidden, because they were not sacred, but unsuspected.

Firstly, because even when they were not used, these ornaments were treasured by families. The word is not an exaggeration, since they were kept with the most cherished possessions, like relics. Among the Baule, some were kept in what they call the *aja*, or *aja dilè* – often incorrectly translated as 'sacred treasure' when the word literally means 'inheritance'. They were part of a group of objects that gave expression to the soul, the spirits of the ancestors, whom the Baule never represent by figurines, preferring to symbolise them with stools, ornaments, jewellery, raw gold or nuggets, and also by the most diverse objects, which are no longer in use but bear the imprint of the deceased. They remain packed in suitcases or bags, in the main bedroom, tucked under the bed: carved walking sticks, fly swats with handles covered in gold leaf, brass bracelets, huge anklets unworn since the thirties, pottery, pieces of cloth, and these decorated combs.

The nature and importance of the *aja* vary according to the size of the family and how ancient it is, with objects being amassed over generations. Contrary to the way the word 'heirloom' is used in the West to refer to a single object, to the Baule it is plural but indivisible and inalienable: no one can take any part of it away, and each portion must be preserved intact and unaltered, because it represents the identity, unity, and continuity of what the Baule call *osu* (incorporating the concepts of 'family', 'kinship', and 'lineage'). In exceptional circumstances – during funerals or at the ceremony for the closing of the period of mourning – these objects are displayed on chairs or cloths, or placed on an altar, then immediately returned to their bags and put away again until the next funeral.

These ornaments were also long neglected, misunderstood, and snubbed by European collectors and by those whom antique dealers in Abidjan or Accra called 'bush runners'. These included Muslim Dyulas, such as the famous Ali, Cissé, and Abdoulaye, who in the 1970s and 1980s scoured villages for them, in search of statues, doors, and masks – objects that were also prized by museum curators.

Relegated to the rank of minor, impermanent art, these ornaments, considered undistinguished, even futile or insignificant, attracted little interest of collectors. Early collectors of African art were keener on what they regarded as 'major' works (modelled on the hierarchy of genres that persisted in the West) to the detriment of other art forms they considered to be subordinate.

In the 1970s, I remember seeing a few old wooden combs – ivory or gold leaf objects were never present – lying around in crates under the stalls in the antiques market that was then held in the Plateau district in the centre of Abidjan. They attracted absolutely no attention, and Samir Borro deserves a lot of credit for his good judgment and sure instinct, not to mention his perseverance in gathering these pieces together in coherent groups, carefully arranged according to type and attractiveness.

But in Africa there is no genre hierarchy, no distinction between 'high art' and 'decorative art', and in any case these two expressions have no equivalent in the local

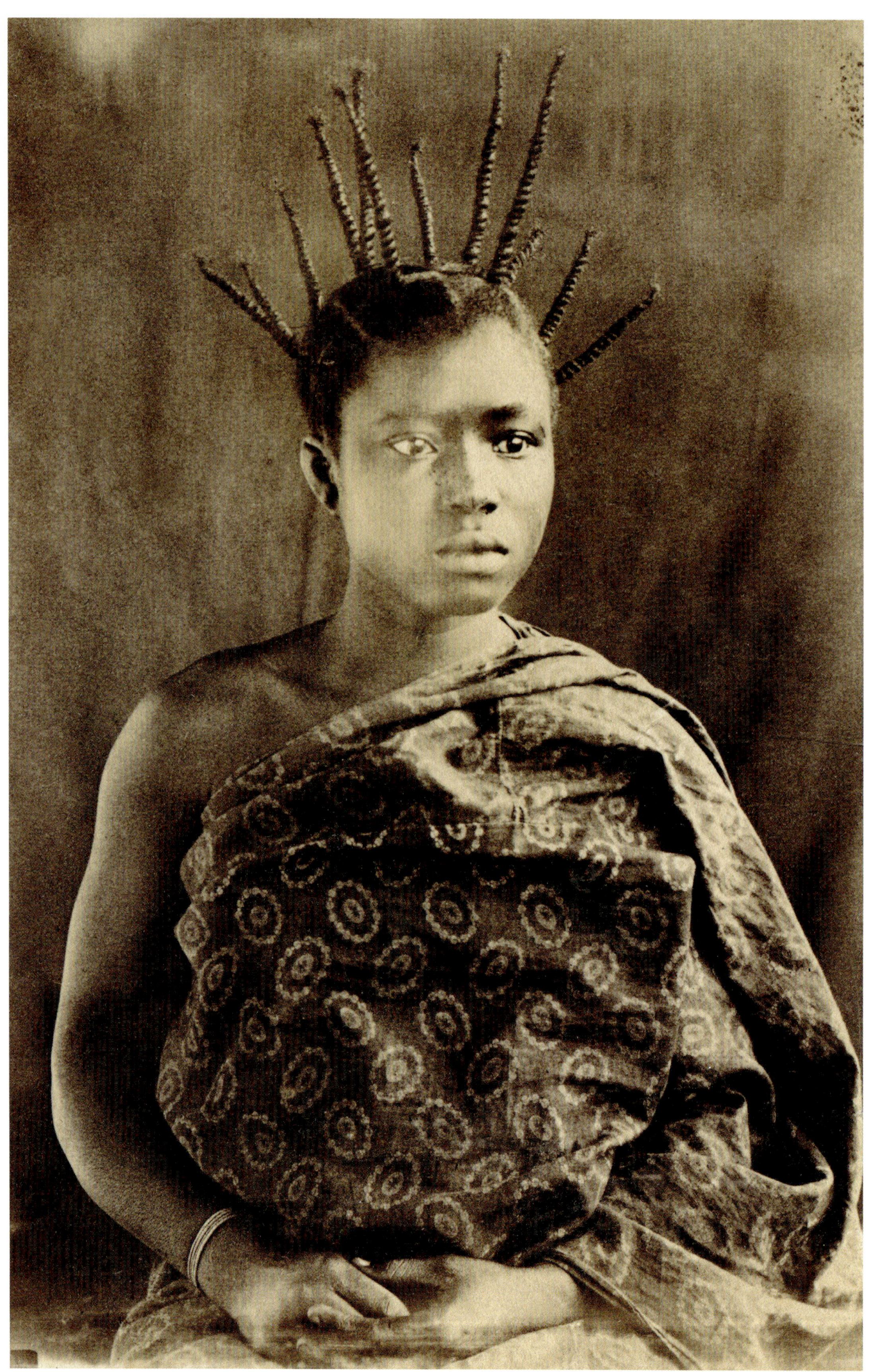

Young woman, Akan, Ghana, 1880–1895
Anonymous photographer
QL-30.013.0101

languages. In the West, the aesthetic canon places enduring works above spontaneous creations, whereas in Africa some of the most sacred and most important ceremonies do not in fact require any sculptural content at all. For instance, among the Senufo, the We, and the Baule, masked dancers are covered from head to toe not with a carved face, but with a costume of mottled fur that matches the shape of the body, with openings only for the eyes and mouth. This outfit is considered to be as sacred as a wooden mask, while everyday objects of no particular distinction – spoons, walking sticks, ointment boxes – are extremely elaborate and are embellished with fine decorations, displaying great refinement. The same is true of these combs, which are a distillation of inventive design.

These adornments illustrate how the sculptors were intent on expressing a human ideal that was as durable and harmonious as the social rules and laws that govern the cycle of the seasons. As physical representations that can be grasped at a glance, they constitute synthesised images through which the sculptor exploits a great sense of rhythm to create a composition that attempts to explore the most eloquent contrasts, bringing space into play. As Michel Leiris wrote of the various 'utilitarian' pieces in Africa, the artist gives material form to 'the harmonisation that could be achieved between the utensil as such and another reality'. And again: 'Just as a tree's cylindrical trunk is turned into a statue by the imagination and dexterity of the craftsman, so an object with a form that is in this case ideally, and not materially, determined is transformed into something other than itself, a creative process that can be described as pure sculpture and goes far beyond mere decoration.'[6]

However, as a result of the social changes affecting African communities, these hair ornaments have unfortunately disappeared, swept away by modernity. Just as the carved doors that used to be plentiful fifty years ago among the Baule and Guro, and ubiquitous at the end of the nineteenth century (judging by early travellers' accounts), no longer exist, so these head adornments have been replaced by combs made of steel, aluminium, or plastic. Admittedly, as mentioned above, one can still find wooden combs on market stalls, with long, thick, well-spaced teeth, but those with added decoration on the handle or back are no longer popular, and all modern specimens are shoddily made, judging by the marks left by the adze and knife, and the lack of polishing.

At the Origins: The Creators

The vast majority of the ornaments in Mina and Samir Borro's collection come from the so-called Akan, a generic term used to describe peoples who settled in the former Gold Coast during the British colonial period. The areas concerned are now known as Ghana (settled by the Ashanti and Fante) and Ivory Coast (Baule, Attie), or else straddling the two countries (Abron, also known as Bron or Brong). Their languages share a number of features and are part of the Kwa language group (sometimes wrongly labelled 'dialects'). One of the distinctive features of the Akan peoples is that they are a matrilineal clan that traces its descent from a common ancestor.

The Ashanti (or Asante), who now number more than eleven million, already had a centralised, rigorously organised state long before British colonisation, with a sovereign reigning in the capital of Kumasi, whose symbol of power was, and still is, a gold stool. Members of the highly ramified administration were recruited from among the aristocracy. The chief aim of the always spectacular ceremonies, which still take place even though the king currently holds no power, was to parade his supremacy, which explains the profusion of objects made of gold or wood covered in gold leaf. These included staffs of office and sceptres, pipes, gilded chairs of European origin, spoons, gold weights, receptacles and pots (finely decorated *kuduo* containers, designed to store gold nuggets and gold dust), and of course ornamental combs, which carry similar incised decorations: criss-crossing, broken lines. There are several more objects, including articles from everyday life – for example, miniature stools with finely carved decorations [Fig. 13] carried at arm's length or placed on the floor [Fig. 1].

In contrast to these relatively heavy pieces of furniture, a long-toothed comb, which has become gigantic, is treated in the same way, as if to worship and glorify it. The decorations are sometimes borrowed from Christianity (Christ on the Cross, Fig. 5), revealing not only the kingdom's syncretic bent but also its vast geographic extent, incorporating as it does an Islamicised north and a coastal area first explored by the Portuguese in 1471. These Europeans came to trade gold for manufactured goods, particularly in the areas they named Costa da Ouro and Costa da Mina (lending its name to the present-day Elmina), and took advantage of the opportunity to convert the local population.

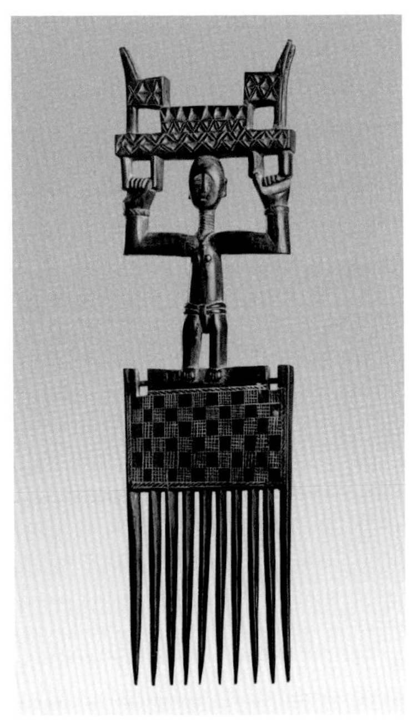

Comb
Ashanti, Akan, Ghana (see Fig. 13, p. 71)

Ghana's other resident population, the Fante (or Fanti), numbering under five million, live along the coast, from the River Sakumo in the east to Ivory Coast. They often found themselves under the sway of the Ashanti Empire, from whom they frequently struggled to free themselves over the centuries. As with the Ashanti, the predominant objects made by the Fante are ceremonial stools, in which the spirits of the ancestors reside, and fertility 'dolls', once worn by pregnant women; in the case of the latter, the shape is different, since the face and coiffure are rectangular. Although the collection has only two Fante pieces, two combs [Figs. 12, 14], they are superb specimens: one depicts a couple with deliberately enlarged arms, as if to stress the power of their embrace, carved in a manner very similar to the ancient gold weights decorated with human figures.

According to oral tradition, the Fante 'came from the north', although it was more likely to have been central Ghana, more precisely in the neighbourhood of the town of Techiman in the former Brong Ahafo region, where they lived for a long time in contact with the Bono (also known as Brong in Ghana and Abron in Ivory Coast). The Bono live on both sides of the border, near the town of Bondoukou, and once ruled the Kingdom of Gyaman, which was modelled on the Ashanti Empire. Once again, we find most of the objects made by the other Akan groups, including fly whisks, swords, and sabres, all covered in gold leaf. The only Abron comb in Mina and Samir Borro's collection [Fig. 103] portrays the same motif of juxtaposed heads, which also adorns their sceptres, other items of regalia, and ceremonial paraphernalia, and testifies to the virtuosity of their artists.

Another people in the Akan group, the Attie (or Atie or Akye), numbering some four hundred thousand, live in the southeast of Ivory Coast, north of the capital Abidjan and around the towns of Anyama, Alépé, and Adzopé, mainly on the banks of the Comoé River. Distantly related to the Baule, the Attie are in fact the result of a split

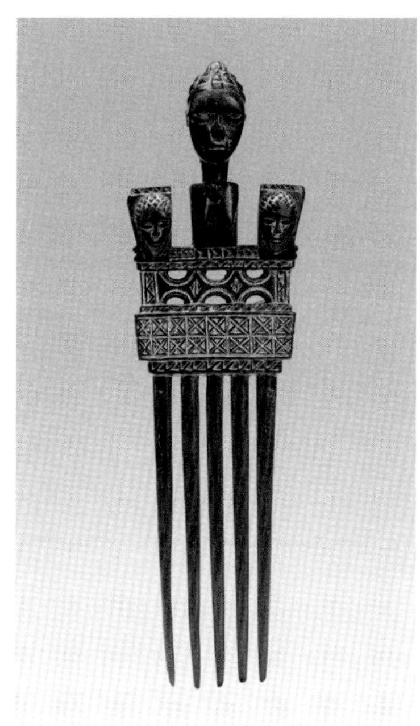

Comb
Abron, Akan, Ivory Coast
(see Fig. 103, pp. 160, 161)

within the Ashanti community (to which they belonged). Following a dynastic quarrel, they left Ghana in the eighteenth century to settle further west. However, unlike other Akan peoples, they never had a centralised state, and organised government never went beyond the local village level. In their case, the stool (*mbesia*), symbolising the lineage and on which sacrifices are performed, is never displayed in public. The Attie did once have figurines too, but their art has now largely disappeared – due to the spread throughout their community of the iconoclastic syncretistic beliefs of the 'prophet' William Harris, who came from Liberia and toured the region from 1914 onwards, roaring 'Burn your fetishes!' and anathematising animist cults, thus putting a stop to all artistic endeavour. While now scarce, four types, all small, can still be found. These include two figurines depicting twins (known as *nda-tinlin* when of the same sex and *takyi-nan-nda* when different); when one dies, another wooden statuette, portraying the *ekanla*, the deceased's double, is given to the survivor, who looks after it. The third type consists of statues of mystical *ebolo* spouses, similar to the *blolo bla* and *blolo bian* of the Baule. The fourth type are statues mediating between diviner-healers and the forest spirits who entered them during the rites of the *Logbu* cult and which were thought to provide answers or cures for serious problems (illnesses, conflicts, etc.). And most of the decorations on these combs, basically human heads, are similar to those on ancient ceremonial canes.[7]

Today, celebrations and festivals are an opportunity to put on display, in the fullest sense of the word, ceremonial objects covered in gold leaf, which are laid out on large cloths to be admired, before being returned to the clan's hidden treasury in the evening. This pleasure taken in ostentation is echoed in their combs, which are particularly numerous, opulent, and refined in their carving, and exist in an astonishing range of materials (horn, ivory, wood), colours, and styles (geometric, even highly stylised, or, in contrast, with almost 'naturalistically' graceful faces).

Like the Attie, the Baule also owe their origins to the split that shook the Ashanti Empire in the eighteenth century. However, theirs is a much larger community (around five million) and their forebears continued their migration from Ghana, forging ahead to the centre of the country and eventually settling in a vast area to the east of the River Bandama, instead of stopping in the southeast corner of Ivory Coast like the Attie. In this fertile territory between the woodland savannah and the tropical rainforest, they imposed their language on the local populations they had conquered and, in return, borrowed from them new traditions, unknown to them in the Ashanti lands from which they came. Foremost among these were religious beliefs, together with the use of ritual wooden figures and, above all, masks, for which the Ashanti had no use at all. To be specific, from the Wan, the Baule borrowed the *Goli* cult and its masks of various shapes (round, with a human face, or with a bull's head), and from the Guro, the Yohoure, and the Tagbana, sacred *bonu amwin* mask-helmets. Baule artists were very productive and this helps to explain the large number of combs collected [Figs. 22, 23, 24, 25, 27, 30, 31, 32, 35, 36, 37, 39, 40, 41, 42, 71, 77, 86], in which we find the same stylistic features as in the statues: the preference for a certain realism, the primacy given to harmony of form, a carefully fashioned hairstyle, a sense of balance, and the high profile accorded to the depiction of protective animals (cockerels, and, above all, a great variety of birds, treated in various ways). These pieces also display a taste for opulence they have retained over the centuries from their Gold Coast origins. Indeed, theirs is a very rare comb whose handle is still covered in gold leaf [Fig. 17] – which may confirm that this comb was little or never used, and that it was kept carefully hidden away in the 'sacred treasure' or heritage (*aja dilè*).

Besides this Akan 'core', various other peoples around its periphery also used this type of long-toothed comb, both as a functional object and as an ornament: to the north, the Koulango; to the west, the Bete and the Dan; to the east of the Ashanti, the Yoruba and the Idoma.

The Koulango have a population of around 150,000 and live in the extreme north-east of Ivory Coast, around the town of Bouna, where they are in close contact with neighbouring peoples: the Lobi, the Ligbi, and the Abron. However, they actually belong to the Gur (formerly Voltaic) ethnic and linguistic group. Artistically, they are best known for their generally anthropomorphic brass figurines, which are placed around the waist, wrist, or even the ankle or neck of a newborn baby, which is considered particularly vulnerable, as a protective lucky charm.[8] This same refined taste and fondness for miniaturisation recur in a superb comb depicting a woman with a long neck adorned with rings [Fig. 104], her hands clasped over her belly, seated on a traditional wide stool in a totally relaxed posture of pensive repose; the crisp, finely incised lines are intended to express restrained energy.

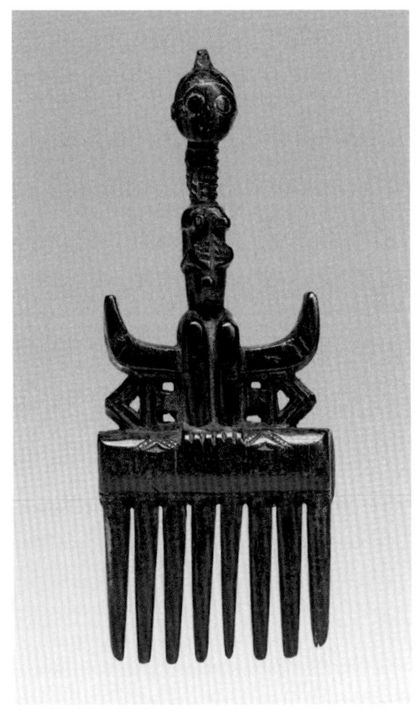

Comb
Koulango, Gur, Ivory Coast
(see Fig. 104, pp. 162, 163)

The art of the Bete, who are renowned for their woodwork, is in stark contrast. Numbering some two million, the Bete live in central western Ivory Coast, around the towns of Gagnoa, Issia, and Daloa. Like the We (also known as Guere, Wobe, and Krahn), they belong to the Kru cultural group, and, like them, they are known particularly for their masks, which are often enormous, while their statues are far scarcer. On the other hand, their huge talent for working on a smaller scale shines through in their combs, where tapering faces perch atop long necks adorned with rings, the handles themselves carved from a comb, in a sort of mise en abyme [Figs. 109, 113]. Another striking piece [Fig. 110] depicts a woman with gigantic, conical, drooping breasts, strangely emerging from the collarbone. Acting as the comb's handle (which is much longer than on other pieces), she holds the object at arm's length, above her head like a trophy, signifying triumph and victory, as if she were the idealised image of the hairdresser.

Even further west, in a mountainous region straddling the border between Ivory Coast and Liberia, live the Dan, a Mande-speaking community of around three million people more commonly known as Gio in Liberia. This people's most distinctive works are their large ceremonial spoons and masks with human faces, of which there are many, sometimes similar in shape but with different functions. Their oval faces and almond-shaped eyes set back in wide sockets, are no longer sculpted in the round as in their masks or statues, but carved in bas-relief and medium-relief on the central part of the comb [Fig. 111], while the teeth and two human bodies are treated in different ways. One portrays a stylised, allusive body with an elongated torso and short legs, with arms crossed in a semicircle; the other, taking abstraction a step further, turns a body into a geometric shape: a trapezoid with a concave base surmounted by a hexagon. These figures wear a comb on top of their head, like a headdress or an emblematic hairstyle.

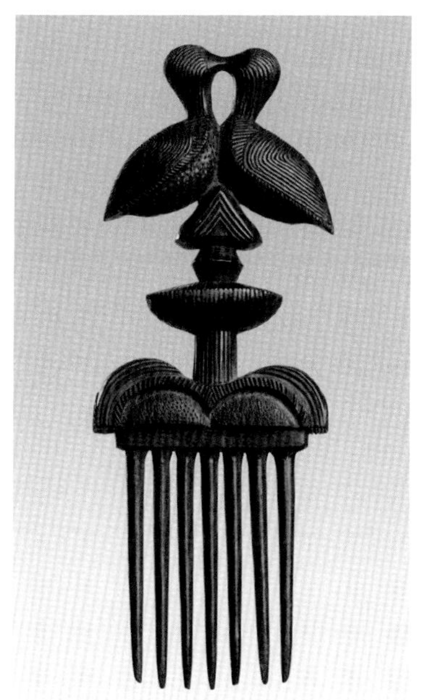

Comb
Baule, Akan, Ivory Coast
(see Fig. 71, pp. 142, 143)

All three million Idoma live in another country, Nigeria, on the opposite side of the 'Akan block' to the east, and a long way from Ivory Coast and Liberia, which are a two-thousand-kilometre drive away. Curiously, they use almost the same type of face as the Dan: in bas-relief, also modelled on several types of mask, but set within an almost perfect circle [Fig. 116]. Besides the outline of the face, this also applies to the eyes and even the (in this case) semi-circular ears. In contrast, the top (or the base, depending on how the figure is held or viewed) of another comb [Fig. 117] is adorned with a female figure with a slender, lithe, graceful body with small breasts and tapering neck and legs, which is totally at variance with the standard appearance of Idoma statues (which feature powerful legs, large breasts, and hands placed firmly on the knees). In this comb [Fig. 117], the disregard for anatomical accuracy and the disproportionately long, loose, skinny, almost threadlike arms, set wide apart from the body, deliberately diverges from the usual approach in Idoma statuary, and this is both for practical reasons – to ensure a firm grip of the anthropomorphic handle – and to add spectacular appeal to this outstanding sculpture.

The Yoruba, who number ten million, also live in Nigeria. The animal motifs on this representative comb [Fig. 116] are similar to those that adorn the top of the metal wands used by diviner-healers to treat their patients and resist 'soul eaters'. Two animals typical of the region and emblematic in Nigeria straddle the comb, one behind the other. At the front is a highly stylised wooden version of the famous bronze Okukor, the cockerel (*okpa*) that since the sixteenth century has stood on the altar dedicated to the queen mother in the palace of the king (*oba*) in Benin City.[9] Right behind, almost glued to it, is a protective monkey, the drill (*Mandrillus leucophaeus*, in the family cercopithecidae), which is closely related to the mandrill. How can anyone, whether man or woman, fail to be delighted to have his or her hair done under the auspicious gaze of these two totemic figures?

The sheer diversity of forms in Mina and Samir Borro's collection bears witness to the fact that these pieces have a wide variety of origins. The range of styles is such that it is possible both to distinguish and identify them, even though it is thanks much less to their overall structure, determined as it is by function, than to their motifs, decorations, and ornaments that these objects stand out. The tiniest details in the appearance of a hairstyle, the balance or exaggerated length of the limbs, the carriage of the head, the shape of a face, the presence or absence of incisions, lend them a certain individuality and an added originality, personality, and aesthetic value.

Judging by the styles, one might think *a priori* that the origins are always clearly and immediately identifiable, just as it is possible, and often easy, to do with masks and statues: it is impossible to mistake a Baule mask for a Dan mask, a Koulango statuette for an Attie statuette, an Idoma mask for a Bete mask.

But when it comes to combs, everything becomes more complex. Firstly, because the peoples who made these works in some cases live very close to each other: the Koulango are in daily contact with the Abron, sometimes even intermingling; the Attie live cheek by jowl with the Baule; and the Fante have been subjugated by the Ashanti on several occasions. It is hard to imagine that there have not been countless aesthetic influences over the centuries, to the point of creating not an overlap but a fusion of styles.

Furthermore, as has always been typical of Africa, it is common for an artist to settle in the territory of a different ethnic group, swapping techniques and borrowing subjects, motifs, and even styles. And renowned sculptors from one population would easily accept commissions from another group, even without leaving their sometimes distant village. Attie artists often made pieces for the Baule, the Yoruba worked for the Idoma, and the Ashanti made objects for the Fante. And this did not even stop short of sacred masks. Why should this not apply to combs, which were never sacred and eminently transportable?

Influences between groups are common, and in Africa they rarely act in one direction only. Indeed, these types of works travelled extensively throughout Ivory Coast, Burkina Faso, Ghana, Togo, Benin, and Nigeria. The same applies to other items of adornment, such as bracelets, anklets, rings, and necklaces. Dealings were numerous and easy along this coast of Guinea, even in inland forested areas, which in any case were cleared earlier in this region than elsewhere in Africa (for example, further west, in Liberia, where the rain forest survived for a long time). This was clearly and magnificently demonstrated by the first two European explorers in the region; one, Thomas Edward Bowdich, travelling from what is now Ghana and crossing the entire country from south to north between 1817 and 1818;[10] and the other, Louis-Gustave Binger,[11] approaching from Mali and Ivory Coast, from the upper reaches of the Niger to the present-day coastal towns of Grand-Bassam and Bingerville, between 1887 and 1889.

Yoruba women from the ruling house of Igbonnibi, Nigeria, 1984
John Pemberton III
Eliot Elisofon Photographic Archives, National Museum of African Art, Washington D.C., USA, Inv. EEPA 2013-015-1829

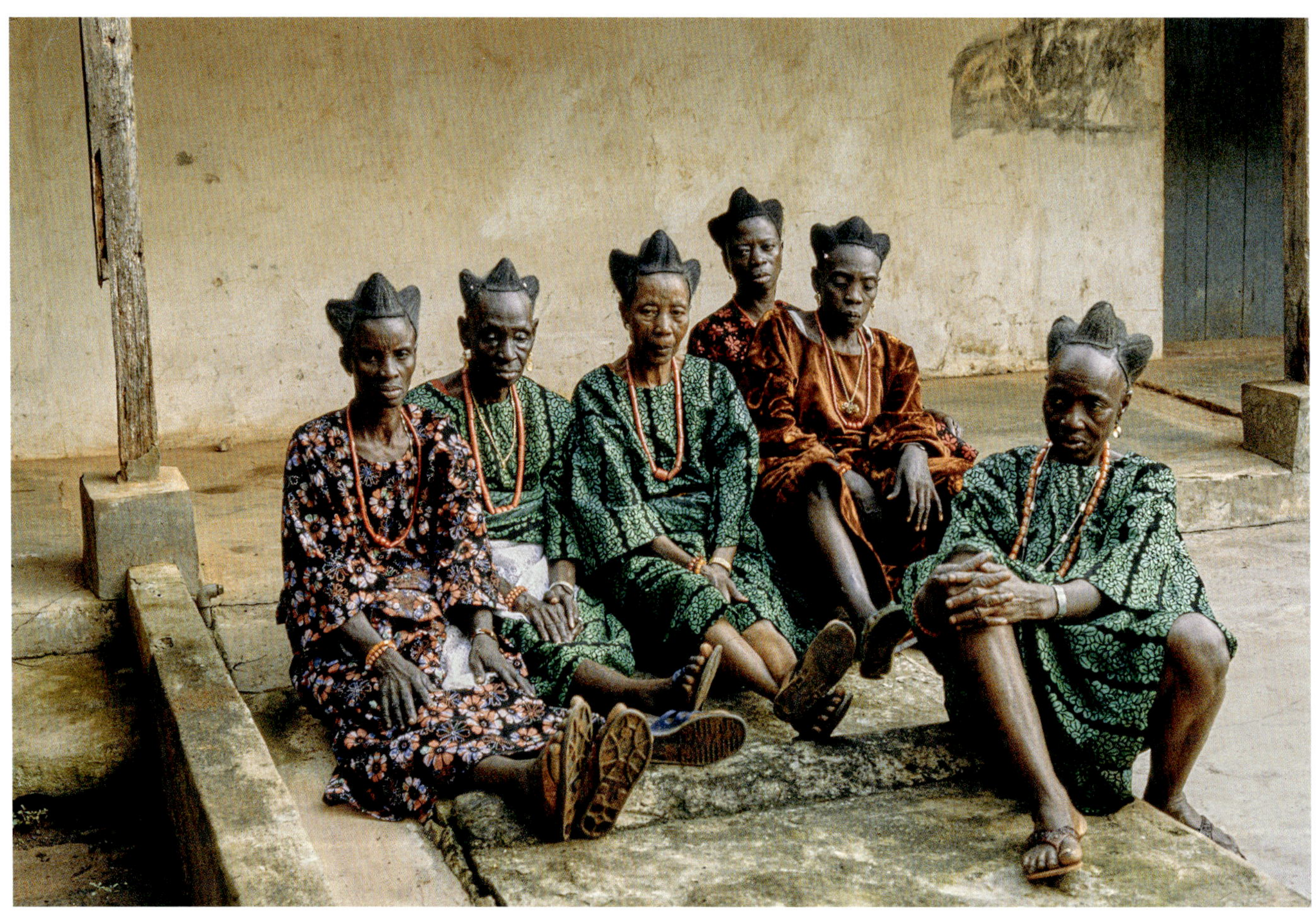

It is important not to overlook the relationships between forms that develop as a result of the endless intermingling of populations as they trade and barter. Since they did not have a precise origin or reflect an absolutely canonical style, many of these ornaments were offerings and came from other villages, different ethnic groups. Adapting to various different requirements and uses, these lightweight objects were easily exchanged for other goods and found themselves at the crossroads of a vast network of social interactions. This is why they are excellent indicators of major changes in style and influences.

A Contrapuntal Art

It hardly bears repeating that many African sculptures – at least the authentic ones – are not designed to be carefully positioned on the shelves of a museum, so they have no plinth or pedestal. All the support they have is an unstable, precarious base, since they are not placed on a flat stone surface during ceremonies, but more or less sunk into loose soil, whether earth or sand.

Another feature of these ornaments is that they actually have two mounts: firstly the teeth of the comb itself, and secondly the hair into which they are slid. And by adding a head, a human body, or an animal at the top of the functional part, the sculptor refuses to compress the forms. The bodies and faces seem to spring from the curve of the handle with astonishing litheness, ready to bound into space, so that the various planes and the different sections come together with a sharp sense of proportion, order, and balance. On the one hand, the perfectly straight, perfectly parallel teeth; on the other, an interplay of curves and counter-curves, which transforms the object by giving it a figurative aspect. But while the teeth, devoid of all ornamentation, stand out in their sharp, tapering gracefulness, they are never unaffected by the gentle curves of the decorations surmounting them, which seem to spring from the top, confident in their elegant economy of form. To deprive these ornaments of their functional purpose would be tantamount to amputating them.

Through a skilful arrangement of the sections, a great sense of rhythm, and a refined interplay that sets just the right tone, the sculptor expresses the concept as a fully realised, coherent object, displaying an astonishing sense of harmony. The overall form is extremely compact and concise, handled as it is with such precision and subtlety that in certain respects it resembles the rigour and discipline of music: the two opposing elements, separate but complementary, thus provide a remarkable example of counterpoint.

Counterpoint is a form of musical notation that marshals two distinct but simultaneous melodic lines. As in polyphony, these ornaments are thus able to make parallel but discrete forms and motifs 'sing' and play seemingly independently of each other, so that when they are seen together, the sculptural meaning and beauty of each can be clearly perceived as part of a coherent whole, while adding an extra dimension created by their synthesis.

If perfect modulation is the result of the fusion of these two forms, which are at once convergent and dissonant, consonant and antithetical, it is because the art of creating such ornaments involves a much wider range of sensibilities than is usually assumed. Since the artist expresses life in movement where matter and spirit mingle, a restrained emotion seems to bubble up from these figures, between the final layers that subordinate the object to the figure or motif and the figure to the object – revealing a profound connection between the individual and the artwork, between sculpture and the expression of existence.

The artist thus turns an aspect of the human body – the torso, neck, and face – into a pure form that he places at the very end of the functional part, as its culmination, its conclusion, and its acme. This harmony between the two 'sections' emphasises their perfect balance in space, as if the better to reach out towards the light and give an impression of ease and lightness – almost weightlessness. Moreover, the beauty of these pieces, exhibiting as they do an acute sense of decisive form, lies in the clear, ethereal volume they are part of and in their perfect sense of harmony in the service of what can only be called *elevation*. Indeed, these elongated objects and beings seem to be suspended between heaven and earth, lifted, drawn upwards, in a sort of state of levitation, on a tricky point of balance, elegantly gripped by an inner dynamic and doubly suspended, since this festive apparel, when worn by a man on special ceremonial occasions, would bestow on him an added majesty and solemnity; and when a woman had the chance to dance, they twirled with her, seeming to float in space, to reach for the sublime. It is worth remembering here that the word 'sublime' does not primarily express magnificence and splendour, but, in accordance with its etymology, an idea of elevation, exaltation, upward movement. In the past, before the word was overused, something was sublime when it was raised, carried upwards, suspended in mid-air, as opposed to something that was lowered.

Levitating Beings

One of the figures on the top of these combs exactly reproduces in miniature the position and style of a mystical spouse, a *blolo bian*, a famous Baule sculpture. Do these ornaments actually gain in range, vibrancy, and, paradoxically, magnificence by re-working certain motifs from larger-scale statues?

And did not Benvenuto Cellini, the creator of *Perseus*, which stands on the threshold of the Loggia dei Lanzi in Florence, introduce into his metalwork many of the practices, motifs, and forms of the 'high' sculpture then in vogue in the Renaissance? Is he not best known for the famous *saliera*, the solid gold saltcellar he made for Francis I, a marvel some twenty centimetres high, which he himself considered his masterpiece?

What are the Baule mystical spouses? According to local beliefs, when someone is born, they leave behind a spouse of the opposite sex in a parallel world (the *blolo*). When problems arise (difficulty in maintaining a stable relationship, sterility, miscarriages), a person consults a diviner, who invariably explains the reason for these ills: they are signs of the mystical spouse's jealousy, who takes revenge by casting spells. The way to bring back the absent spouse and appease any feelings of anger and abandonment is to make him or her real. A sculptor will have to represent this mystical spouse in the form of a figurine in order to exorcise the evil spells. The object will have to be worshipped (keeping it close at least one night a week, making offerings, dressing it up, stroking it like a doll, etc.). In view of this, what could be better than to ask an artist to decorate a comb with such a figure – or rather a hairpin (since in this case it only has three teeth)?

The outcome in the present example is admirable, and it is worth pointing out that the effectiveness of a figure representing a spirit spouse also depends on its ability to please the disgruntled supernatural being. It is sculpted in accordance with the prevailing standards of beauty to increase the chances of success, and it is extraordinarily well made. The piece exhibits a supreme confidence in its fine lines, combined with a remarkable sense of volume and a vibrant elegance that hints at the possibility of a real intake of breath. The sculptor has accurately rendered the structure of the human body, while striving to describe the perfect lines of an ideal form.

Standing on its support, this harmoniously curving statue gives absolute priority to its vertical aspect, and it is distinguished by its long, smooth outline, as if the sculptor had wanted to make the most of the full length of his initial block of wood. A number of features stand out: the daring fluidity of the body, with its graceful curves; the hair gathered in a single bun, with the lightest striations, perhaps to make it easier to handle; the protruding navel, to emphasise the concept of lineage or descent; and the rather short legs, a not uncommon characteristic, which are bent to suggest movement and remove any hint of solemn remoteness in the figure.

As photographs from the 1920s and 1930s attest, it used to be the custom in villages to grow an extremely long, carefully plaited beard. The elderly say that these traditional beards were known as *akansa tenden* and explain that they were coated with shea butter to keep them so long. The same attribute is found on other works in the collection [Figs. 30, 31]. In this case, the beard lends the man an air of dignified maturity and a certain sense of superiority. This dignity is underlined by the extremely complex hairstyle, created with the same painstaking meticulousness as the beard, and which the sculptor has reproduced with the utmost care. It was a practice typical of the patriarchs and has since been abandoned. Carefully crafted, such hair could only be worn by those who no longer worked in the fields and had the leisure to patiently put up with its being painstakingly looked after by expert hands – in other words very elderly men.

This is why certain patriarchs, and even younger but high-ranking and respectable men, might sometimes wear a comb in their meticulously constructed hairstyle just like women, so as to proclaim their detachment from the daily grind.

Other ornaments have even slimmer bodies that are elongated to the nth degree, turning their vertical nature into the supreme virtue [Figs. 42, 104, 105]. This is certainly true of the Baule, but it also applies to the Ashanti [Fig. 3], the Fante [Fig. 12], the Koulango [Fig. 104], and even the Bete, who are known for their particularly huge statues and masks [Figs. 113, 114]. Such adornments clearly reveal the extent to which this type of object, which uses a person's image to achieve its vigorous equilibrium, is attached to anthropomorphic parameters, and how much these remain the model and goal of all metamorphosis.

Faces in Space: Single Heads Facing Each Other

The favourite motif in these ornaments is not always a standing or seated figure – these complete figures are called 'wooden beings' (*waka sona* among the Baule, and *nkpasopi* among the Attie in southeastern Ivory Coast) – but one, two, or even three human heads. The Attie have a specific term for this type of decoration: *tsanhen*. From the practical point of view, a head used as a handle offers a perfect grip.

One of the first thoughts that come to mind is that this art is in stark contrast to the codes and canons that govern representation in West Africa. Statues in this region always depict standing figures or spirits of nature seated – and therefore retaining their physical features. With the exception of the practice of placing commemorative terracotta heads on tombs – something that has long since disappeared, and which no one in the twentieth century witnessed, since it flourished on the coast, to the east of Ivory Coast and west of Ghana, between the sixteenth and nineteenth centuries – there are virtually no examples of heads displayed alone. Statues used for worship or divination, which would be made of wood, never consisted of a single part of the body.

On the other hand, these hair ornaments very rarely had complete anthropomorphic figures. In African art, the head is always given prominence – hence the importance of the mask on this continent. On statues and decorations, the head is almost always enlarged, because African art has always reflected a hierarchical concept of the body, rather than seeking morphological 'truth'; it has never aimed for anatomical 'accuracy'. These are iconographic, symbolic proportions. The head is considered to be the seat of thought and a communicator of vitality and social power. It is therefore imbued with emblematic significance and its expressive power is emphasised in these hair ornaments. As the seat of a person's identity, it is a summary, a representation of their essence, an epitome of their main features.

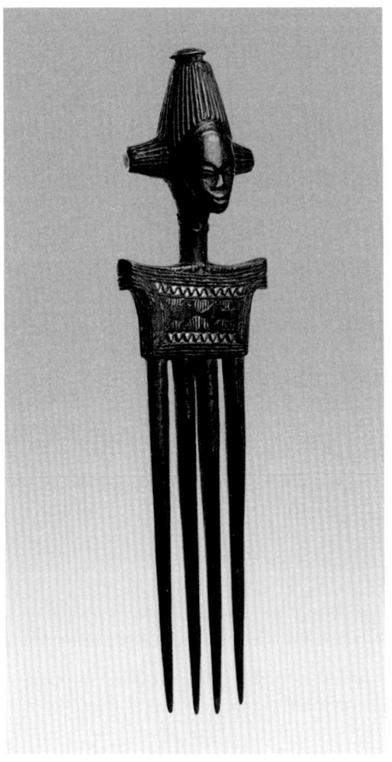

Comb
Baule, Ivory Coast (see Fig. 35, p. 100)

Sometimes it is perched at the top of a long neck [Figs. 33, 38, 40], which is an unambiguous criterion of beauty among the Baule (and all the Akan: Agni, Attie, Ashanti alike), amounting to an artistic and human ideal. In everyday life, value judgements even find kinship between art and a person's body, especially the slight curve of a wonderfully long, graceful neck. Young Baule, Attie, and Agni women are very proud of the elegance of their slender, willowy necks, and they always make the most of them.

But above all, adding an extra face just over that of the person wearing a comb ornament is a stunning manoeuvre: the doubling of the human figure, placing one over the other, makes it clear the extra face is no portrait, but an ideal image that displays an amazing inventiveness in its positioning. In this refined, restrained art there is nothing abstract or stylised about the expressions. The features are perfectly defined: the high, rounded forehead projects over the heart-shaped face set over the gentle protruding mouth; almond-shaped eyes with heavy, closed or half-closed eyelids, seem to focus on a secret or on the ephemeral nature of human affairs; the short chin is sometimes extended by a beard – a subtle effect of life's unfolding. The most commonly seen features are two lines that follow the eyebrow arches, meeting at the root of a straight, slim nose and separating again before following the shape of the nostrils, thus repeating the double upper curve, on a smaller scale. Their expressiveness is accentuated by the pinched shapes and the strength of the lines describing each volume.

In short, these objects display multiple configurations that are adapted to the hand, making them extremely easy to handle and conveying a sense of balance, rigour, and controlled momentum. They exploit all the techniques of wood carving without turning these ornaments merely into pretty bibelots. They are thus testaments to the astonishing mastery of the sculptors, their gift for getting to the heart of an object, their ability to rely on a system of constraints in order to attain a greater artistic effect. For while the ornament respects functional requirements, it also transcends them, imposing a vibrant tension that does not emerge from a plain whim of the sculptor's. Exalting and amplifying the magnificence of the coiffures, making them even more resplendent, combs tower over them like plumes or wings. The better to take flight?

Real Hairstyles, Carved Hairstyles, Dreamt Hairstyles

A further doubling: the hairstyles which, with their chiselled braids, buns, and plaits, lend form to volume and add to the magnificence of these adornments. Hairstyle upon hairstyle: the ornament seems to repeat the woman's hairstyle, like a raised mirror. Did they serve as models for mothers and friends, who held them in their hands before getting down to work with the comb? Mina and Samir Borro's collection offers a rich array of hairdos. Painstakingly modelled and reproduced down to the tiniest detail, they seem to vary ad infinitum, and it is enlightening to note that African sculptors, disparaged a century ago because they seemed unable to make 'objective' representations, display astonishing precision and scrupulous realism when it comes to depicting hair arrangements – especially in these miniature works, as if trying to rival goldsmiths in the fine detailing of their plaits.

But if the most talented sculptors have been able to draw inspiration from the most ingenious creations of hairdressers, reproducing them meticulously and with the utmost precision, this is because the two fields have always interacted and fed off each other.

It bears repeating that in the absence of photographs, or at least their extreme rarity, sculptures are the only means of becoming acquainted with the coiffures of the past. If one looks at the masks of the Baule, the Yohoure, the Wan, and the Guro, one can see that at the beginning of the twentieth century both women and men, especially the patriarchs, usually wore their hair in high buns, forming three pronounced conical protuberances. Some of these impressive structures have become obsolete, swept away by the modern world; but they are rarely forgotten when one takes the time to interview hairdressers today, in Abidjan, Accra, Kumasi, or Bouaké – especially in the villages, where traditions have survived – and show them catalogues from collections and museums. But the fact that sculptures and carvings can perfectly reproduce the most complex forms is also thanks to the malleability of wood, which mimics to perfection, in the tiniest detail, all the swirls and arabesques of these extraordinary edifices.

In Africa, the techniques and methods used are as varied as the hairstyles they create. Smoothing, twisting, and separating to fashion fine plaits, multiple braids – side or frontal, arranged in a fan or in parallel ridges, divided into clusters or shells, or gathered in buns or in chignons, erected in the form of crests, horns, or a pointed cone set at the top of the head, perhaps finished off with structures held in place by buttresses, rods, fibres. The procedure was so systematised that, for example, among the Baule, renowned artists living in central Ivory Coast, each element of the traditional hairstyle had a specific name and applied to coiffures that adorned the women as well as some of the men. For instance, the arc of braided hair at the top of the forehead, running from one temple to the other, was called *tre ba* [Figs. 33, 34, 35, 36]. Another extremely eye-catching feature on both wooden [Fig. 42] and ivory [Fig. 43] ornaments is the *ko glo* [Fig. 46], a unique, elaborately pointed crest that adorns the highest part of the head.

Other hairstyles are even more elaborate, in the form of tiaras or crowns that stand erect like crests, veritable monuments made of hair that increase the size of the head [Figs. 18, 19, 20, 21]; or others that include long chignons, the *tré si kpolé*, which flow down from the nape of the neck [Figs. 39, 40]; or the conspicuous plaits arranged in a fan [Fig. 44] that are found mainly on ivory pieces; braids gathered up at the top of the head; or again, jutting protuberances and bristly pigtails, sometimes curled in a ring and even more voluminous [Figs. 50, 51].

Each type of hairstyle also had its own name, which might paradoxically be quite prosaic: *gyira tre*, the 'lion style', resembled a lion's mane; *bwa wè*, 'ram's horns', arranged the hair into two long pigtails at the temples, tapering towards the bottom; *alowa kofie*, 'yam mounds', built the hair into a checkerboard of small clumps, like the piles of this tuber found in the fields; and so on. But within the great variety of styles, the artist could also give free rein to his imagination in a wealth of details.

Several of these ornaments feature an even more remarkable design [Figs. 57, 58]: the faces portrayed in solemn majesty are sometimes encircled by wide, methodically striated aureoles, in a network of finely engraved scarifications enhanced by the deep patina of use. Indeed, these halos – the discs of light that sculptors in other civilisations placed around the heads of sacred figures, deified heroes, gods and saints – offer proof of the active role played by this finery in building the social body. These nimbi, then, lend the figures a hieratic expression and a royal appearance, as if they have been transformed into fabulous apparitions [Figs. 45, 62, 70].

Carried away by his own inventiveness, one artist has even carved out a small ivory bowl on the top of a figure's head [Fig. 56]. This is a rare, though wonderfully executed and highly effective, conceit, which here symbolises the idea of making an offering (as occurs on several ceremonial figurines in West Africa, among the Attie, the Senufo, and the Guro). However, it is clearly empty here and illustrates almost cheekily the receptacle that a woman could under no circumstances carry when wearing this hairstyle – as we saw earlier.

Some of the hairstyles are huge and can be even as high as the face [Figs. 47, 48, 64, 66], but thanks to the play of curves and incisions, they consist of clean, simple forms that display an absolute mastery of volume and a perfect balance between flamboyance and restraint. The perfectly judged proportions, the softness of the modelling, and the skilled carving are testament to the mastery of the sculptors, who strive to encapsulate a being's imperious presence in a motionless form. This proves once again that the role of the figurative component, whether anthropomorphic or stylised, and in any case harmoniously adapted to the overall form, is to link the object to its users, to make it one with its function, by highlighting a serene power accentuated by the subtlety of the modelling.

Scenes of Daily Life: Decorative Features

In their formal diversity, these works bear witness to the inventiveness of the artists who conceived them; they display an extraordinary range of formal solutions and divergent approaches. Despite the constraints imposed by their function, they encompass a wide variety of styles, as well as displaying great skill in handling the material and an unquestioned originality. Since they are not bound by sacred codes, nor, unlike masks and statues, conditioned by religious or social prescriptions, artists have been able to give free rein to their verve and inspiration: each creator, unhampered by liturgical

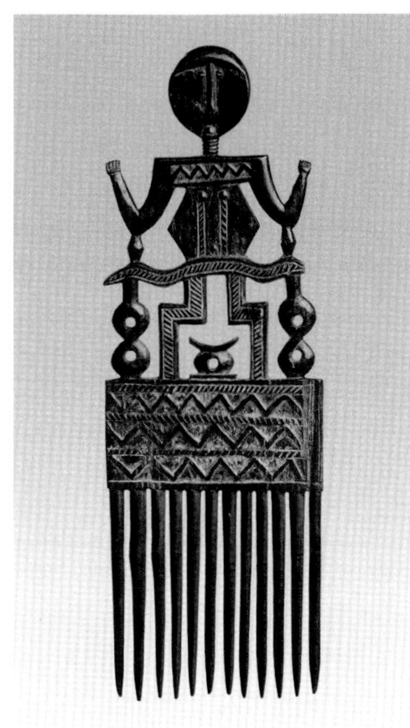

Comb
Ashanti, Akan, Ghana (see Fig. 1, pp. 56, 57)

constraints, has constantly pushed back the boundaries of representation in terms of motifs, subjects, and forms.

These works are further enhanced by the extreme care taken in their decoration, in which scenes from everyday life are depicted with meticulous attention to the details of social context. It can be said that to a certain extent each of these adornments tells a story, recalls a legend, or passes on the memory of a myth.

One of them [Fig. 4] includes two scenes on the upright separating the top decoration from the teeth: two facetious sequences in which the Lilliputian forms take on the nigh-impossible challenge of achieving architectural monumentality, thanks to the imaginative use of closed and open space. The aesthetic principle here is that of the tableau vivant. The artist has created this highly expressive example by multiplying the descriptive details, of which he gives a personal interpretation. On one side of the front is portrayed a remarkable, almost Cézanne-like dining scene: bottles and jugs are lined up on a table, a maid brings a dish, a guest is arriving late and holds out his arms in greeting as he gets ready to join someone already seated next to a wary dog. On the back we find the same characters, but this time a gigantic bird has appeared and is crossing the room, while the dog has leapt up and become as large and aggressive as a wild beast; the dishes are flying all over the place and the two guests have stood up, stunned and amazed. One can only imagine the success that the young woman wearing this ornament must have enjoyed, the admiration she must have aroused, the exclamations, the laughter, her village friends whirling round to see how the story unfolds.

One of these items of furniture stands out on other ornaments: the seats. Stools, chairs, and thrones, in a variety of shapes, are used to enliven the setting and lend it a geometric rigour: a small circle within a square, a square within a rectangle, stocky or rounded cubes with supports, and even a tiny 'dwarf' stool placed between a figure's legs [Fig. 1]. However, there is nothing fanciful about these articles, for each of these seats has a specific name, function, and purpose. A stool is more than merely a utilitarian object: in Africa, at least in a village, one does not sit just anywhere, or on any type of seat, even as a guest. Especially since, stylistically speaking, far from diminishing a person, a stool actually contributes to his status, boosting his authority.

This is the case with the first type of stool, the most common in the region and on these ornaments. Its rectangular base, which is rather small, as if to emphasise an impression of flight, is echoed by a tray that is the same shape, but wider and curved at both ends, which is supported by a single cylindrical central pillar. Known as an *asesedwa* by the Ashanti and *ulimbi bia* by the Baule, who adopted the design, it played an important role in rites performed at an enthronement or in memory of a deceased dignitary. It would also confirm the prestige or power of its owner, and enhance his or her rank. A tangible expression of cultural values and a mark of hospitality, it immediately revealed the hierarchical position within society of the owner, host, or guest. It appears on an ornament in its role as a throne [Fig. 31], on which sits a chief or dignitary in the posture of someone with the power to decide on matters regarding the community and ready to address any grievances. This role can also be assumed by a woman [Fig. 104], which is hardly surprising in a culture where matrilineal descent prevails.

Another model is that of European-style chairs with high backs, which might seem incongruous. However, they have a long history among the Ashanti, dating back to the sixteenth century. Known as *asipim* ('I stand erect', an allusion to the stability of the chiefdom or the state), they are said by the Ashanti to have no spiritual value. Yet, when not in use, they remain turned to face the wall. Superstition? When asked about the reason for this, the answer is: 'It has always been so.'

On one of these ornaments, a figure is shown holding a set of two *asipim* chairs above his head in his outstretched arms [Fig. 12]. This is actually a precise transposition of a normal scene in an Ashanti princely home, as it still might be witnessed today: on important occasions (offering condolence, meetings, formal exchanges, ceremonies, etc.), young girls, usually nieces of the chief or dignitary, solemnly carry the personal chair of the honoured person high above their heads, as if it were a king's palanquin. Once they have carefully placed it in front of the house, the guest or host can sit down in it, protected by a parasol.

This is an opportunity to examine this surprising motif, rarely represented in West African art: figures holding objects up towards the sky. While Atlases and caryatids are common in the art of the Hemba and the Luba peoples in the Democratic Republic of Congo, they are unexpected among the Ashanti, the Baule, and the Agni – except on these hair ornaments, where they occasionally appear. With aplomb, assurance, and no particular effort, a person holds up two seats – one like a standard [Fig. 13], the other like a drum [Fig. 107]; a woman raises above her head the very comb on which she is the decoration [Fig. 110]; or again, several figures have become the Atlases for the combs they are responsible for decorating. Their appearance clearly indicates that they represent an image of power and authority, a sign of distinction, for the women who wear this ornament.

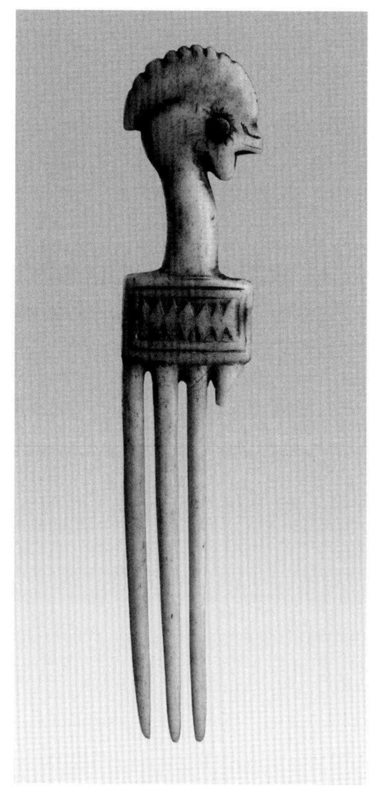

Comb
Baule, Akan, Ivory Coast (see Fig. 80, p. 149)

The *asipim*, *asesedwa*, and *ulimbi bia* seats are reserved for men among the Ashanti, Agni, and Baule, both in theory and in practice; when they die, they are used as altars for ancestor worship.

Pipes, which used to be the attributes of dignitaries in Africa – as can be seen in old photographs – reflect the same desire to incorporate an emblem of masculinity into the female realm. A magnificent ornament shows an old man sitting on an *asesedwa* stool drawing on a big pipe. Finely and accurately carved, with a smooth finish and astonishingly true to life in the pose, this small sculpture, which sacrifices anatomical precision in favour of emotional realism, eschews all minor details [Fig. 31]. On another astonishing sculpture, the beard, plaited right down to its roots, merges with the pipe stem, which is also oversized [Fig. 30]. In contrast, two pipes carved with great skill stand side by side alone on a hairpin [Fig. 29], and one cannot help thinking of the man or woman who (cheekily?) wore these two male attributes at the top of their hairdo . . .

Another motif has been appropriated that is usually set aside for the masks of male brotherhoods: birds perched delicately on the top of ornaments in pairs and side by side [Figs. 74, 75, 76]. Together, they conjure up a dream of peace and harmony, of mankind and the natural world miraculously reconciled [Fig. 71].

It then spread further east, first to the Baule, in the area near Yamoussoukro, and was later adopted in certain Agni sculptures – which is why some claim that it was actually the Baule who created it.

These astonishing carvings of oxpeckers, passerines, and curlews exploit a skilful interplay of light and shadow to create infinite variations in style that often make use

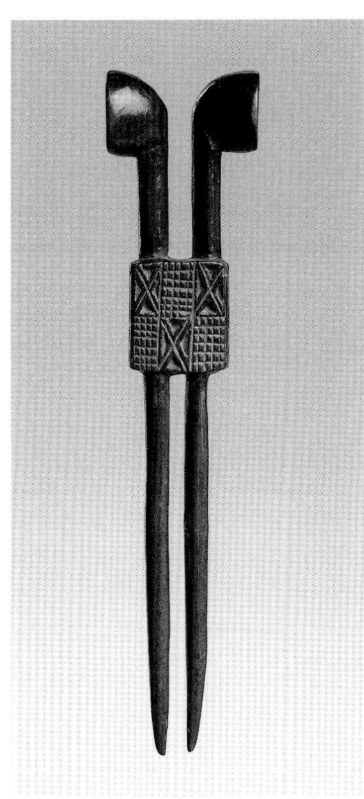

Comb
Baule, Akan, Ivory Coast
(see Fig. 29, p. 92)

of foreshortening. The African artist selects, reinterprets, and stylises, never breaking completely free of naturalistic representation. The cockerel predominates, not only among the Yoruba, but also among the Attie [Fig. 90] and the Baule [Figs. 82, 83, 84]. Symbolising life and revival, it is a favourite sacrificial animal almost everywhere in Africa. On these occasions, the animal's throat is slit and its blood poured over a statuette or sacred mask to welcome an eminent guest, to celebrate a funeral, or to ask for a spirit's protection. Another advantage of the cockerel is that it is thought to live on the border between the civilised world of the village and the deepest wild bush it originally came from.

In combinations that are at once discreet and bold, vigorous and uncluttered, the humanised bush thus comes to represent a harmony that has finally been attained.

The Lure of Geometry: Towards Abstraction?

A testament to the ancient traditions they spring from and demonstrating a high technical standard in their execution, these works unequivocally illustrate the magnificent eclecticism of this little-known art. As we have seen, their original craftsmanship, freedom of execution, and astonishing creativity can be explained in part by the fact that these ornaments had no ritual or magical significance. Unaffected by religious stipulations, they answer to the artists' desire for fantasy, their wish to compete with one another, their instinct for emulation, but also in some cases their willingness to meet the demands of their patrons – as we can guess from the occasional depiction of Christ. Besides respecting certain conventions concerning statues (the figures of mystical spouses), or readopting carving techniques sometimes similar to those of the ivory pommels long in use along the Gulf of Guinea, sculptors exploited their subject in an entirely new way, to the extent that these ornaments went through a whole series of experiments that testify to the degree of inventiveness that was brought to bear. The range of styles is also very broad: from ascetic simplification to a search for exuberance, from minimalism to extravagance, from highly expressive realism to the lure of geometry.

Many ornaments make no attempt to create a sense of volume and indeed eschew all work in the round, which actually prevails in this region's sculpture. As a result, the sculptor's approach is turned upside-down. He views form in terms of planes, edges, and angles, and studies the surface of the wood or ivory and the shadows that surround the figures and highlights them with graphic sharpness while the light plays gently over them. By abandoning volume and favouring bas-reliefs or graphic techniques, the sculptor gives engraving and incising the lion's share in fashioning these forms. He takes us to the threshold of geometric abstraction by working in two-dimensions and, in consequence, adopting an extreme approach to the representation of real life. The sculptor's work is reduced to the essentials, with a neat, even rendering of lines in dazzling combinations, sliding into one another, criss-crossing, and intertwining.

But although these works are pared down in the extreme, the flat surfaces, criss-crossed by subtle modulations, come constantly to life in the play of the grain, the changing texture, the skilfully exploited effect of the knots, creating such sharp outlines that their mutual relationships impress themselves on the eye with force and precision.

Alongside the large openwork decorations [Figs. 1, 2] there is a wealth of hatching, serrated friezes, twists, meanders, and more subtle motifs, all picked out with infinite delicacy and according to a very clearly defined pattern. Vibrant incisions describe a multitude of juxtaposed squares, a frieze of crosses [Fig. 6], architectural frameworks, arches, concentric curves [Fig. 4], and granules set into the polished wood in highly rhythmic broken lines, animated by spirals, zigzags, and loops.

Aided by optical effects, these ingenious combinations are enlivened by a network of dotted lines and a wide variety of motifs, carved and incised with a knowing use of ellipsis. What is immediately striking is the supple treatment of the flowing outlines and harmonious proportions that lend the object its sense of physical presence, a restrained power combined with great expressiveness. The ancient secret of the regulations and the precise meaning of the sculptural conventions are thus made plain, telling us that in these ornaments allusion supersedes affirmation.

Beyond this play of broken lines and arabesques, almost all the geometric shapes can be found and reflect a constant passion for concision. Thus, here are multiple examples of circles, both full and empty; semi-circles, whether facing each other or overlapping; hexagons with a base set on a rectangle; trapezoids whose small base ends in a circle; rhombi; and tight grid patterns, crisply embellished with tiny punch marks.

This geometric approach is applied to the figures too, and the features of the human form are confidently transmuted accordingly: breasts become pyramidal or conical; legs and torsos are carved in straight lines; some arms describe a perfect arc, with the hands resting on rounded hips, while other arms are stretched out in the shape of a *W* over an inverted *N*. At the extreme, all that remains is a circle with other circles made up of dots inside [Fig. 4]. These correspondences between the body and abstract shapes lend the decoration both a certain austerity and vitality.

The various instances of stylisation, a radical method of representing reality, affect figures in a number of ways. Both human figures [Figs. 1, 2] and animals are stylised and drawn as silhouettes, their outlines sharply defined within a strictly circumscribed, frontal architectural framework built around a single axis.

These figures, frozen in a series of calculated gestures, are depicted in a way that isolates them in a kind of heraldic clarity, as if to transform them into icons or conversely, incorporate them into a decoration in order to determine the outlines of symmetrical compositions, meanwhile always striving for a clarity of form and pared-down volumes. The artists have been wonderfully adept at carving wood and ivory so as to create an unbreakable interconnection between the representation of an individual and the abstract ornament.

However complex they might be, the forms make up intelligible groups: extremely slender figures, circular heads, round eyes. By rendering the body with such clean, spare lines, elongation becomes surreal and a face retains only a few details from perceived reality that are related to each other through an interplay of echoing shapes: eyes, mouth, and nose.

This two-dimensionality and simplification of features really comes into its own in the collection's several examples of replicas of a famous sculpture, the *Akua'ba* of the Ashanti of Ghana [Figs. 9, 11]. This widespread model features a disc-shaped

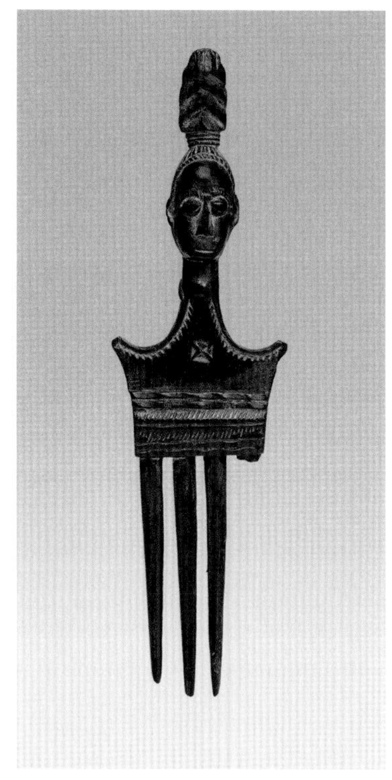

Comb
Attie, Akan, Ivory Coast
(see Fig. 38, p. 105)

Young Akan women, Ghana/Ivory Coast
Late 19th to early 20th century
Archives no. 182
American Colonization Society Collection

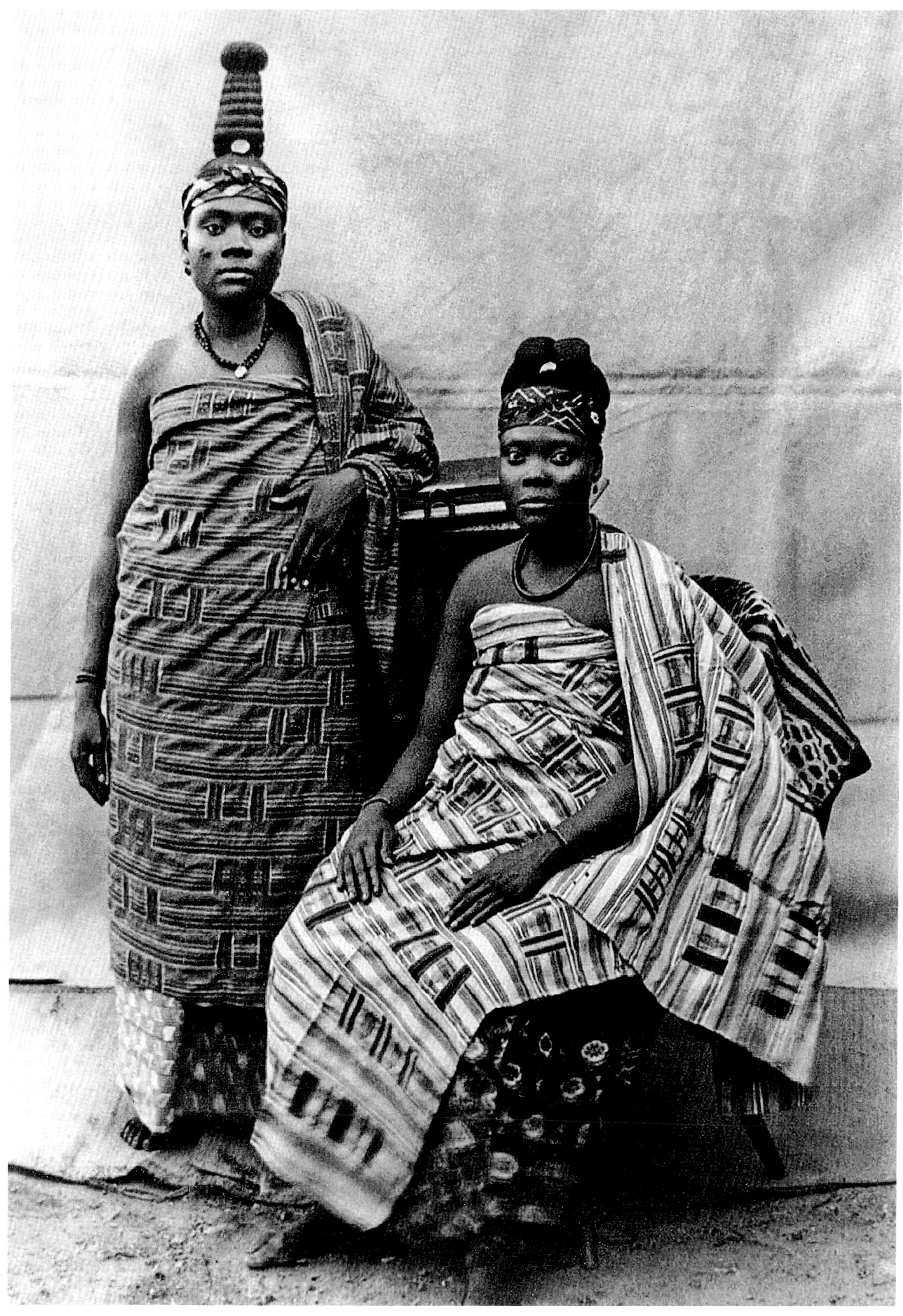

head incised on a flat surface, which is disproportionately large compared with the small cylindrical body; a ringed neck, a sign of wealth and well-being; a truncated cone-shaped torso; and smooth, outstretched arms. Beneath the high, oval forehead, which takes up more than half the face, the broad eyebrow arches meet to form a straight, triangular nose, while the mouth, set very low, is merely suggested by a cleft. In the past, these dolls might be adorned with belts, necklaces, earrings, and multi-coloured beads.

The *Akua'ba* (plural: *Akua'ma*) takes its name from a legendary girl called Akua ('Wednesday' in Ashanti, the custom being to name a child after its day of birth). She was having trouble conceiving (the sure sign of a curse, in Africa) and went to consult a diviner, who recommended that her father or husband carve a tiny child out of wood. When her neighbours saw that she was also feeding it, they started to tease her, making fun of 'Akua's baby [*ba*]'. But as soon as she gave birth to a perfect little girl, these same women began to follow her example. As a result, many women who were childless, or were pregnant but wanted to ensure their newborn would be healthy, used to carry these fertility dolls wrapped in cloth and strapped to their backs, just like a real baby. When they were not carrying the doll, they would look after it, washing and dressing it. They then gave them to children to play with, like the Baule's mystical spouse statues in Ivory Coast.

However, when added at the top of a hair ornament, this motif had no apotropaic value. It was not a charm, just a decorative element. When interviewed, women said: 'On a comb, it's just there to look pretty.' The *Akua'ba* habit has also long since disappeared, but this figure's stylised form has perhaps made it the most recognisable of all African sculptures.

Conclusion

As André Leroi-Gourhan establishes in *Le Geste et la parole*, form does not suggest function completely; there is always a 'residue' that we can call *style*. However clear an object's purpose may be, it is not true that the images and motifs that adorn that object can be reduced to its function. The demands of style remain crucial, even in cases where a particular configuration is thought to depend solely on functional considerations. Beauty, then, lies in the freedom with which life seeks and finds its forms, in the way wood, ivory, bone, or horn are transformed by sculpture, in the way artists, even for a utilitarian object, combine a love of perfect forms with the desire to produce ever-new variants.

Simplified volumes, virtuoso craftsmanship, meticulous detailing in the carving, concern for the overall form and spatial relationships: the figures, animals, and geometric designs that crown these hair ornaments with confident breadth never diminish or upstage them. The outlines never become academic, bland, or redundant. This art includes all the elements typical of African sculpture and its conventions: the carefully considered composition and distribution of parts, the graceful modelling that exploits a rare ingenuity, the unexpected resources and surprisingly precise detailing.

However, despite and no doubt because of their small size, these sober, restrained compositions, which are often pared down to the essentials yet filled with a lively expressiveness, sharpen artists' architectural instincts more than other works. These master craftsmen take pleasure in creating light, airy forms so as to offer a clear, uniform artistic approach and define solid frameworks that are governed by an age-old care taken over the distribution of volumes. By superbly combining the subtlety of the lines and the harmony of the composition, these artists succeed, with the greatest sculptural confidence and a fluid, assertive style, in creating an impression of elegance and majesty, sensuality and rigour, combining the genius of ellipsis with a sense of grace. By seeming to manifest the mysterious fluid that ensures the world's seamless continuity, one form leading to another, these carved figures achieve a magnificence expressed through an unerring sense of rhythm and an innate respect for proportions, as if each were seeking the essence of pure form.

1 See George Schweinfurth, *Au cœur de l'Afrique (1868–1871), Voyages et découvertes dans les régions explorées de l'Afrique centrale* (Paris: Hachette, 1875).
2 One need only read the very first books about these sumptuous courts: Richard Austin Freeman's *Travels and Life in Ashanti and Jaman* (Constable Publishers, London), about the kingdom of Ashanti and Gyaman, published in 1898; Maurice Delafosse's many works, written in the early twentieth century, about the Baule in the Ivory Coast; and above all, for all these kingdoms, especially the opulent monarchy of Benin, the astonishing work by Olfert Dapper (1636–1689) entitled *Description de l'Afrique*, published in 1668, with many splendid engravings depicting magnificent ceremonies.
3 On this topic, see Alain-Michel Boyer, 'Un art ostentatoire, de l'Ethiopie au Sud Soudan', in *Arts & Cultures* 13, (2012): 84–103.
4 'L'Ethnographie de la Côte d'Ivoire', 1900'.
5 On these masks and their summit ornament, see five books (including illustrations) by the author: *Arts premiers de Ivory Coast* (Saint-Maur: Editions Sépia, 1997); *Baule, L'Esthétique de l'harmonie dans la dissemblance* (Milan: 5 Continents Editions, 2008); *Le Sacré, le Secret: les Wan, les Mona et les Koyaga de Ivory Coast* (Paris: Éditions Hazan, 2011); *Les Yohouré de Ivory Coast, Faire danser les dieux* (Lausanne: Éditions Ides et Calendes, 2016); and *We (Guéré, Wobé, Kran), un art d'Afrique entre assemblage et constructivisme* (Milan: 5 Continents Editions, 2019).
6 Michel Leiris and Jacqueline Delange, *Afrique Noire. La création plastique* (Paris: Gallimard, 1967), 196.
7 See Jean-Paul Barbier-Mueller, *Arts de la Côte d'Ivoire dans les collections du musée Barbier-Mueller* (Geneva: Musée Barbier-Mueller, 1993), 175–76.
8 See Alain-Michel Boyer, *Les Figurines Kulango: Les esprits mystérieux de la brousse de la collection Pierluigi Peroni* (Milan: 5 Continents Editions, 2017).
9 It was purloined by the British in 1897 and returned to Nigeria by Cambridge University in 2021.
10 Thomas Edward Bowdich, *Mission from Cape Coast Castle to Ashantee, with a statistical account of that kingdom, and geographical notices of other parts of the Interior of Africa* (London: J. Murray, 1819).
11 Louis-Gustave Binger, *Du Niger au golfe de Guinée par le pays de Kong et le Mossi par le capitaine Binger (1887–1889)* (Paris: Hachette, 1892).

Young Akan women, Ghana, 1880–1888
Anonymous photographer
QL-30.013.0050

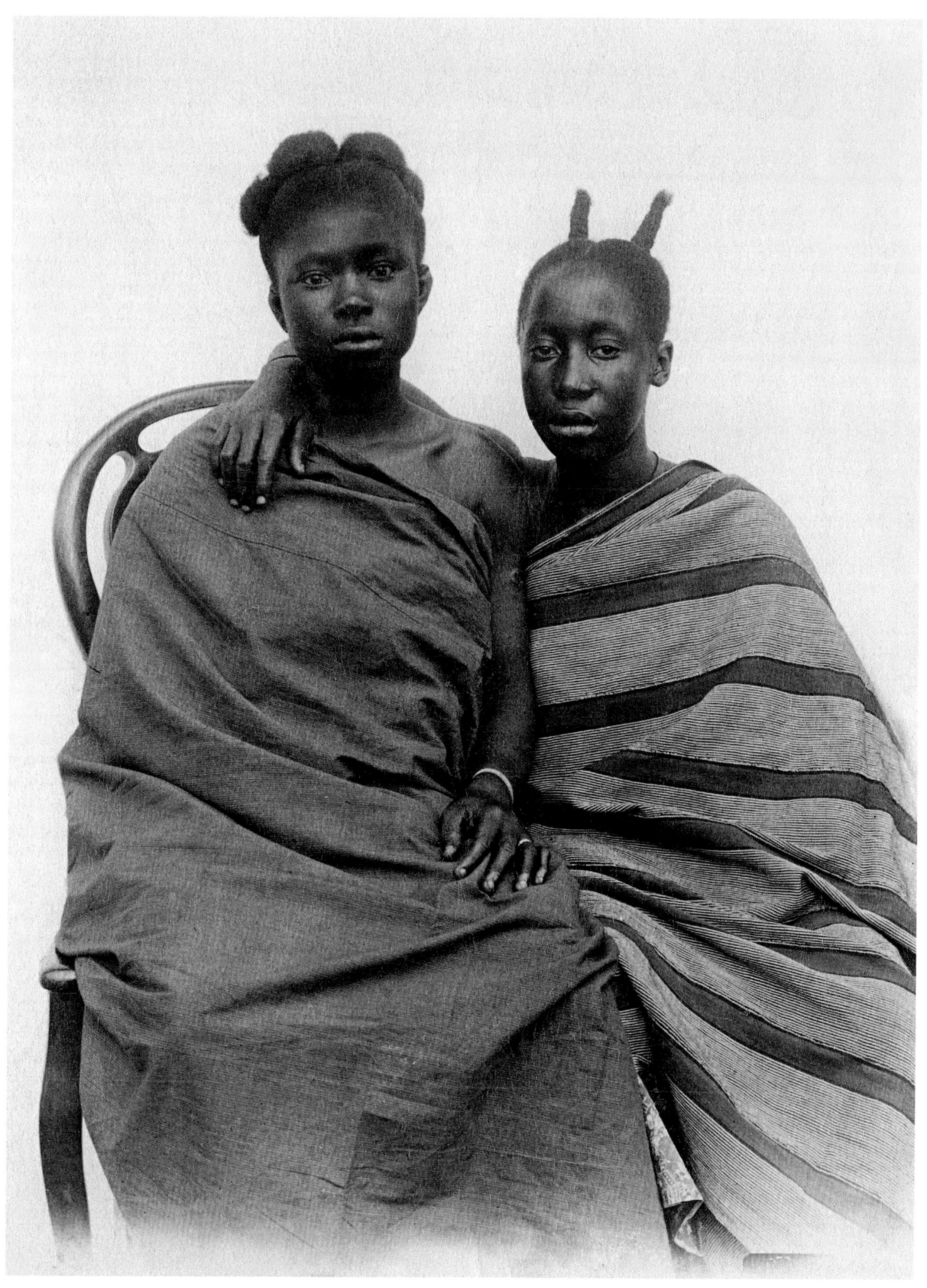

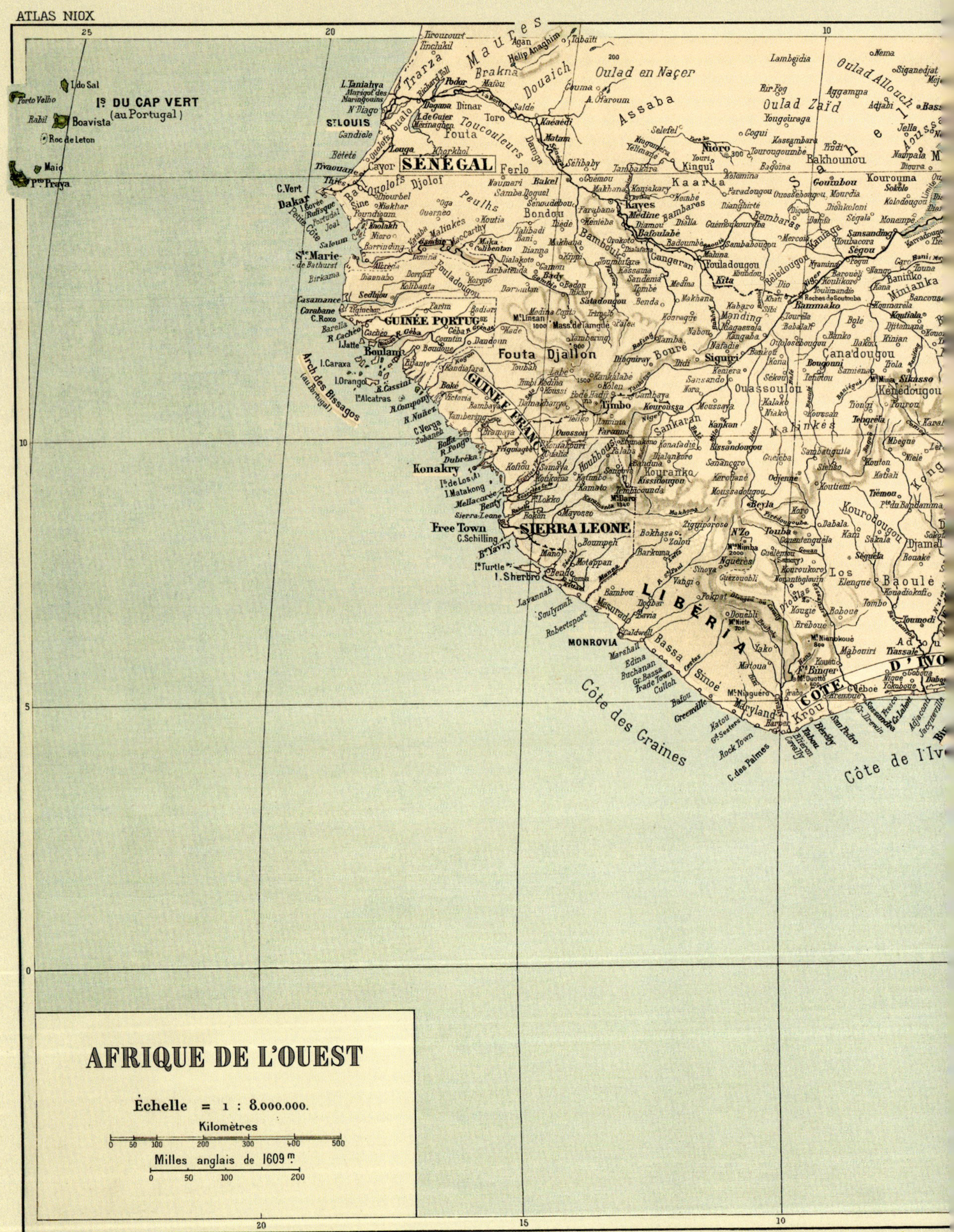

Imp. Dufrénoy, Paris.

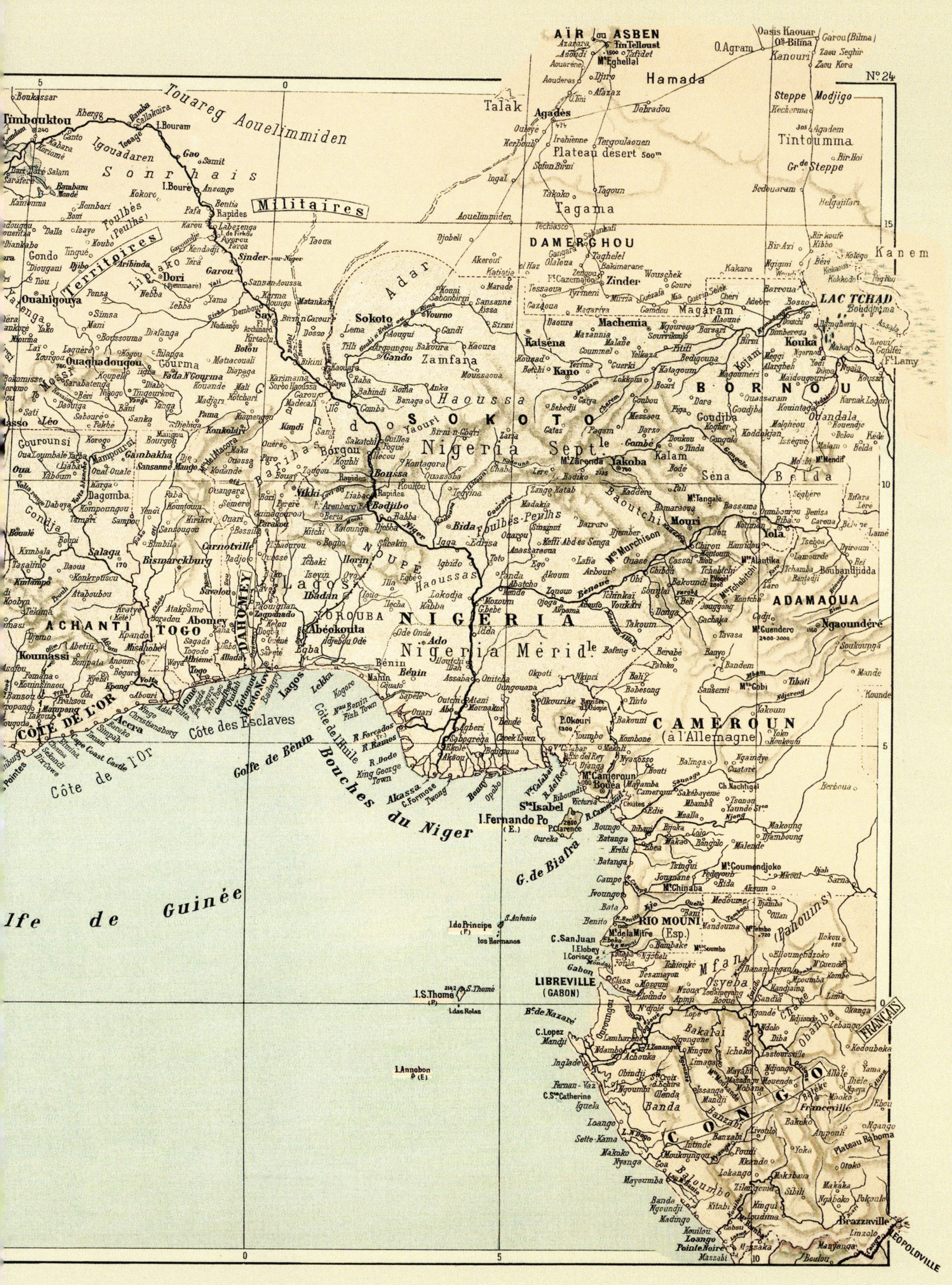

N° 24
AÏR ou ASBEN
Agades
Plateau desert
Tagama
Hamada
Tintoumma
Kanem
LAC TCHAD
Touareg Aouelimmiden
Timbouktou
Sonrhais
Militaires
Territoires
DAMERGHOU
Zinder
Sokoto
Kano
Katsena
Zamfana
Haoussa
SOKOTO
Nigeria Septle
BORNOU
Kouka
Yola
ADAMAOUA
Ngaoundéré
Mossi
Ouahigouya
Ouaghadougou
Gourma
Dori
Dagomba
Salaga
ACHANTI
Koumassi
TOGO
DAHOMEY
Abomey
Lagos
Abéokouta
YOROUBA
NUPÉ
NIGERIA
Nigeria Mérid.le
Bénin
Côte des Esclaves
Golfe de Bénin
Bouches du Niger
G. de Biafra
Golfe de Guinée
Côte de l'Or
CÔTE DE L'OR
CAMEROUN
(à l'Allemagne)
I. Fernando Po
RIO MOUNI
(Esp.)
LIBREVILLE
(GABON)
I. S. Thomé
I. do Principe
I. Annobon
CONGO
FRANÇAIS
Brazzaville
LÉOPOLDVILLE
Loango

WEST AFRICAN COMBS

Fig. 1 Peigne | Comb
Ashanti, Akan, Ghana
Bois | Wood
26 × 8,5 cm | 26 × 8.5 cm

Publication
Aspects, Akan Cultures in Ghana, Gemeentemuseum Den Haag, 2002, p. 64, n° 39

Exposition | Exhibition
La Haye | The Hague, Gemeentemuseum Den Haag, *Aspects, Akan Cultures in Ghana*, 29 septembre 2001 – 6 janvier 2002 | 29 September 2001 – 6 January 2002 (n° de référence | ref. no. F61)

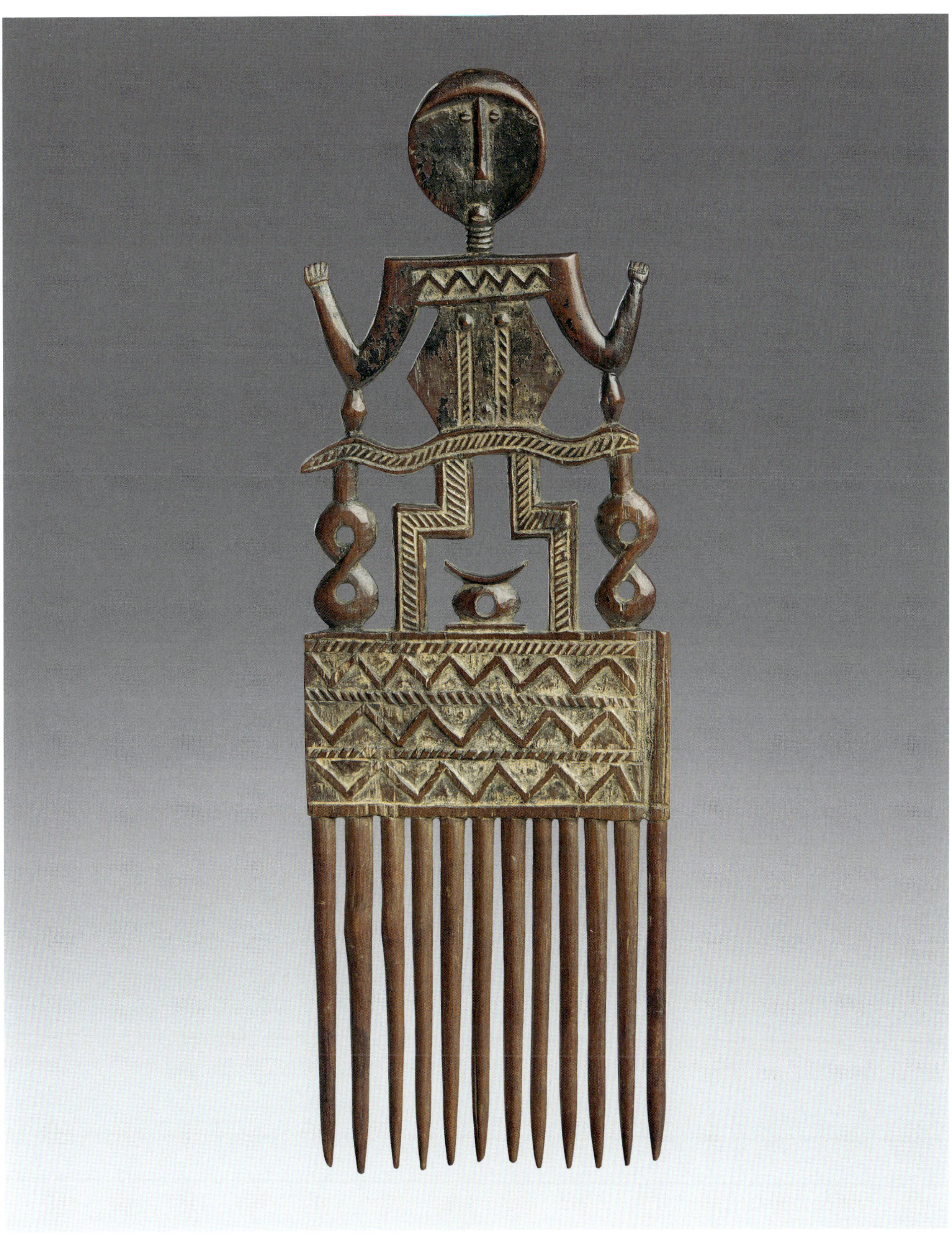

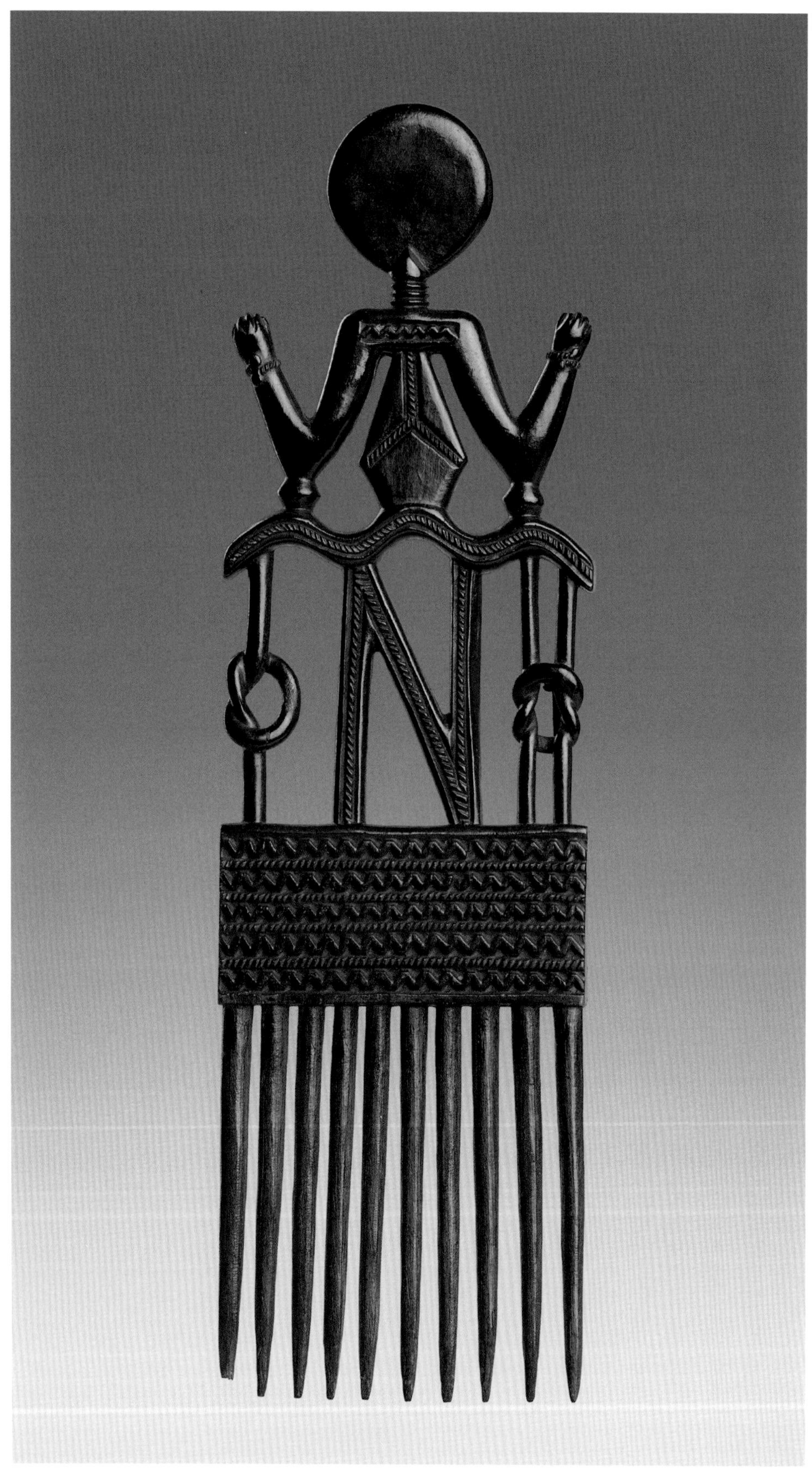

Fig. 2 Peigne | Comb
Ashanti, Akan, Ghana
Bois | Wood
28,5 × 8,4 cm | 28.5 × 8.4 cm

Provenance
Aimé Kerchache

Publication
Antoine Ferrari de la Salle, *Le Taureau qui aime les masques d'hommes. Regards sur Samir Borro*, Bruxelles, Beyrouth, Oser Dire Éditions, 2018, p. 77

Exposition | Exhibition
La Haye | The Hague, Gemeentemuseum Den Haag, *Aspects, Akan Cultures in Ghana*, 29 septembre 2001 – 6 janvier 2002 | 29 September – 6 January 2002 (n° de référence | ref. no. F62)

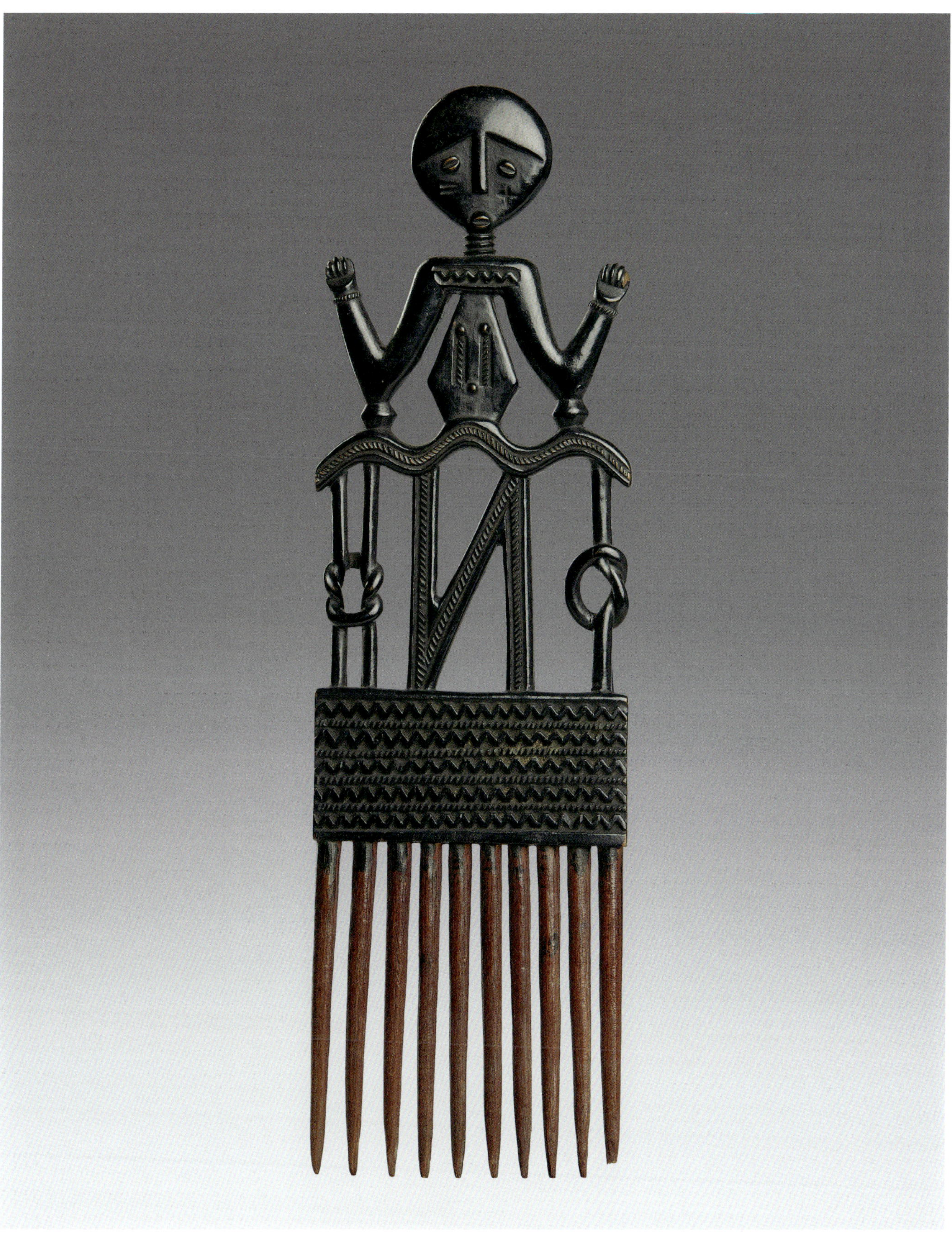

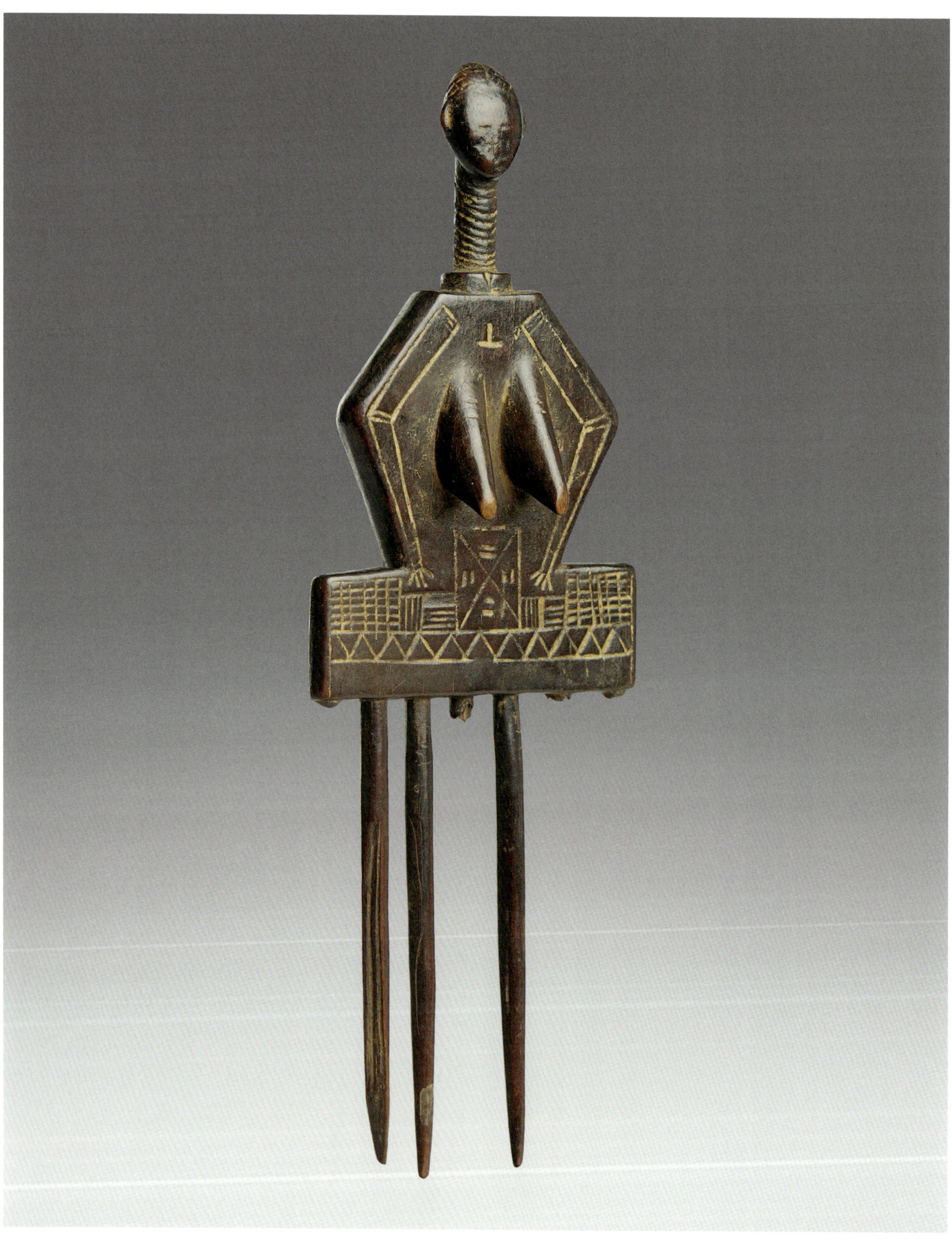

Fig. 3 Peigne | Comb
Ashanti, Akan, Ghana
Bois | Wood
21,5 × 7,5 cm | 21.5 × 7.5 cm

Provenance
André Blandin

Exposition | Exhibition
La Haye | The Hague,
Gemeentemuseum Den Haag,
Aspects, Akan Cultures in Ghana,
29 septembre 2001 – 6 janvier 2002 |
29 September 2001 – 6 January
2002 (n° de référence | ref. no. F63)

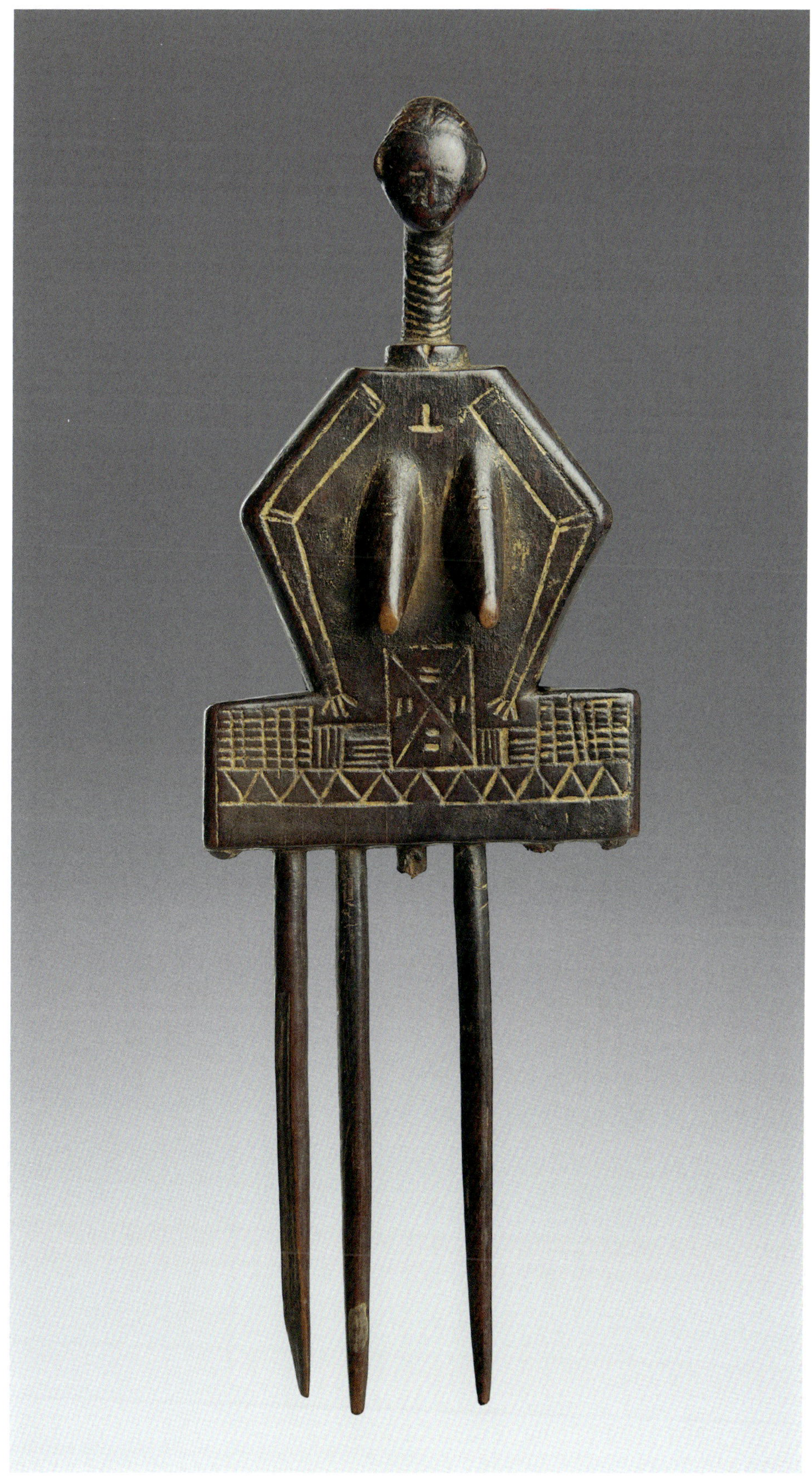

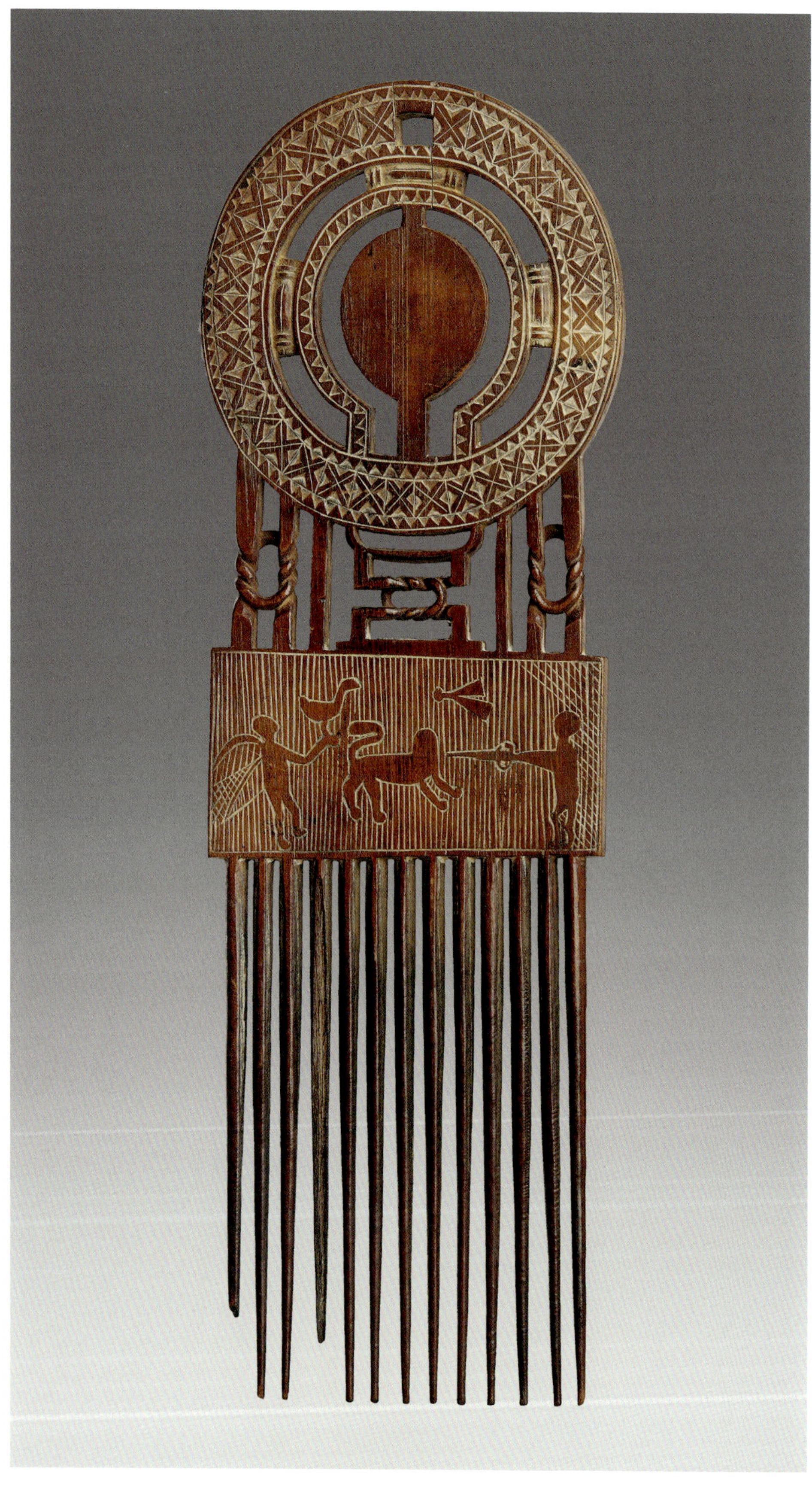

Fig. 4 Peigne | Comb
Ashanti, Akan, Ghana
Bois | Wood
37 × 13 cm

Provenance
Ali Barry

Publication
Jean-Yves Augel, Valentine Plisnier, *Coiffures africaines en majesté*, Sainte-Foy-lès-Lyon, Galerie Vallois, 2024, fig. 1, p. 118

Exposition | Exhibition
Sainte-Foy-lès-Lyon, Espace culturel Jean Salles, *Coiffures africaines en majesté*, 6 – 21 avril April 2024

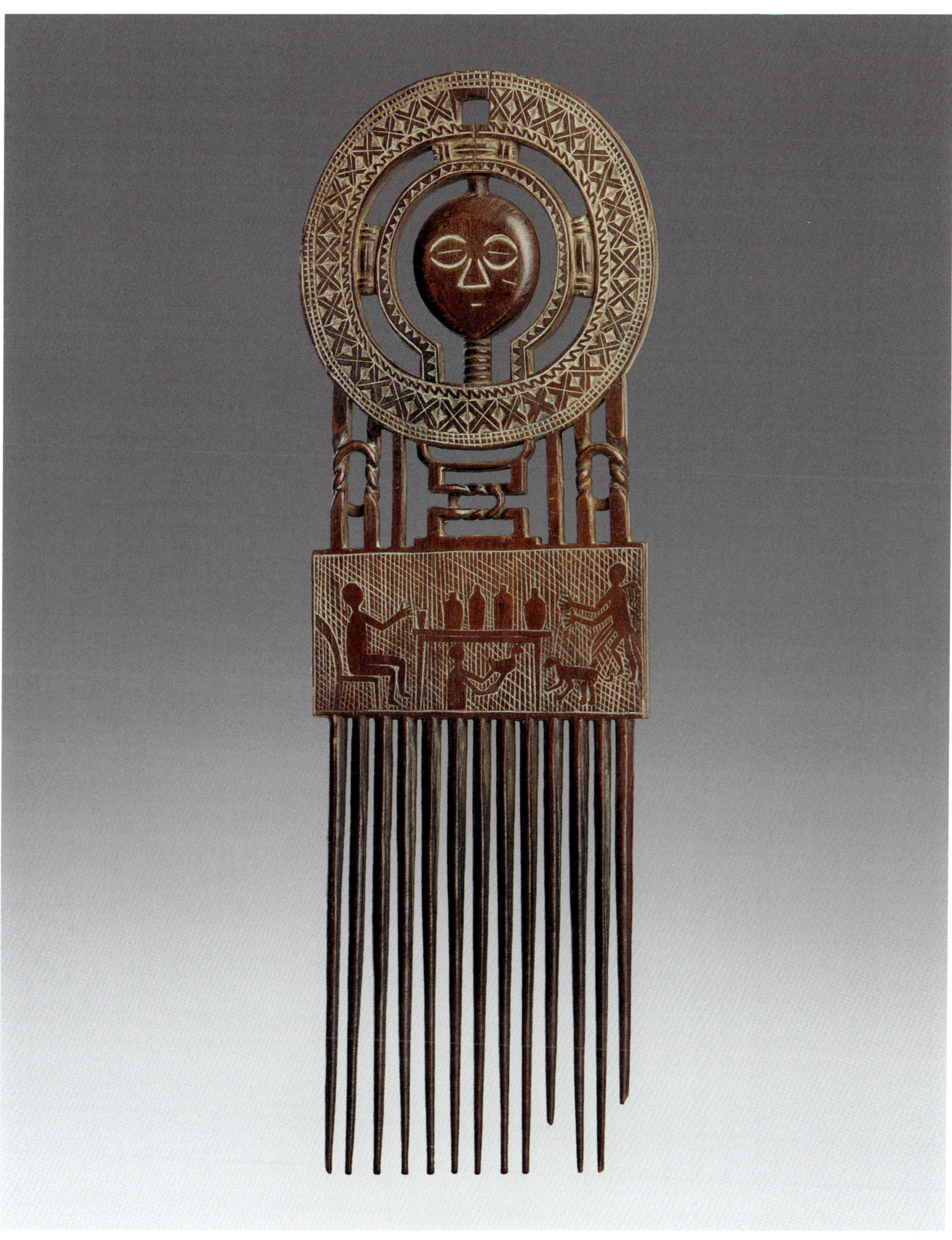

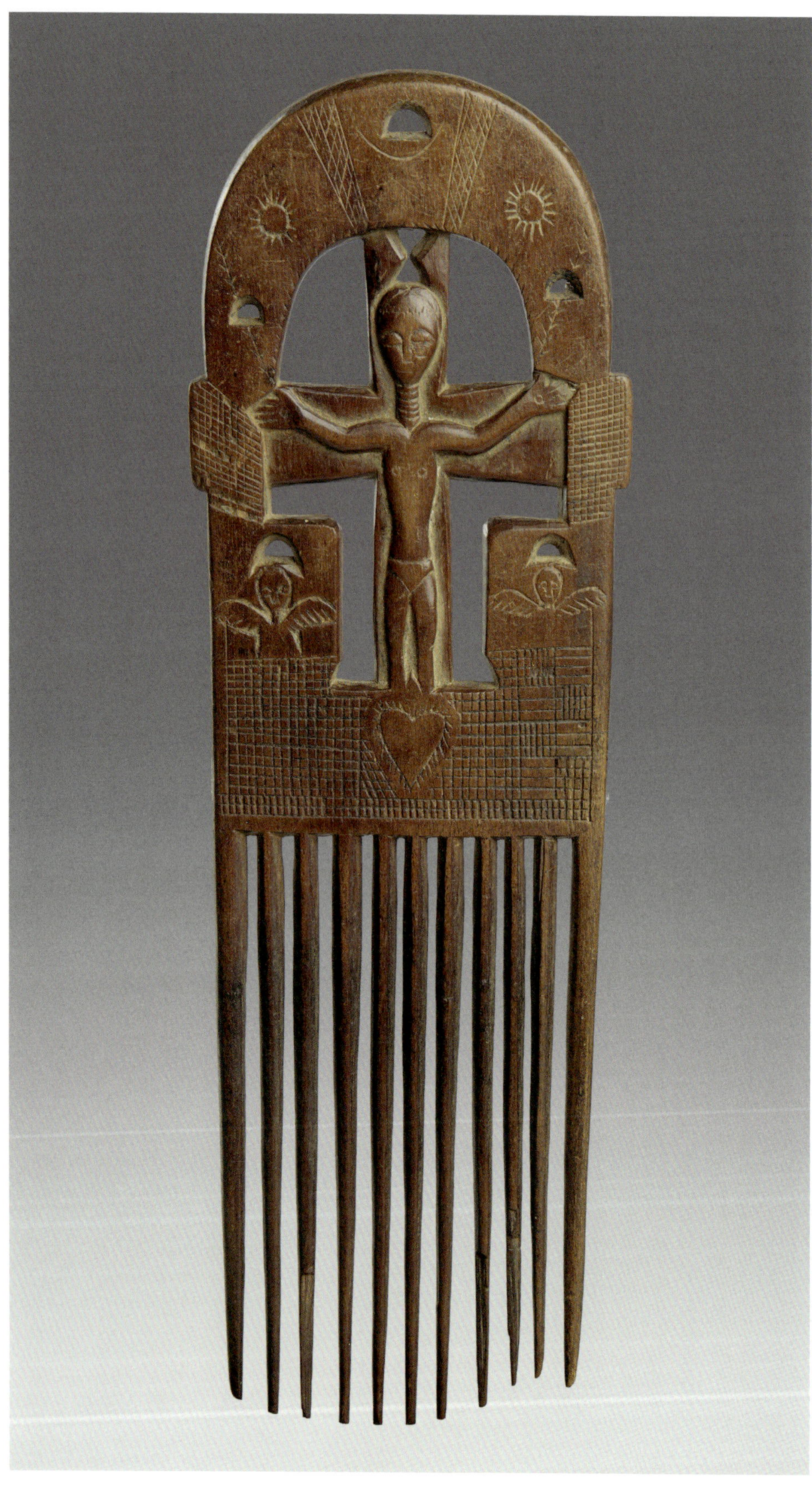

Fig. 5 Peigne | Comb
Ashanti, Akan, Ghana
Bois | Wood
30 × 9,5 cm | 30 × 9.5 cm

Exposition | Exhibition
La Haye | The Hague,
Gemeentemuseum Den Haag,
Aspects, Akan Cultures in Ghana,
29 septembre 2001 – 6 janvier 2002
| 29 September 2001 – 6 January
2002 (n° de référence | ref. no. C15)

Fig. 6 Peigne | Comb
Ashanti, Akan, Ghana
Bois | Wood
35,5 × 13,5 cm | 35.5 × 13.5 cm

Exposition | Exhibition
La Haye | The Hague,
Gemeentemuseum Den Haag,
Aspects, Akan Cultures in Ghana,
29 septembre 2001 – 6 janvier 2002 |
29 September 2001 – 6 January
2002 (n° de référence | ref. no. F70)

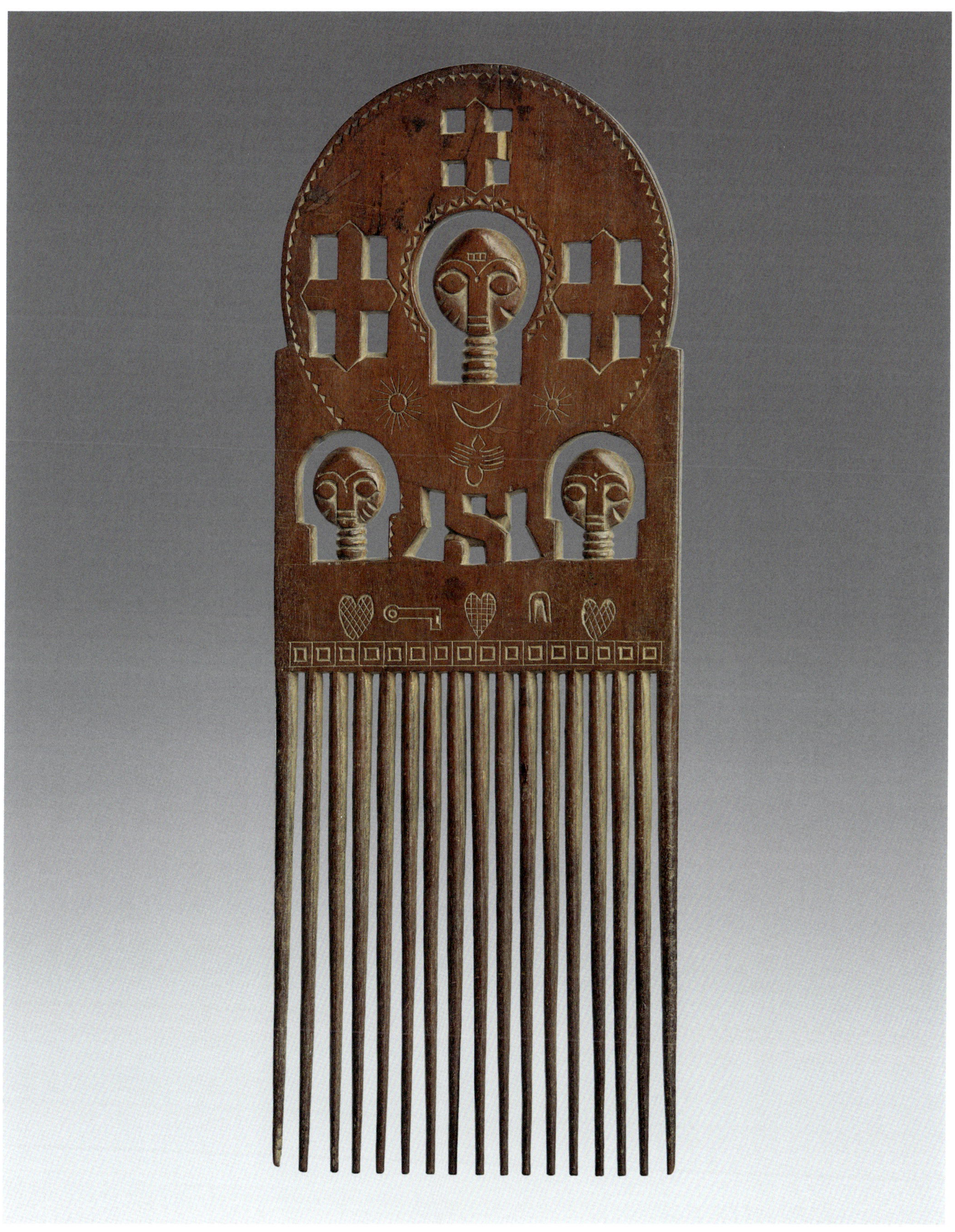

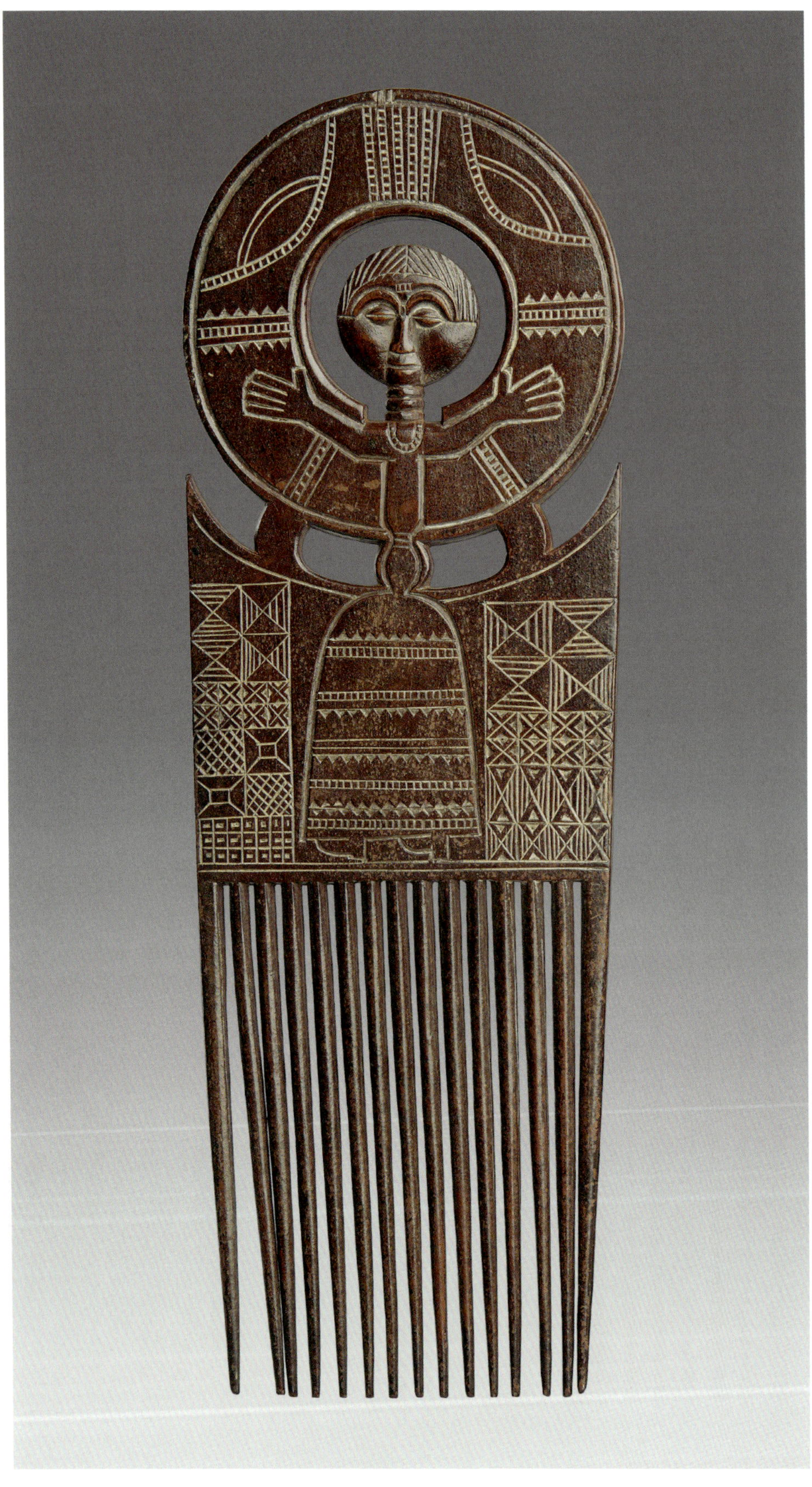

Fig. 7 Peigne | Comb
Ashanti, Akan, Ghana
Bois | Wood
30 × 10,5 cm | 30 × 10.5 cm

Provenance
Ali Barry

Fig. 8 Peigne | Comb
Ashanti, Akan, Ghana
Bois | Wood
37 × 12 cm

Provenance
Ali Barry

Exposition | Exhibition
La Haye | The Hague,
Gemeentemuseum Den Haag,
Aspects, Akan Cultures in Ghana,
29 septembre 2001 – 6 janvier 2002 |
29 September 2001 – 6 January 2002 (n° de référence | ref. no. F71)

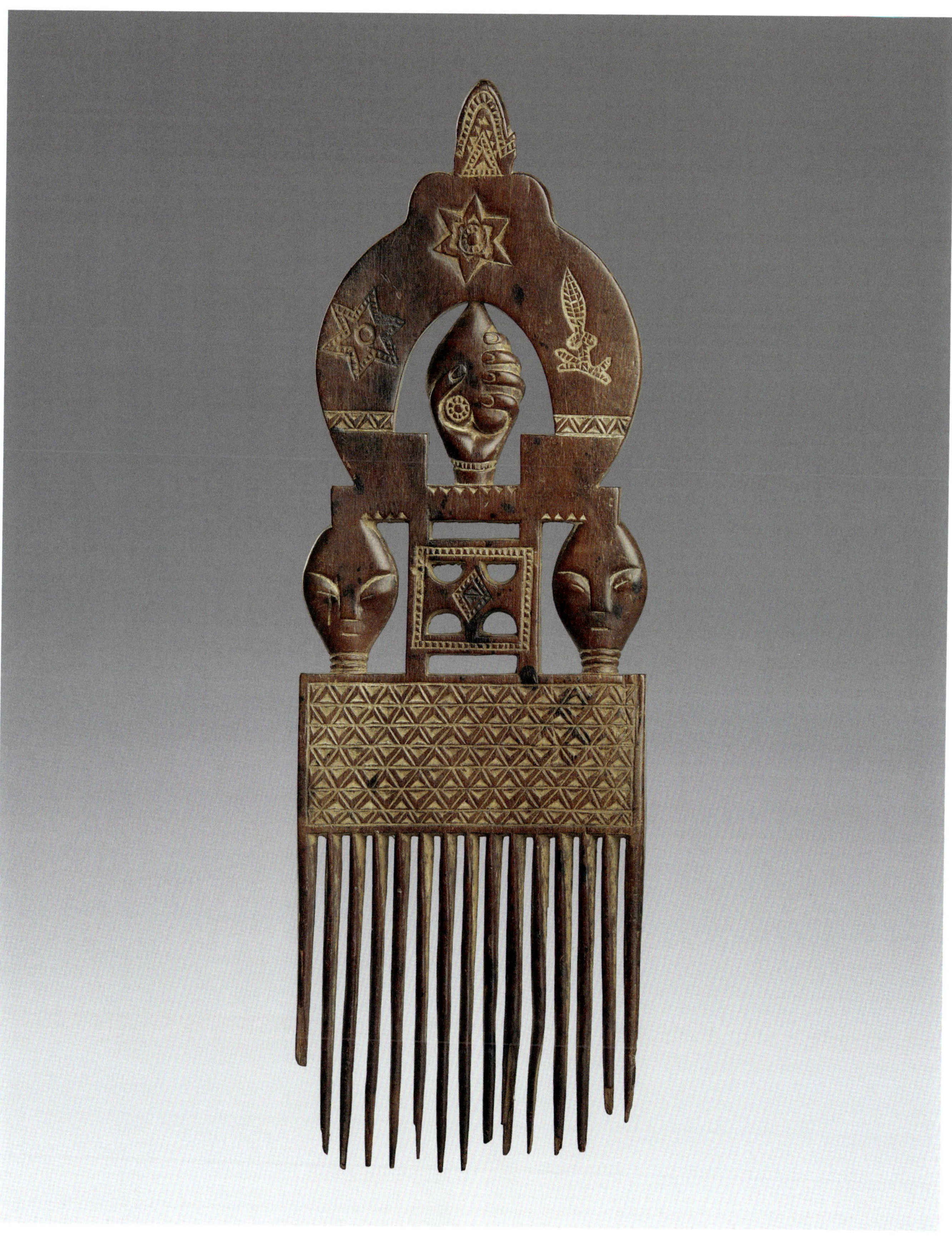

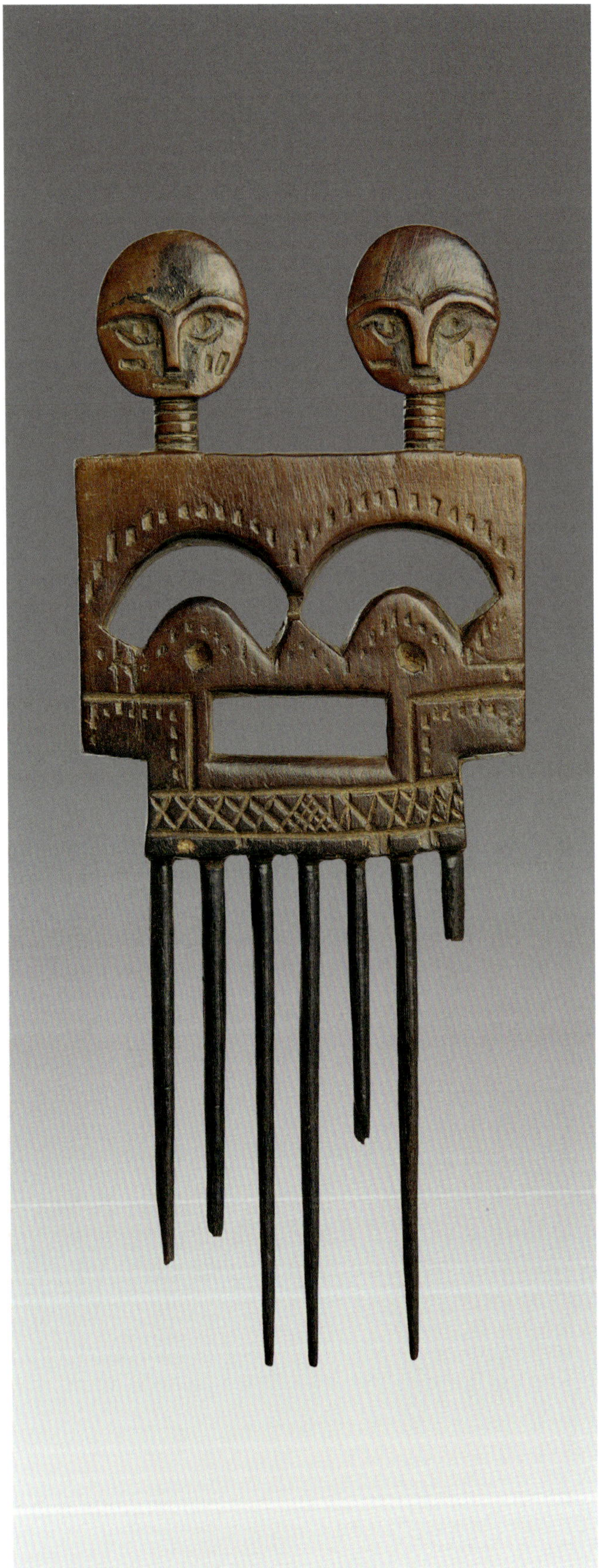

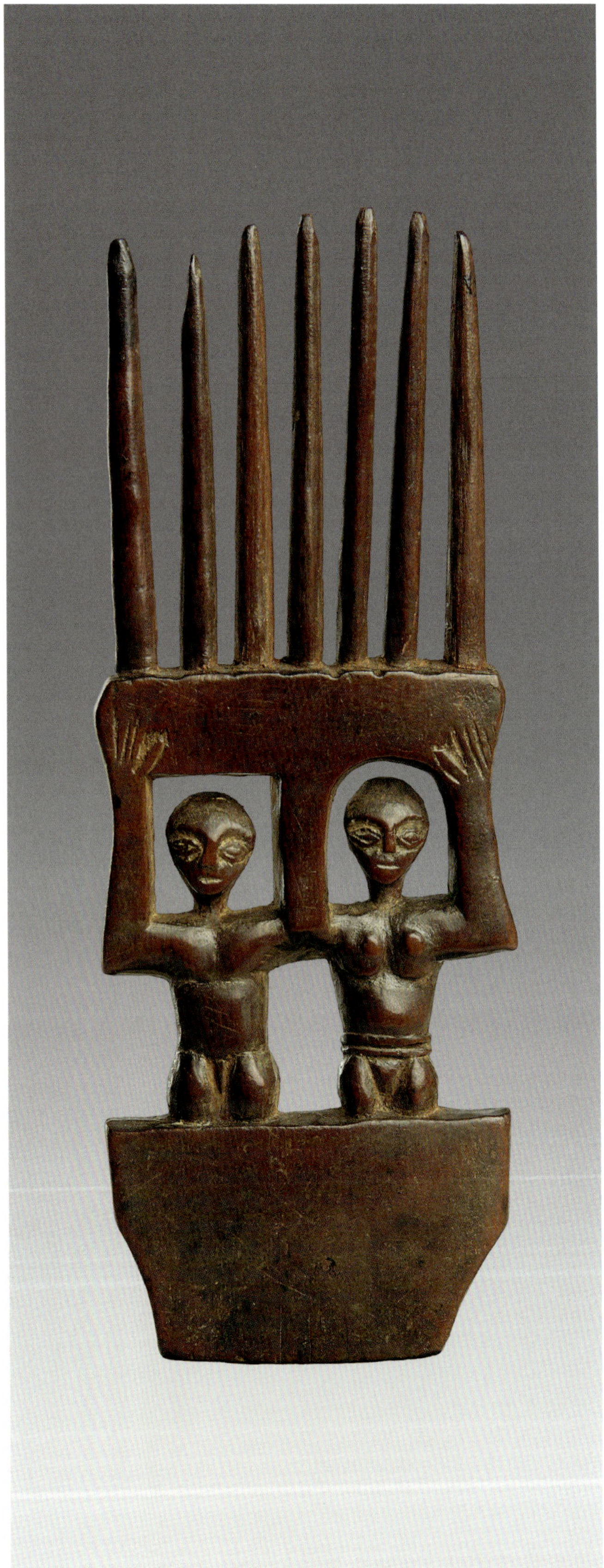

Fig. 9 Peigne | Comb
Ashanti, Akan, Ghana
Bois | Wood
17 × 7 cm

Provenance
Ali Barry

Exposition | Exhibition
La Haye | The Hague,
Gemeentemuseum Den Haag,
Aspects, Akan Cultures in Ghana,
29 septembre 2001 – 6 janvier 2002 | 29 September – 6 January 2002 (n° de référence | ref. no. F66)

Fig. 10 Peigne | Comb
Ashanti, Akan, Ghana
Bois | Wood
16 × 6 cm

Provenance
Ali Barry, 1965

Exposition | Exhibition
La Haye | The Hague,
Gemeentemuseum Den Haag,
Aspects, Akan Cultures in Ghana,
29 septembre 2001 – 6 janvier 2002 | 29 September – 6 January 2002 (n° de référence | ref. no. F67)

Fig. 11 Peigne | Comb
Ashanti, Akan, Ghana
Bois | Wood
27 × 6 cm

Provenance
Maine Durieu

Publication
Aspects, Akan Cultures in Ghana,
Gemeentemuseum Den Haag,
2002, p. 65, n° 40

Exposition | Exhibition
La Haye | The Hague,
Gemeentemuseum Den Haag,
Aspects, Akan Cultures in Ghana,
29 septembre 2001 – 6 janvier 2002 | 29 September – 6 January 2002 (n° de référence | ref. no. F60)

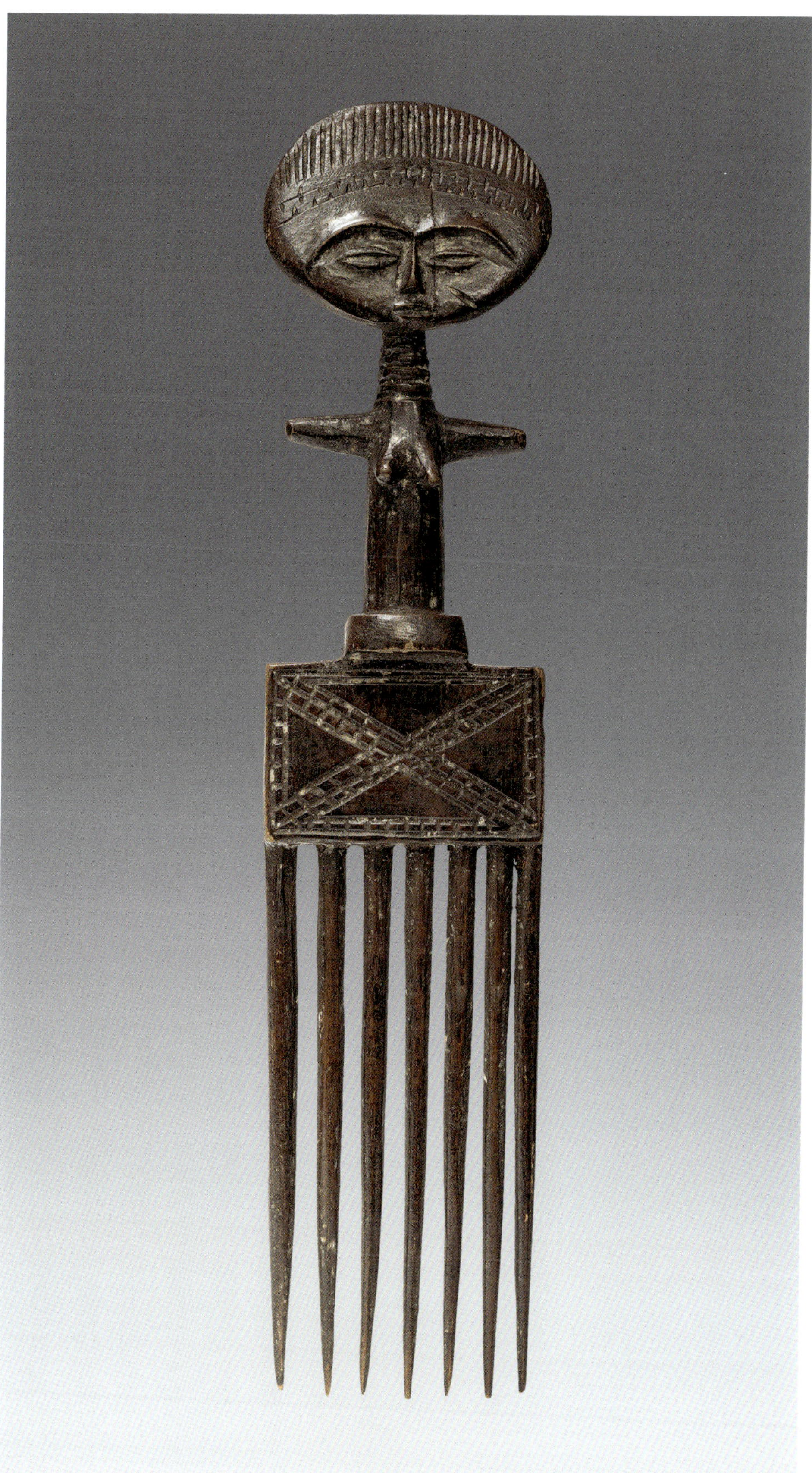

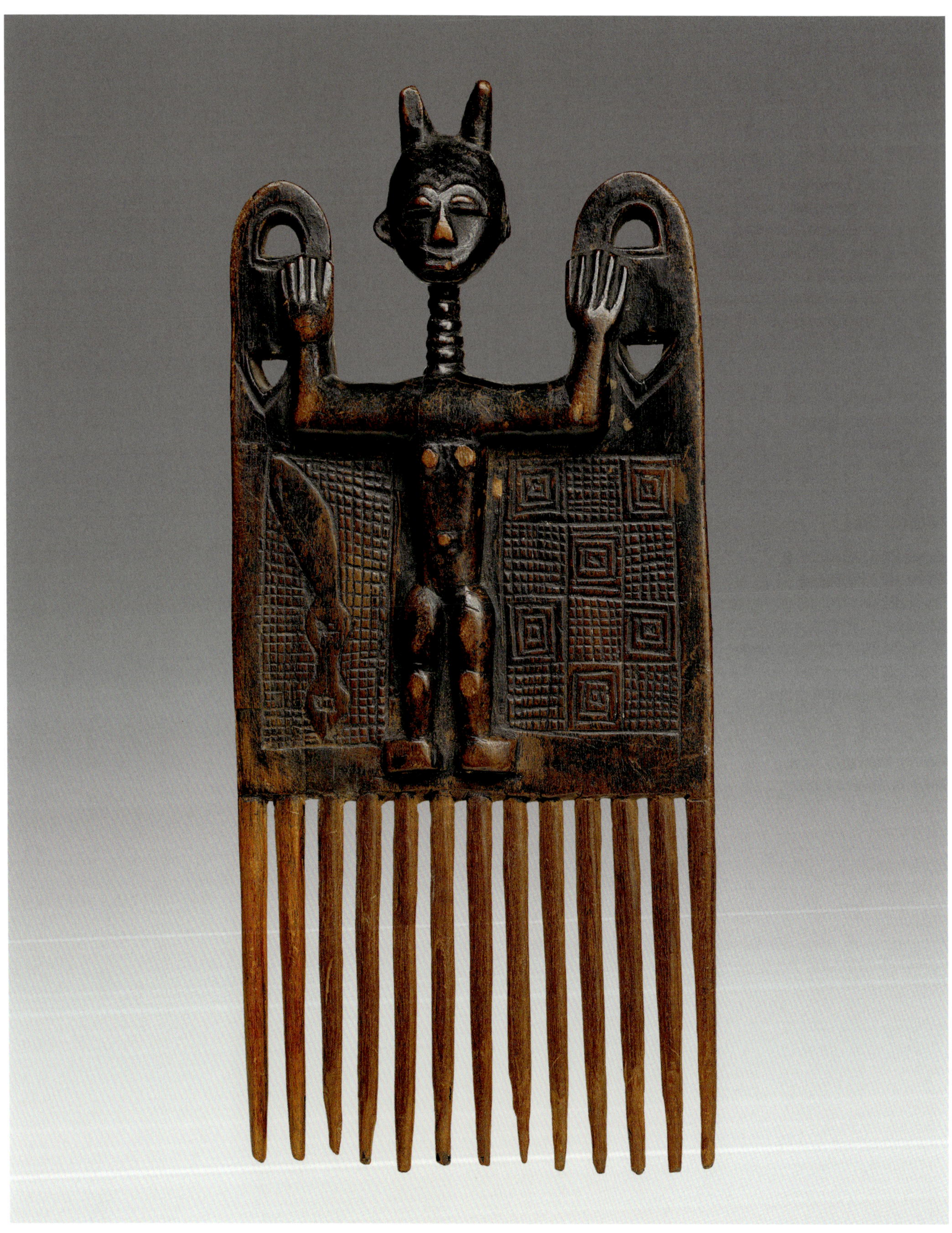

Fig. 12 Peigne | Comb
Fanti, Akan, Ghana
Bois | Wood
22,5 × 10,5 cm | 22.5 × 10.5 cm

Provenance
Maine Durieu

Exposition | Exhibition
La Haye | The Hague,
Gemeentemuseum Den Haag,
Aspects, Akan Cultures in Ghana,
29 septembre 2001 – 6 janvier 2002 |
29 September 2001 – 6 January
2002 (n° de référence | ref. no. F64)

Fig. 13 Peigne | Comb
Ashanti, Akan, Ghana
Bois | Wood
34 × 10 cm

Provenance
Ali Barry

Exposition | Exhibition
La Haye | The Hague,
Gemeentemuseum Den Haag,
Aspects, Akan Cultures in Ghana,
29 septembre 2001 – 6 janvier 2002 |
29 September 2001 – 6 January
2002 (n° de référence | ref. no. F65)

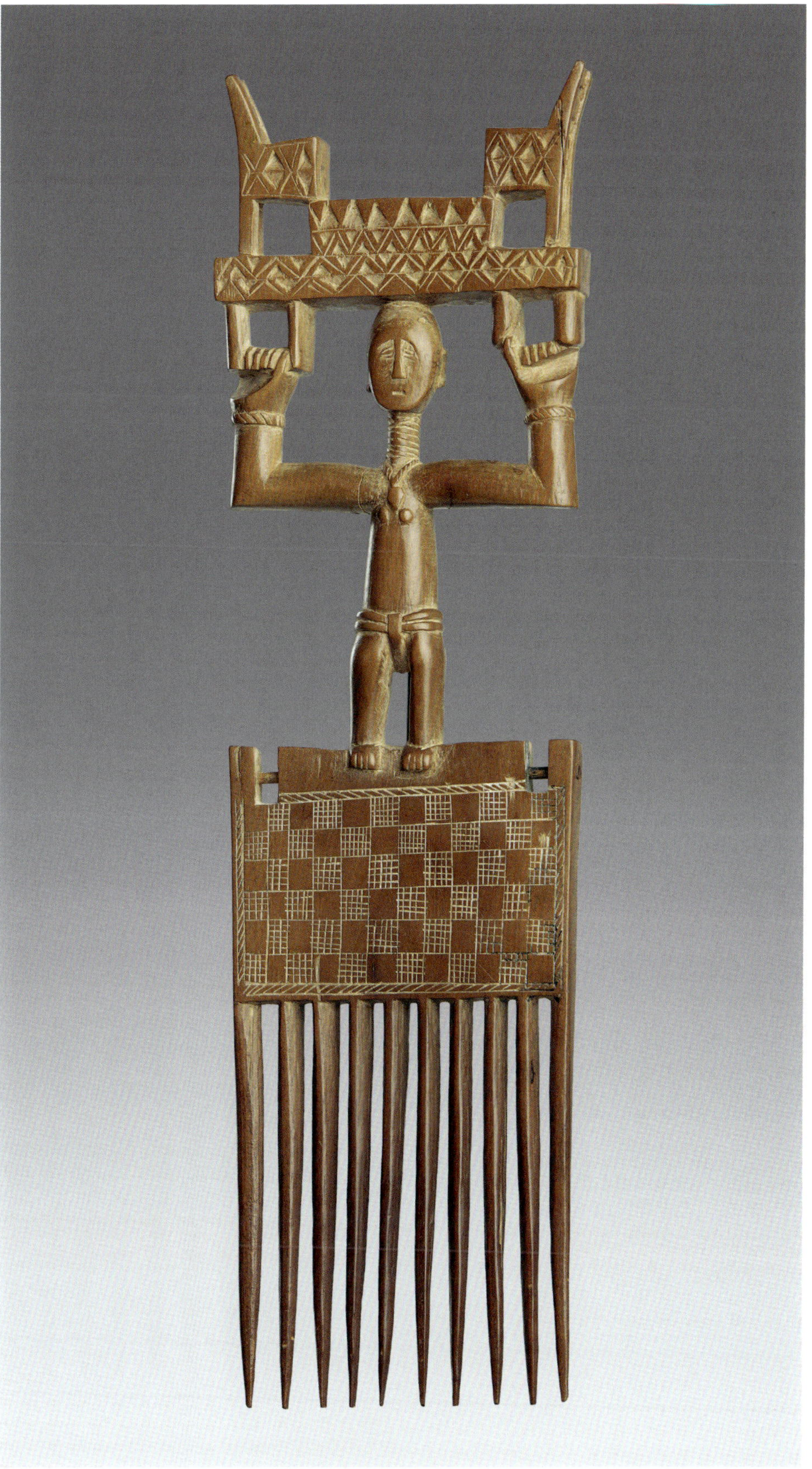

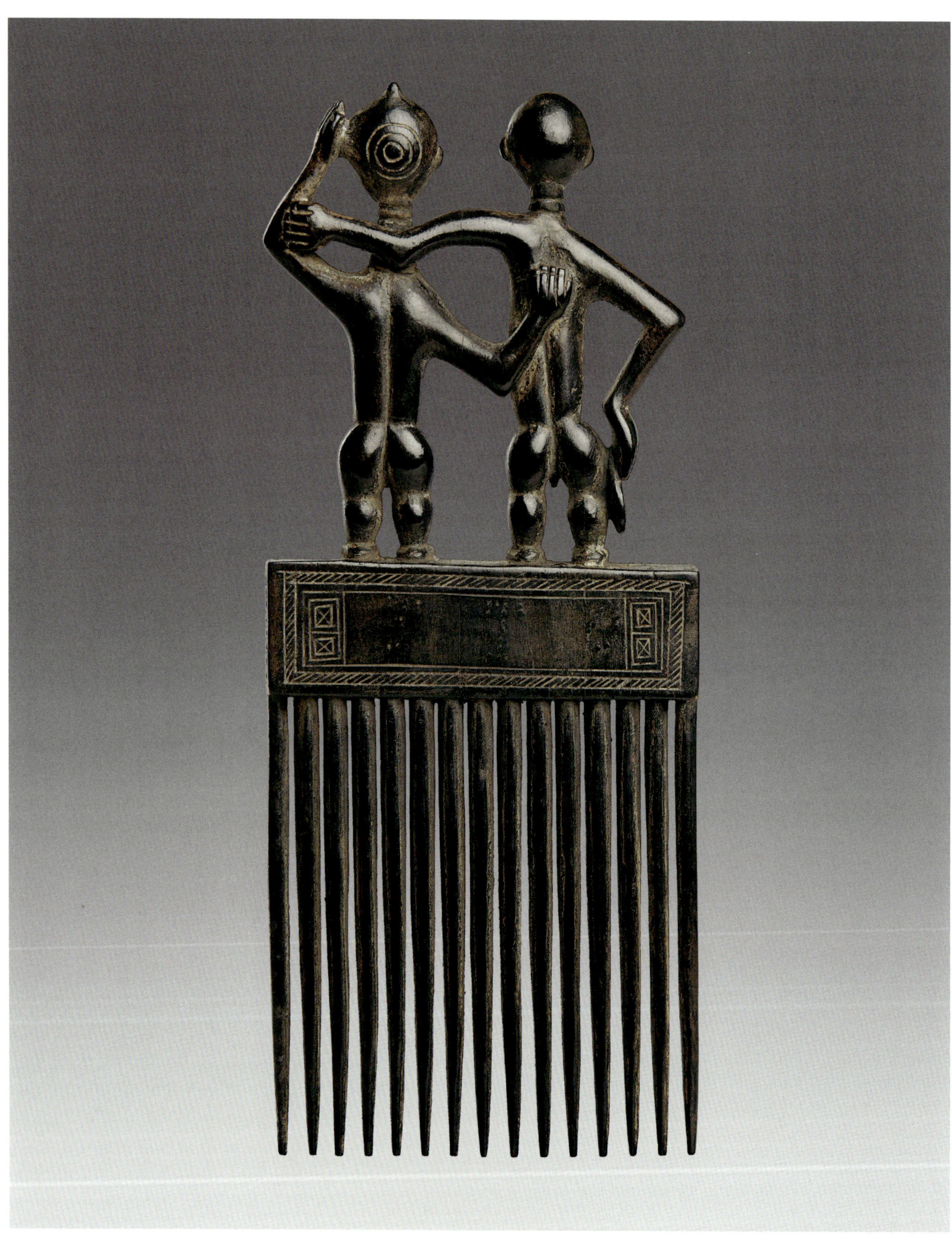

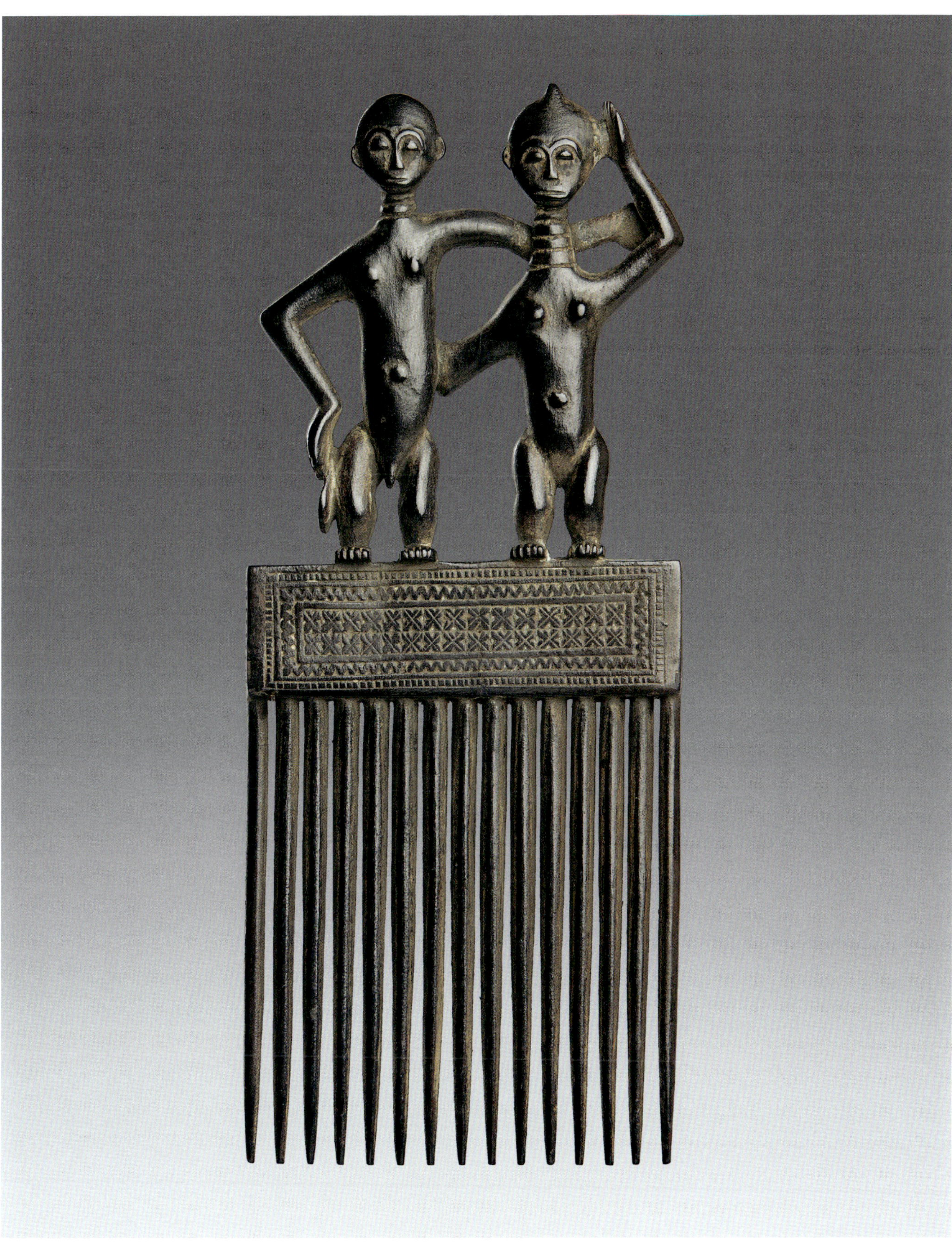

Pages 72, 73
Fig. 14 Peigne | Comb
Fanti, Akan, Ghana
Bois | Wood
25 × 10,5 cm | 25 × 10.5 cm

Provenance
Aimé Kerchache

Publications
Nicolas Rolland, Najwa Borro, Sarah Boukamel, « Samir Borro, une quête absolue », in *Tribal Art Magazine,* n° 106, hiver 2022, p. 100, fig. 14 ; Antoine Ferrari de la Salle, *Le Taureau qui aime les masques d'hommes. Regards sur Samir Borro*, Bruxelles, Beyrouth, Oser Dire Éditions, 2018, p. 77 ; *Aspects, Akan Cultures in Ghana*, Gemeentemuseum Den Haag, 2002, p. 64, n° 39

Exposition | Exhibition
La Haye | The Hague, Gemeentemuseum Den Haag, *Aspects, Akan Cultures in Ghana*, 29 septembre 2001 – 6 janvier 2002 | 29 September 2001 – 6 January 2002 (n° de référence | ref. no. F68)

Fig. 15 Peigne | Comb
Ashanti, Akan, Ghana
Bois, perles | Wood, pearls
29,4 × 9,1 cm | 29.4 × 9.1 cm

Provenance
Merton Simpson

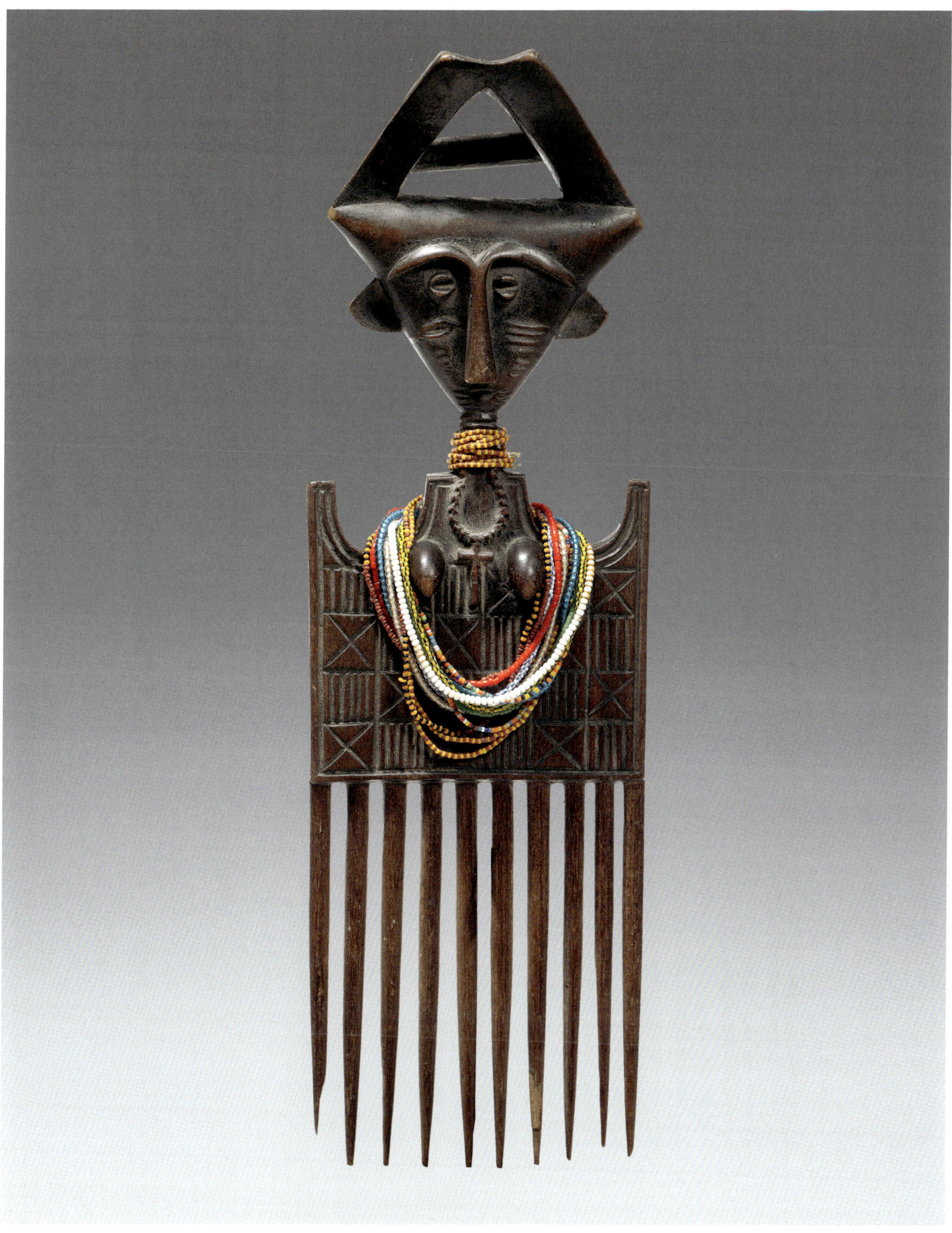

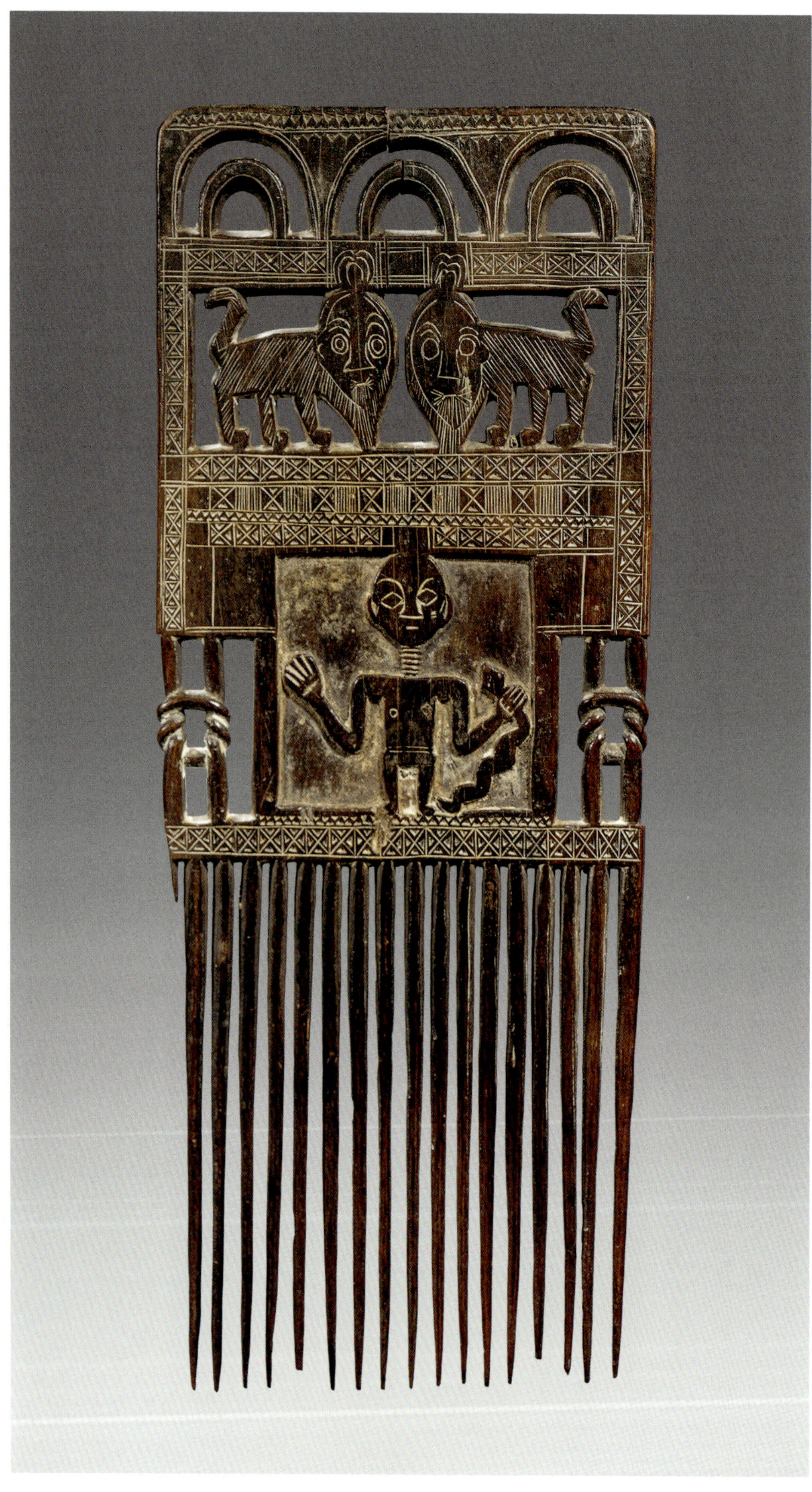

Fig. 16 Peigne | Comb
Ashanti, Akan, Ghana
Bois | Wood
36,5 × 14,4 cm | 36.5 × 14.4 cm

Publication
Aspects, Akan Cultures in Ghana,
Gemeentemuseum Den Haag,
2002, p. 65, n° 40

Exposition | Exhibition
La Haye | The Hague,
Gemeentemuseum Den Haag,
Aspects, Akan Cultures in Ghana,
29 septembre 2001 – 6 janvier 2002 |
29 September 2001 – 6 January
2002 (n° de référence | ref. no. F69)

Fig. 17 Peigne | Comb
Ashanti, Akan, Ghana
Bois, garance, feuille d'or | Wood,
madder, gold leaf
22,8 × 8 cm | 22.8 × 8 cm

Provenance
Georges Brou

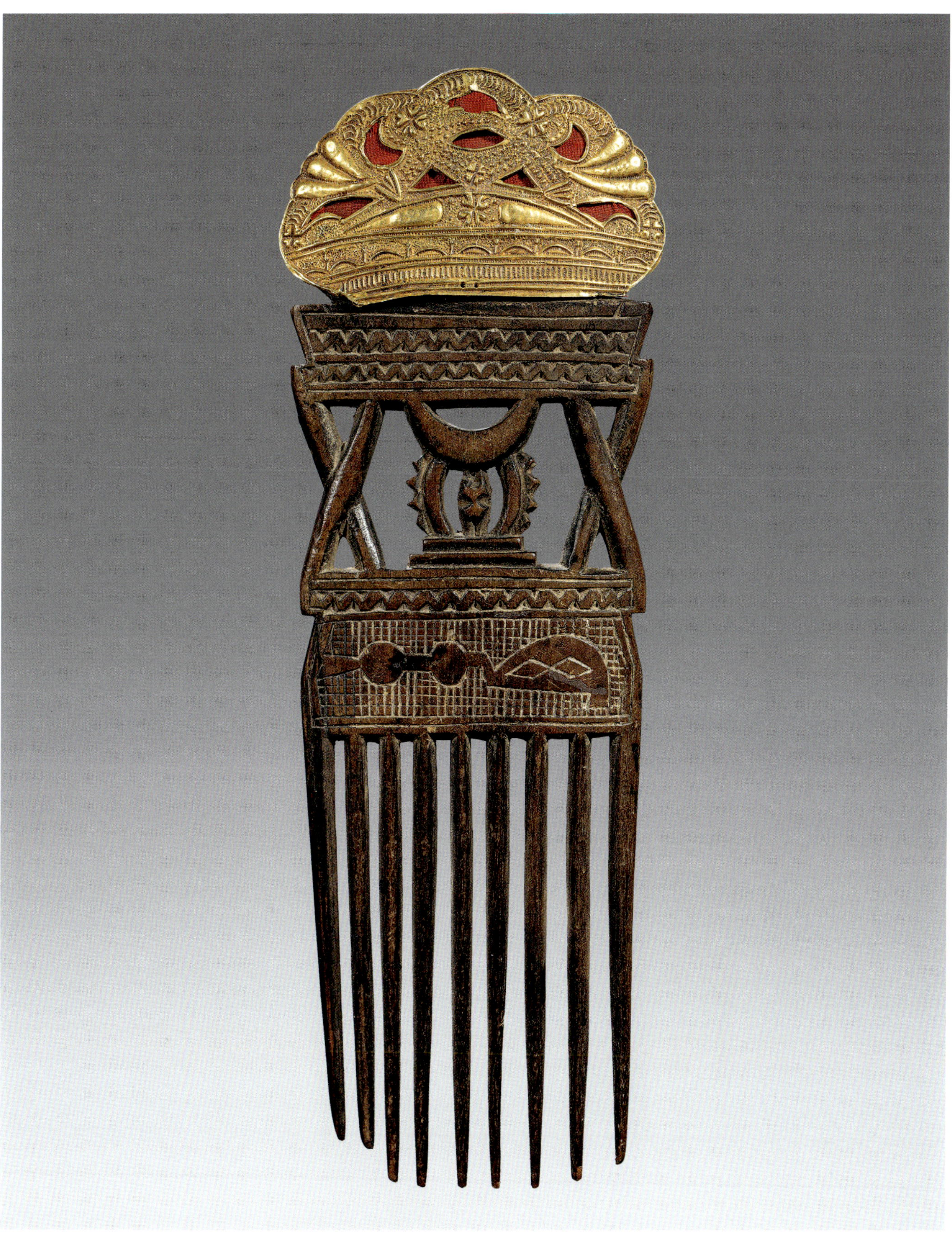

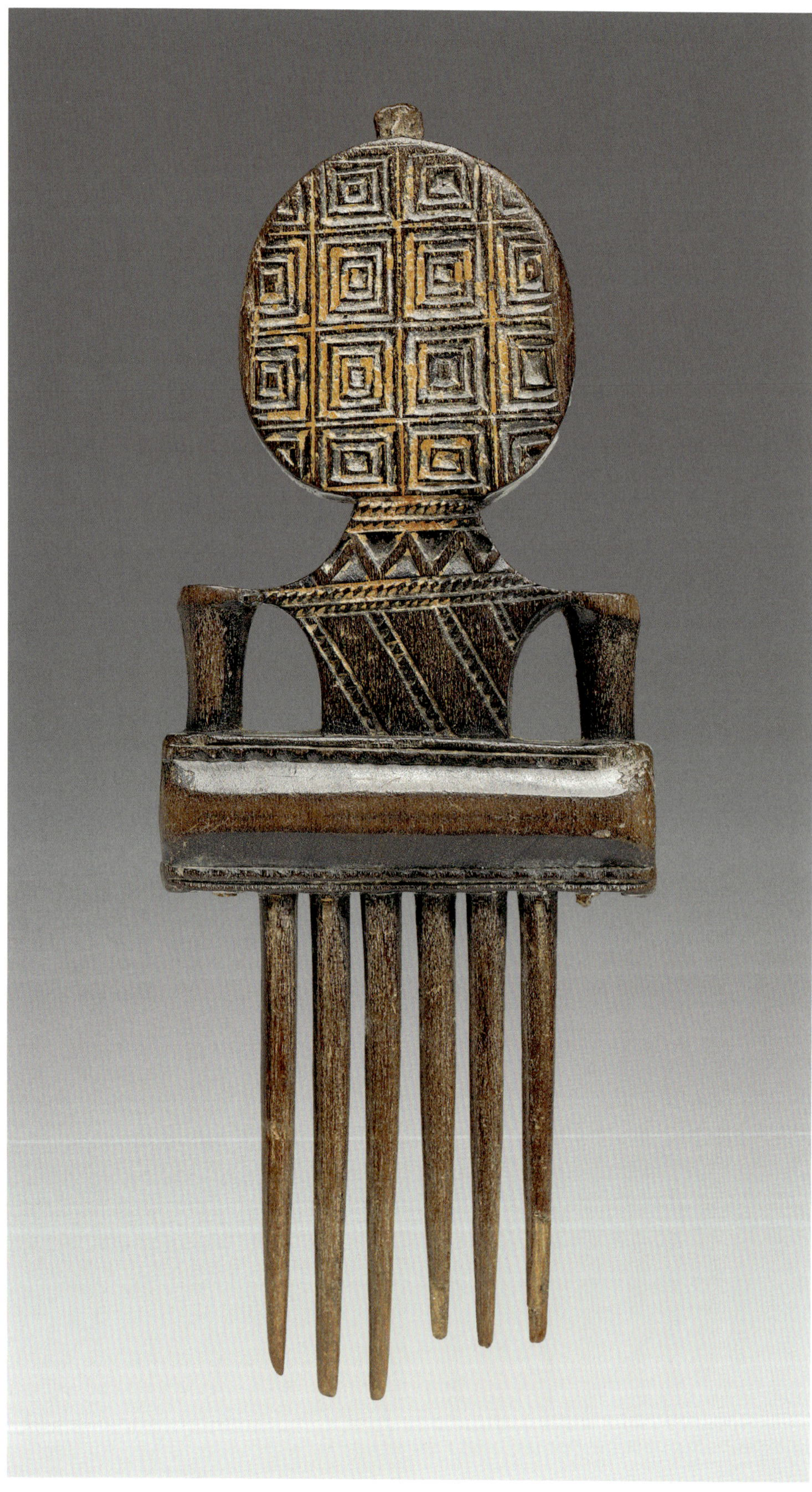

Fig. 18 Peigne | Comb
Attié | Attie, Akan,
Côte d'Ivoire | Ivory Coast
Bois | Wood
17,5 × 7 cm | 17.5 × 7 cm

Provenance
Jean-Paul Delcourt

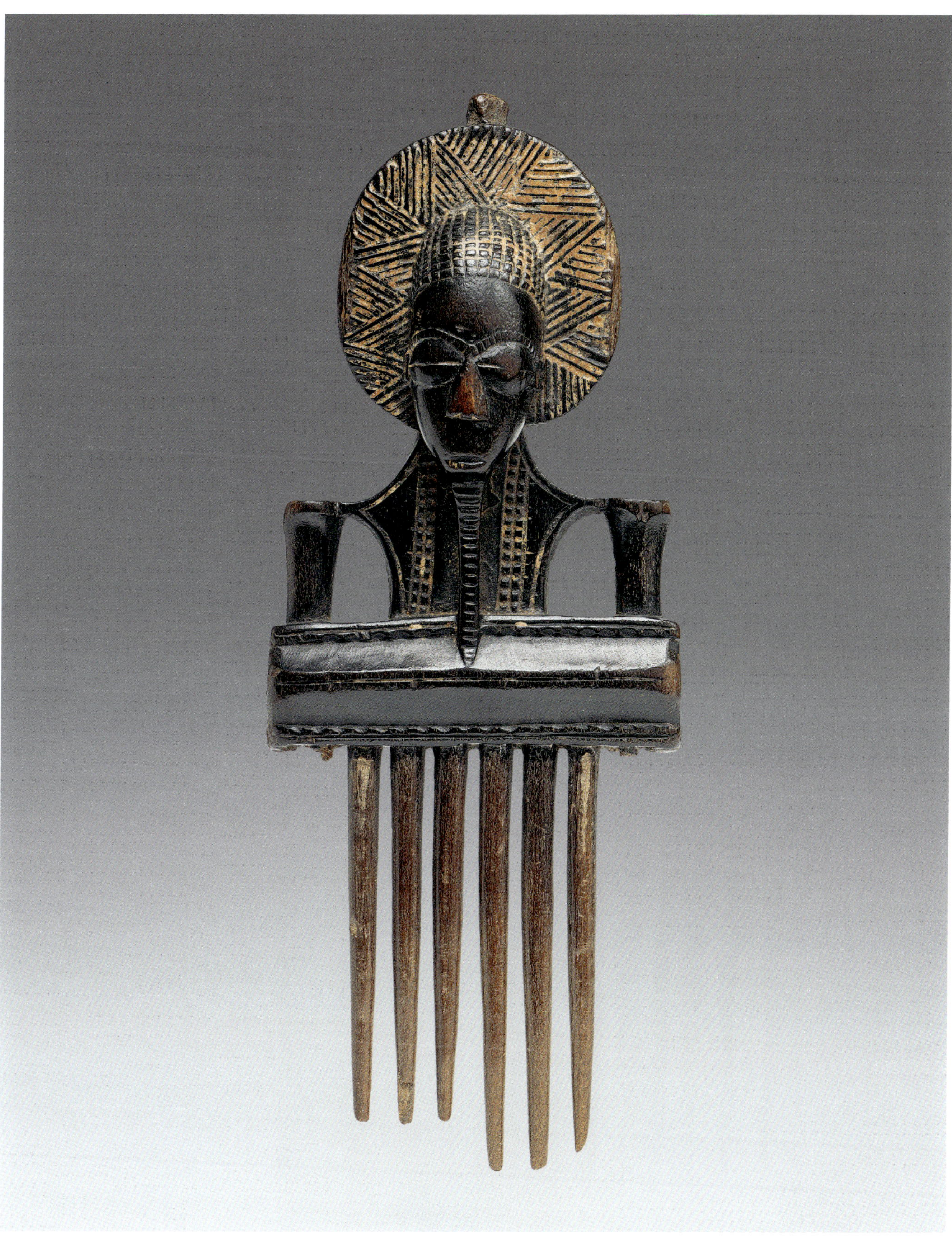

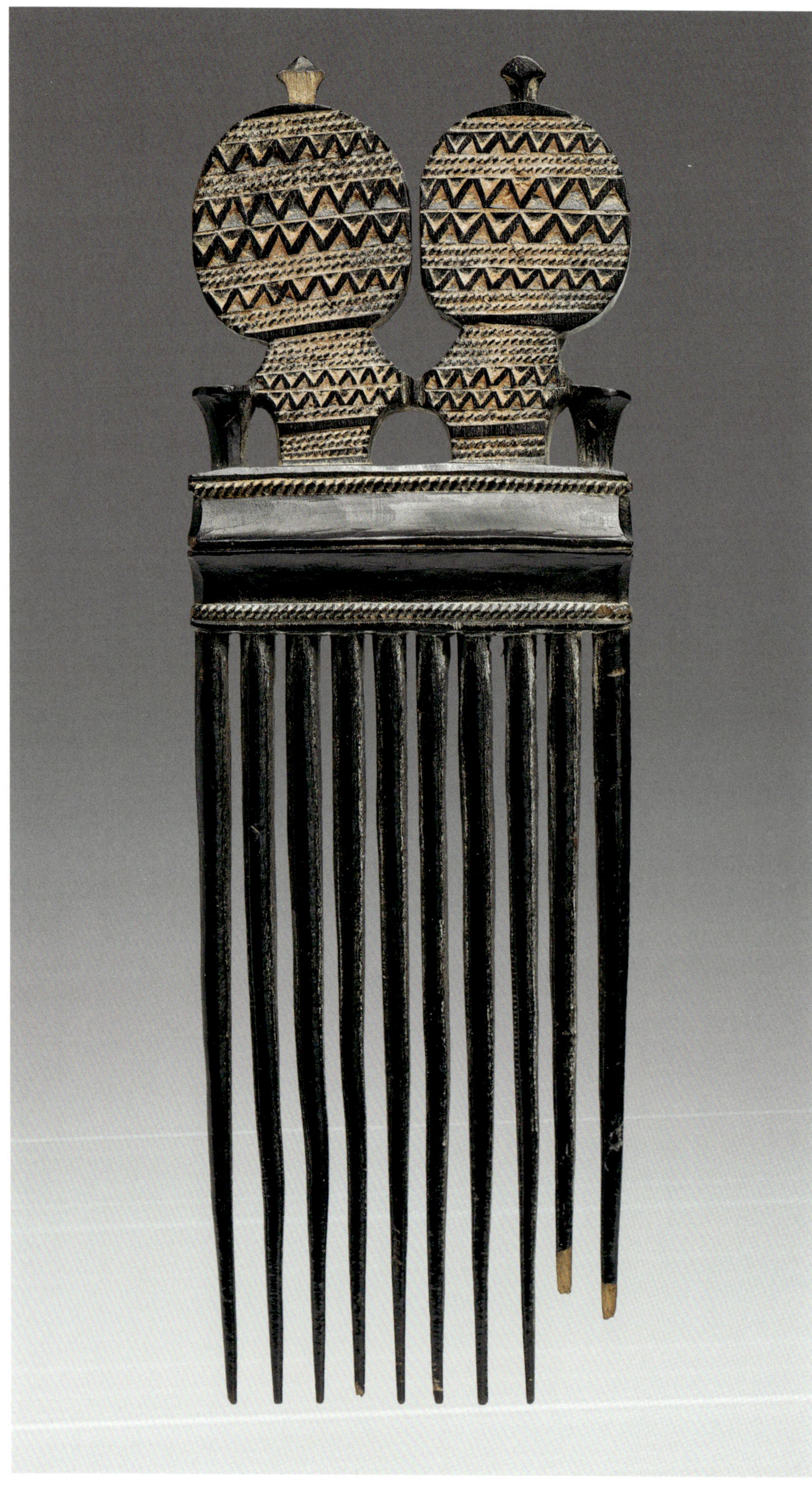

Fig. 19 Peigne | Comb
Attié | Attie, Akan,
Côte d'Ivoire | Ivory Coast
Bois | Wood
20 × 7 cm

Provenance
Merton Simpson

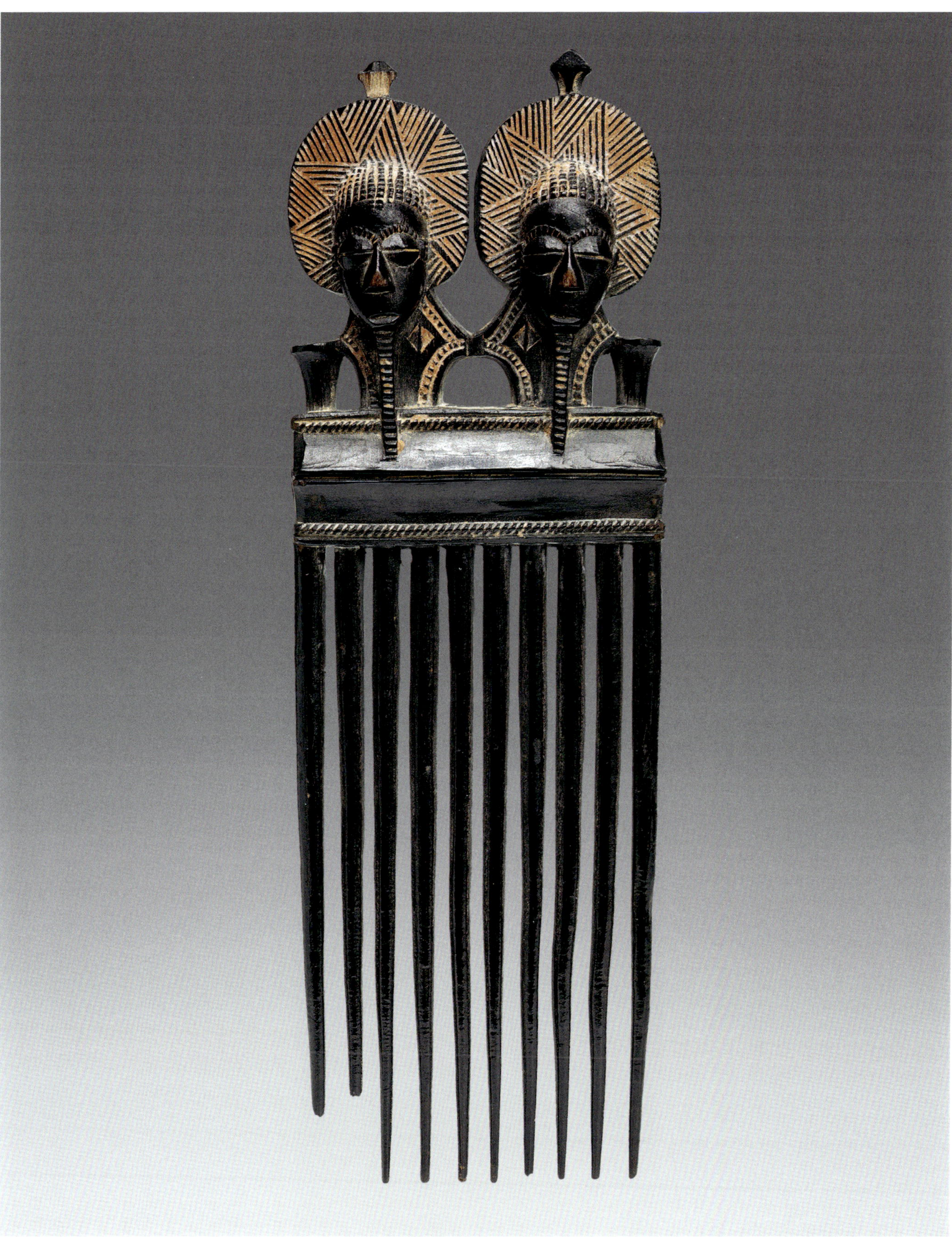

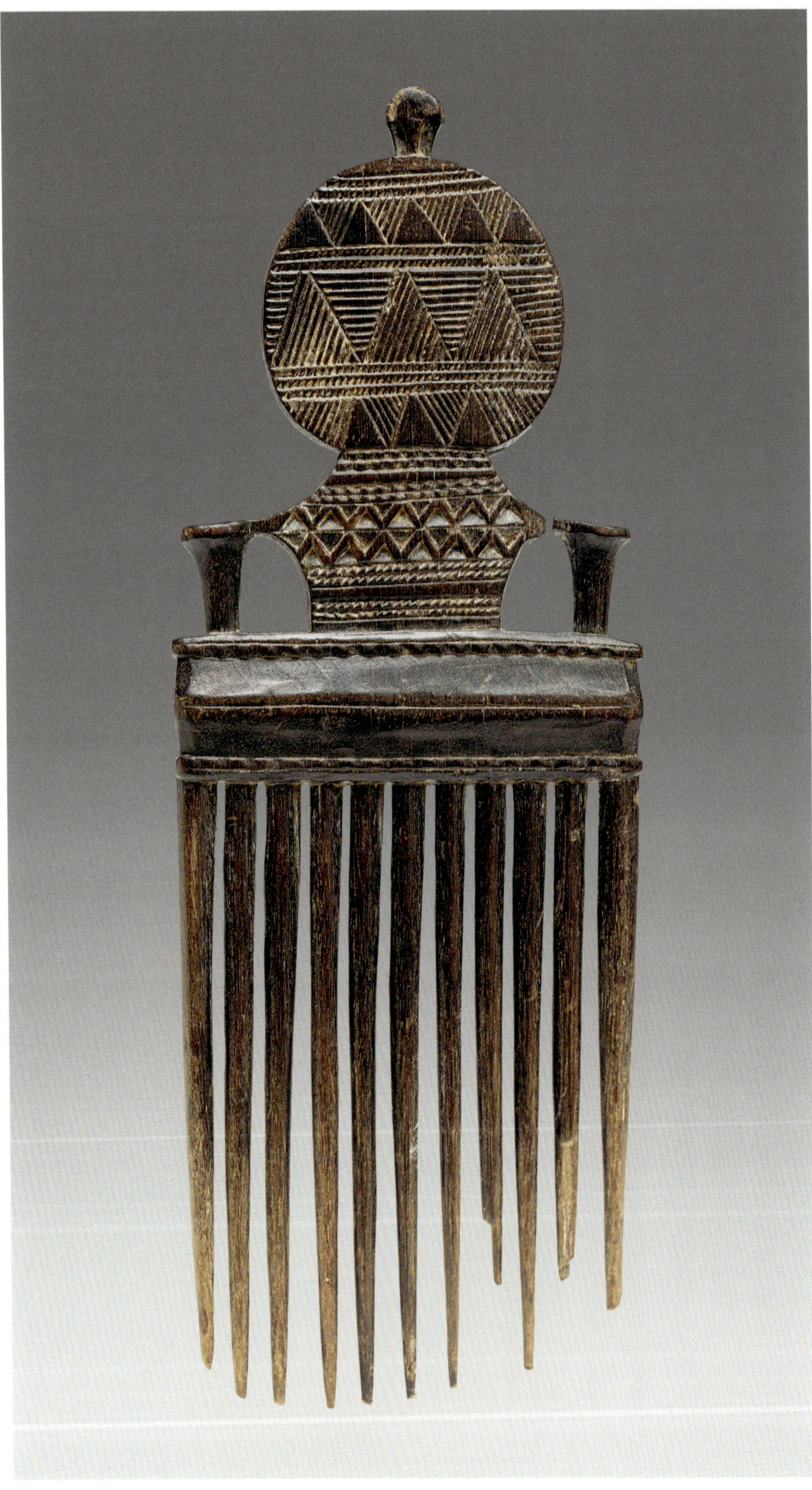

Fig. 20 Peigne | Comb
Attié | Attie, Akan,
Côte d'Ivoire | Ivory Coast
Bois | Wood
18,5 × 6,8 cm | 18.5 × 6.8 cm

Provenance
Robert Duperrier

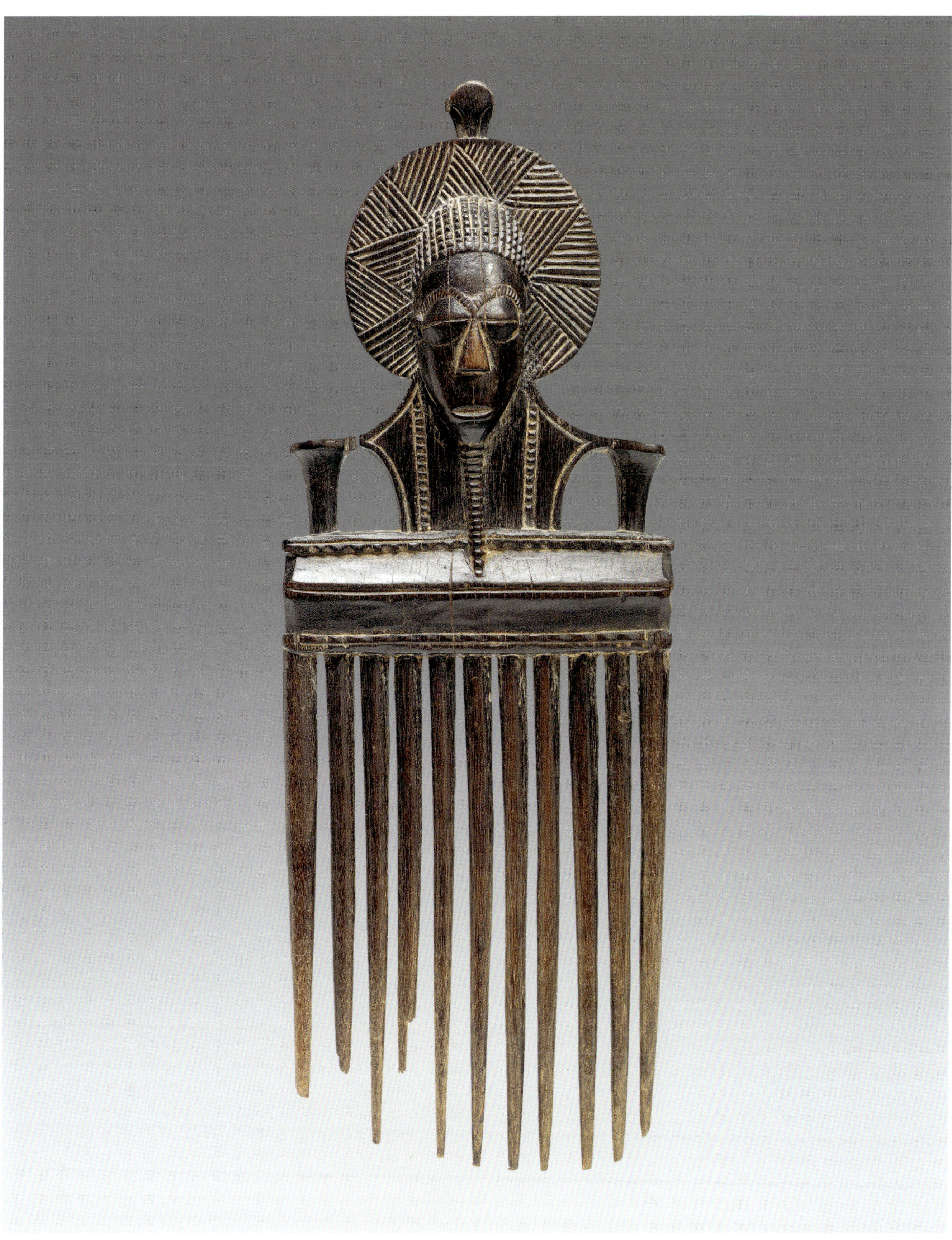

Fig. 21 Peigne | Comb
Attié | Attie, Akan, Côte d'Ivoire | Ivory Coast
Bois, or | Wood, gold
14,6 × 6 cm | 14.6 × 6 cm
Provenance
René Rasmussen

Publication
Hélène Joubert, Jean-Paul Chazal, *Visions d'Afrique*, Taiwan, National Museum of History, 2003, fig. 106, p. 156

Exposition | Exhibition
Visions d'Afrique, Taïwan | Taiwan, National Museum of History, 6 décembre 2003 – 22 février 2004 | 6 December 2003 – 22 February 2004

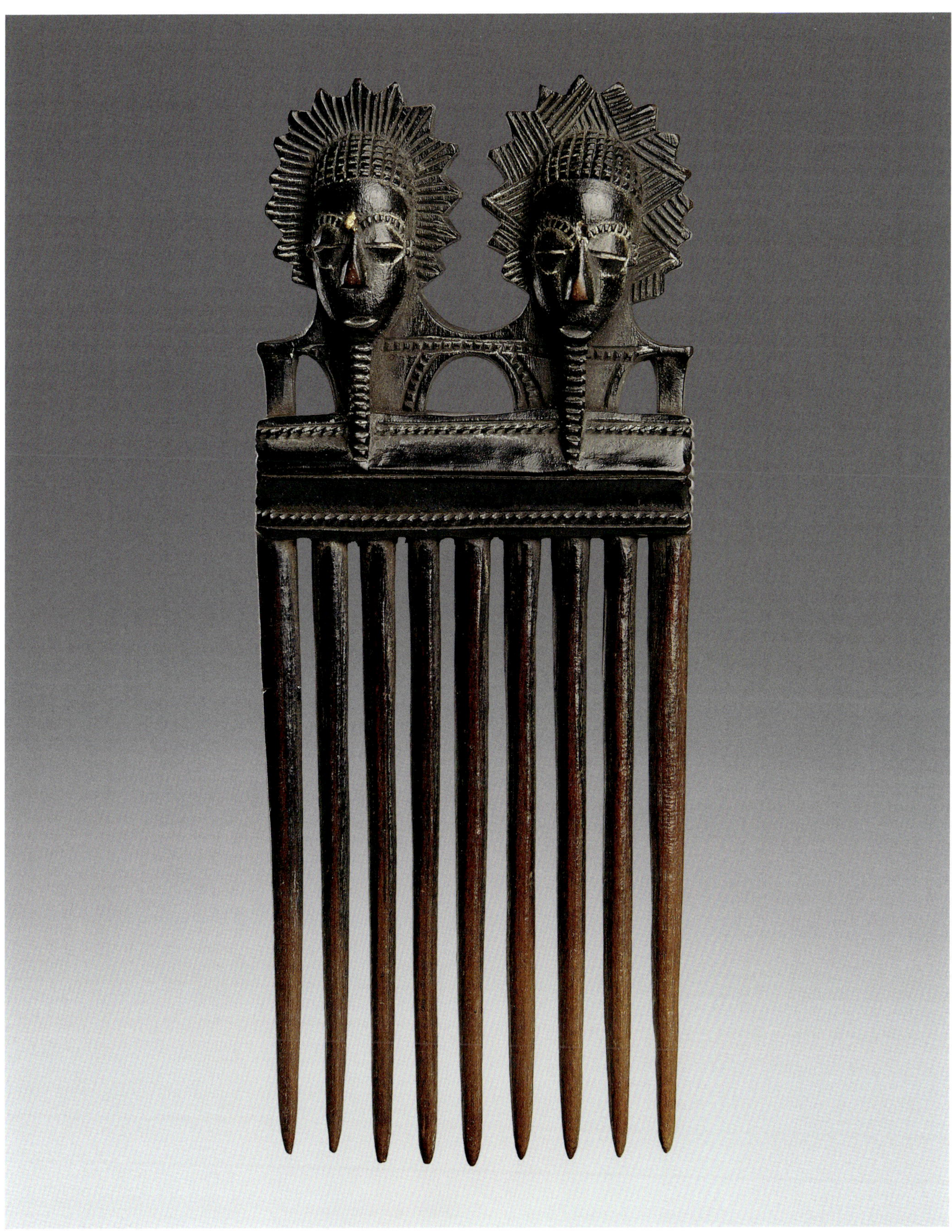

Fig. 22 Peigne | Comb
Baoulé | Baule, Akan, Côte d'Ivoire | Ivory Coast
Bois | Wood
19,5 × 7,5 cm | 19.5 × 7.5 cm

Fig. 23 Peigne | Comb
Baoulé | Baule, Akan, Côte d'Ivoire | Ivory Coast
Bois | Wood
15 × 6,5 cm | 15 × 6.5 cm

Provenance
Jean-Paul Delcourt

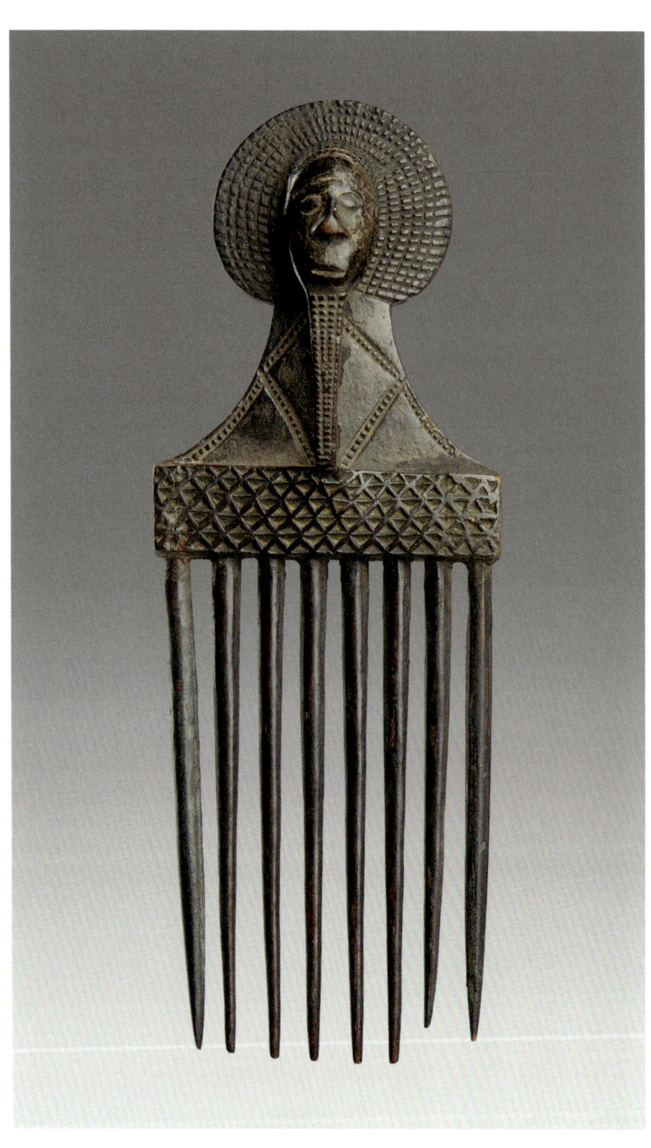

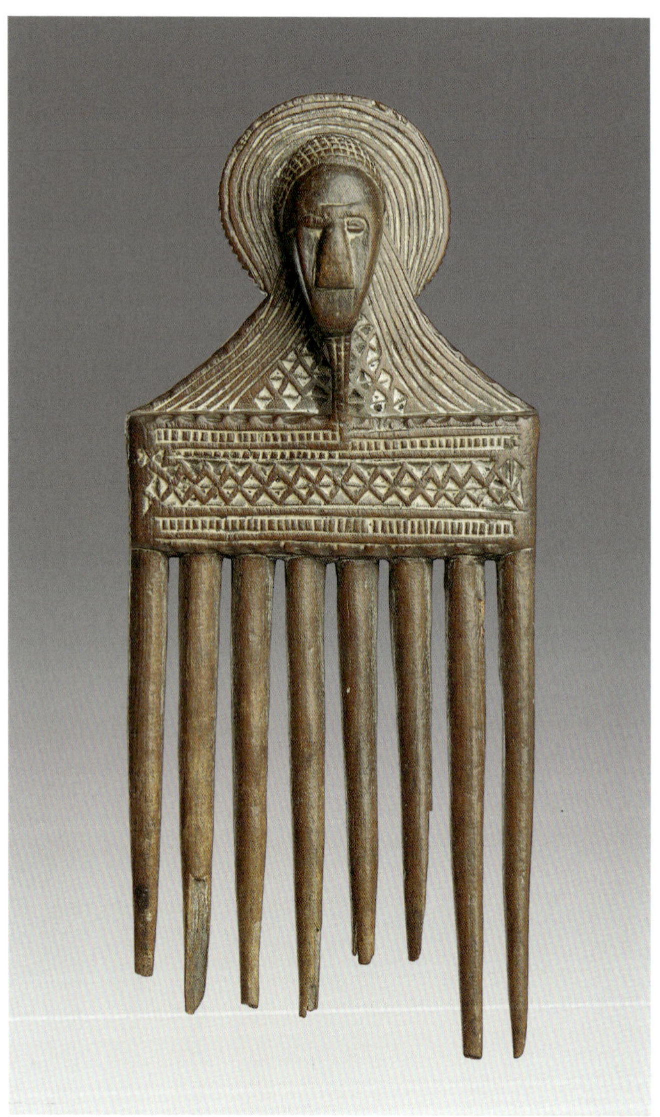

Fig. 24 Peigne | Comb
Baoulé | Baule, Akan, Côte d'Ivoire | Ivory Coast
Bois | Wood
14 × 5,6 cm | 14 × 5.6 cm

Provenance
Jean-Pierre Laprugne

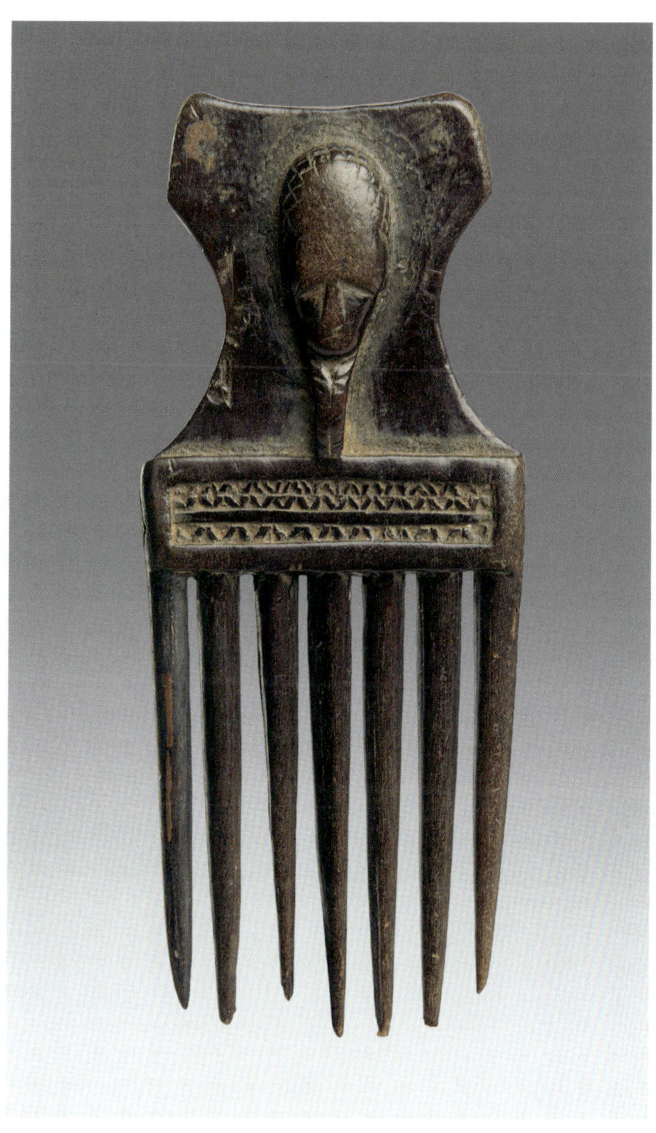

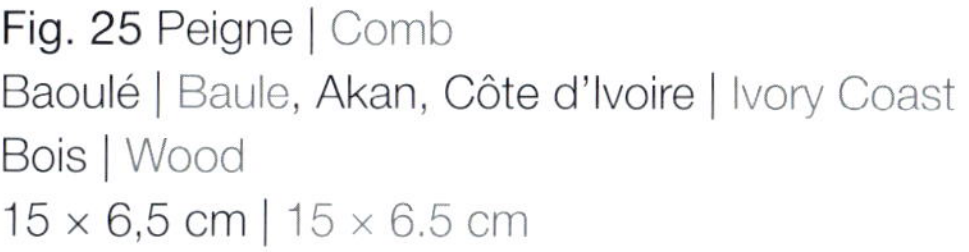

Fig. 25 Peigne | Comb
Baoulé | Baule, Akan, Côte d'Ivoire | Ivory Coast
Bois | Wood
15 × 6,5 cm | 15 × 6.5 cm

Provenance
Issaka Zango

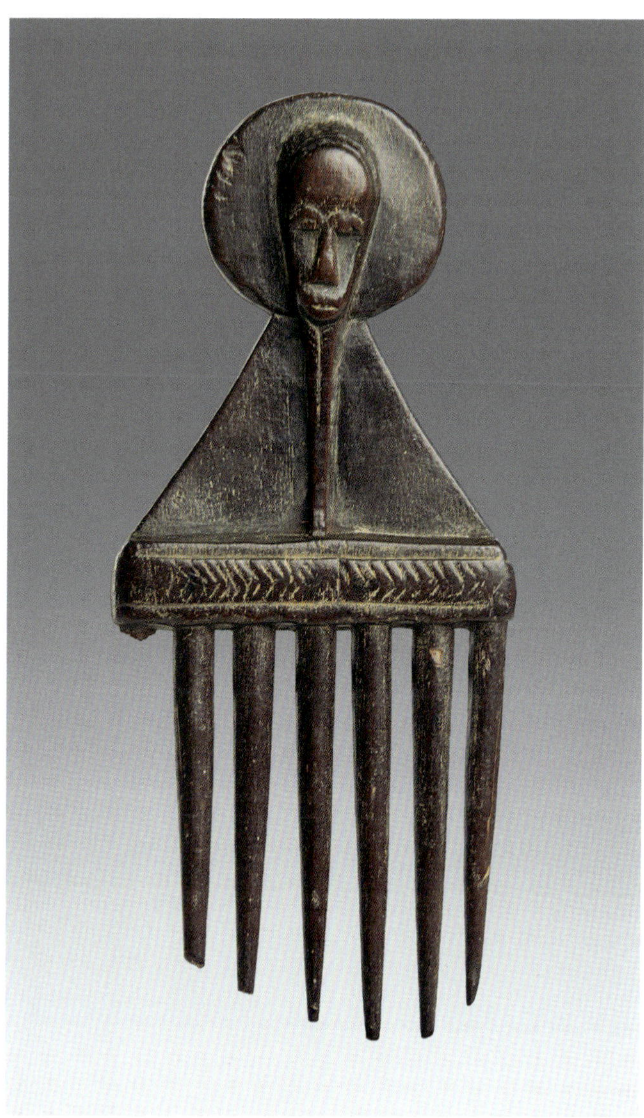

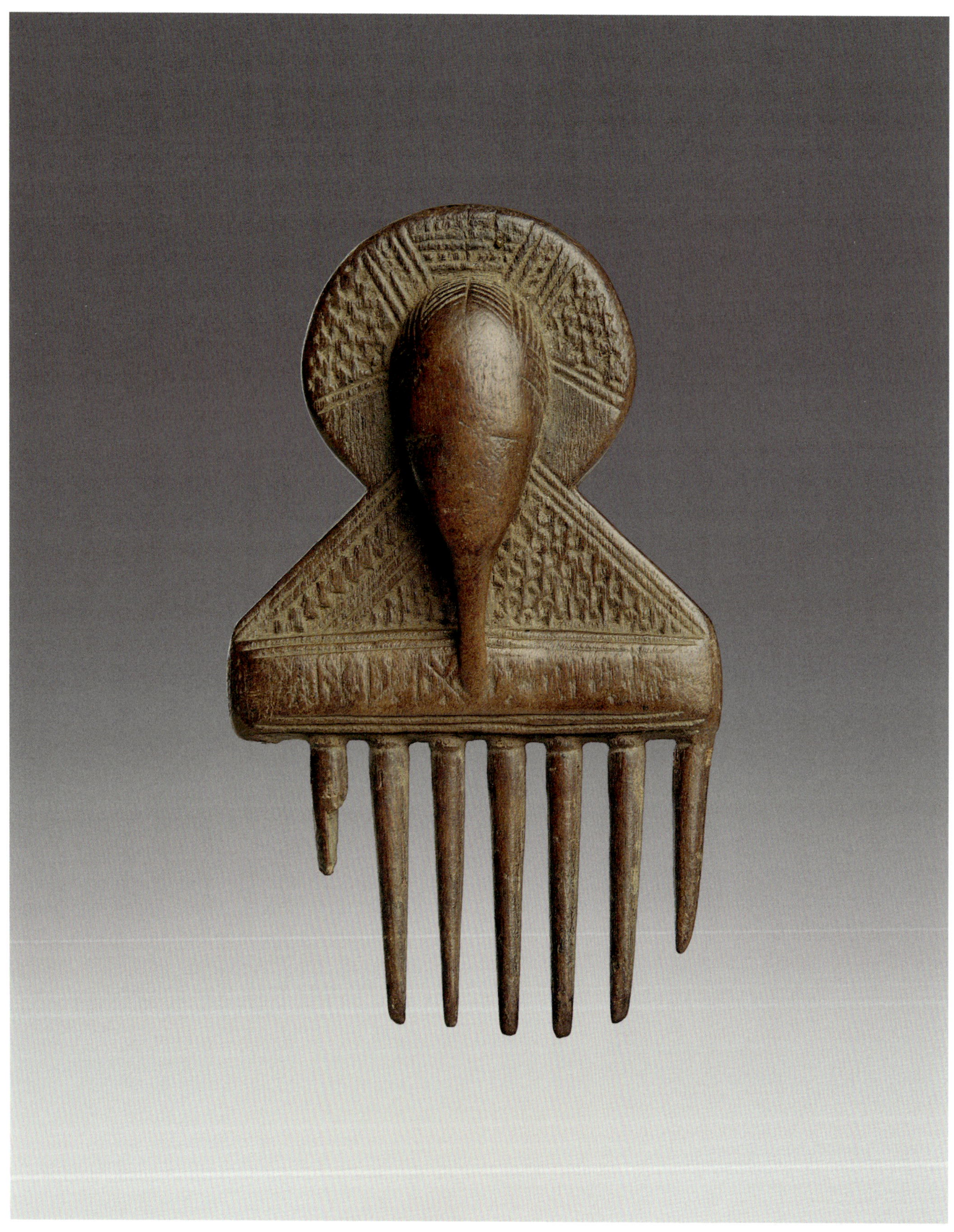

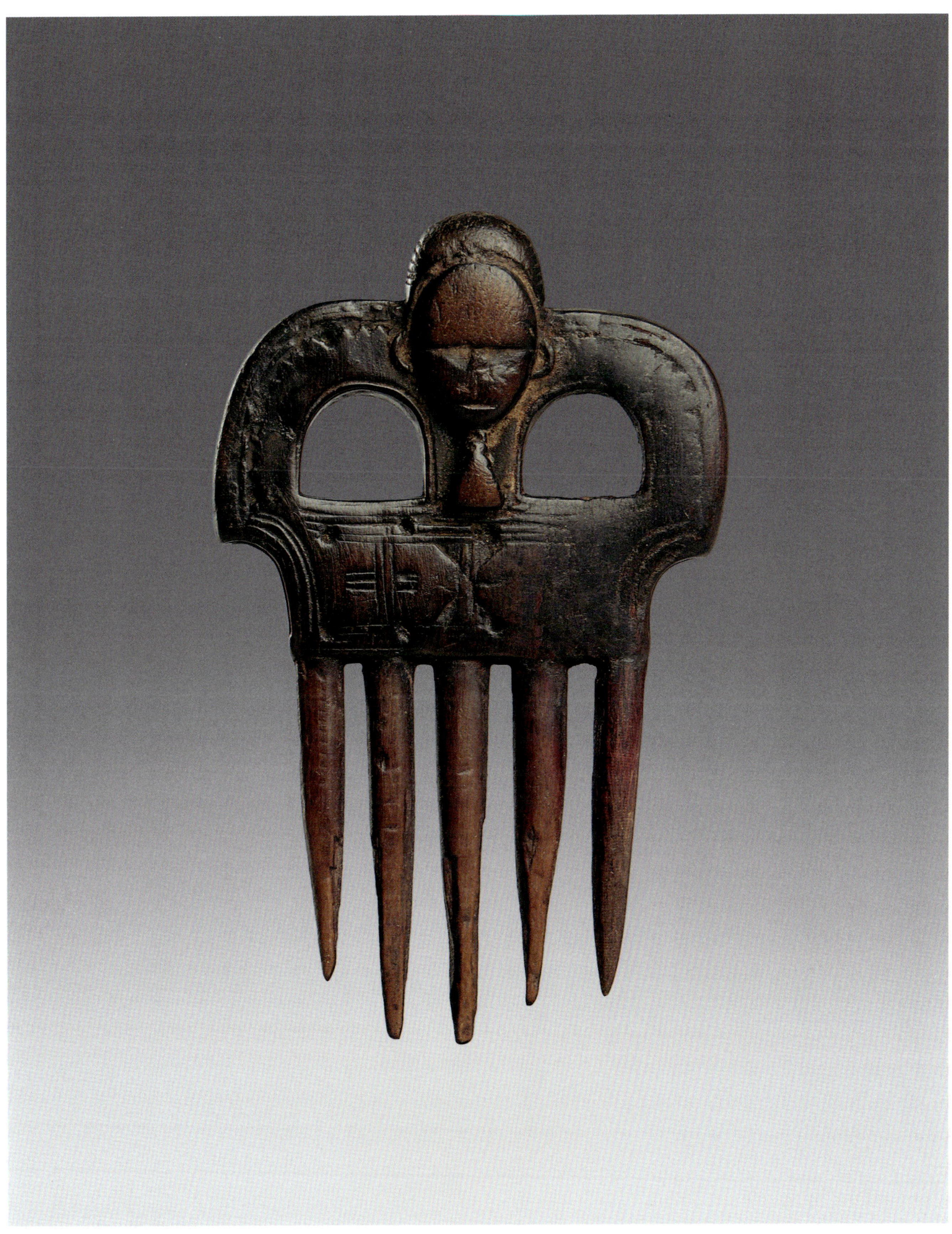

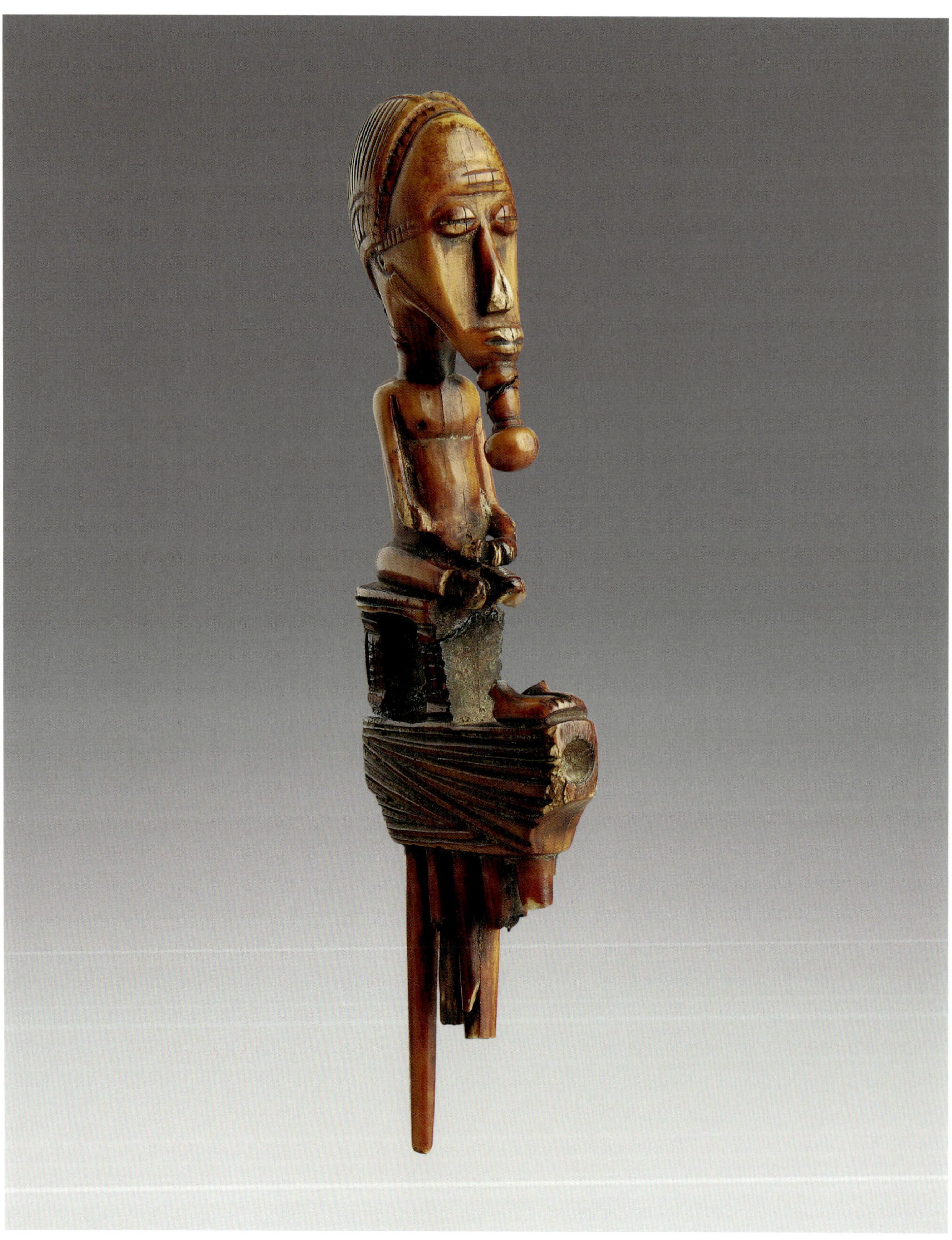

Page 88
Fig. 26 Peigne | Comb
Baoulé | Baule, Akan, Côte d'Ivoire | Ivory Coast
Bois, clou de tapissier (au dos du peigne) |
Wood, upholstery tack (on the back of the comb)
10,5 × 6,8 cm | 10.5 × 6.8 cm

Provenance
Jean-Paul Delcourt

Fig. 28 Peigne | Comb
Baoulé | Baule, Akan, Côte d'Ivoire | Ivory Coast
Ivoire | Ivory
12,5 × 4 cm | 12.5 × 4 cm

Provenance
Jean-Pierre Laprugne

Page 89
Fig. 27 Peigne | Comb
Baoulé | Baule, Akan, Côte d'Ivoire | Ivory Coast
Bois | Wood
10 × 6,1 cm | 10 × 6.1 cm

Provenance
Henri Kamer

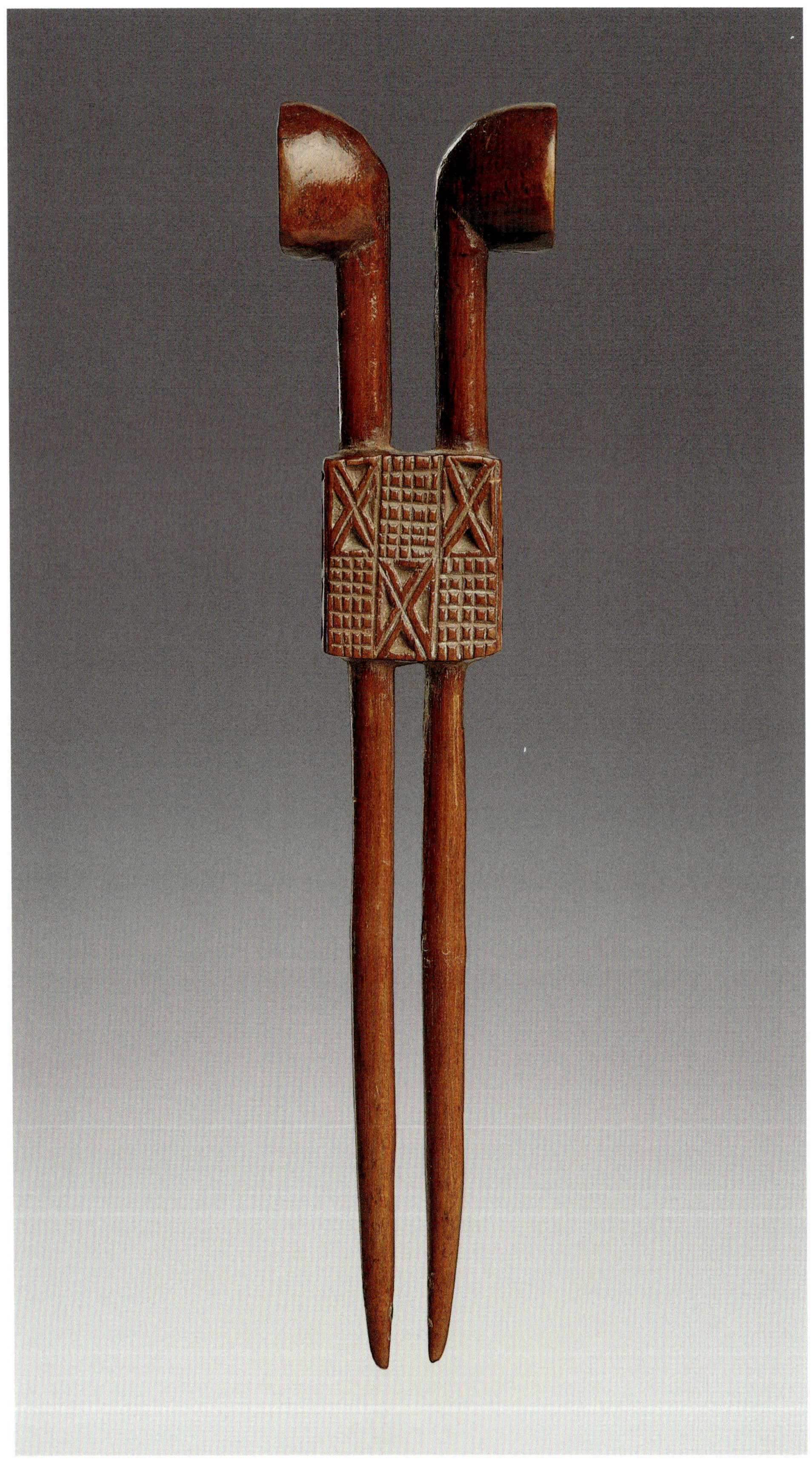

Fig. 29 Peigne | Comb
Baoulé | Baule, Akan,
Côte d'Ivoire | Ivory Coast
Bois | Wood
12 × 2,5 cm | 12 × 2.5 cm

Provenance
Koussi Nzi

Fig. 30 Peigne | Comb
Baoulé | Baule, Akan,
Côte d'Ivoire | Ivory Coast
Bois | Wood
20 × 4 cm

Provenance
Koussi Nzi

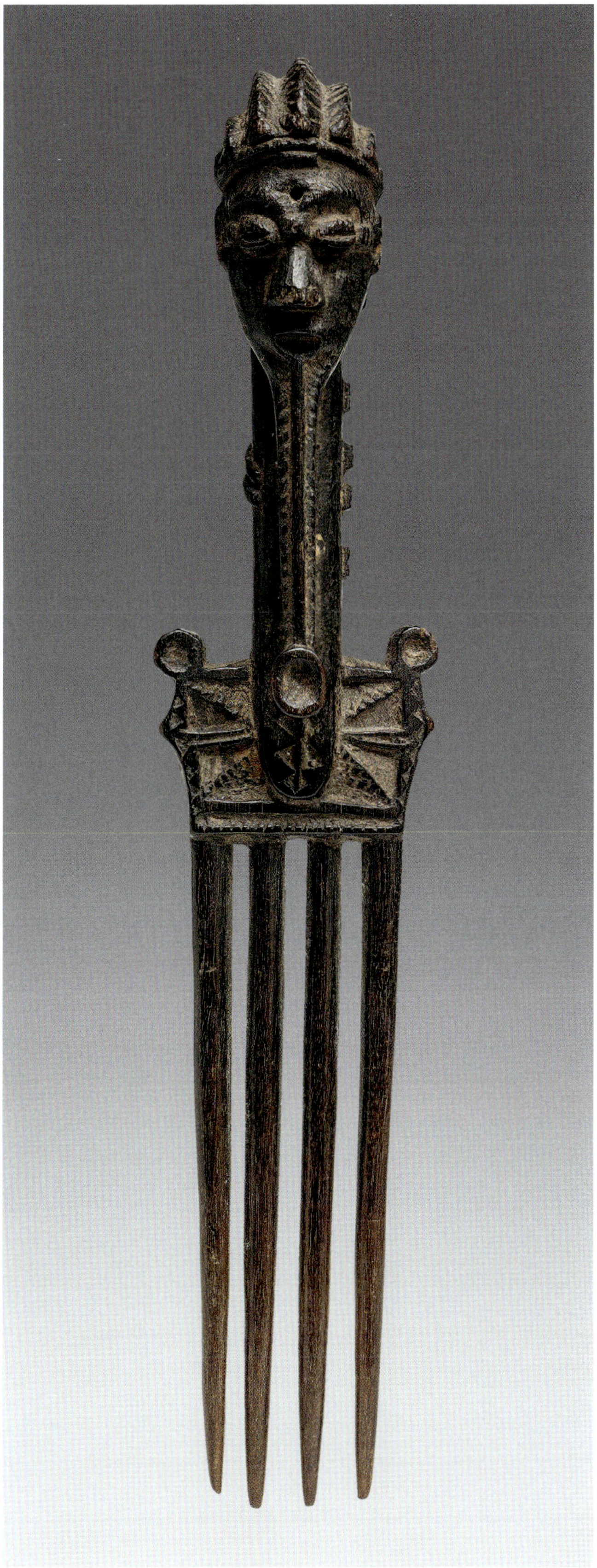

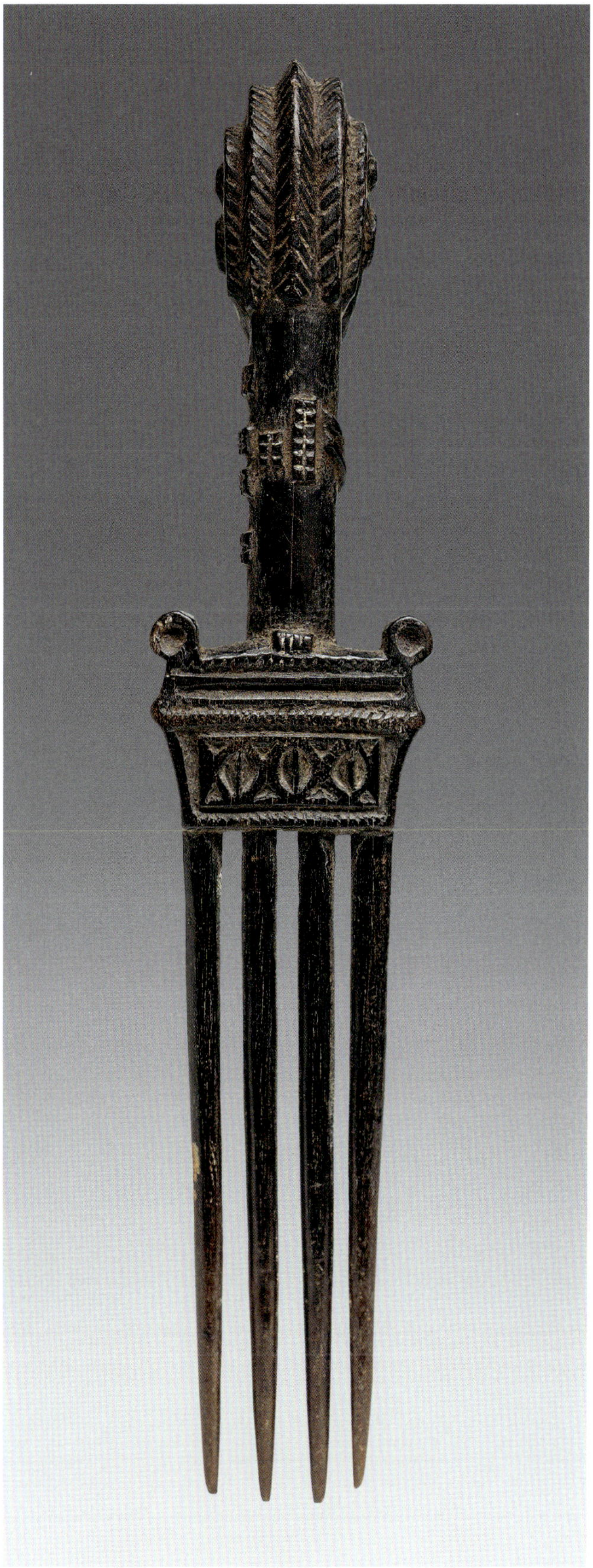

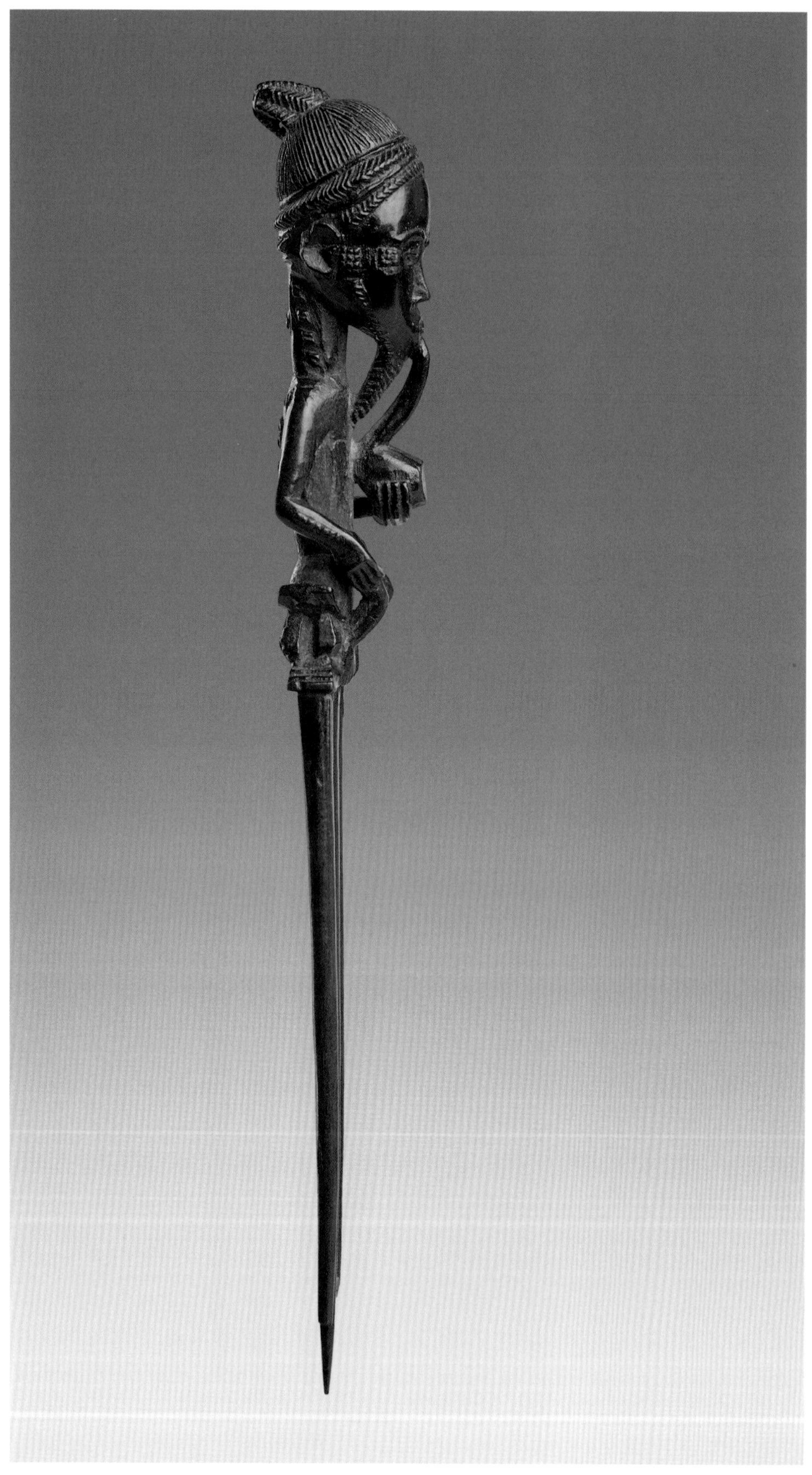

Fig. 31 Peigne | Comb
Baoulé | Baule, Akan,
Côte d'Ivoire | Ivory Coast
Bois | Wood
19,5 × 2,5 cm | 19.5 × 2.5 cm

Provenance
René Rasmussen, Maurice Pinto

Publications
Raoul Lehuard, « Visions d'Afrique à Taïwan », in *Arts d'Afrique Noire*, n° 130, eté 2004, p. 21 ; Hélène Joubert, Jean-Paul Chazal, *Visions d'Afrique*, Taiwan, National Museum of History, 2003, fig. 107, p. 157

Exposition | Exhibition
Visions d'Afrique, Taïwan | Taiwan, National Museum of History, 6 décembre 2003 – 22 février 2004 | 6 Decembe 2003 – 22 February 2004

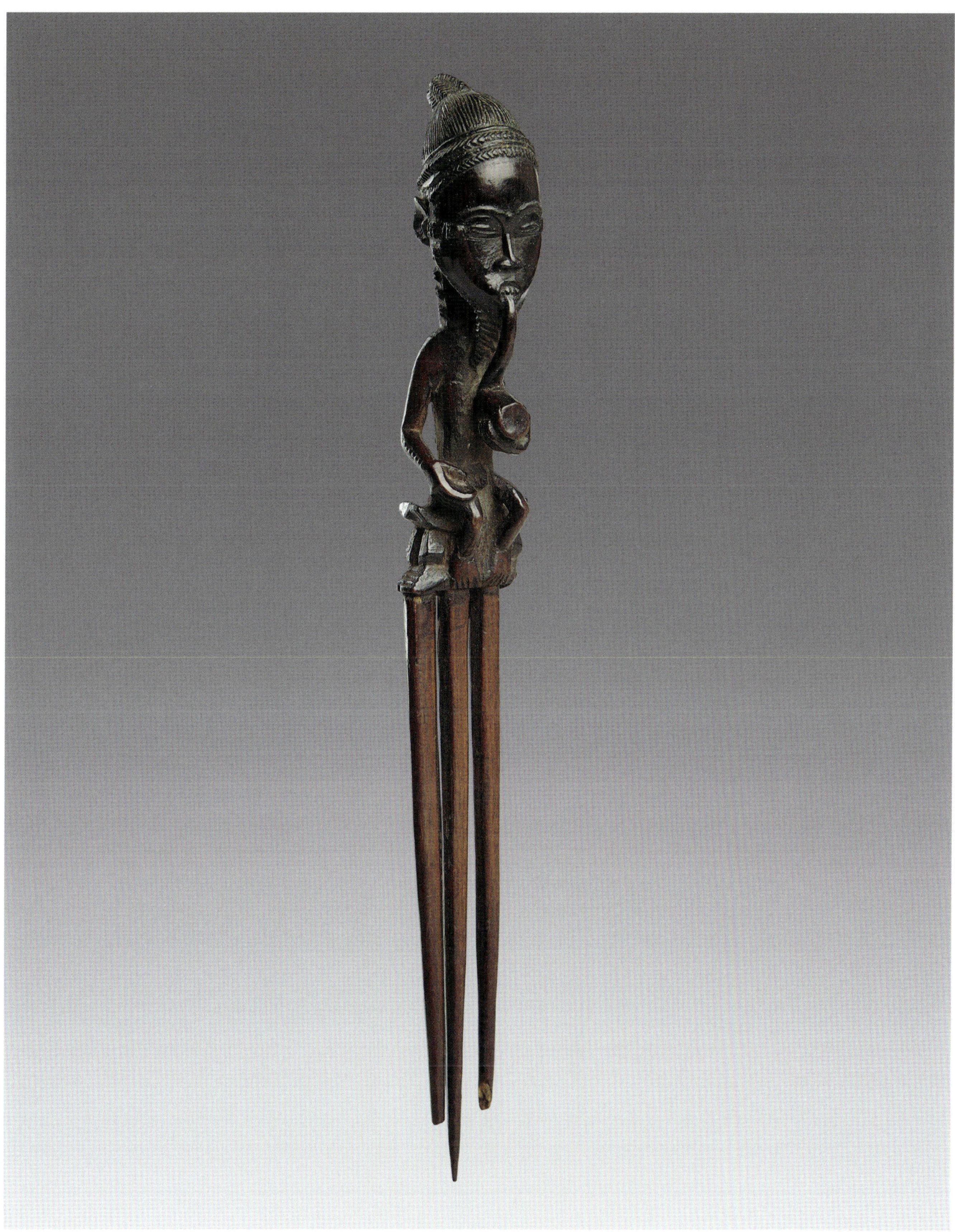

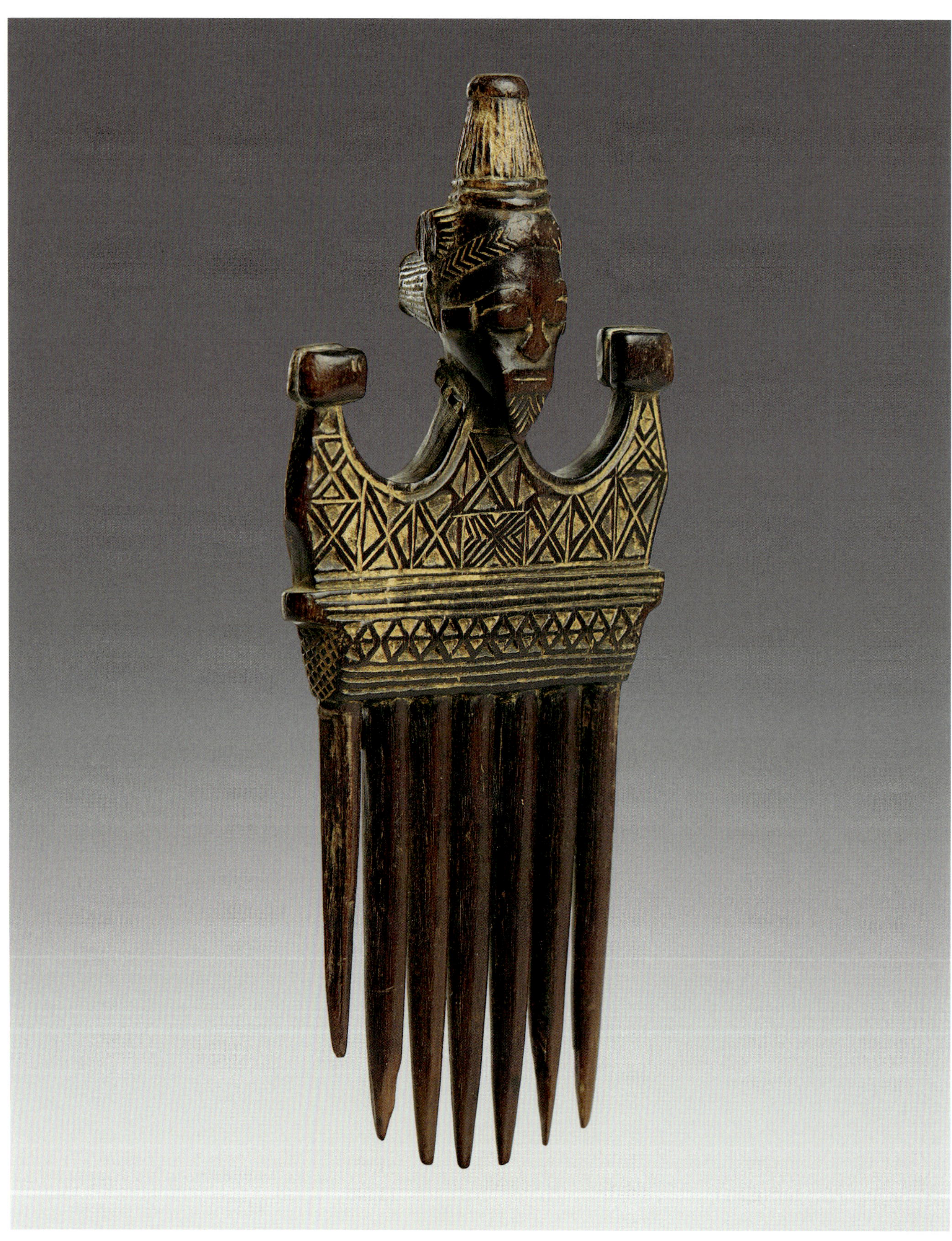

Fig. 32 Peigne | Comb
Baoulé | Baule, Akan, Côte d'Ivoire | Ivory Coast
Bois | Wood
16 × 7 cm

Publication
Jean-Yves Augel, Valentine Plisnier, *Coiffures africaines en majesté*, Sainte-Foy-lès-Lyon, Galerie Vallois, 2024, fig. 3, p. 119

Exposition | Exhibition
Sainte-Foy-lès-Lyon, Espace Culturel Jean Salles, *Coiffures africaines en majesté*,
6 – 21 avril | 6 – 21 April 2024

Fig. 33 Peigne | Comb
Baoulé | Baule, Akan, Côte d'Ivoire | Ivory Coast
Bois | Wood
13,5 × 2,5 cm | 13.5 × 2.5 cm

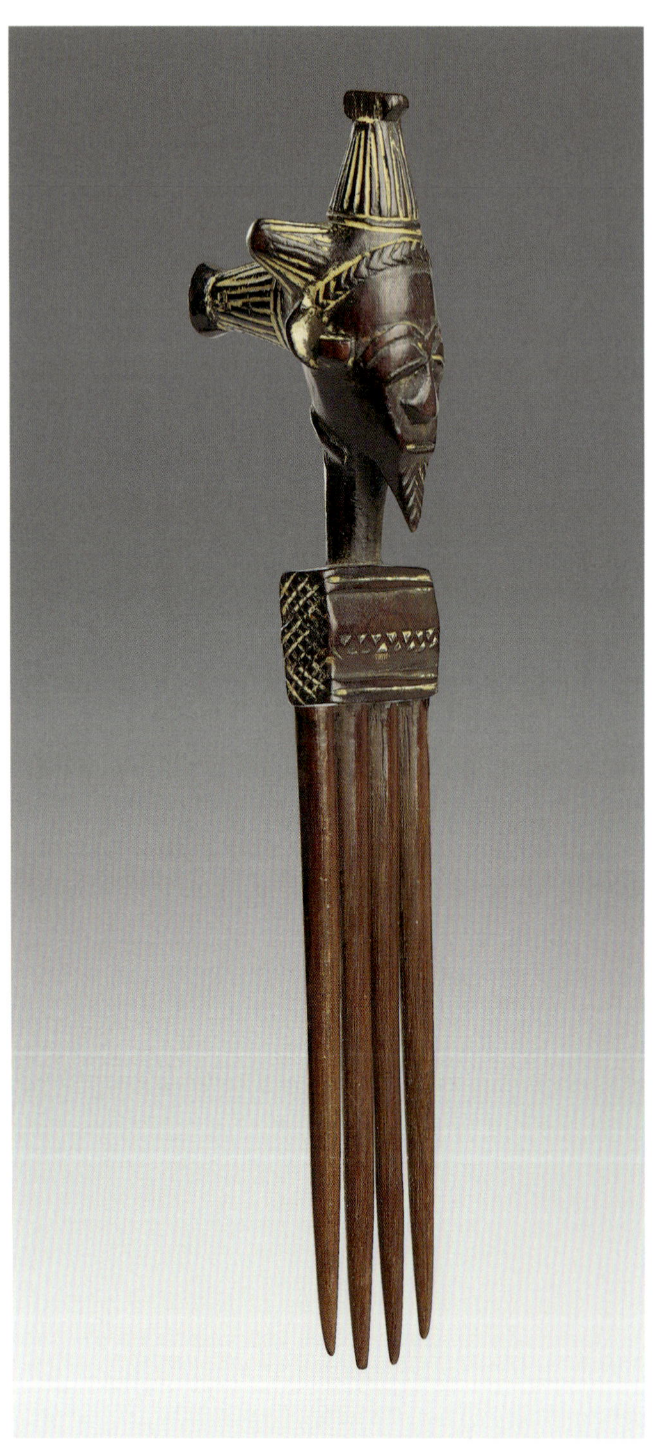

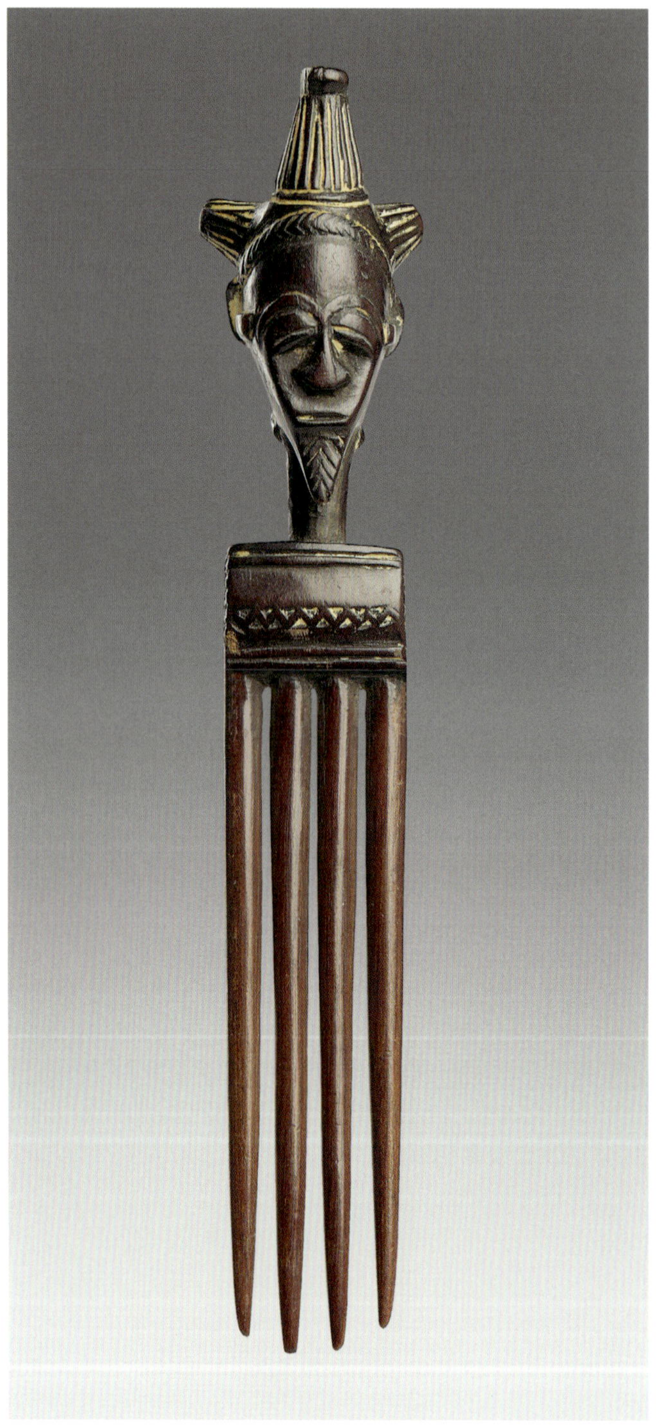

Fig. 34 Peigne | Comb
Baoulé | Baule, Akan, Côte d'Ivoire | Ivory Coast
Bois | Wood
17,5 × 3,5 cm | 17.5 × 3.5 cm

Provenance
Jonas De Boeck

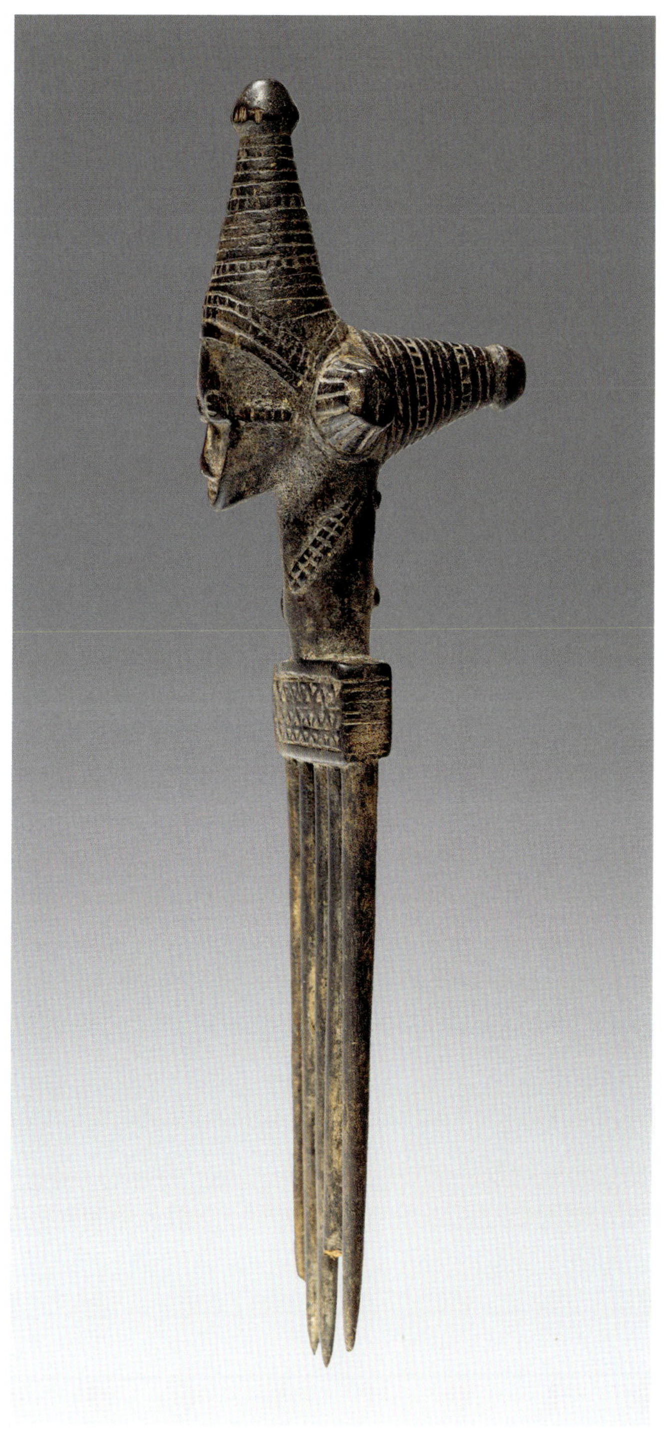

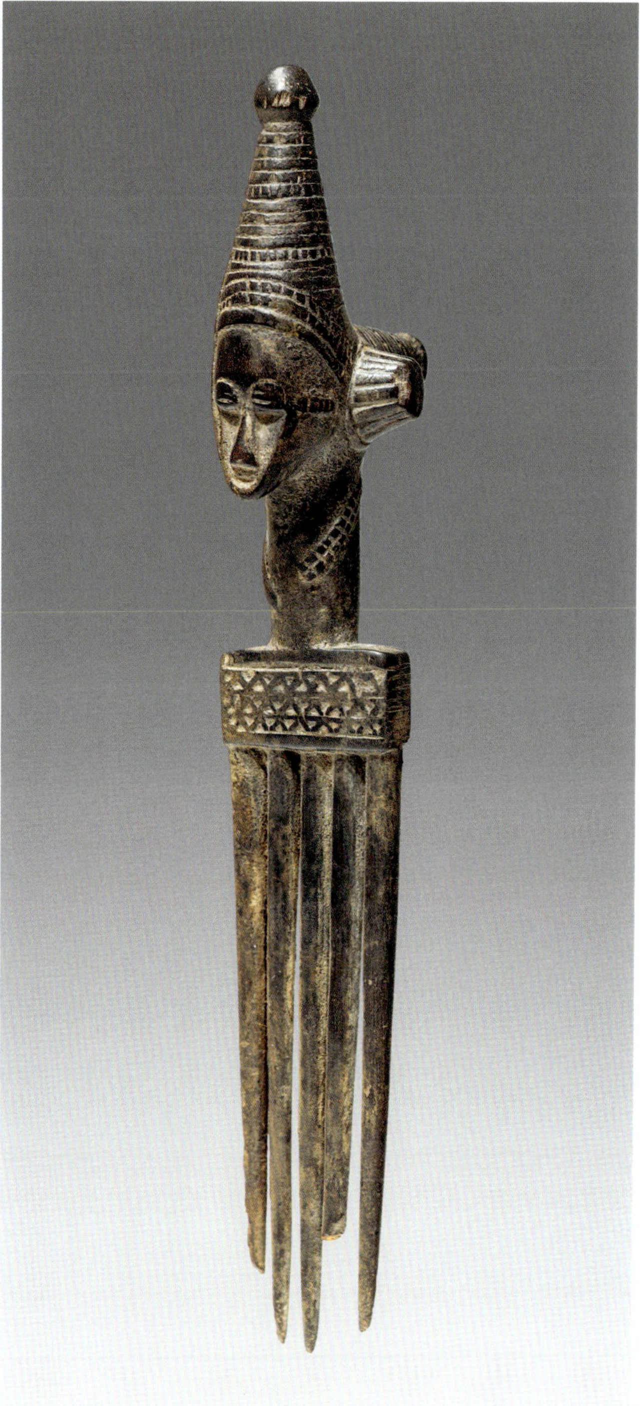

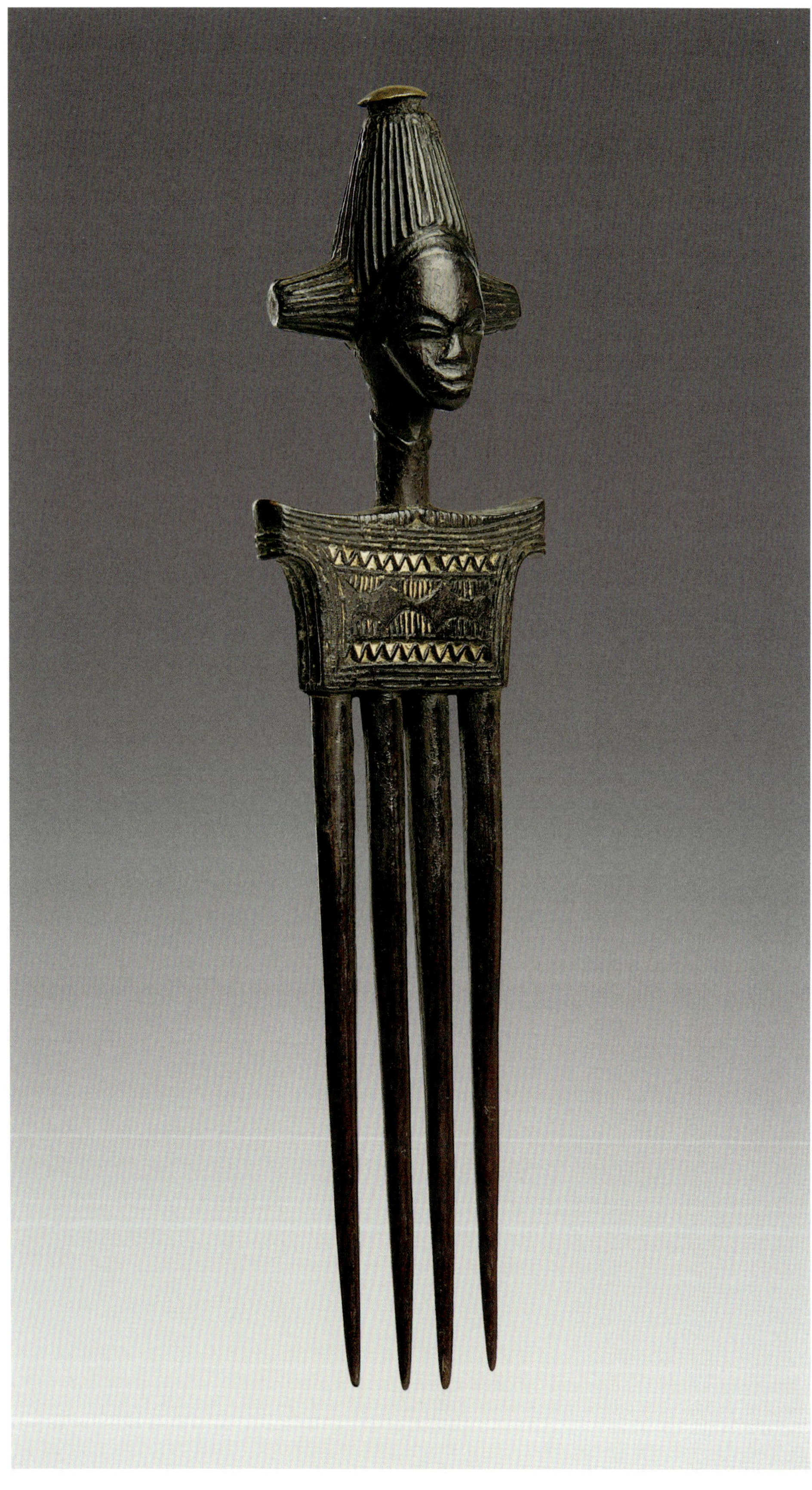

Fig. 35 Peigne | Comb
Baoulé | Baule, Akan,
Côte d'Ivoire | Ivory Coast
Bois, clou de tapissier | Wood, upholstery tack
15,5 × 4,5 cm | 15.5 × 4.5 cm

Publication
Jean-Yves Augel, Valentine Plisnier, *Coiffures africaines en majesté*, Sainte-Foy-lès-Lyon, Galerie Vallois, 2024, fig. 4, p.119

Exposition | Exhibition
Sainte-Foy-lès-Lyon, Espace Culturel Jean Salles, *Coiffures africaines en majesté*, 6 – 21 avril | 6 – 21 April 2024

Fig. 36 Peigne | Comb
Baoulé | Baule, Akan, Côte d'Ivoire | Ivory Coast
Bois | Wood
13,5 × 5 cm | 13.5 × 5 cm

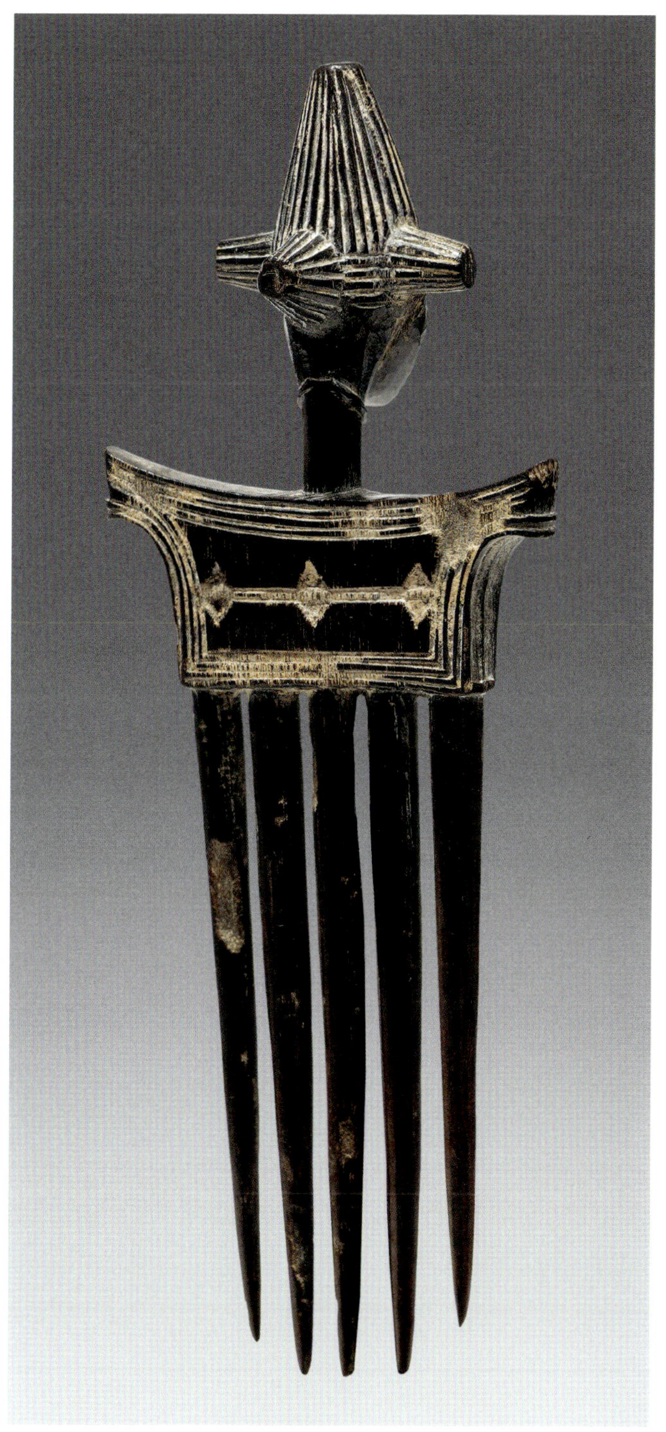

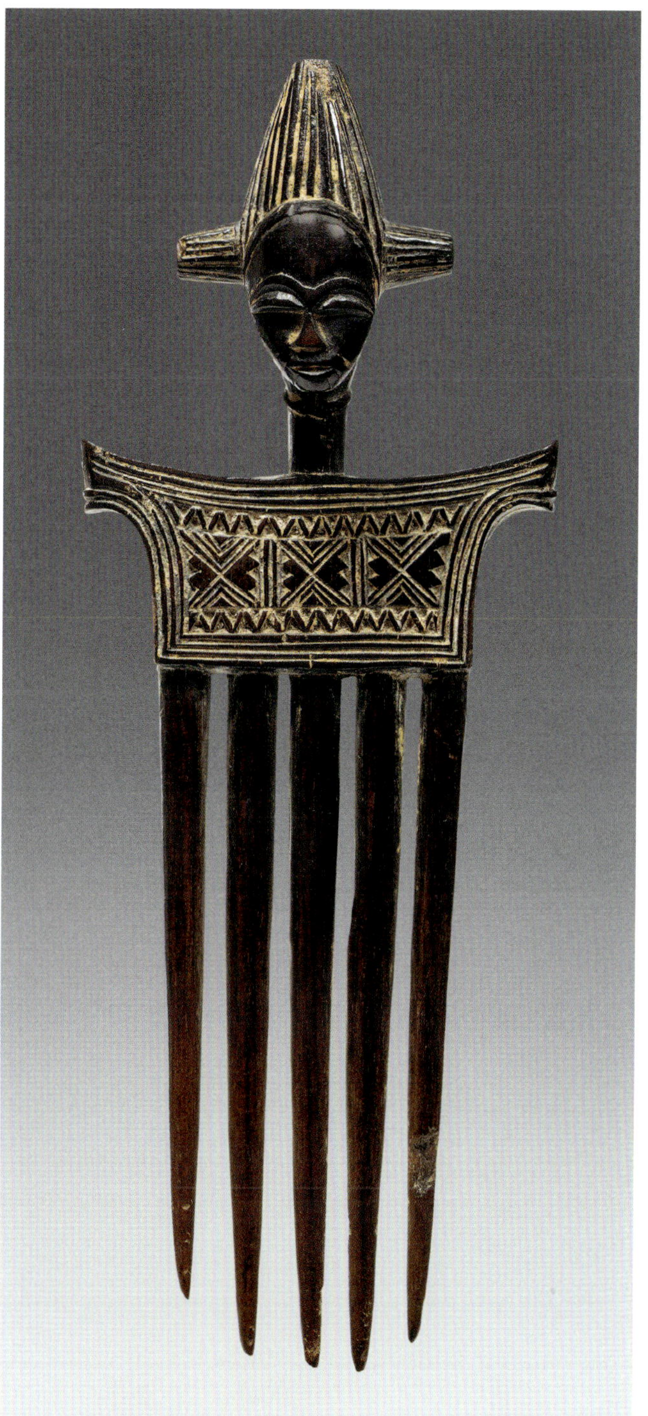

Fig. 37 Peigne | Comb
Baoulé | Baule, Akan, Côte d'Ivoire | Ivory Coast
Bois | Wood
14,7 × 3,6 cm | 14.7 × 3.6 cm

Provenance
Maine Durieu

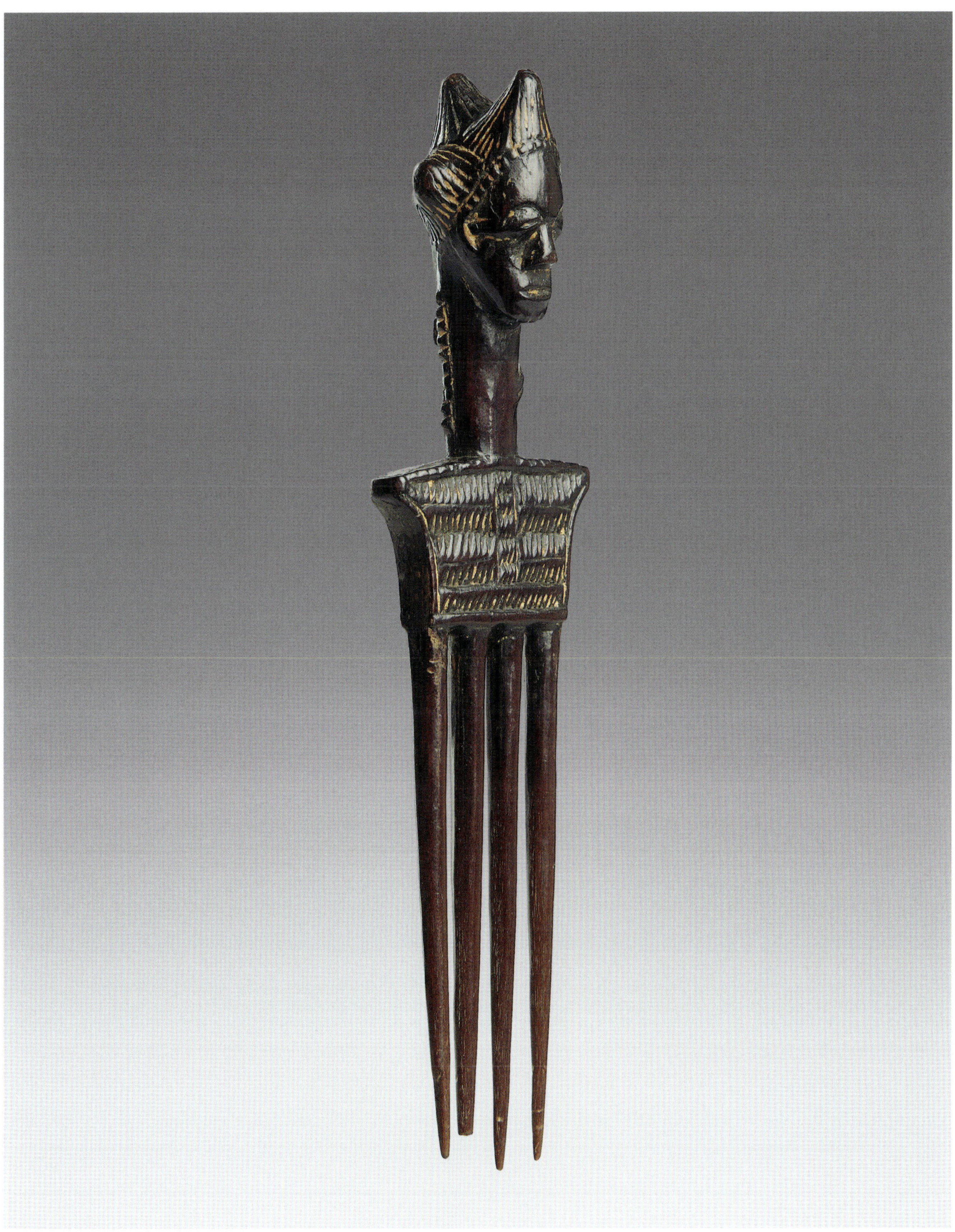

Fig. 38 Peigne | Comb
Attié | Attie, Akan, Côte d'Ivoire | Ivory Coast
Bois | Wood
17,5 × 4,5 cm | 17.5 × 4.5 cm

Provenance
Henri Kamer

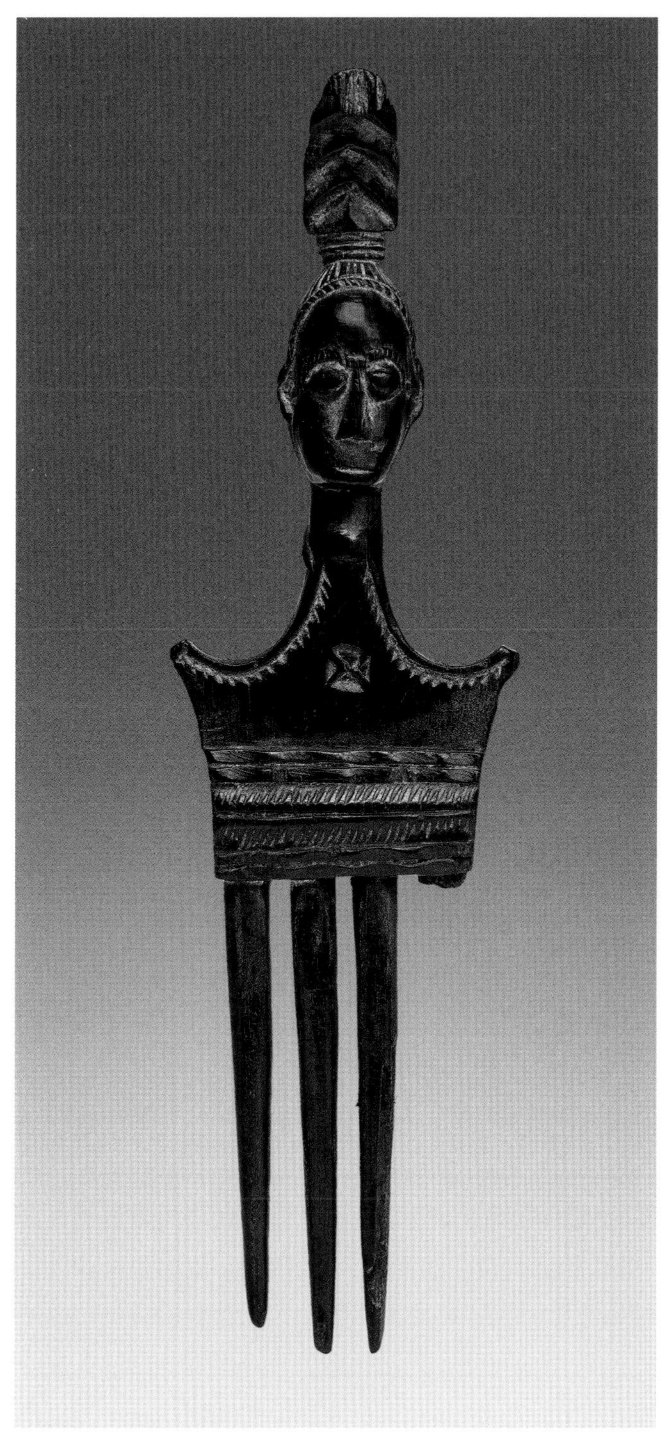

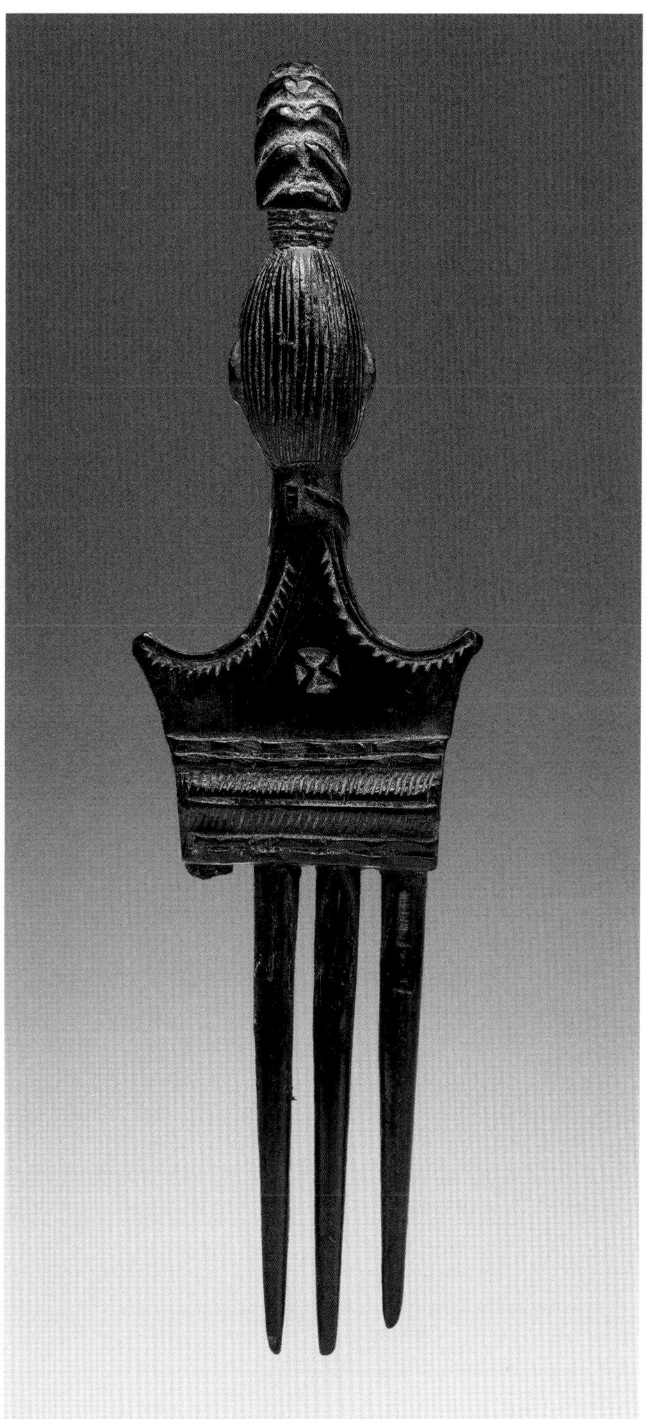

Fig. 39 Peigne | Comb
Baoulé | Baule, Akan, Côte d'Ivoire | Ivory Coast
Bois | Wood
19 × 5 cm

Provenance
Robert Duperrier

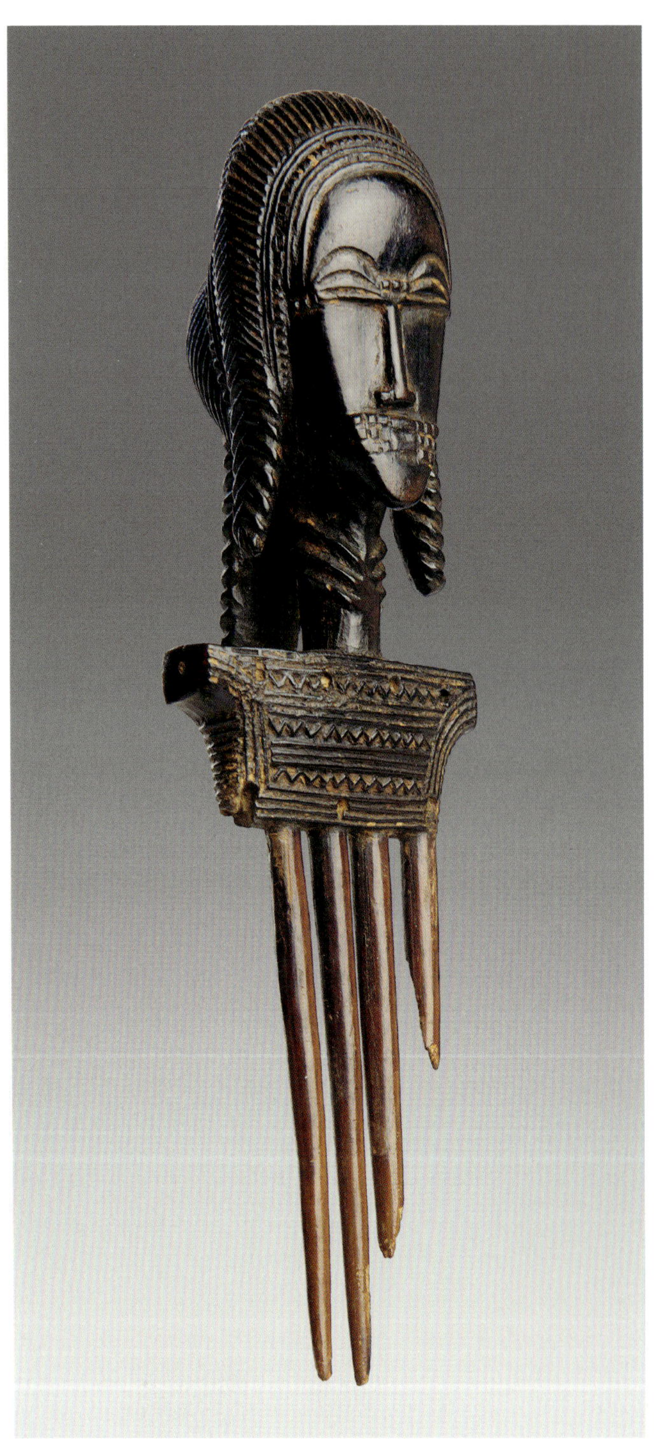

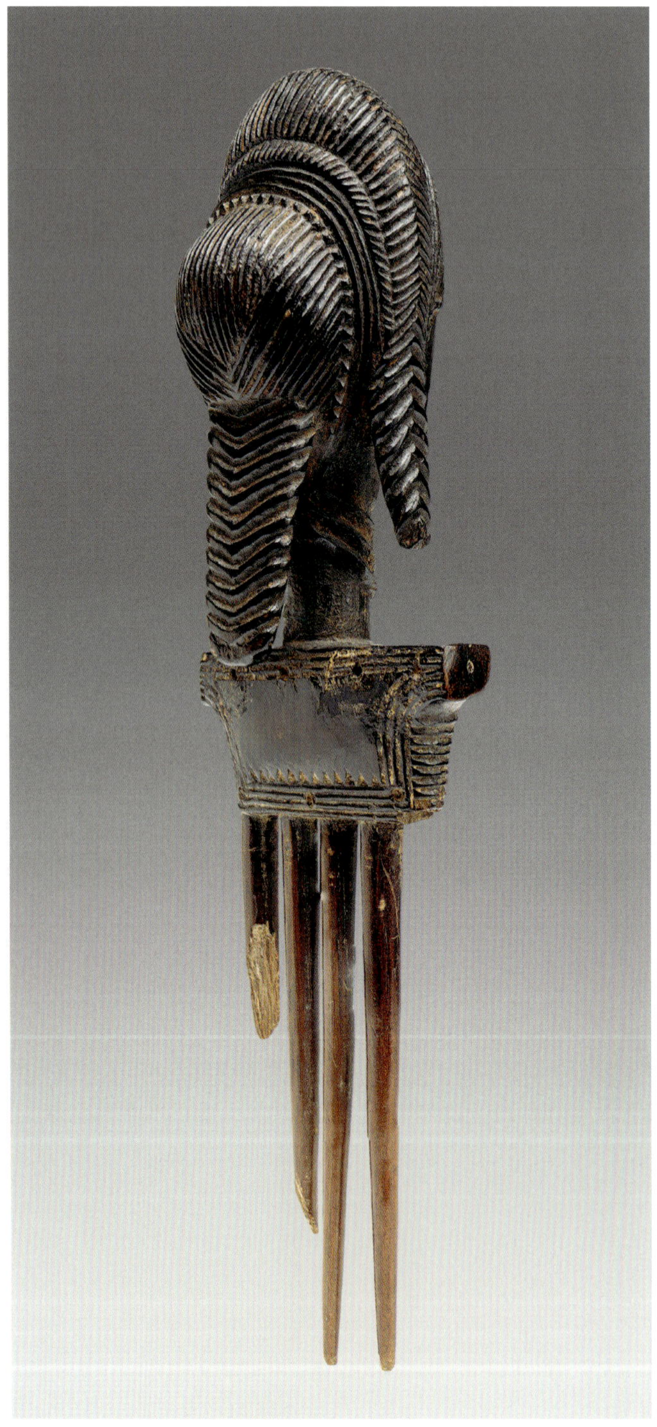

Fig. 40 Peigne | Comb
Baoulé | Baule, Akan, Côte d'Ivoire | Ivory Coast
Bois, clous de tapisserie | Wood, upholstery tacks
12,5 × 5 cm | 12.5 × 5 cm

Provenance
Baba Keïta

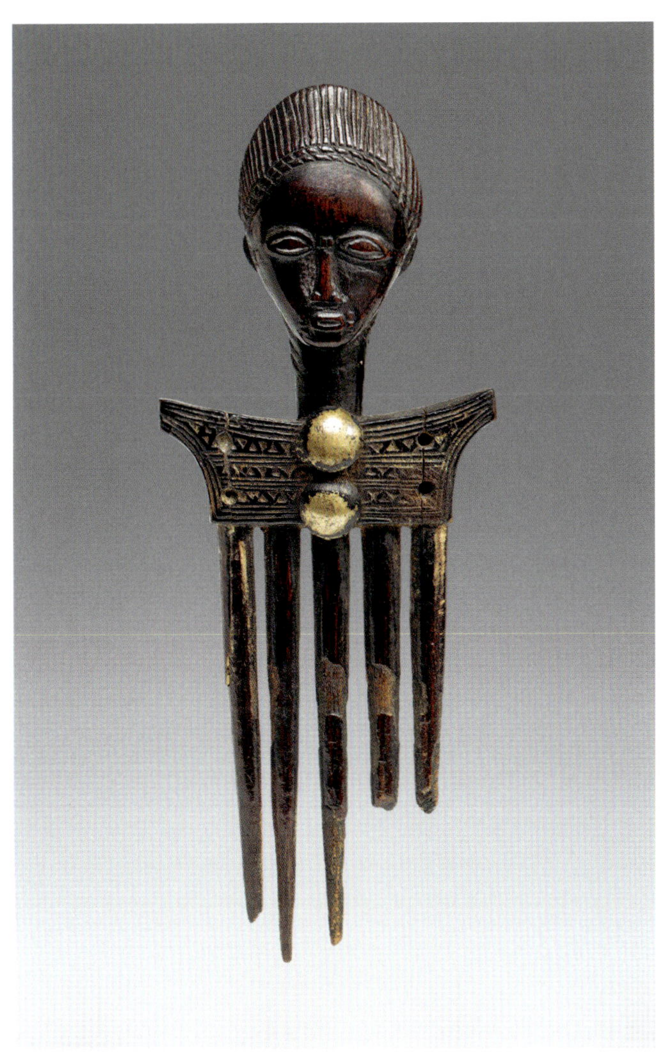

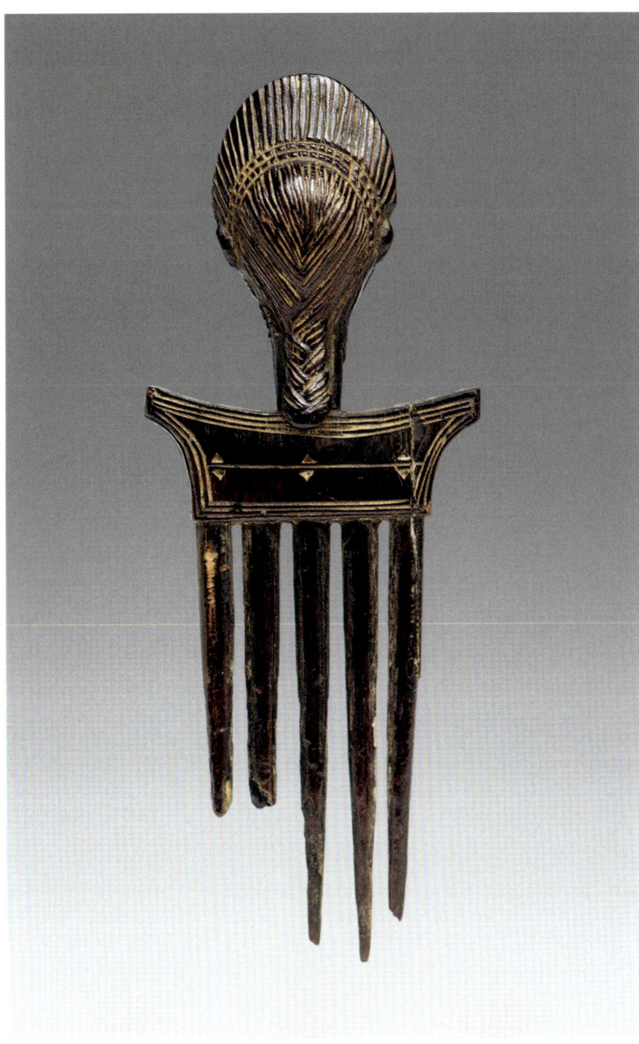

Fig. 41 Peigne | Comb
Baoulé | Baule, Akan, Côte d'Ivoire | Ivory Coast
Bois | Wood
17 × 5,5 cm | 17 × 5.5 cm

Provenance
Paul Mossi

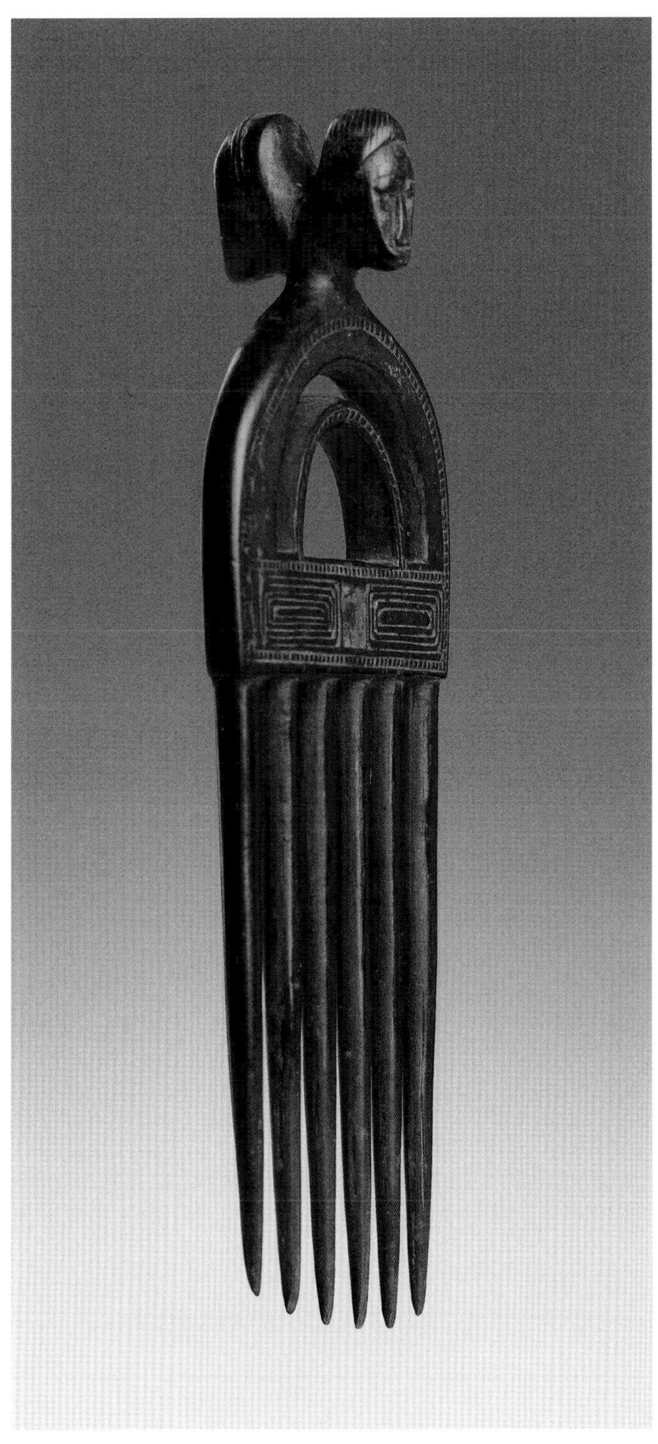

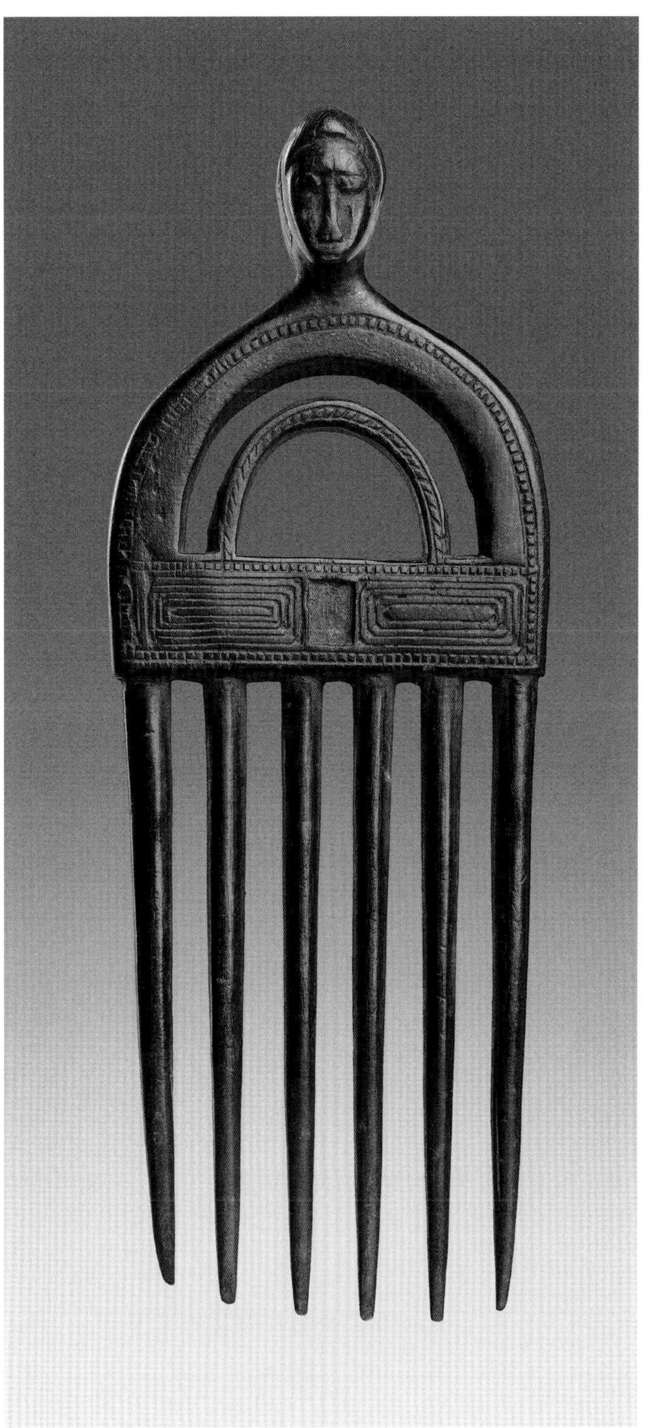

Fig. 42 Peigne | Comb
Baoulé | Baule, Akan, Côte d'Ivoire | Ivory Coast
Bois | Wood
15 × 5 cm

Provenance
Maurice Nicaud

Fig. 43 Peigne | Comb
Baoulé | Baule, Akan, Côte d'Ivoire | Ivory Coast
Ivoire | Ivory
7,6 × 3 cm | 7.6 × 3 cm

Provenance
Dramane Ouedraougo

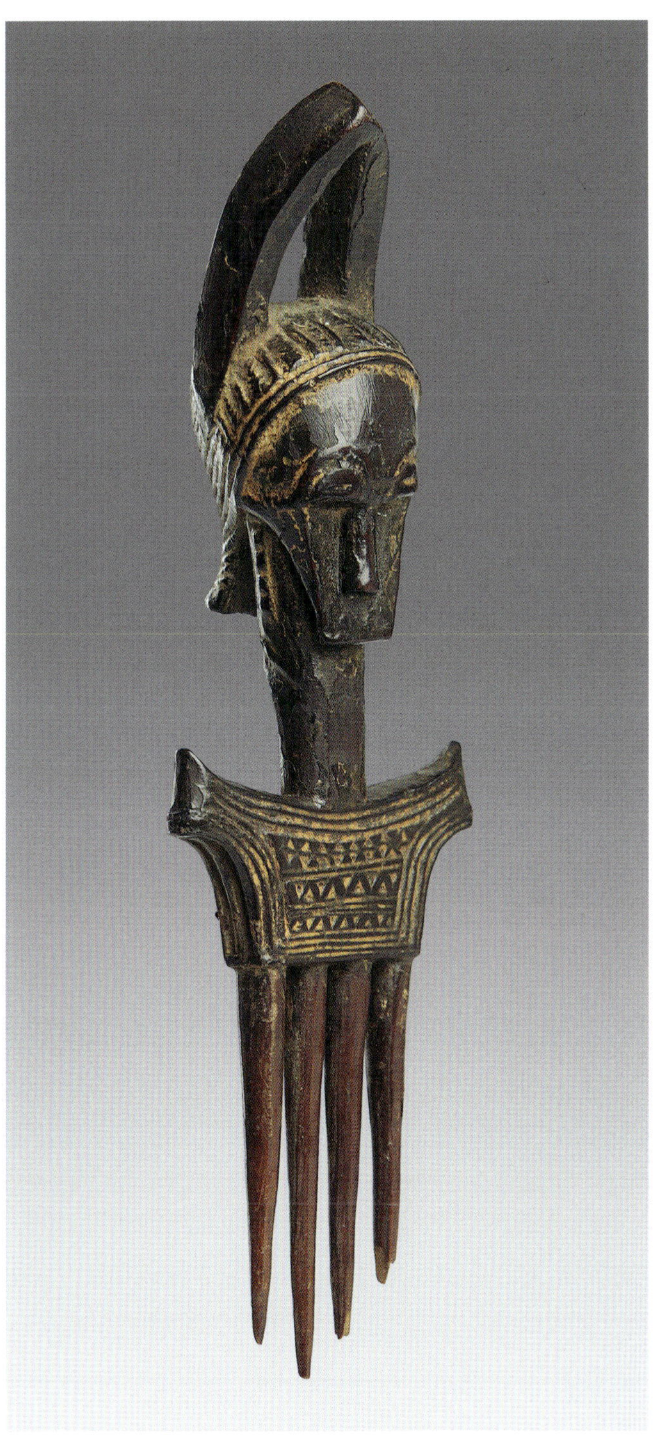

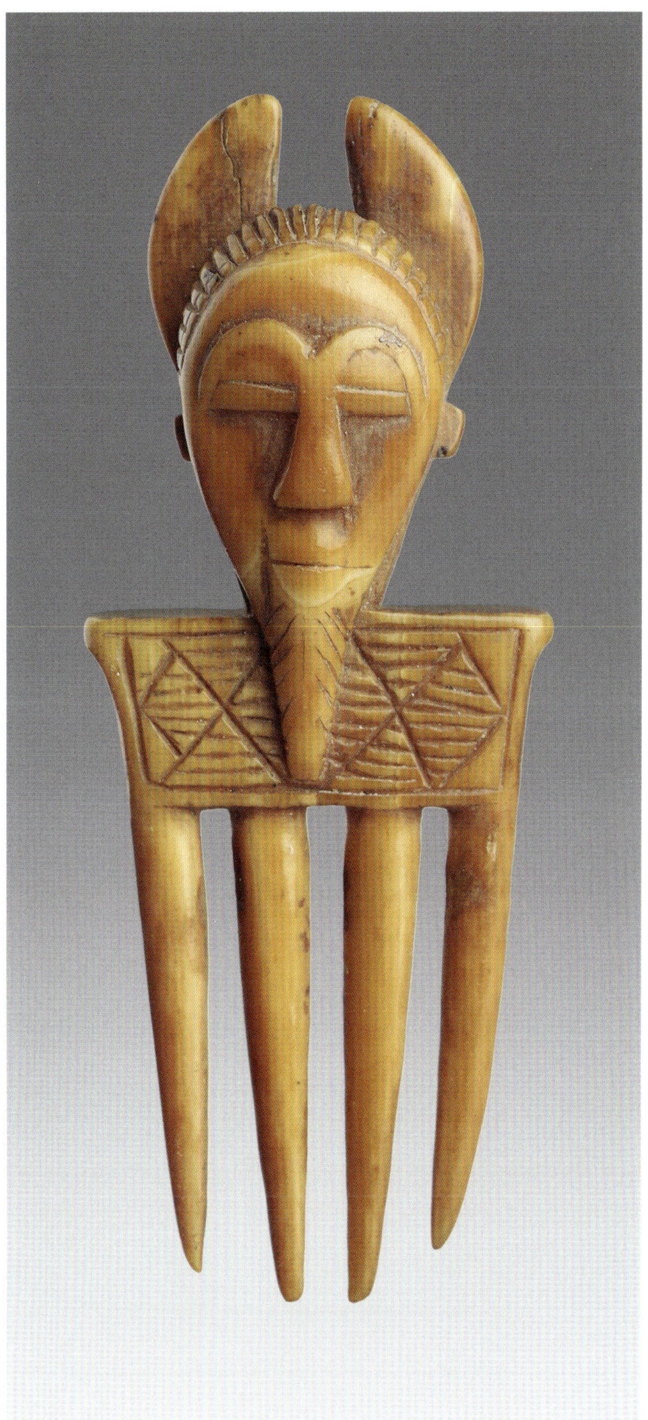

Fig. 44 Peigne | Comb
Attié | Attie, Akan, Côte d'Ivoire | Ivory Coast
Ivoire | Ivory
16 × 5,4 cm | 16 × 5.4 cm

Provenance
Baba Keïta

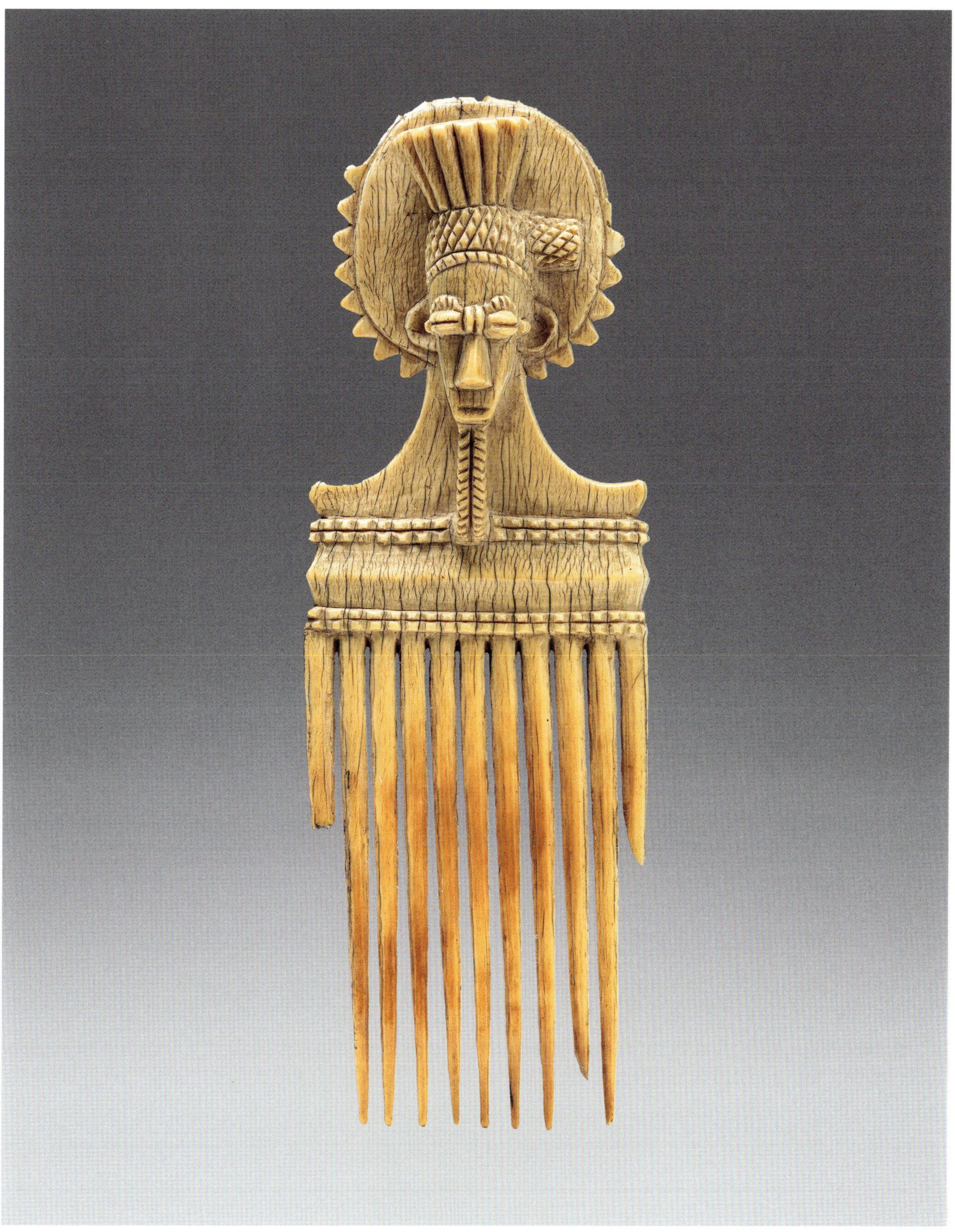

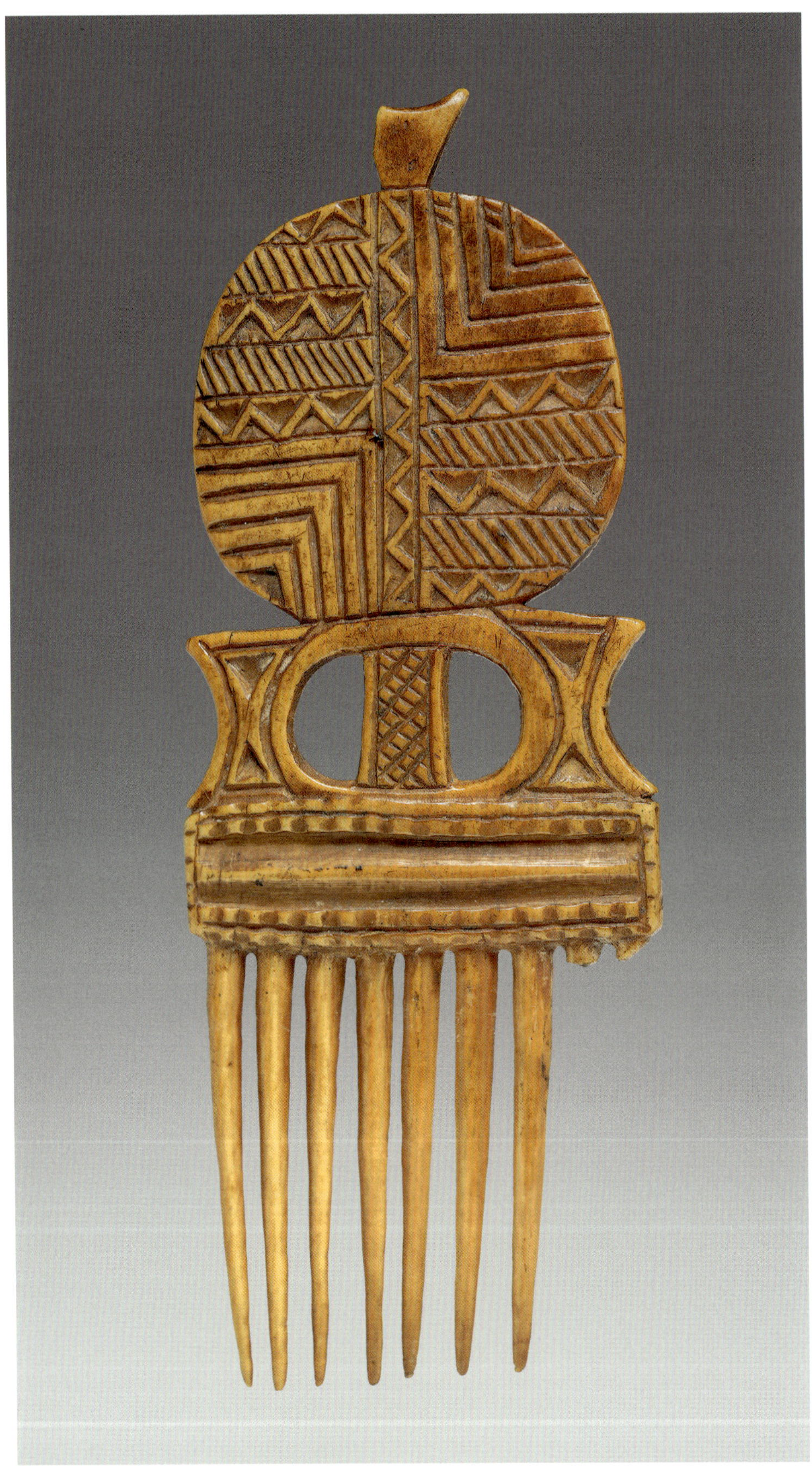

Fig. 45 Peigne | Comb
Attié | Attie, Akan, Côte d'Ivoire | Ivory Coast
Ivoire | Ivory
14 × 6,5 cm | 14 × 6.5 cm

Provenance
Mr Bombey

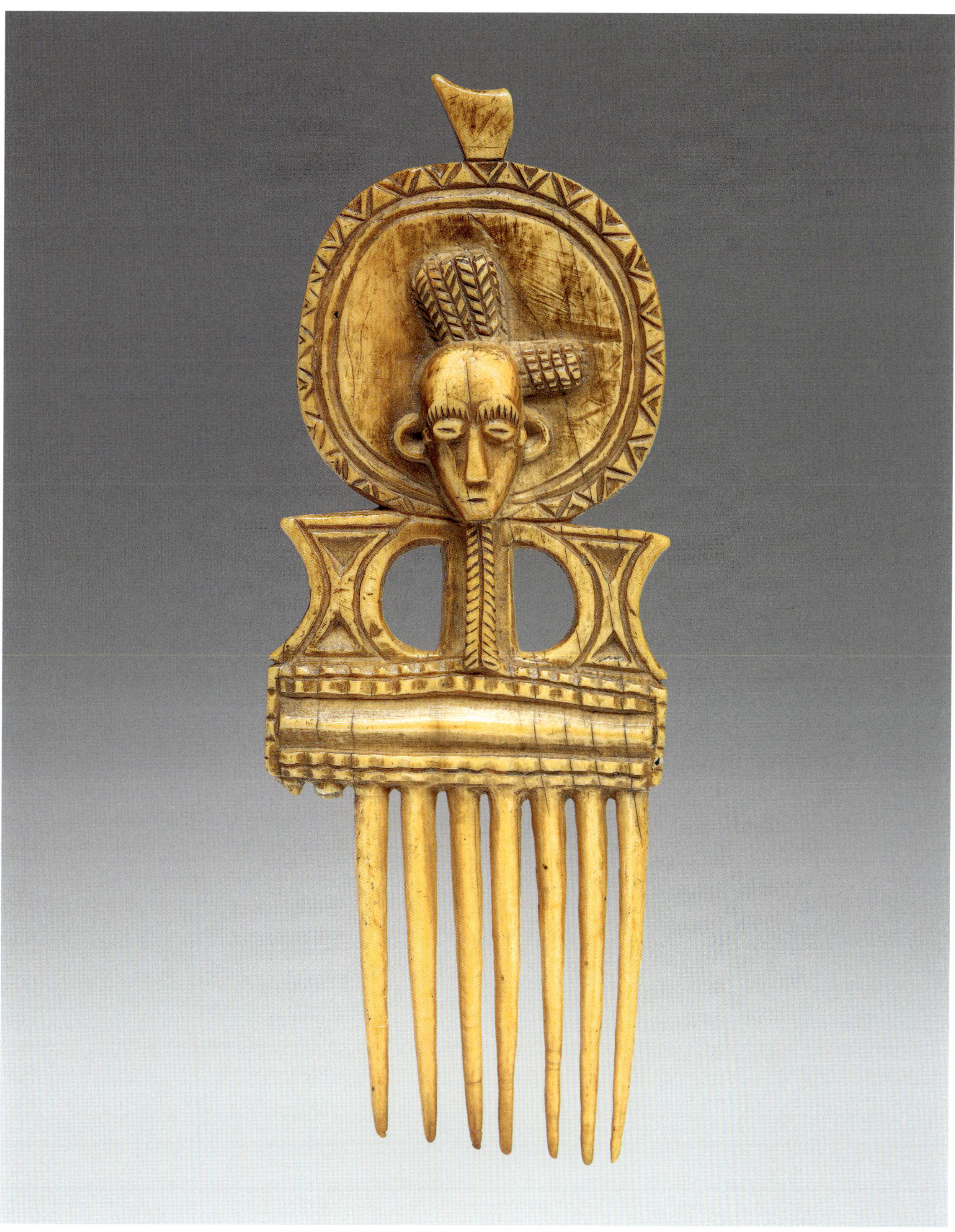

Fig. 46 Peigne | Comb
Attié | Attie, Akan, Côte d'Ivoire | Ivory Coast
Ivoire | Ivory
16,5 × 5,5 cm | 16.5 × 5.5 cm

Provenance
Hélène Leloup

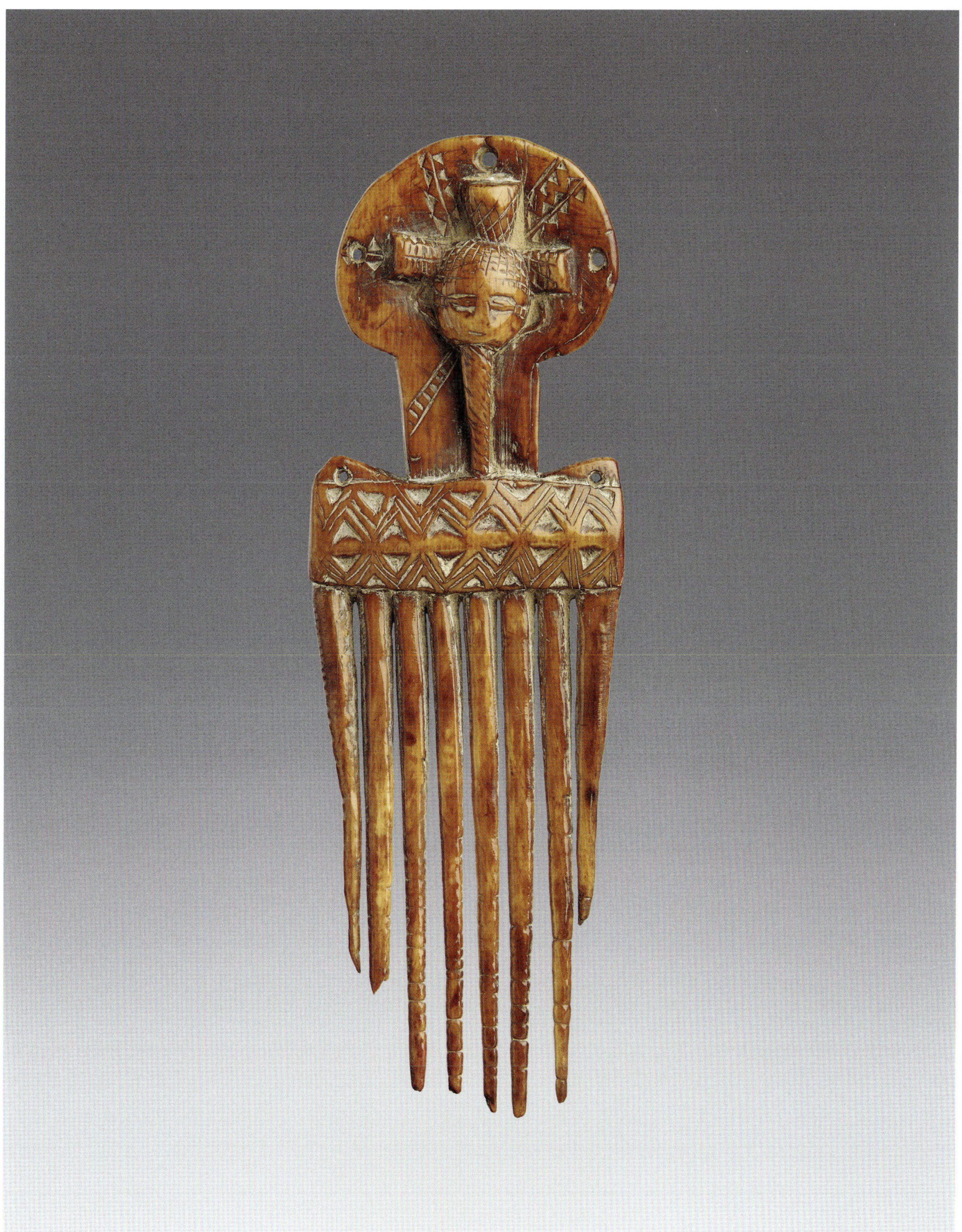

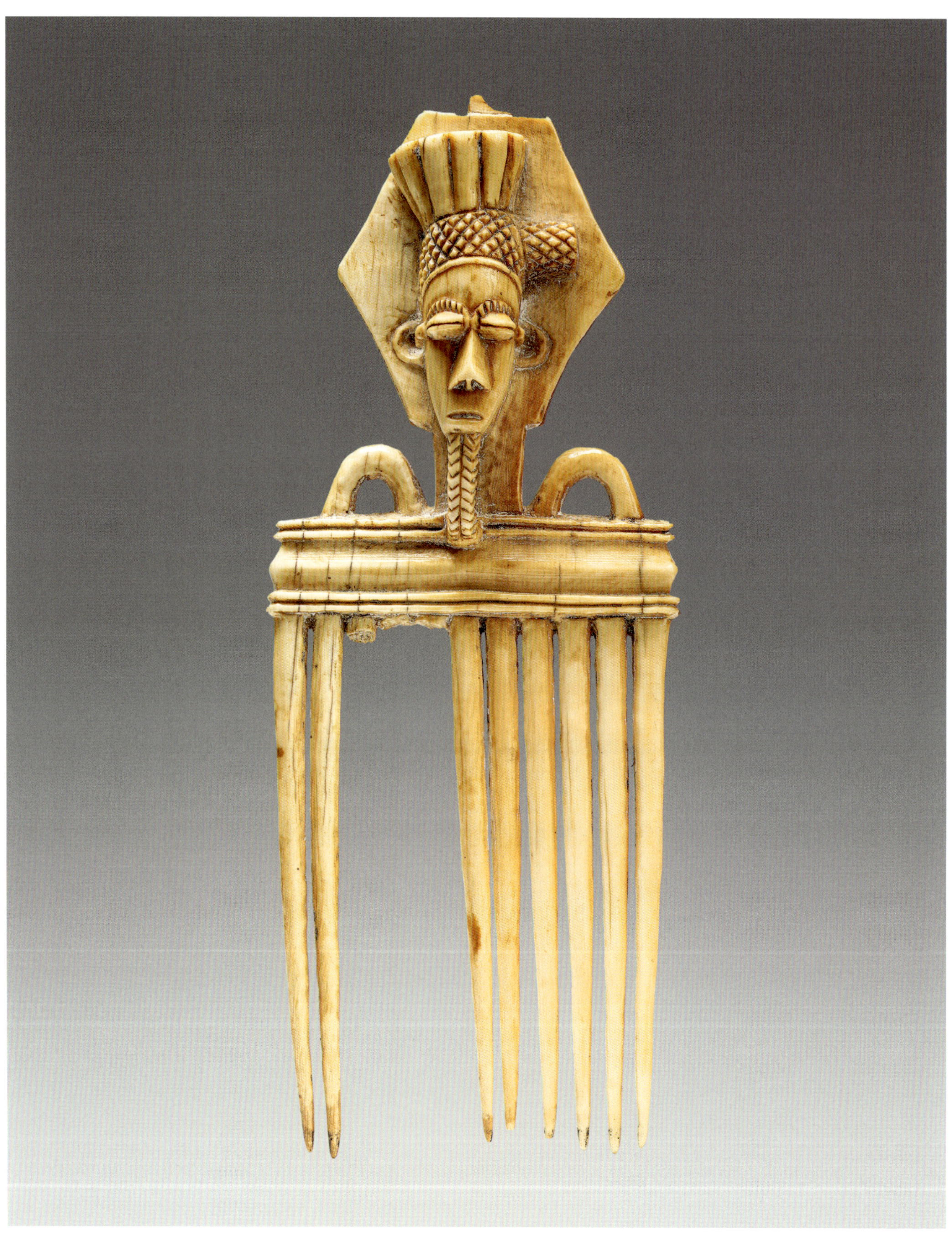

Fig. 47 Peigne | Comb
Attié | Attie, Akan, Côte d'Ivoire | Ivory Coast
Ivoire | Ivory
16 × 6,5 cm | 16 × 6.5 cm

Provenance
Ali Diaby

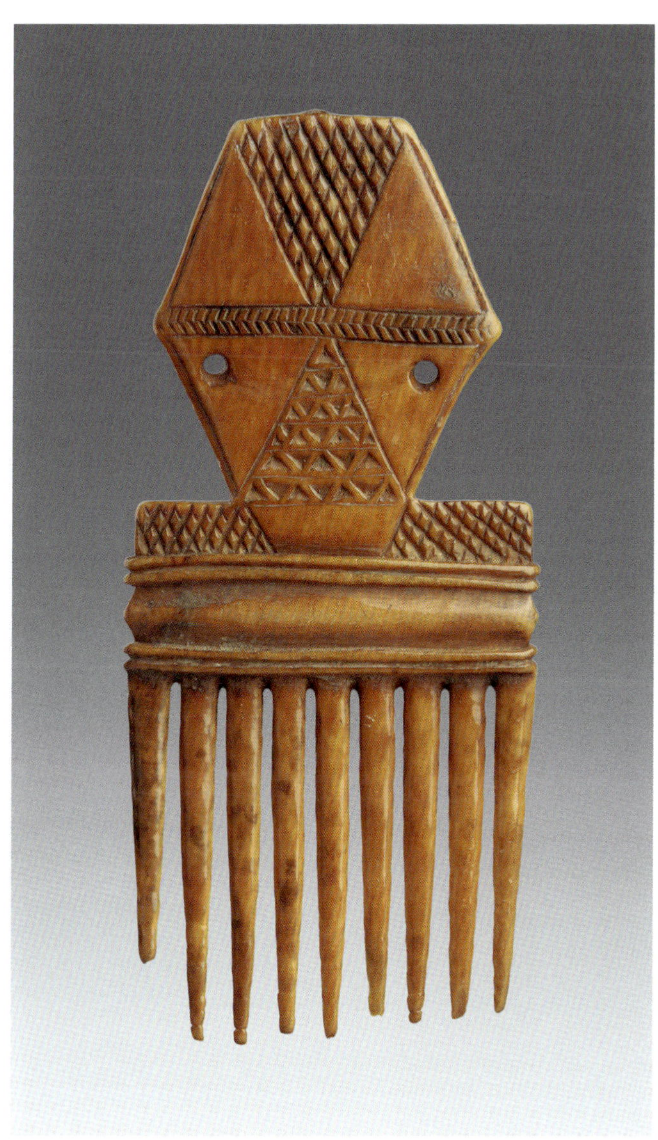

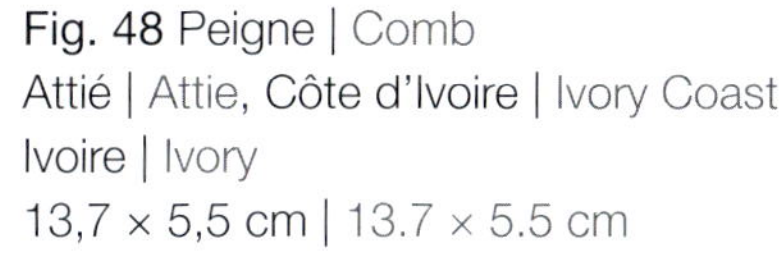

Fig. 48 Peigne | Comb
Attié | Attie, Côte d'Ivoire | Ivory Coast
Ivoire | Ivory
13,7 × 5,5 cm | 13.7 × 5.5 cm

Provenance
Issaka Zango

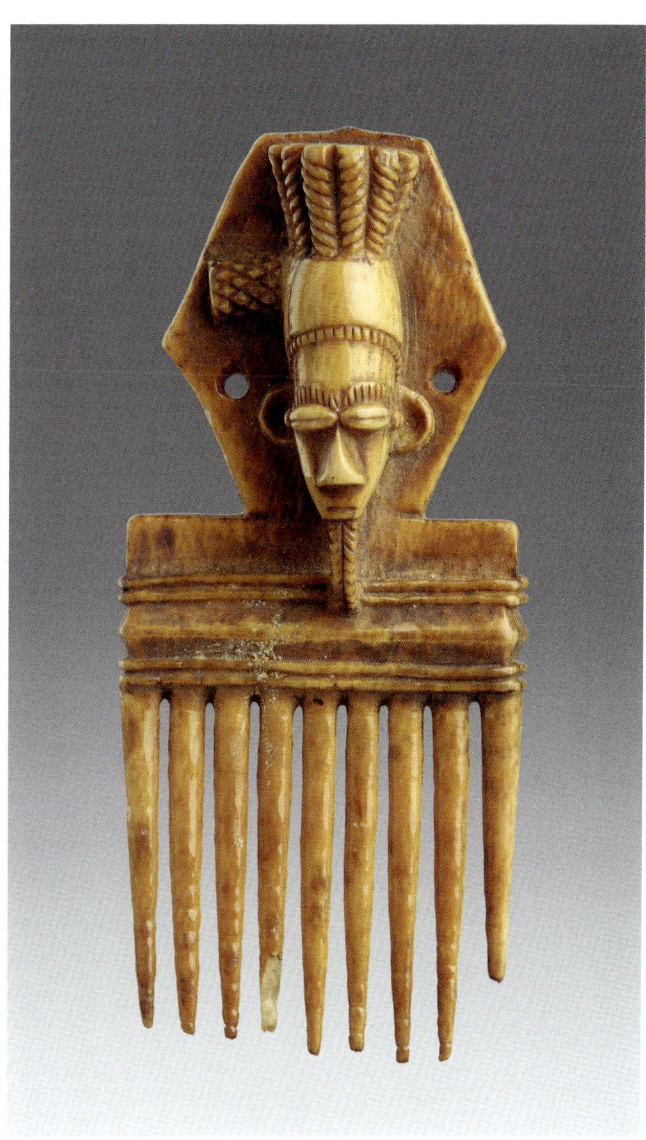

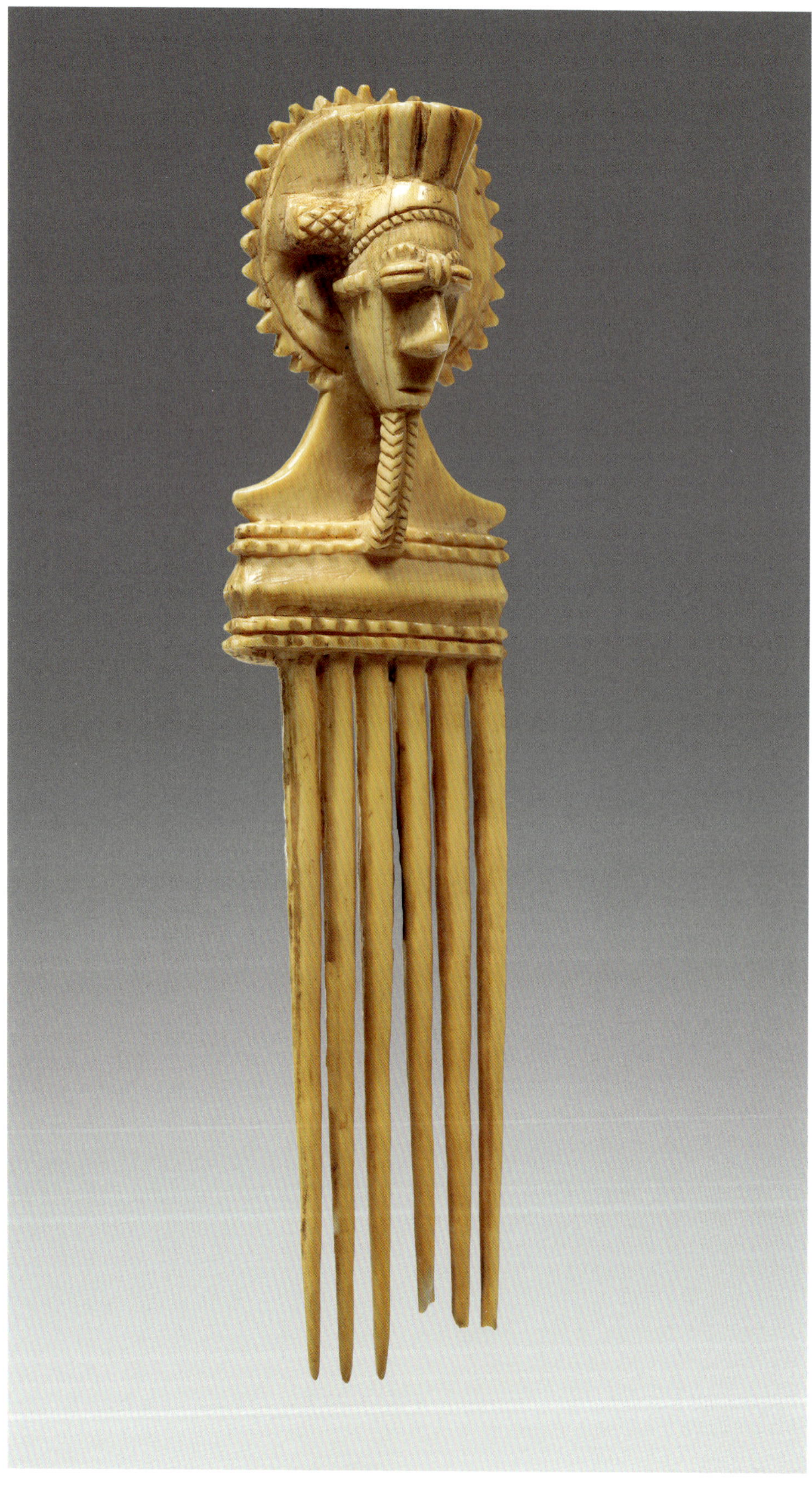

Fig. 49 Peigne | Comb
Attié | Attie, Akan, Côte d'Ivoire | Ivory Coast
Ivoire | Ivory
15,5 × 4,5 cm | 15.5 × 4.5 cm

Fig. 50 Peigne | Comb
Attié | Attie, Akan, Côte d'Ivoire | Ivory Coast
Ivoire | Ivory
17 × 5 cm

Provenance
Jean Kouamé

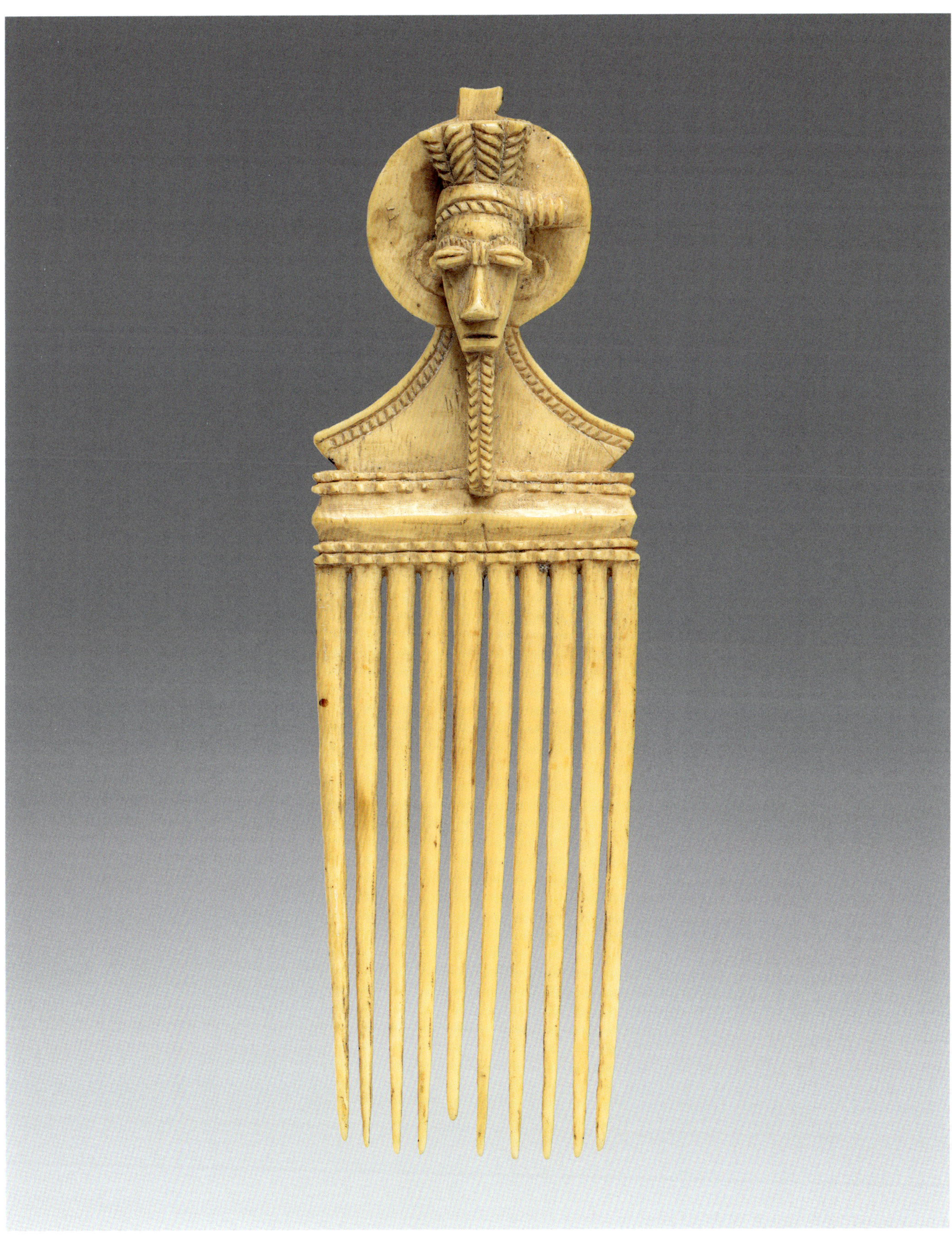

Fig. 51 Peigne | Comb
Attié | Attie, Akan, Côte d'Ivoire | Ivory Coast
Ivoire | Ivory
15 × 3,7 cm | 15 × 3.7 cm

Provenance
Paul Mossi

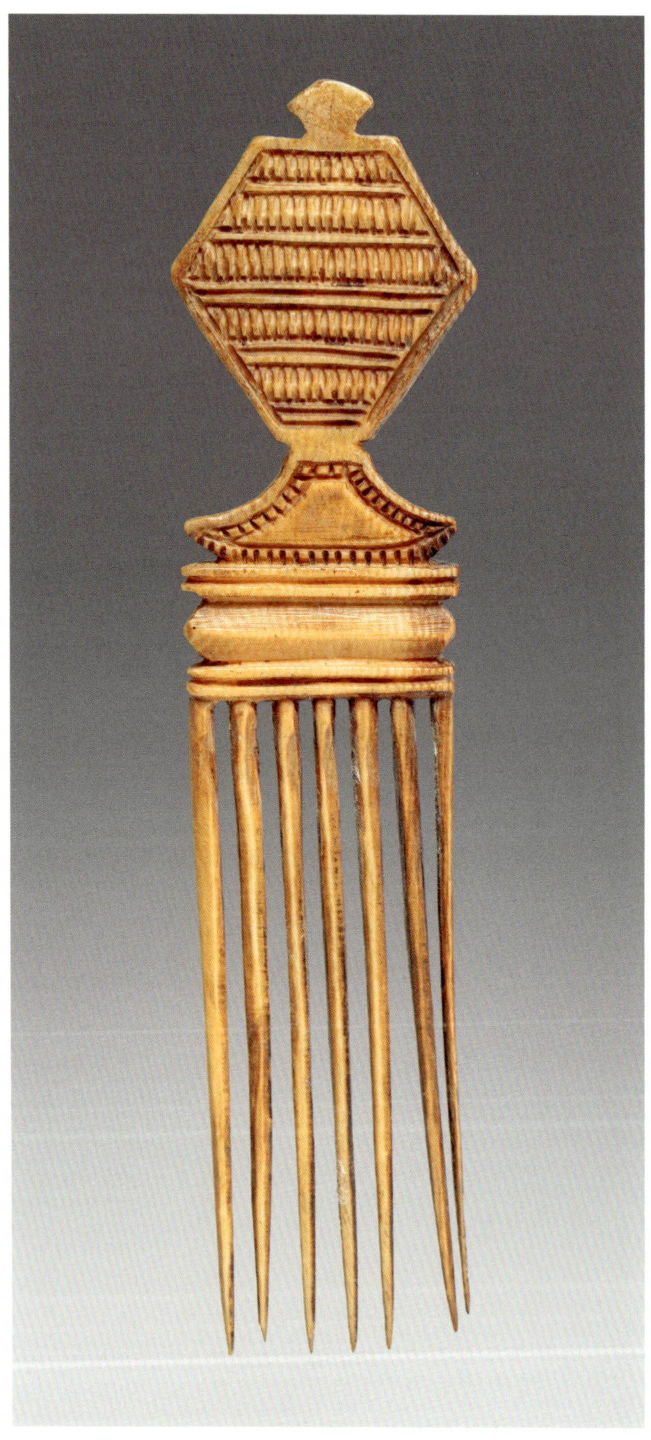

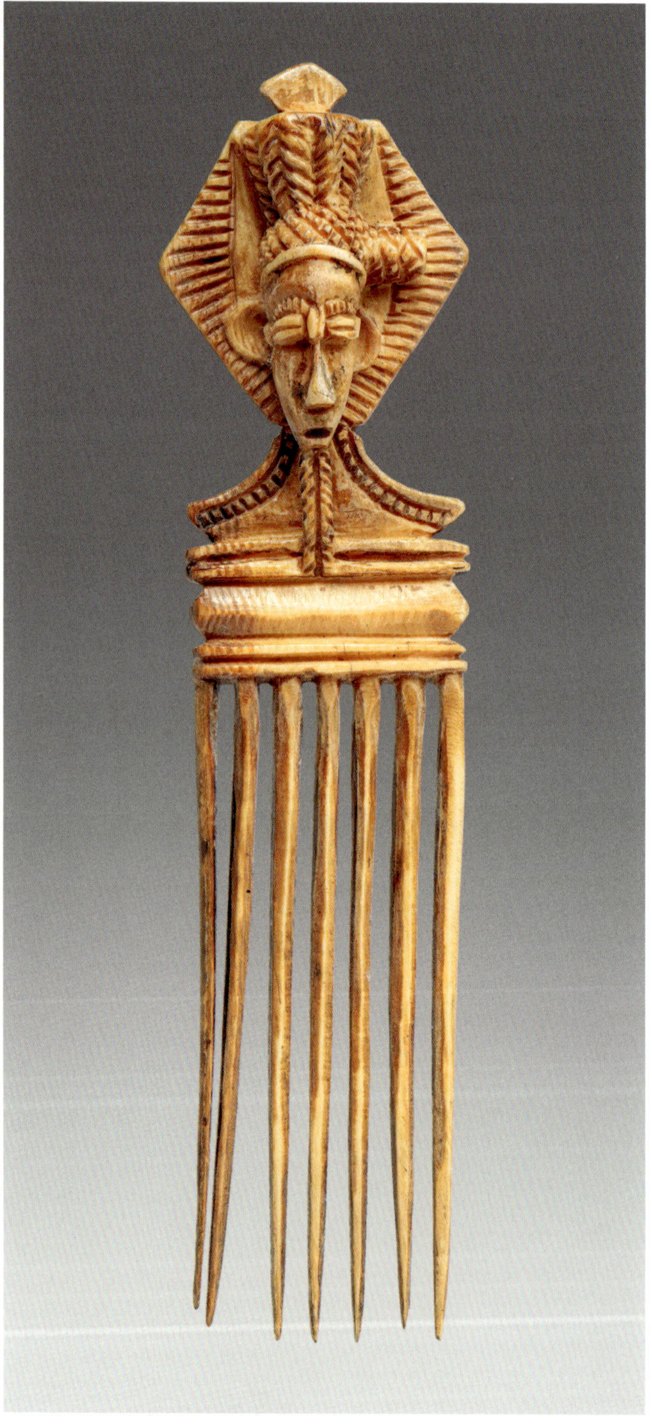

Fig. 52 Peigne | Comb
Attié | Attie, Akan, Côte d'Ivoire | Ivory Coast
Ivoire | Ivory
16 × 5 cm

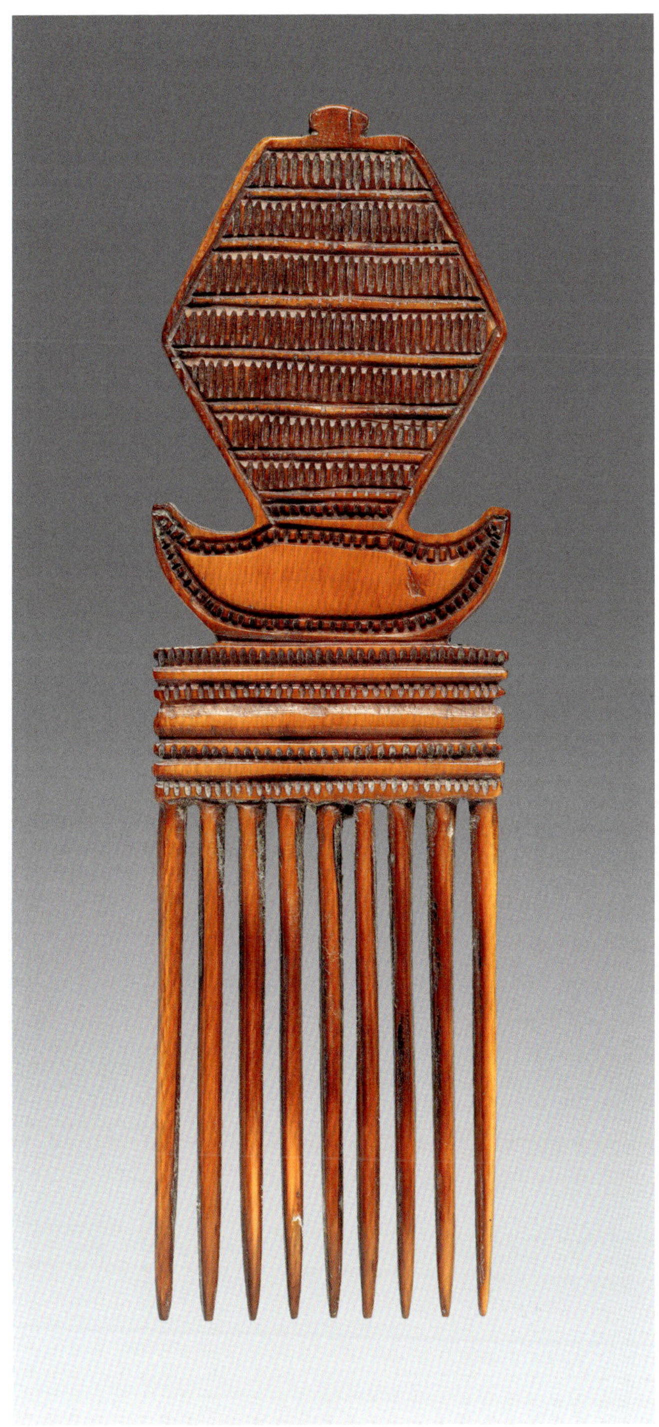

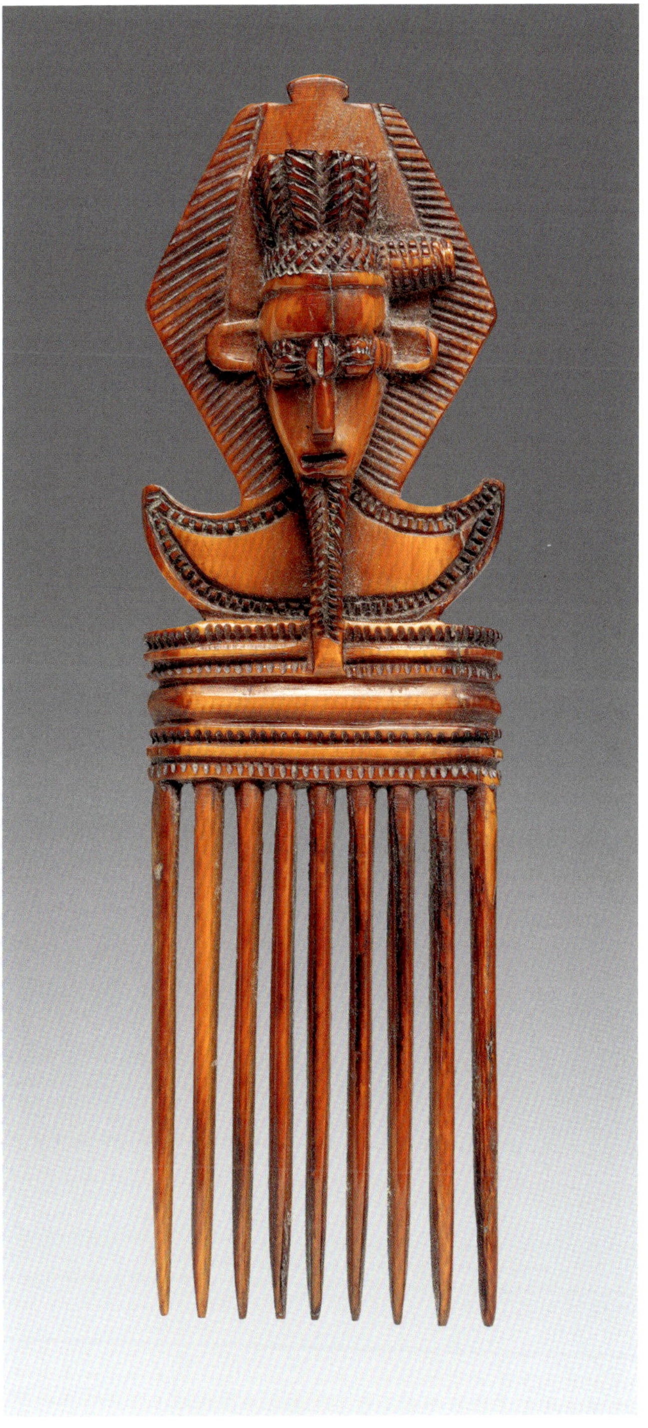

Fig. 53 Peigne | Comb
Attié | Attie, Akan, Côte d'Ivoire | Ivory Coast
Ivoire | Ivory
16 × 6,5 cm | 16 × 6.5 cm

Provenance
Ali Diaby

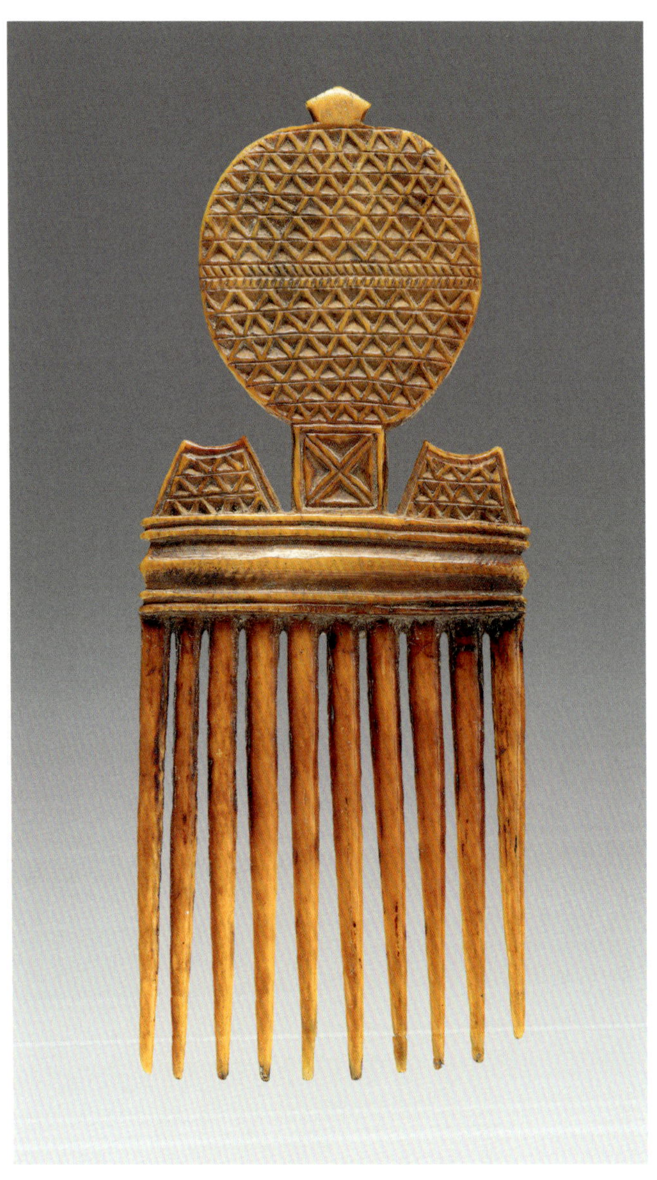

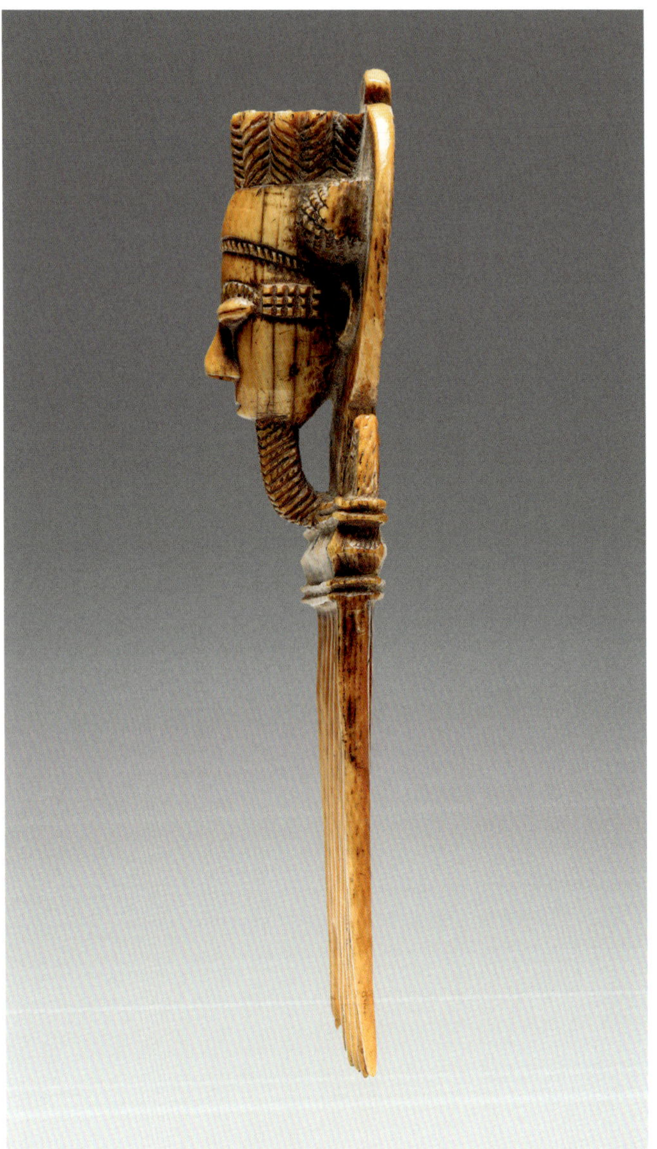

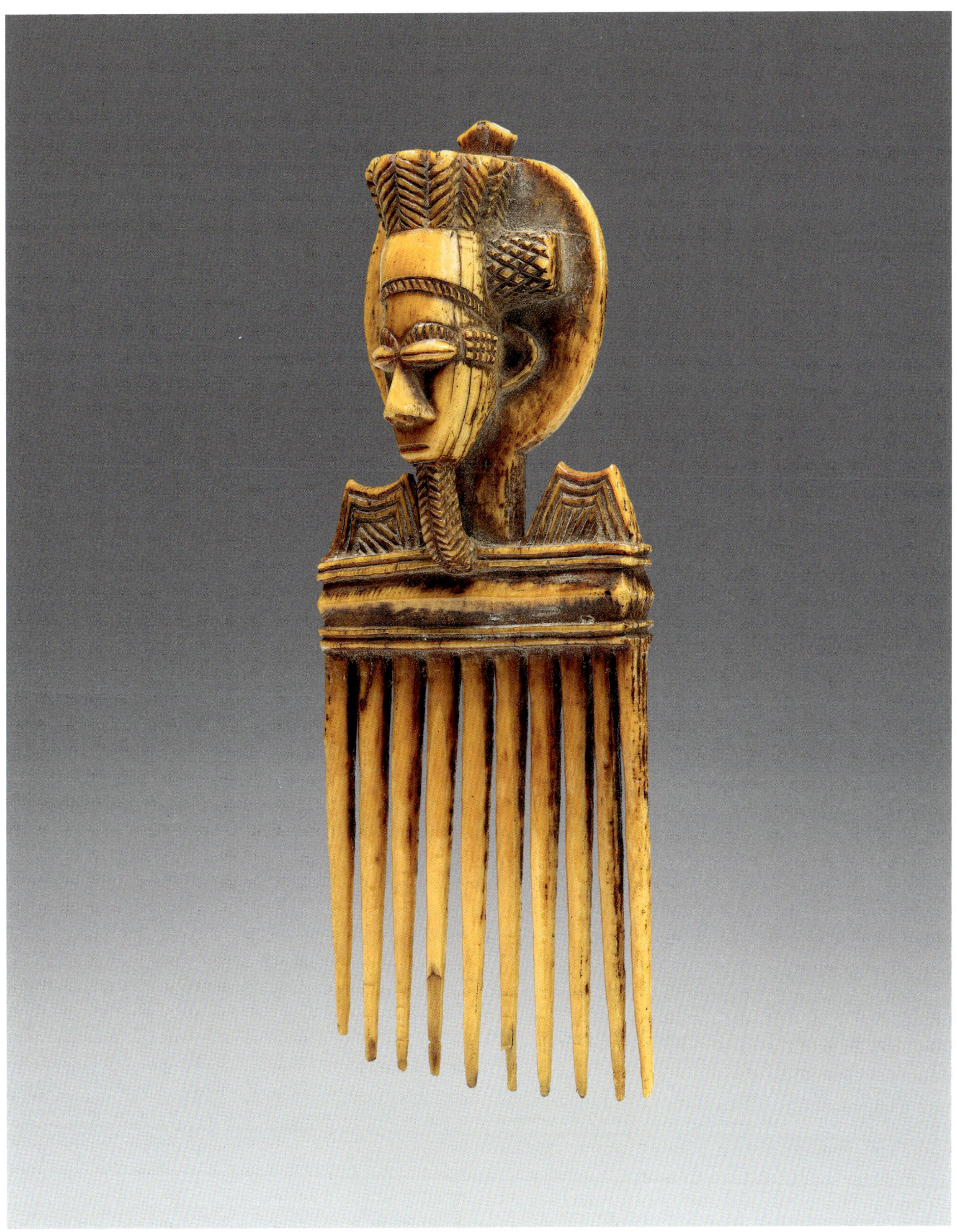

Fig. 54 Peigne | Comb
Attié | Attie, Akan, Côte d'Ivoire | Ivory Coast
Ivoire | Ivory
13,5 × 5 cm | 13.5 × 5 cm

Provenance
Samory Diabaté

Fig. 55 Peigne | Comb
Attié | Attie, Akan, Côte d'Ivoire | Ivory Coast
14 × 3,5 cm | 14 × 3.5 cm
Ivoire | Ivory

Provenance
René David

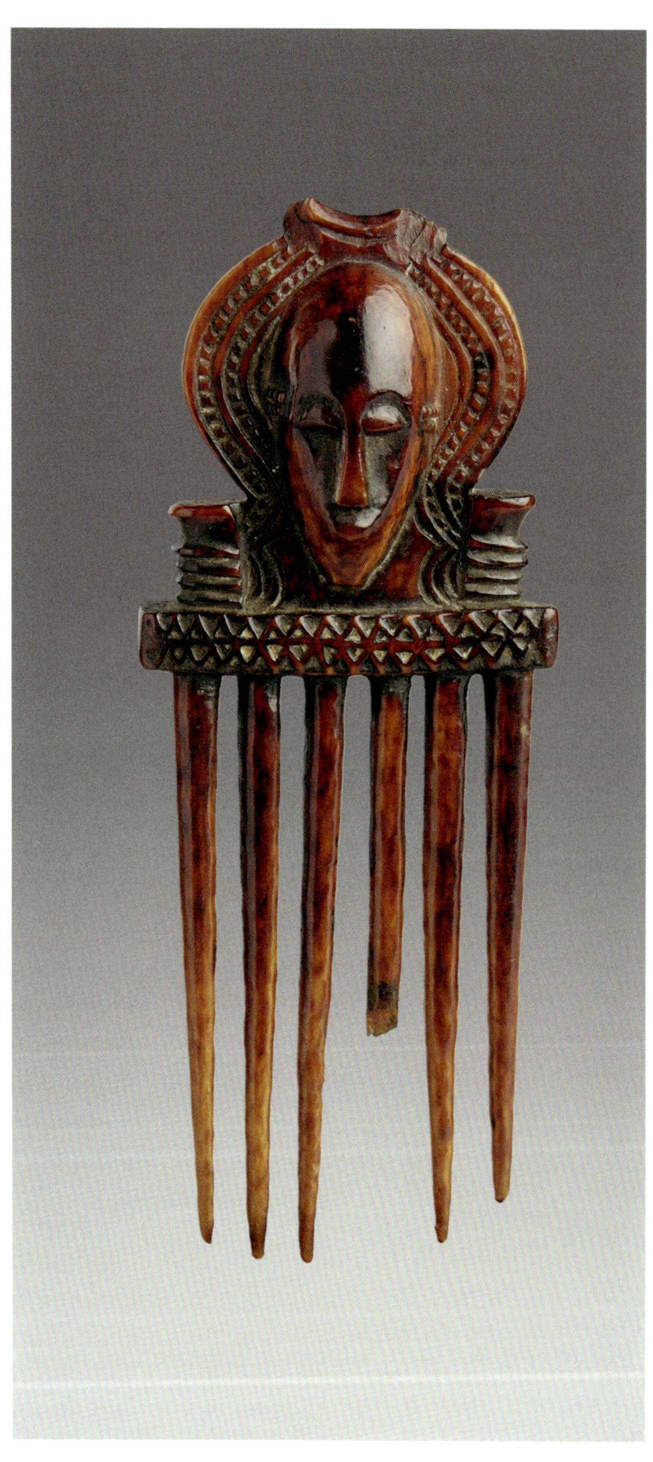

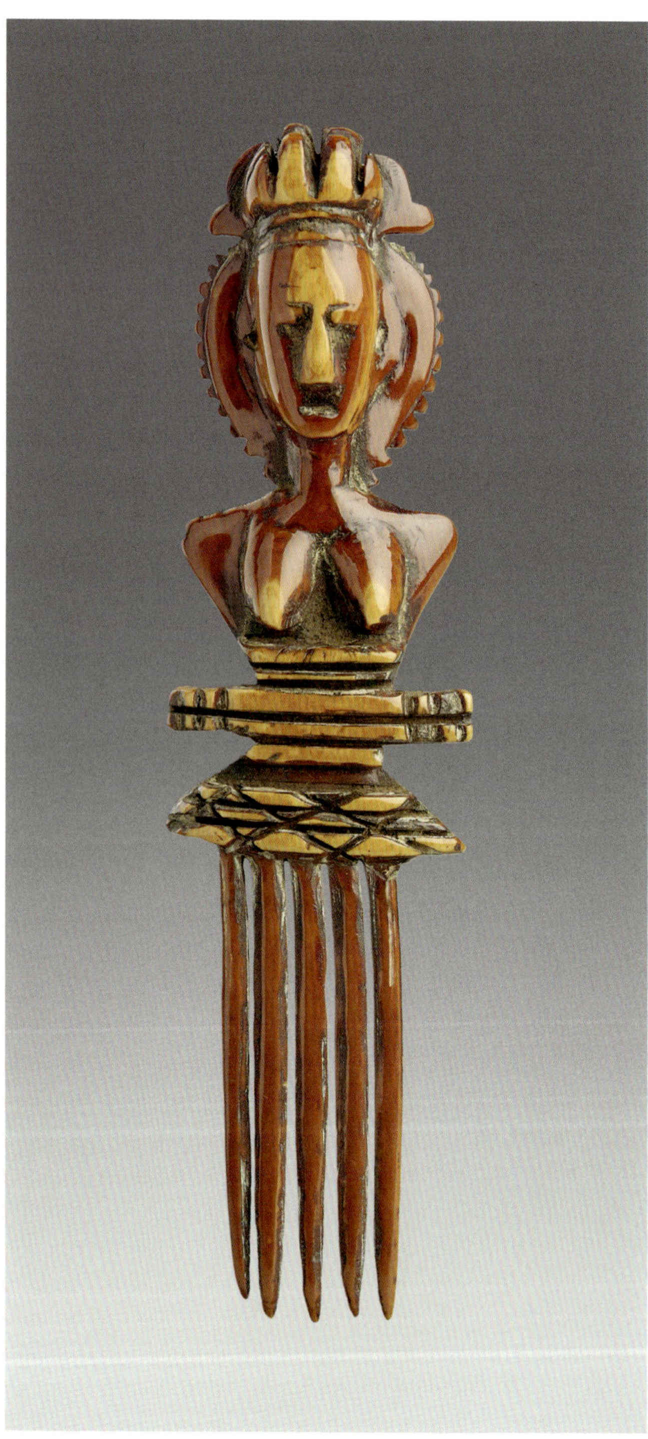

Publication
Jean-Yves Augel, Valentine Plisnier, *Coiffures africaines en majesté*, Sainte-Foy-lès-Lyon, Galerie Vallois, 2024, fig. 2, p. 120

Exposition | Exhibition
Sainte-Foy-lès-Lyon, Espace culturel Jean Salles, *Coiffures africaines en majesté*, 6 – 21 avril | 6 – 21 April 2024

Fig. 56 Peigne | Comb
Attié | Attie, Akan, Côte d'Ivoire | Ivory Coast
Ivoire | Ivory
11 × 4,5 cm | 11 × 4.5 cm

Provenance
Charles Ratton, Marceau Rivière

Publication
Marceau Rivière, *Les chefs-d'œuvre africains des collections privées françaises*, Paris, Editions Philbi, 1975, fig. 17

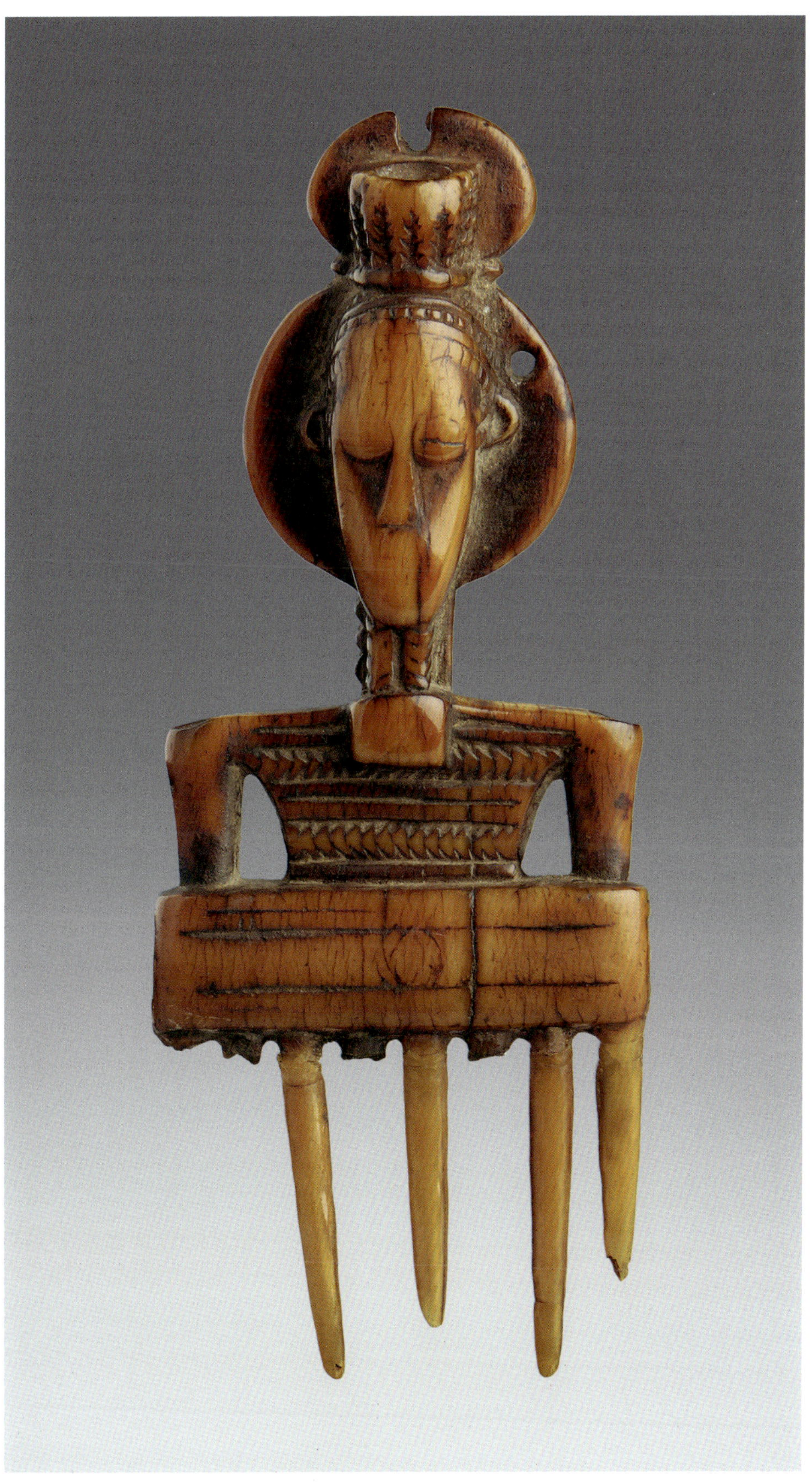

Fig. 57 Peigne | Comb
Attié | Attie, Akan, Côte d'Ivoire | Ivory Coast
Bois | Wood
16 × 9 cm

Publication
Hélène Joubert, Jean-Paul Chazal, *Visions d'Afrique*, Taiwan, National Museum of History, 2003, fig. 107, p.157

Exposition | Exhibition
Visions d'Afrique, Taïwan | Taiwan, National Museum of History, 6 décembre 2003 – 22 février 2004 | 6 December 2003 – 22 February 2004

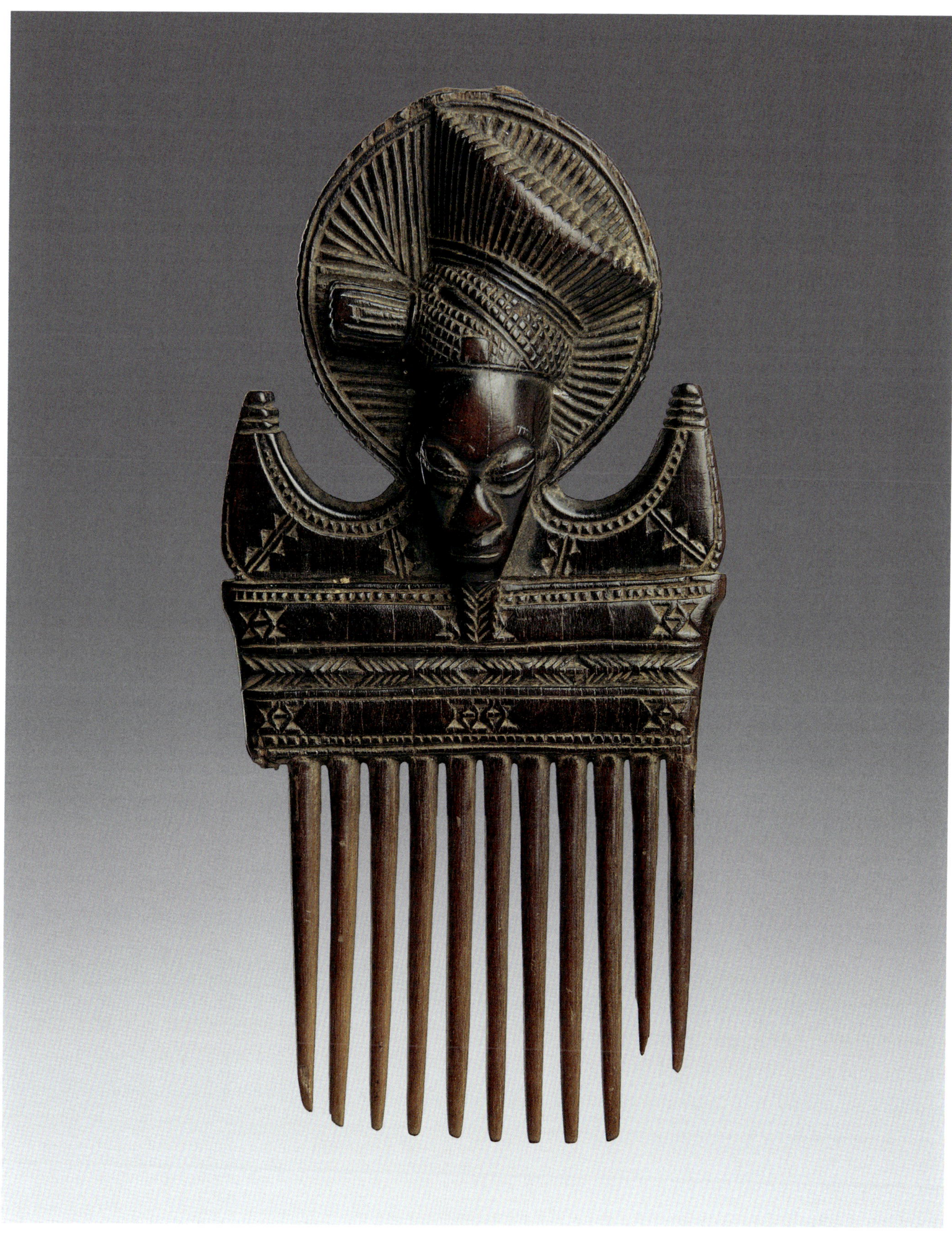

Fig. 58 Peigne | Comb
Attié | Attie, Akan, Côte d'Ivoire | Ivory Coast
Bois, or | Wood, gold
17 × 8 cm

Provenance
Merton Simpson

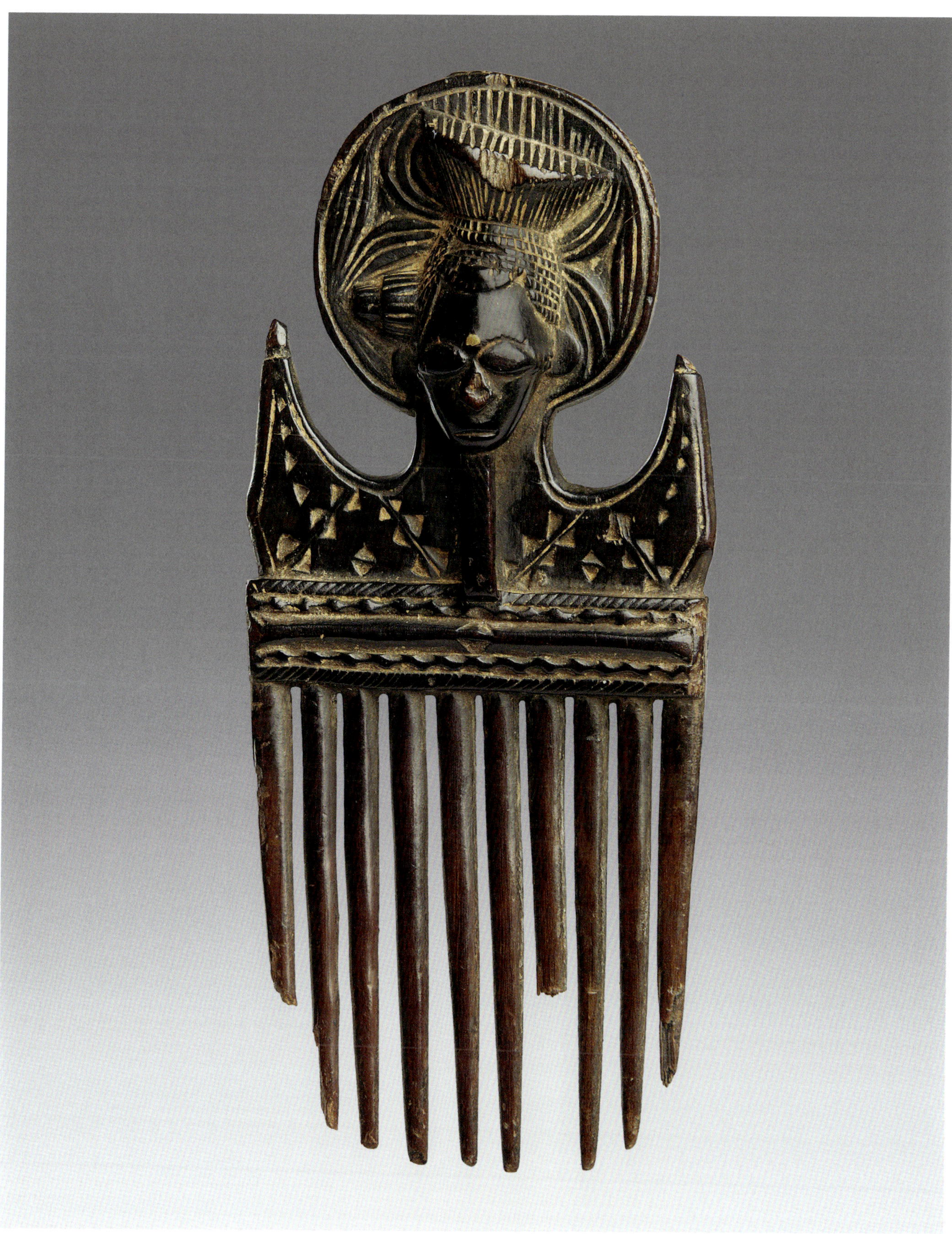

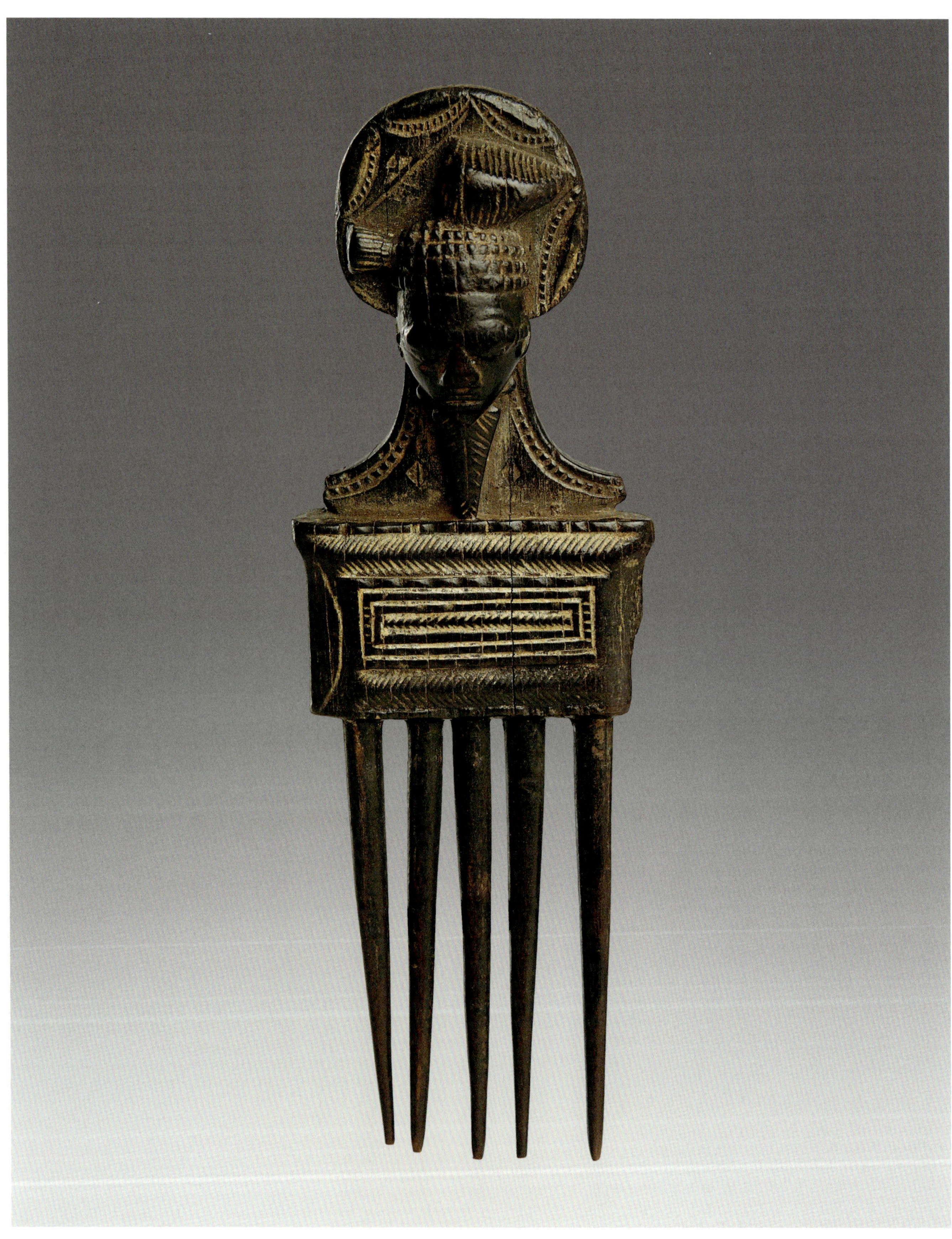

Fig. 59 Peigne | Comb
Attié | Attie, Akan, Côte d'Ivoire | Ivory Coast
Bois | Wood
16,6 × 6 cm | 16.6 × 6 cm

Provenance
Don Bosco

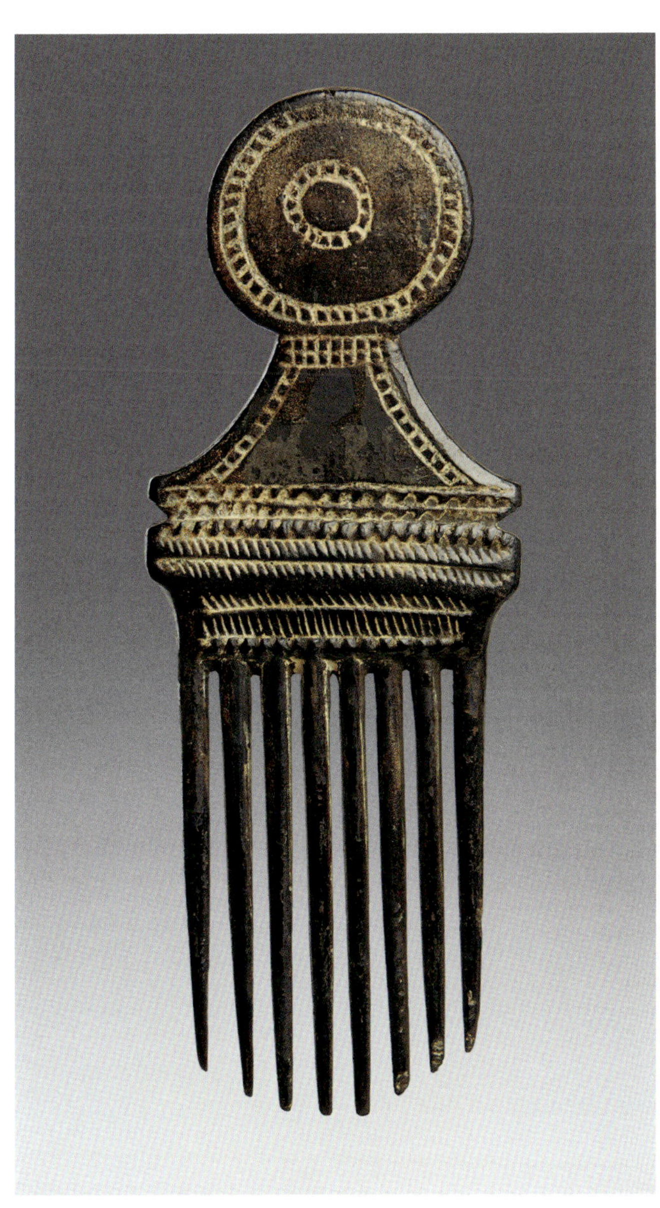

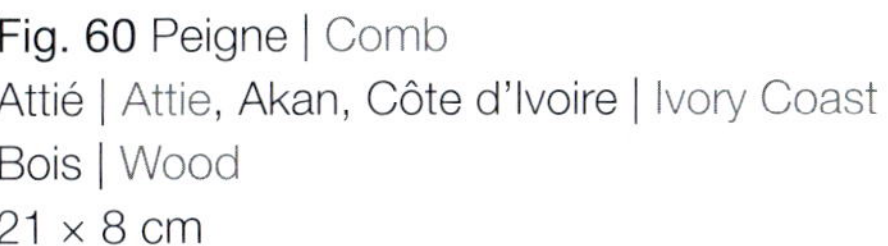

Fig. 60 Peigne | Comb
Attié | Attie, Akan, Côte d'Ivoire | Ivory Coast
Bois | Wood
21 × 8 cm

Provenance
Georges Brou

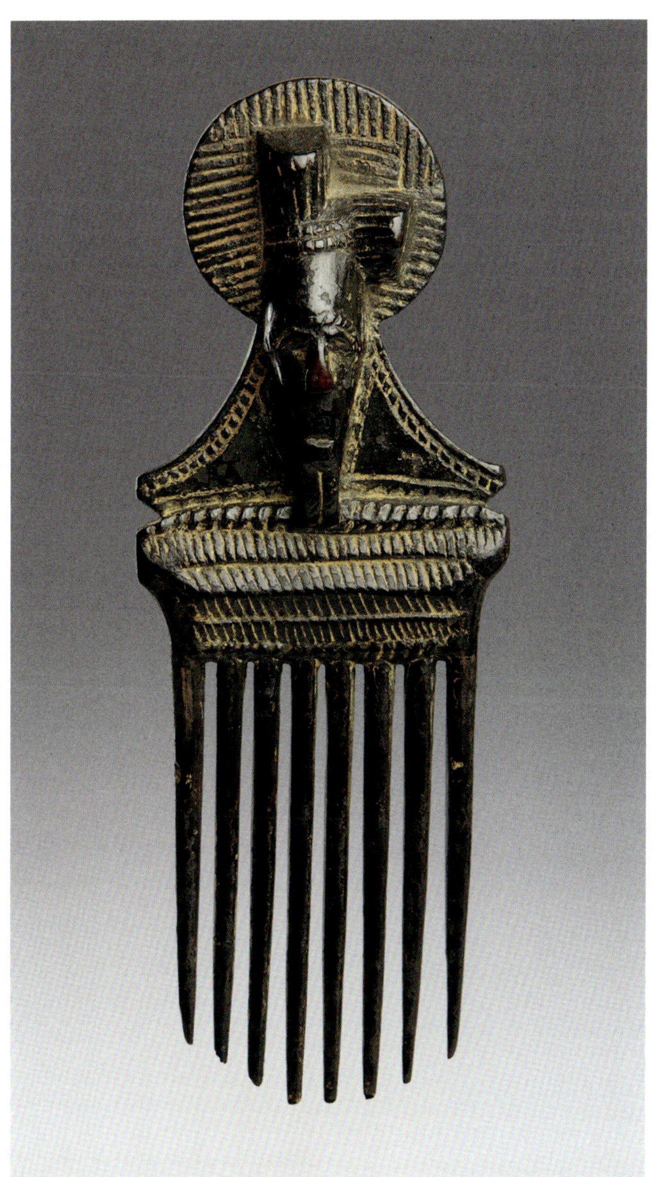

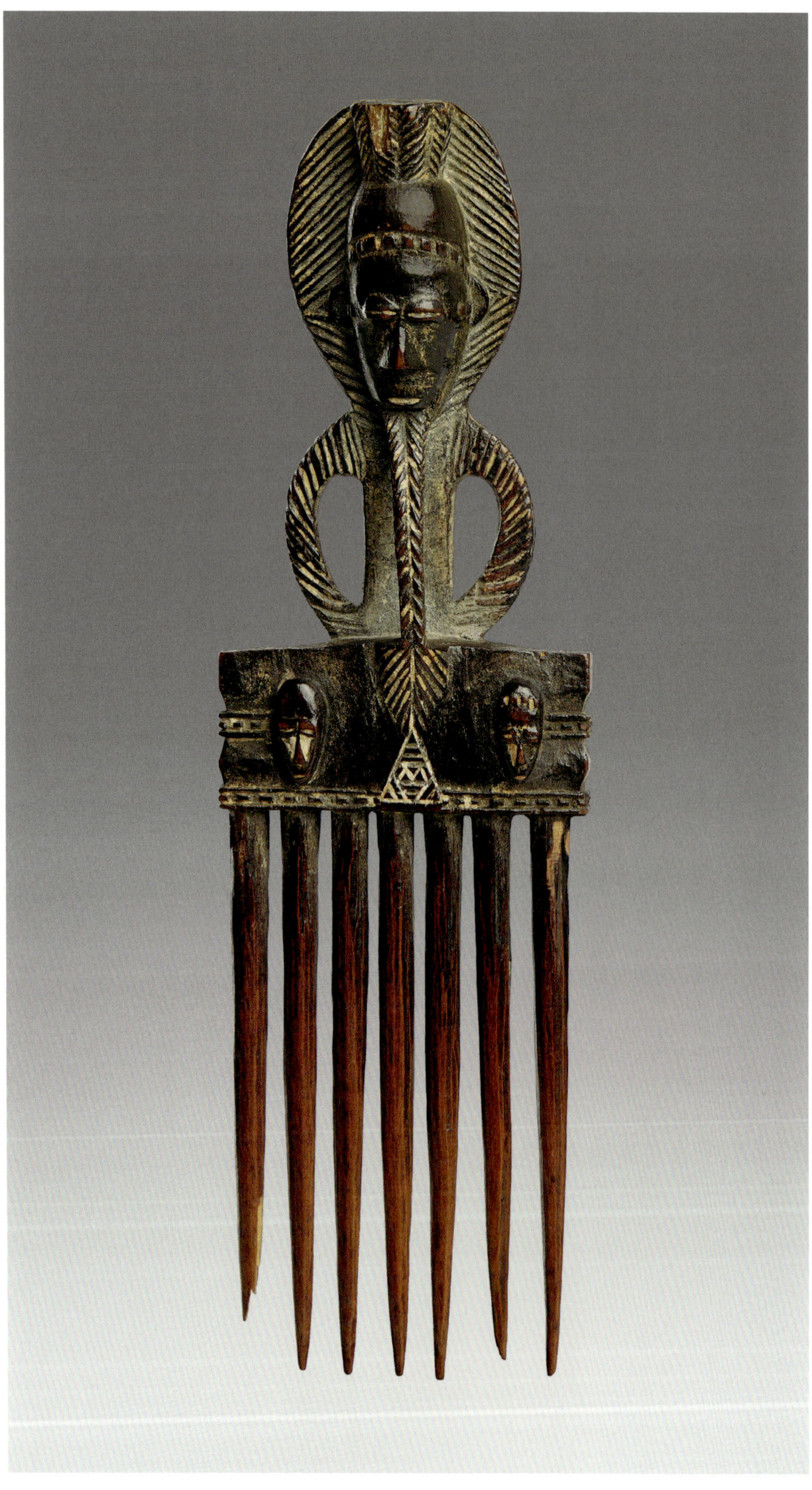

Fig. 61 Peigne | Comb
Attié | Attie, Akan, Côte d'Ivoire | Ivory Coast
Bois | Wood
17,5 × 5,5 cm | 17.5 × 5.5 cm

Provenance
Galerie l'Accrosonge, Paris

Fig. 62 Peigne | Comb
Attié | Attie, Akan, Côte d'Ivoire | Ivory Coast
Bois, clous de tapisserie | Wood, upholstery tacks
16 × 5 cm

Provenance
Hélène Yapo

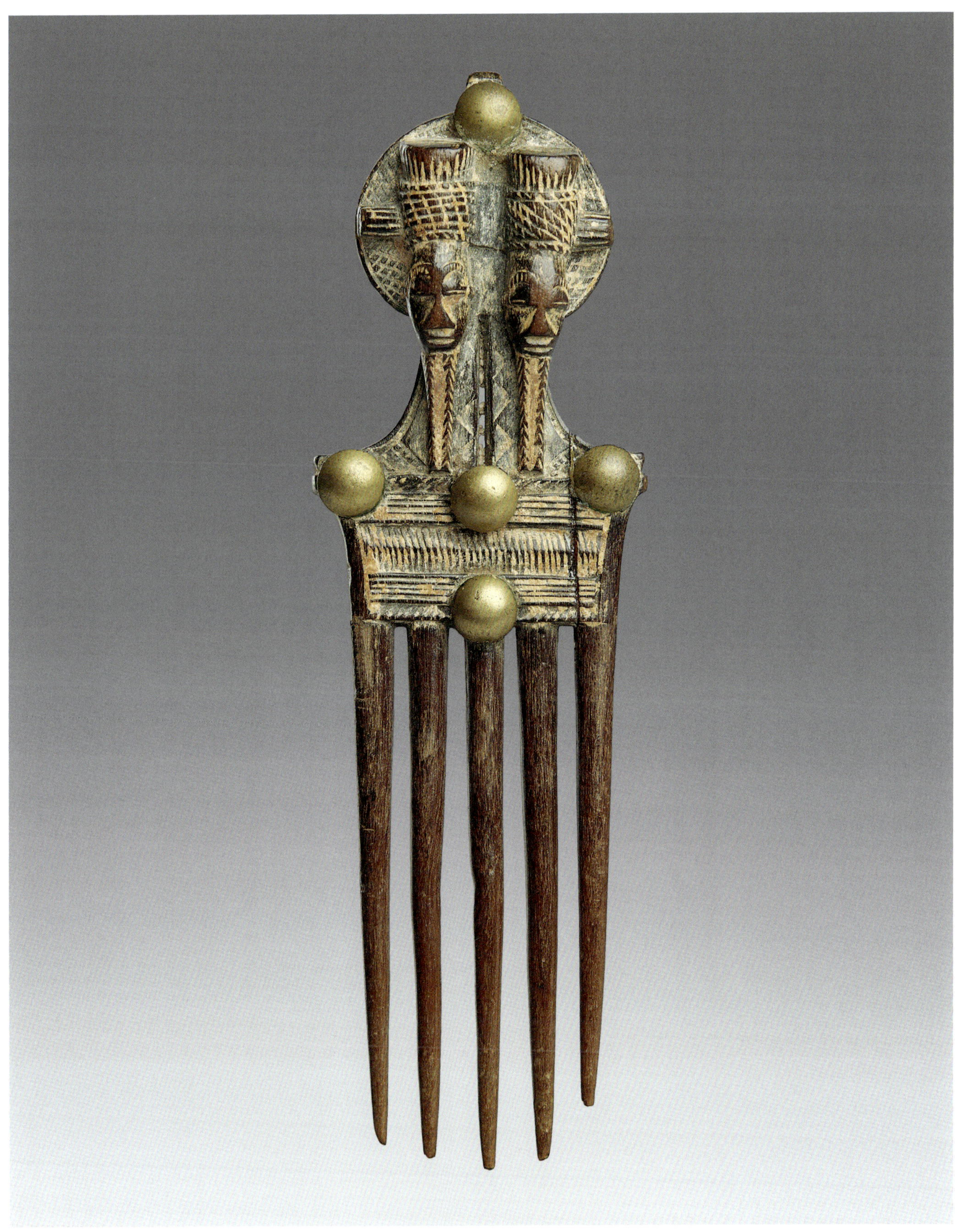

Fig. 63 Peigne | Comb
Attié | Attie, Akan, Côte d'Ivoire | Ivory Coast
Bois, or | Wood, gold
16 × 3,5 cm | 16 × 3.5 cm

Provenance
André Blandin

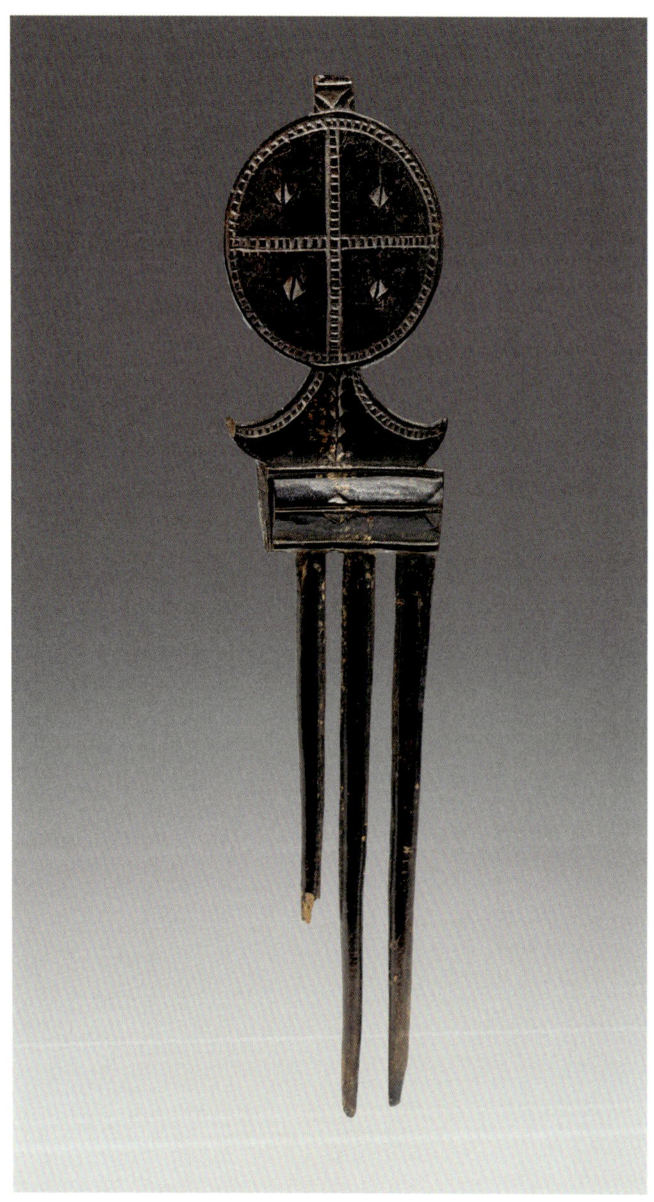

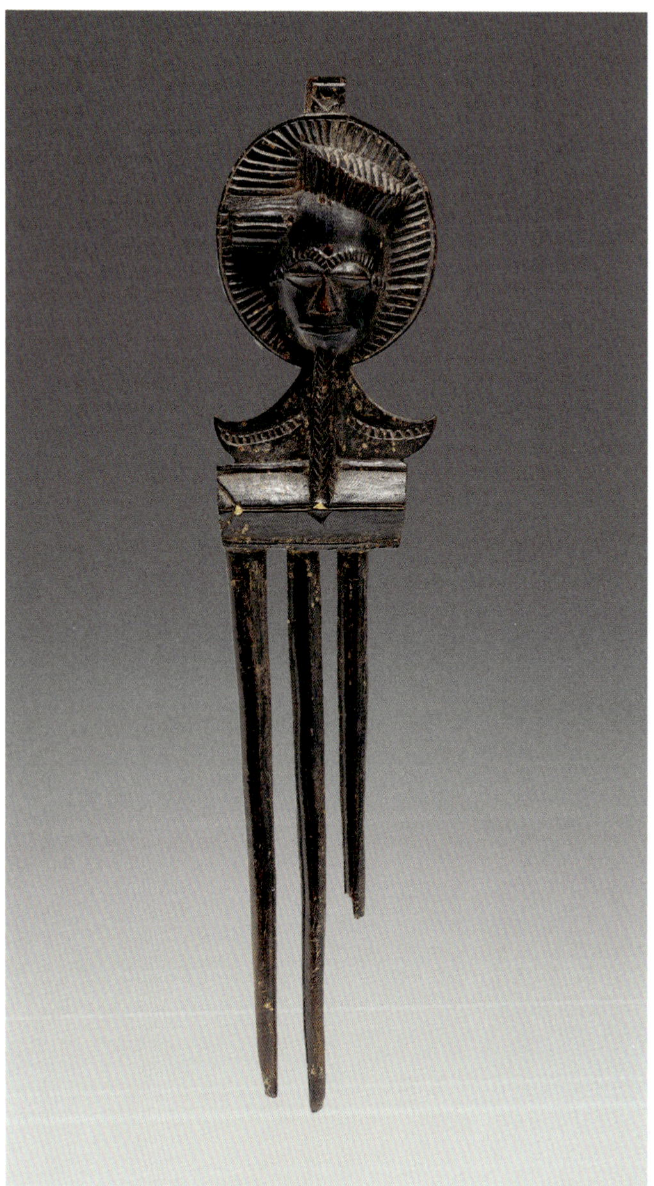

Fig. 64 Peigne | Comb
Attié | Attie, Akan, Côte d'Ivoire | Ivory Coast
Bois | Wood
14,5 × 4,5 cm | 14.5 × 4.5 cm

Provenance
Georges Brou

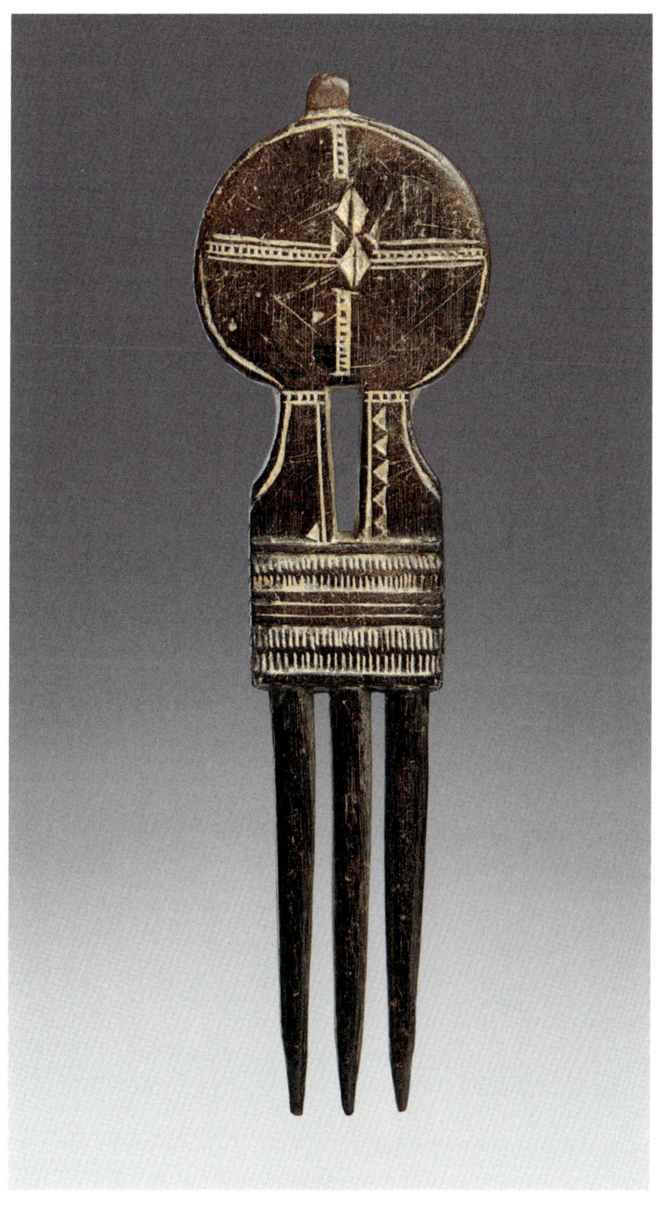

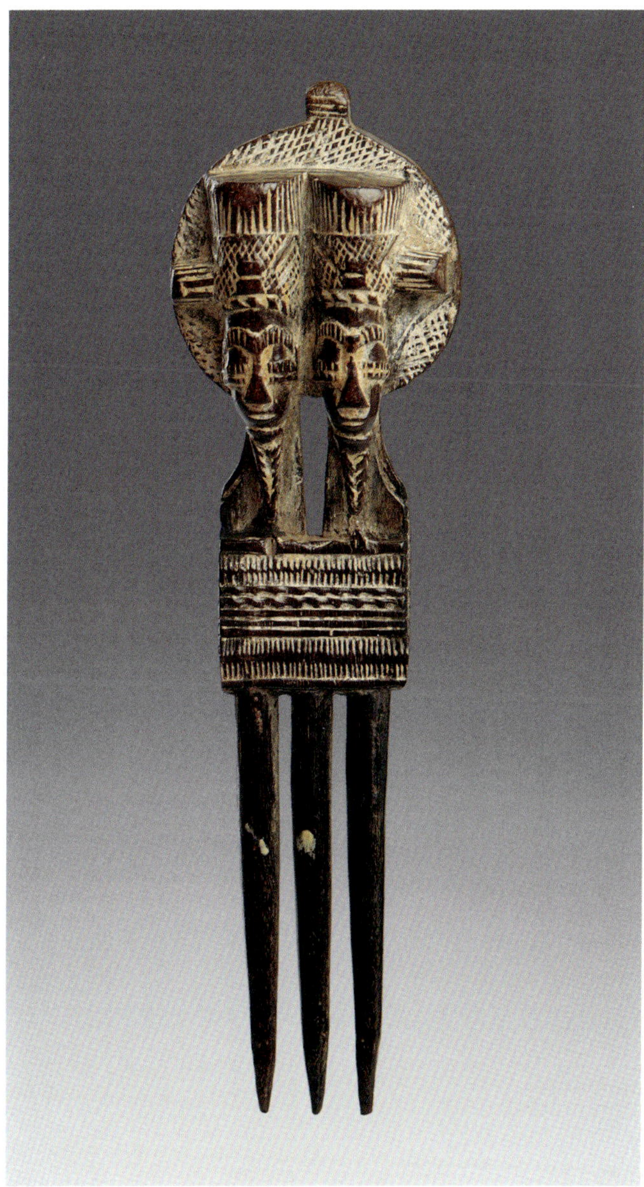

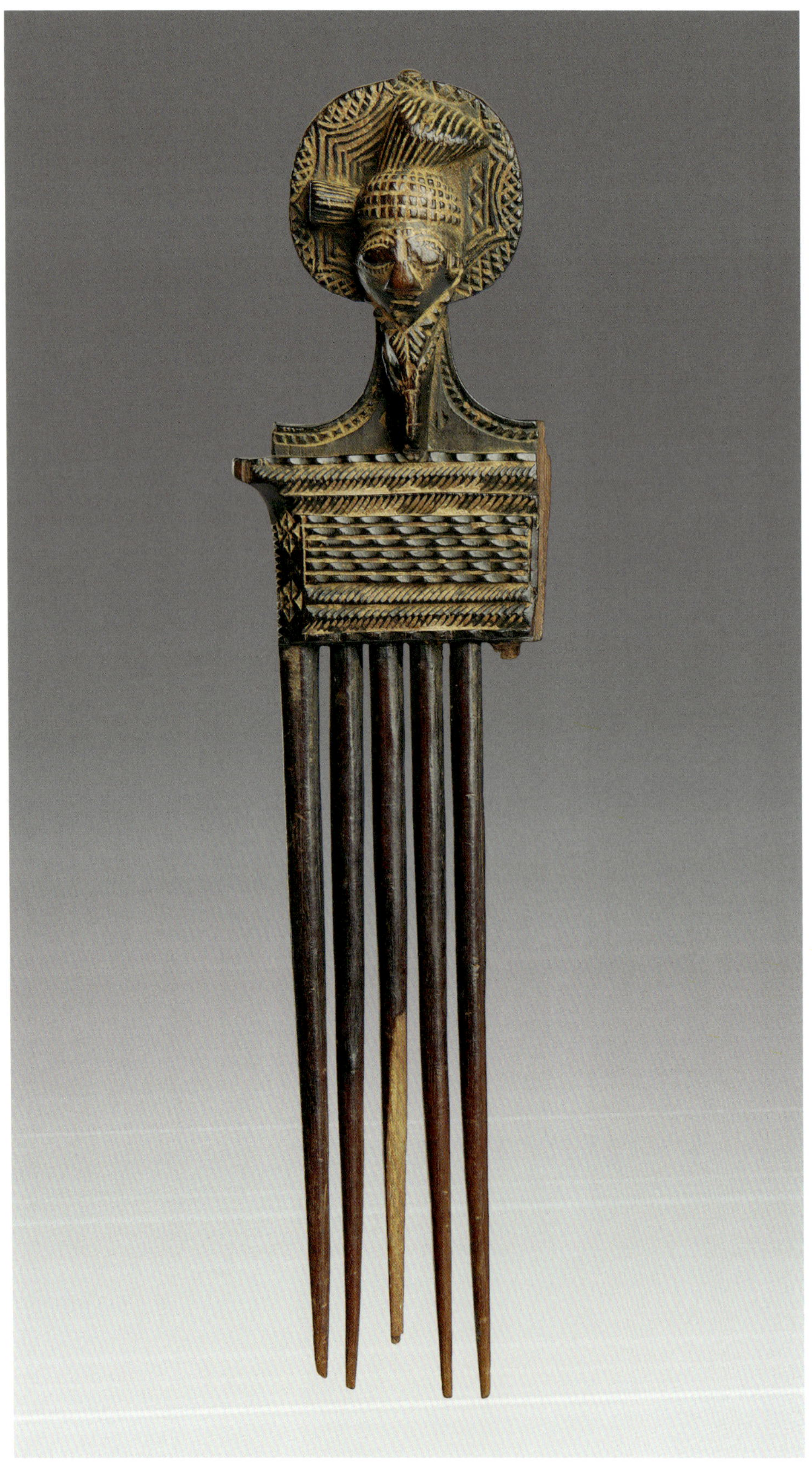

Fig. 65 Peigne | Comb
Attié | Attie, Akan, Côte d'Ivoire | Ivory Coast
Bois | Wood
21 × 5,8 cm | 21 × 5.8 cm

Provenance
Yao Yao

Fig. 66 Peigne | Comb
Attié | Attie, Akan, Côte d'Ivoire | Ivory Coast
Bois | Wood
20 × 6 cm

Provenance
Paul Nguessan

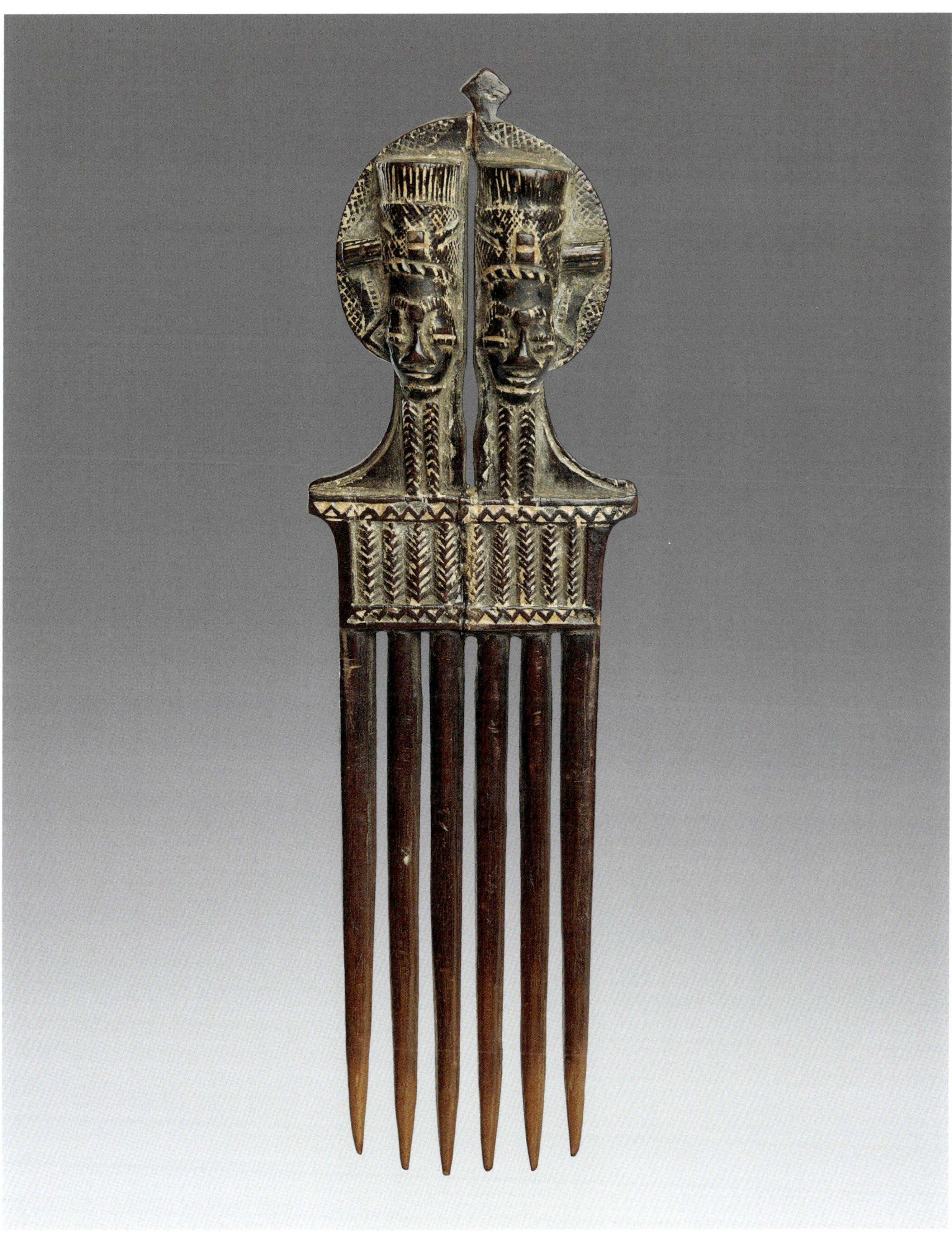

Fig. 67 Peigne | Comb
Baoulé/Attié | Baule/Attie, Akan,
Côte d'Ivoire | Ivory Coast
Corne | Horn
13,6 × 4,5 cm | 13.6 × 4.5 cm

Fig. 68 Peigne | Comb
Baoulé/Attié | Baule/Attie, Akan,
Côte d'Ivoire | Ivory Coast
Corne | Horn
12,6 × 4 cm | 12.6 × 4 cm

Provenance
Baba Keita

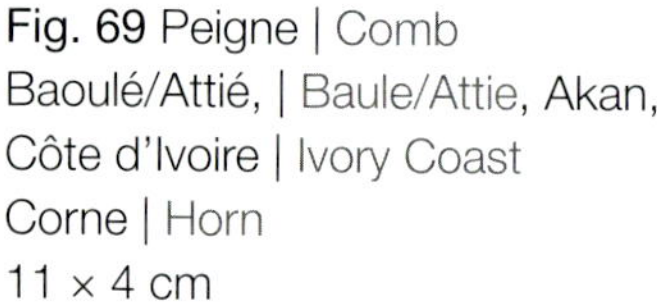

Fig. 69 Peigne | Comb
Baoulé/Attié, | Baule/Attie, Akan,
Côte d'Ivoire | Ivory Coast
Corne | Horn
11 × 4 cm

Provenance
Baba Keita

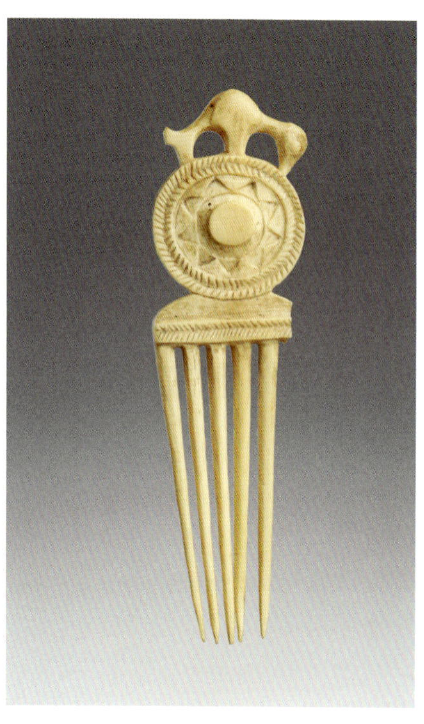

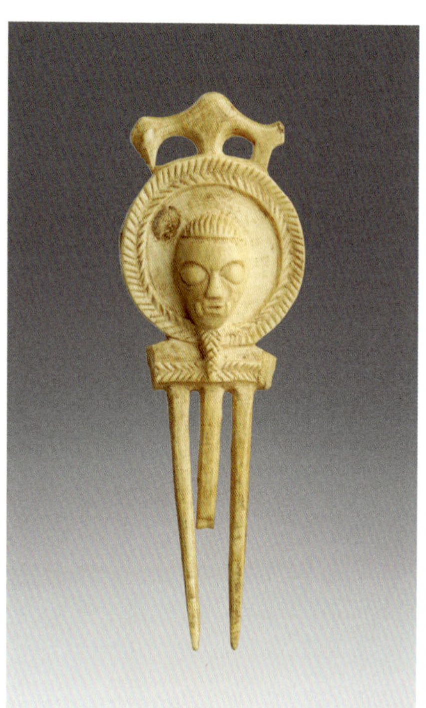

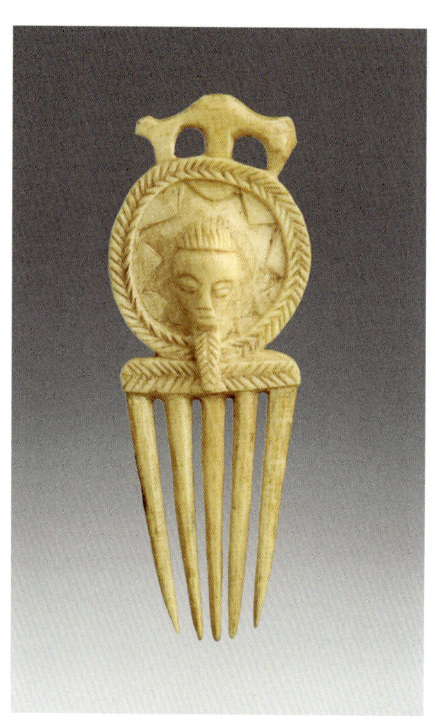

Fig. 70 Peigne | Comb
Baoulé/Attié | Baule/Attie, Akan,
Côte d'Ivoire | Ivory Coast
Ivoire | Ivory
10,6 × 5 cm | 10.6 × 5 cm

Provenance
Robert Duperrier

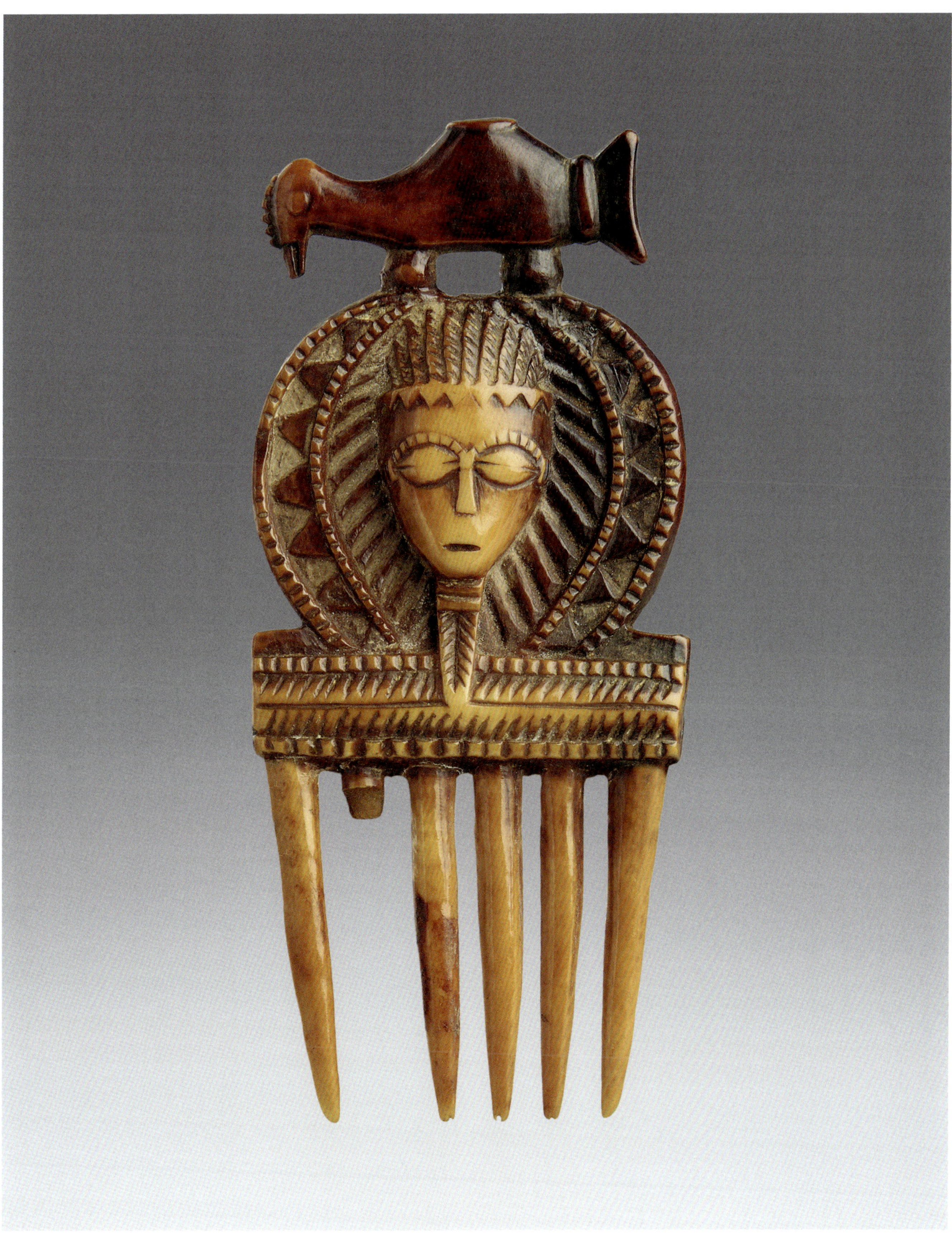

Fig. 71 Peigne | Comb
Baoulé | Baule, Akan, Côte d'Ivoire | Ivory Coast
Bois | Wood
25,3 × 9,5 cm | 25.3 × 9.5 cm

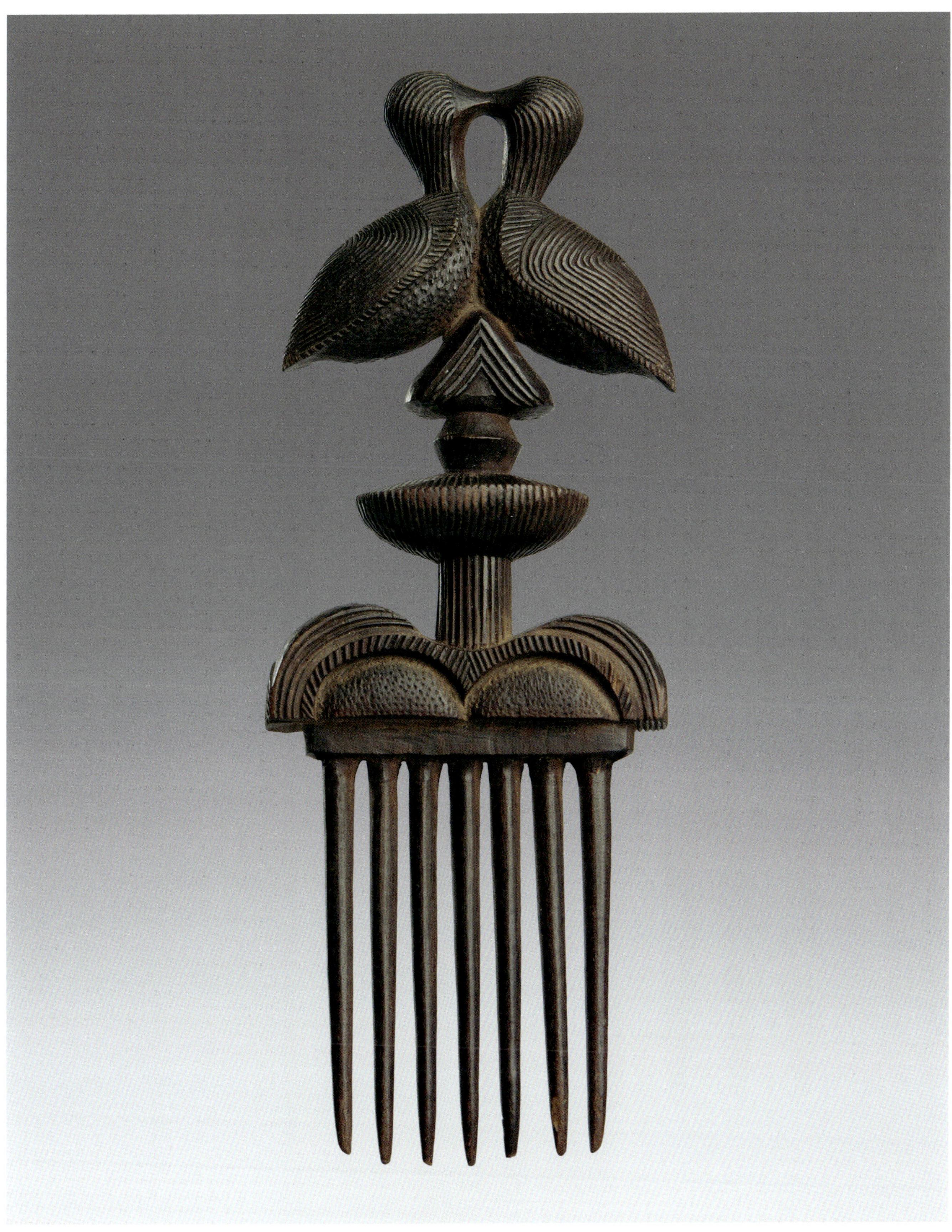

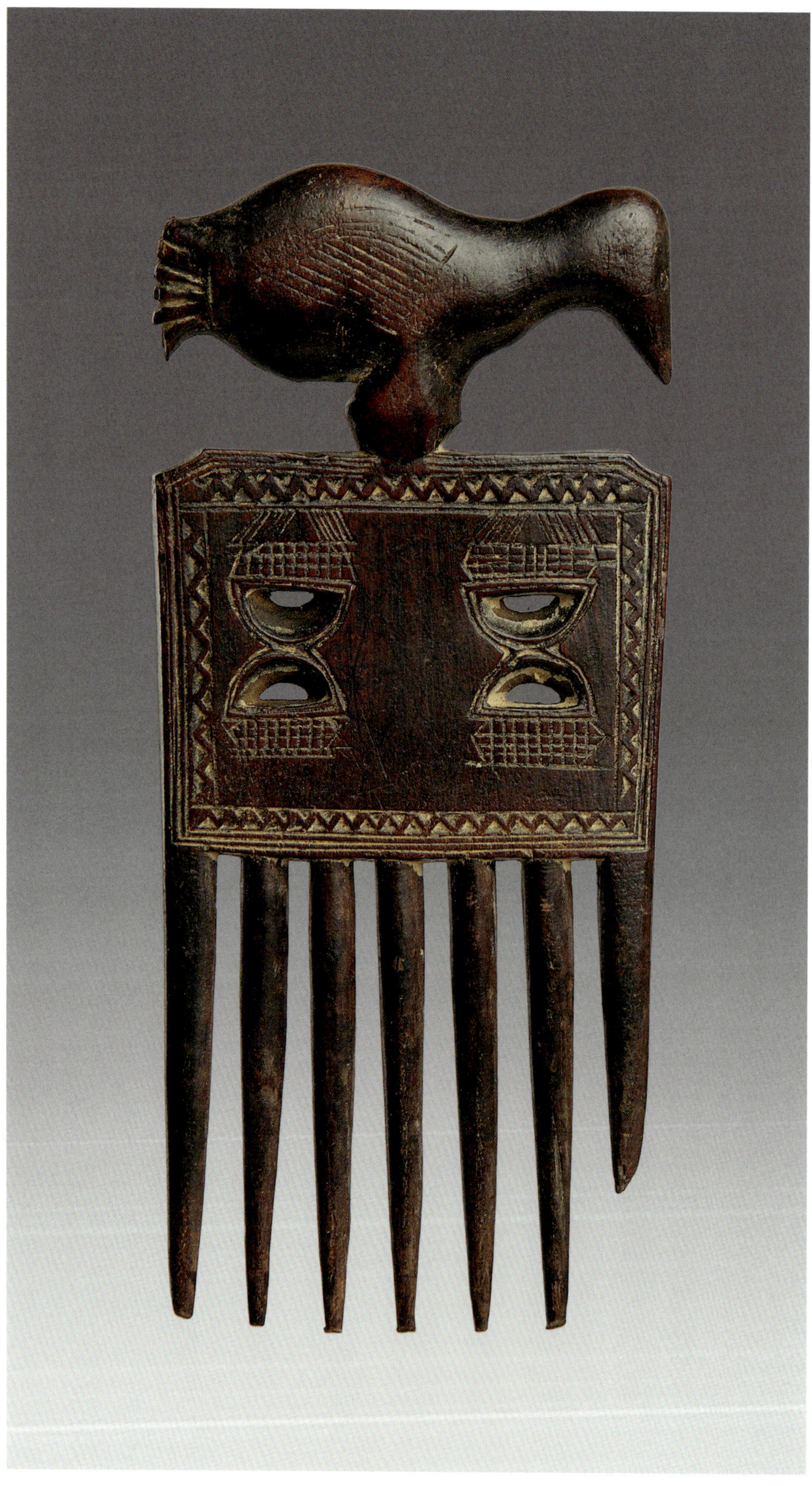

Fig. 72 Peigne | Comb
Baoulé | Baule, Akan, Côte d'Ivoire | Ivory Coast
Bois | Wood
15 × 8 cm

Provenance
Hassan Hassan

Fig. 73 Peigne | Comb
Baoulé | Baule, Akan, Côte d'Ivoire | Ivory Coast
Bois | Wood
22 × 10,5 cm | 22 × 10.5 cm

Provenance
Saramory Diabaté

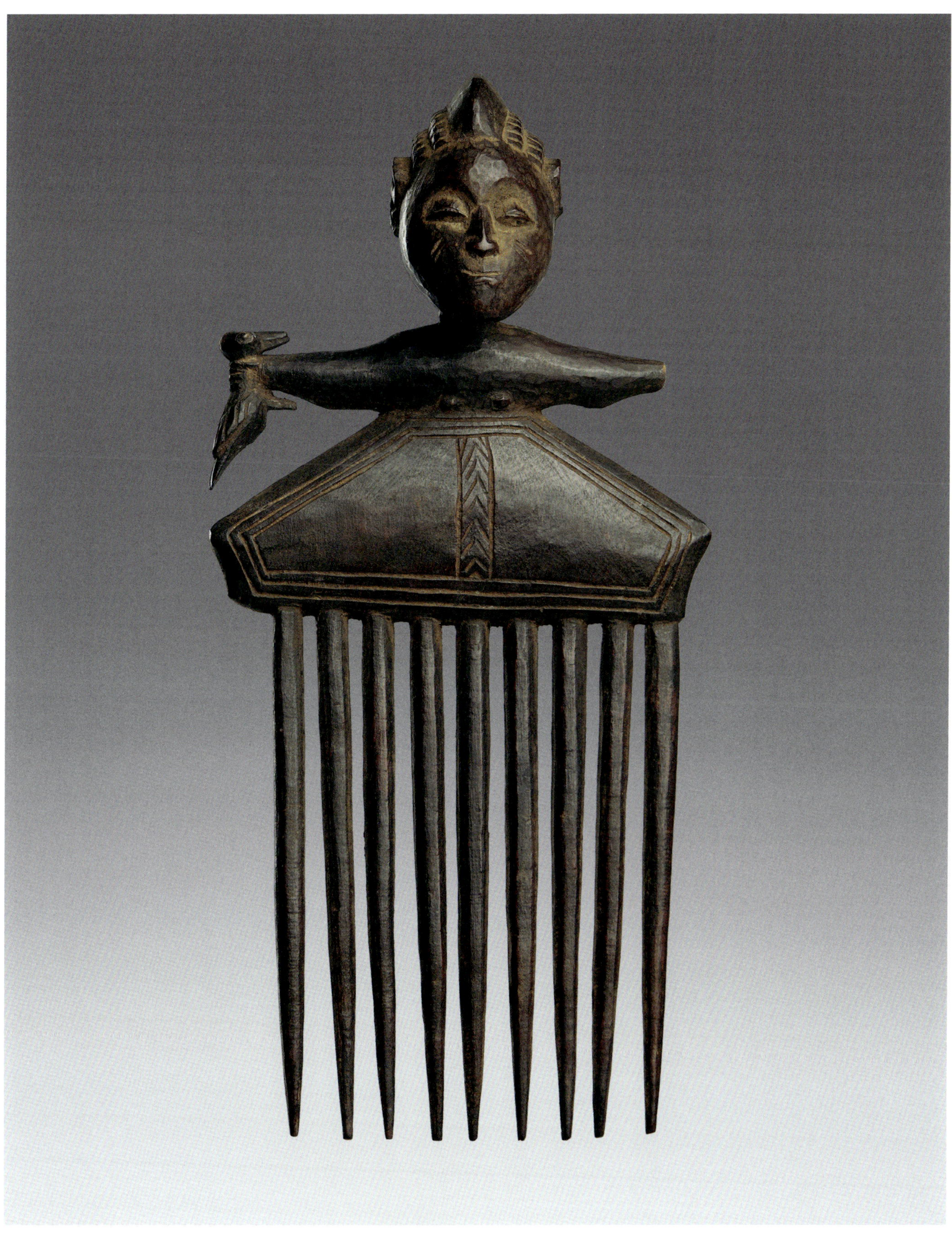

Fig. 74 Peigne | Comb
Baoulé | Baule, Akan, Côte d'Ivoire | Ivory Coast
Bois | Wood
14 × 7 cm

Fig. 75 Peigne | Comb
Baoulé | Baule, Akan, Côte d'Ivoire | Ivory Coast
Bois, feuille d'or | Wood, gold leaf
14 × 5 cm

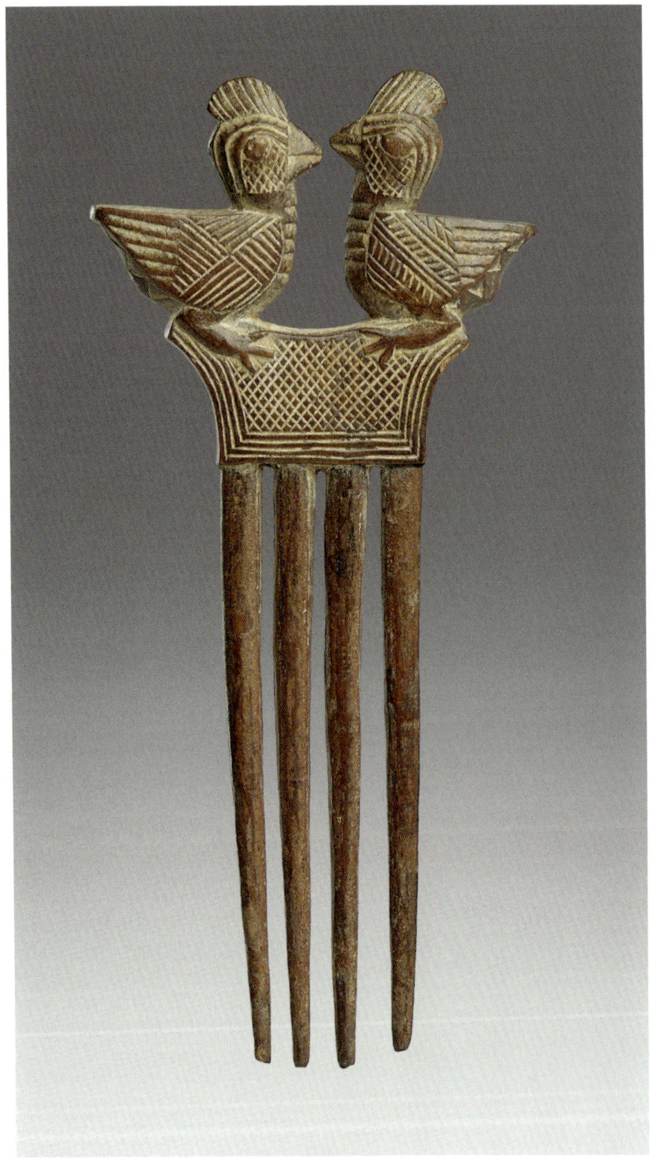

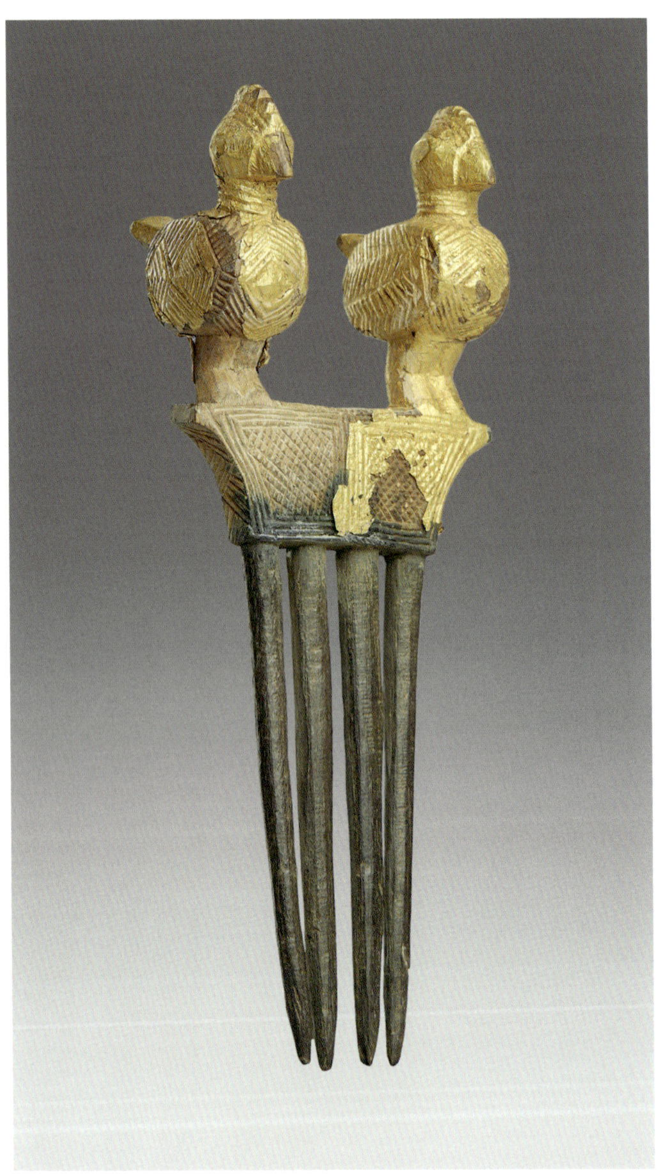

Fig. 76 Peigne | Comb
Baoulé, Akan, Côte d'Ivoire | Ivory Coast
Bois | Wood
14,5 × 5,5 cm | 14.5 × 5.5 cm

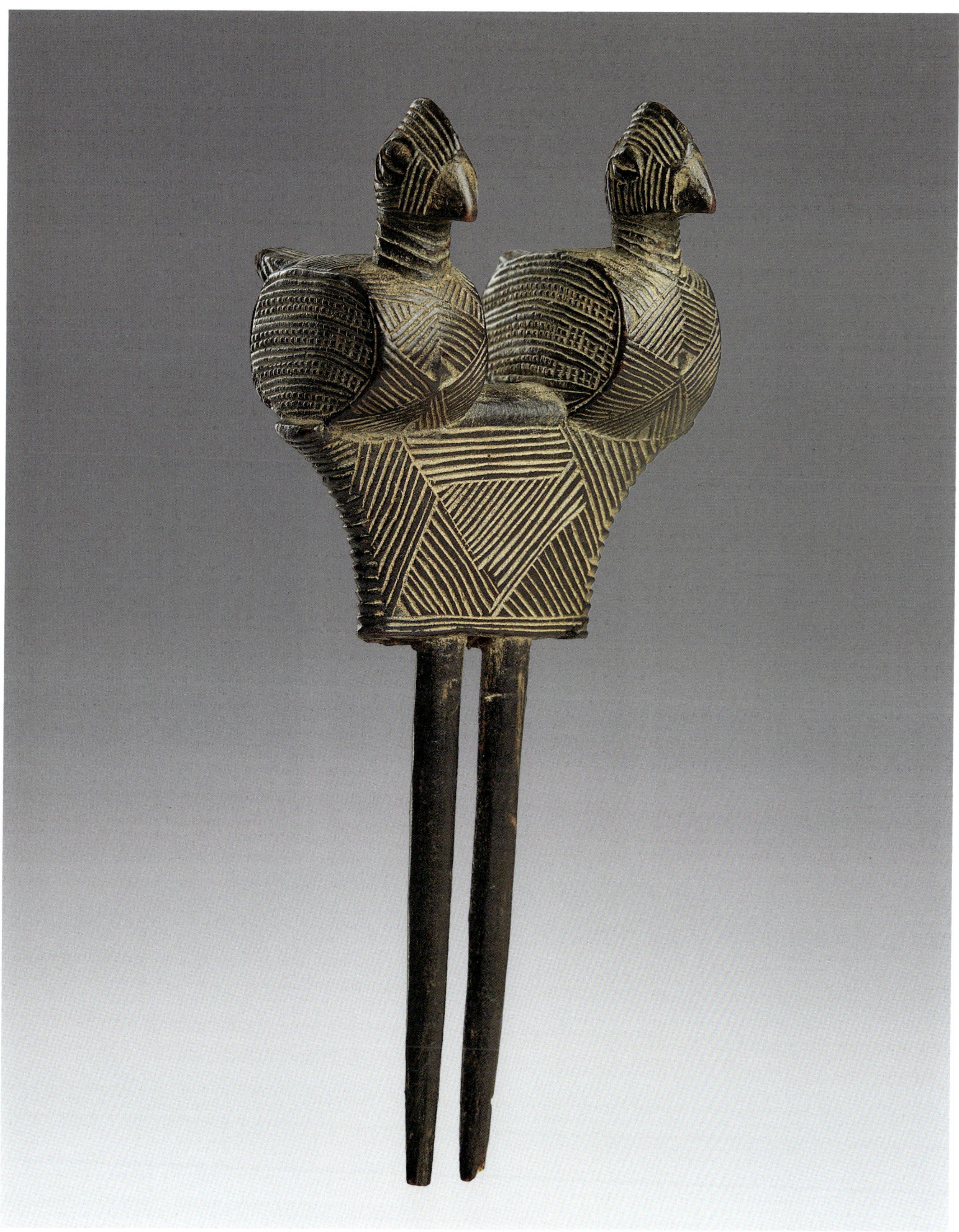

Fig. 77 Peigne | Comb
Baoulé | Baule, Akan, Côte d'Ivoire | Ivory Coast
Ivoire, métal | Ivory, metal
13 × 3 cm

Fig. 78 Peigne | Comb
Baoulé | Baule, Akan, Côte d'Ivoire | Ivory Coast
Ivoire, métal | Ivory, metal
12,5 × 3,5 cm | 12.5 × 3.5 cm

Fig. 79 Peigne | Comb
Baoulé | Baule, Akan, Côte d'Ivoire | Ivory Coast
Ivoire, métal | Ivory, metal
17 × 3,3 cm | 17 × 3.3 cm

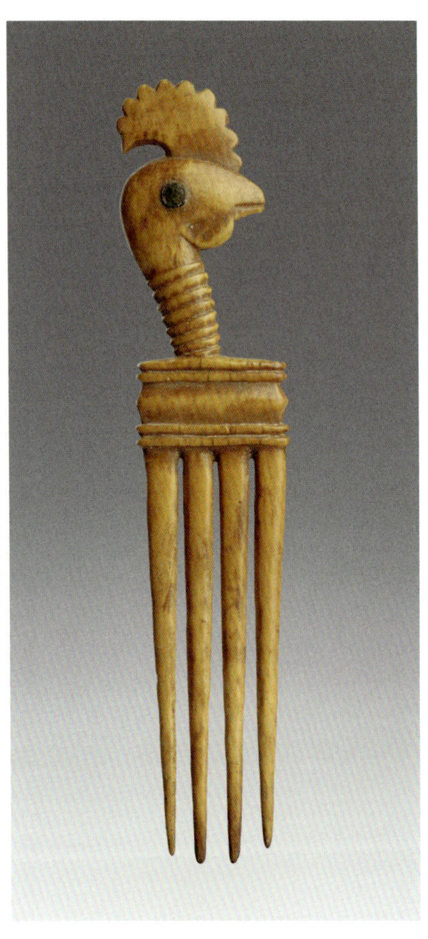

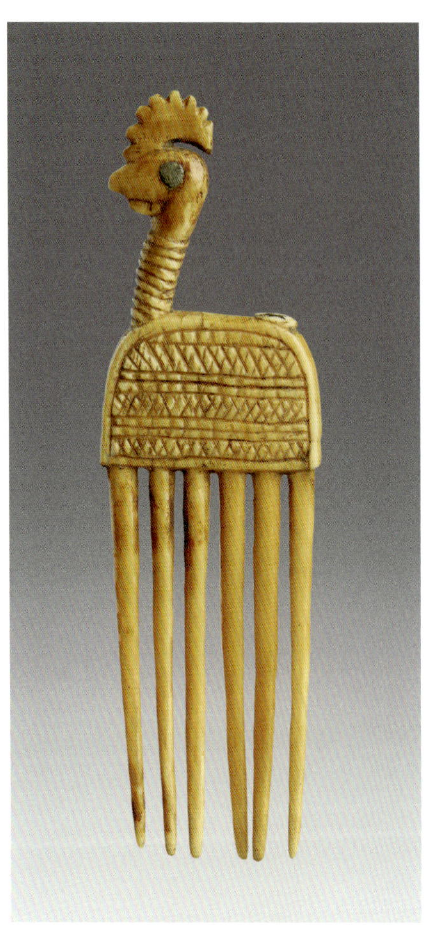

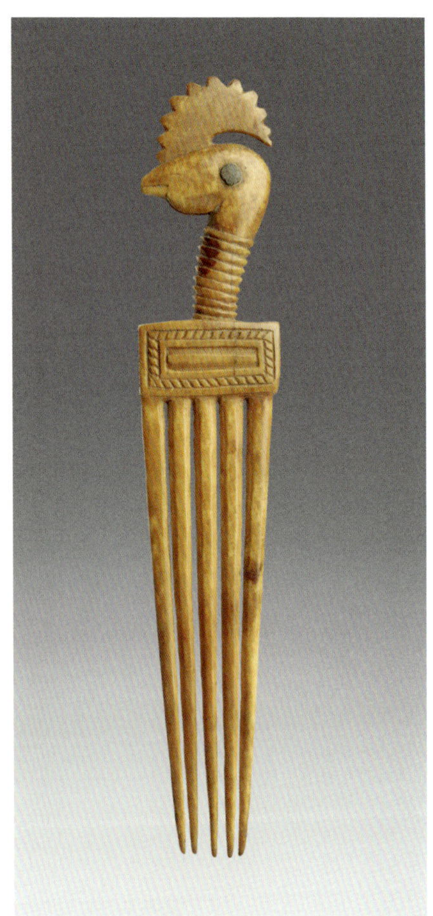

Fig. 80 Peigne | Comb
Baoulé | Baule, Akan, Côte d'Ivoire | Ivory Coast
Ivoire, métal | Ivory, metal
9,1 × 2,1 cm | 9.1 × 2.1 cm

Fig. 81 Peigne | Comb
Baoulé | Baule, Akan, Côte d'Ivoire | Ivory Coast
Ivoire | Ivory
9,8 × 2,2 cm | 9.8 × 2.2 cm

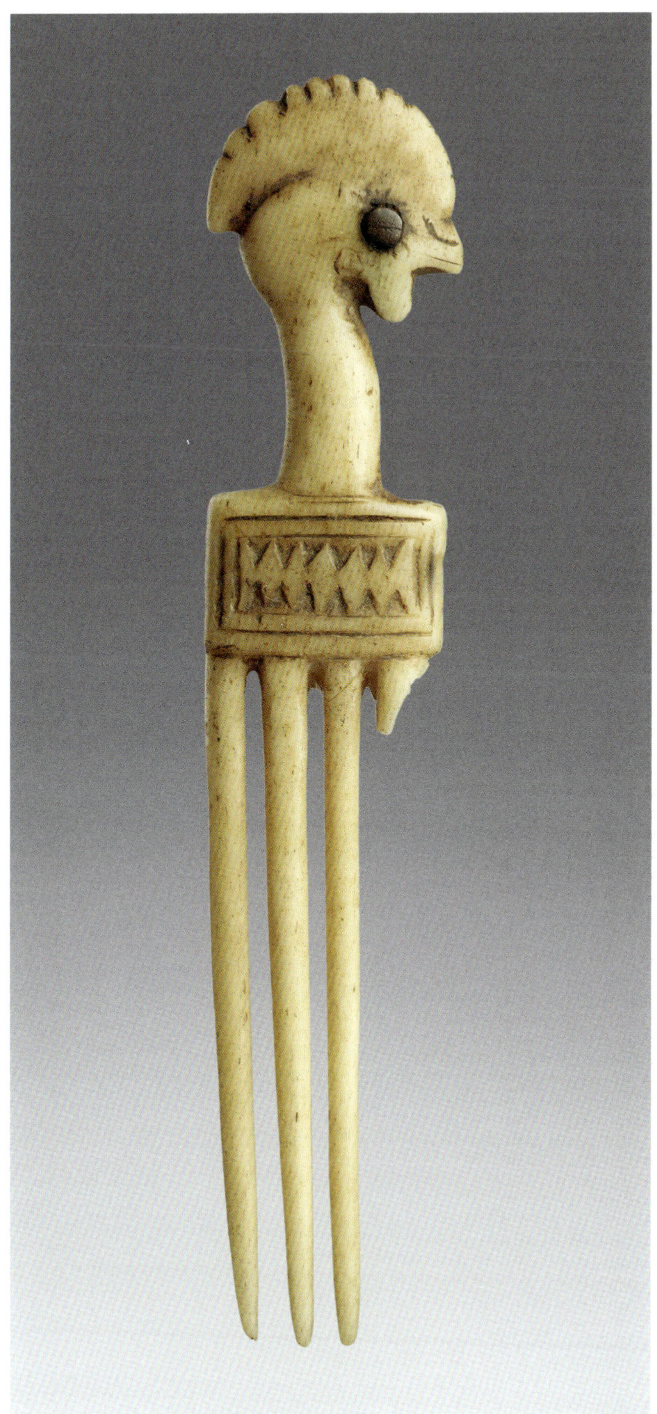

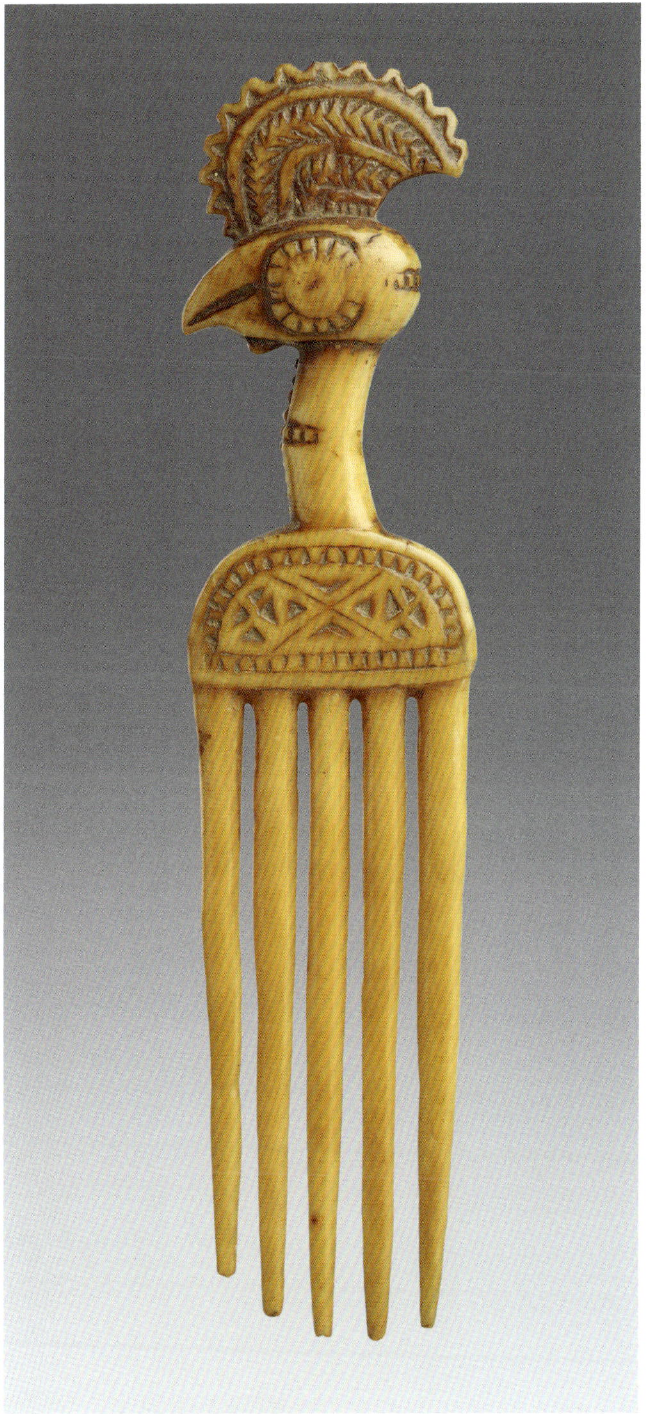

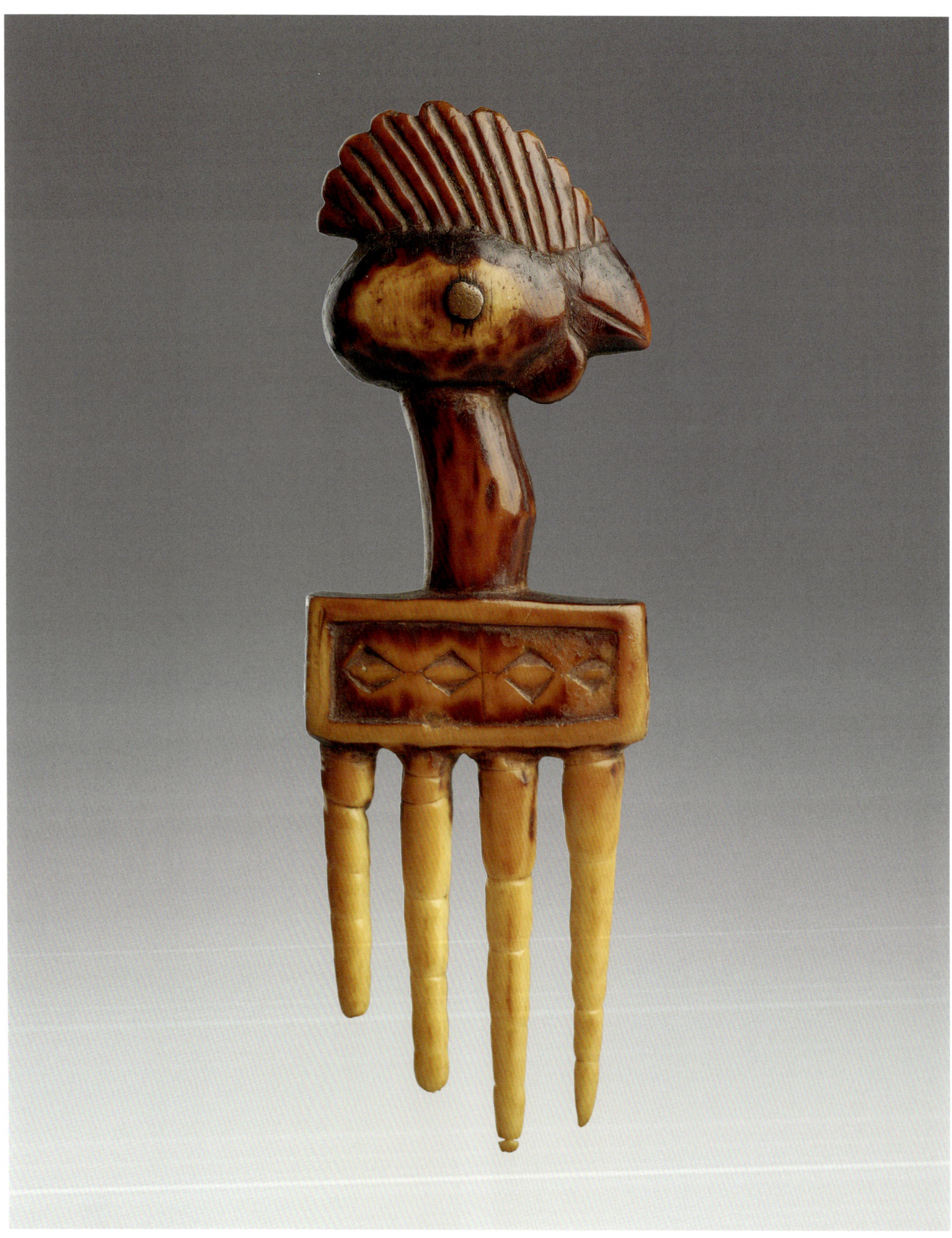

Fig. 82 Peigne | Comb
Baoulé | Baule, Akan, Côte d'Ivoire | Ivory Coast
Ivoire, cuivre | Ivory, copper
9 × 2,8 cm | 9 × 2.8 cm

Provenance
Baba Keita

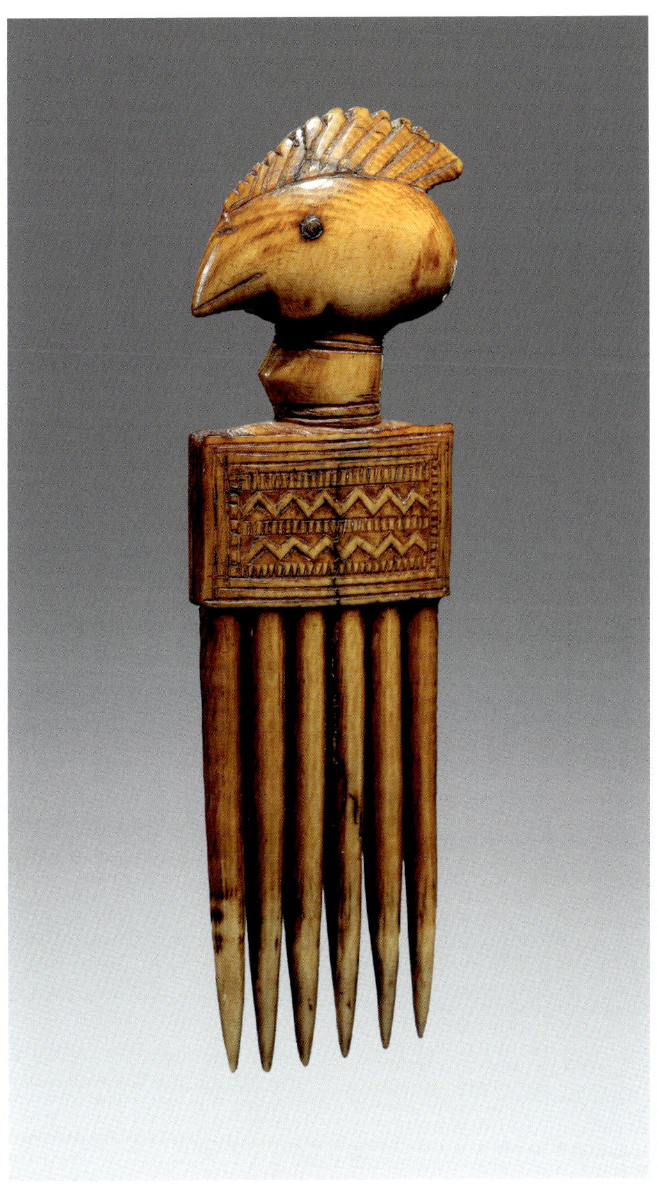

Fig. 83 Peigne | Comb
Baoulé | Baule, Akan, Côte d'Ivoire | Ivory Coast
Ivoire | Ivory
14,5 × 5 cm | 14.5 × 5 cm

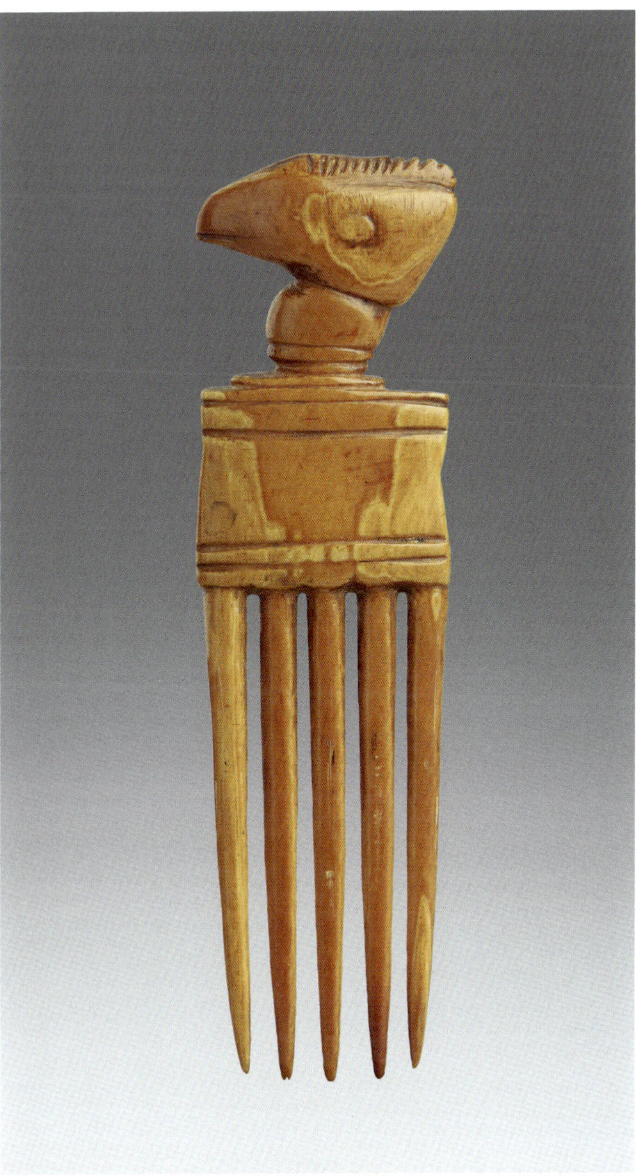

Fig. 84 Peigne | Comb
Baoulé | Baule, Akan, Côte d'Ivoire | Ivory Coast
Ivoire | Ivory
12,5 × 3,9 cm | 12.5 × 3.9 cm

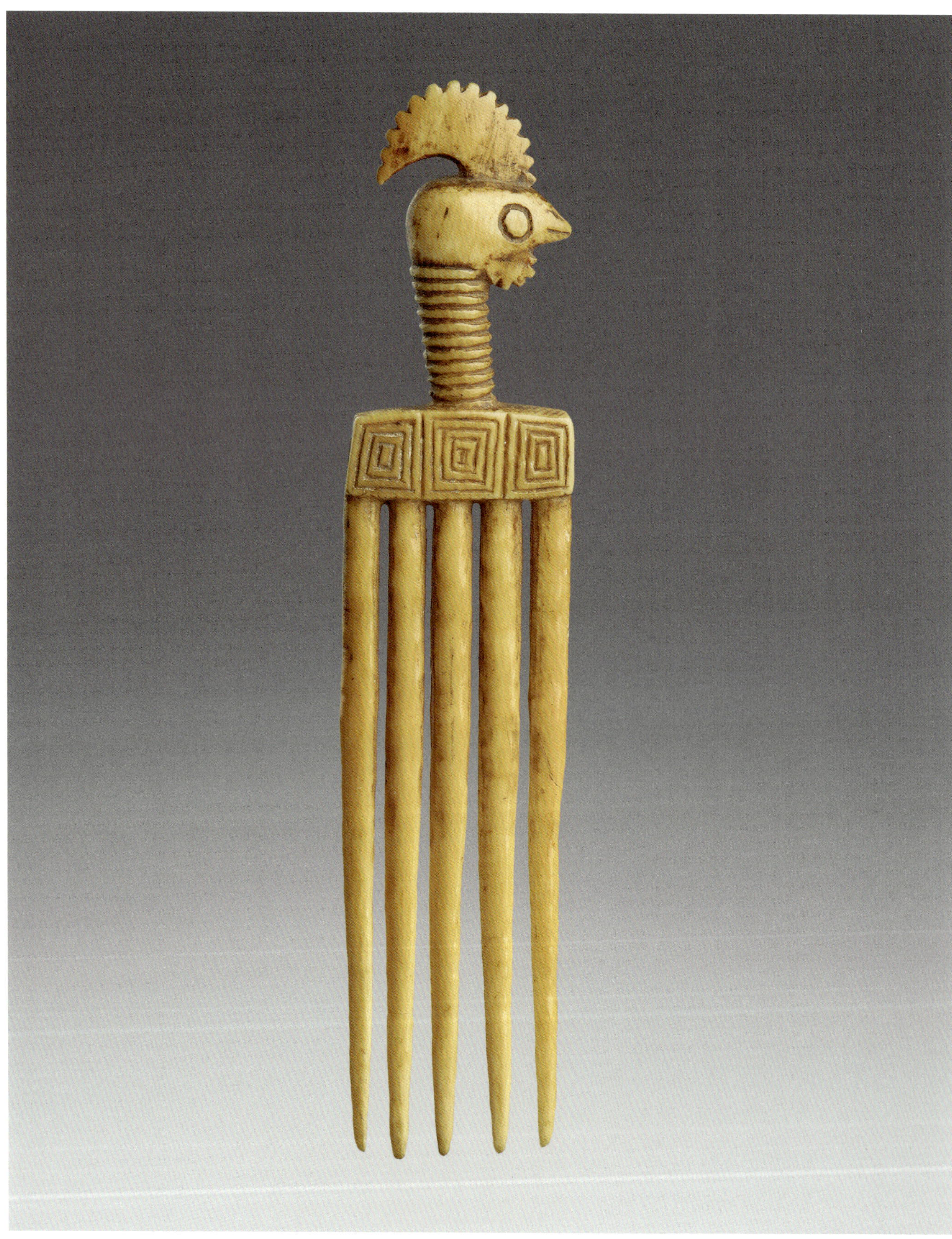

Fig. 85 Peigne | Comb
Baoulé | Baule, Akan, Côte d'Ivoire | Ivory Coast
Ivoire | Ivory
13,5 × 2,9 cm | 13.5 × 2.9 cm

Provenance
Dramane Ouedraougo

Fig. 86 Peigne | Comb
Baoulé | Baule, Akan, Côte d'Ivoire | Ivory Coast
Ivoire, métal | Ivory, metal
8,6 × 2,9 cm | 8.6 × 2.9 cm

Provenance
Issaka Zango

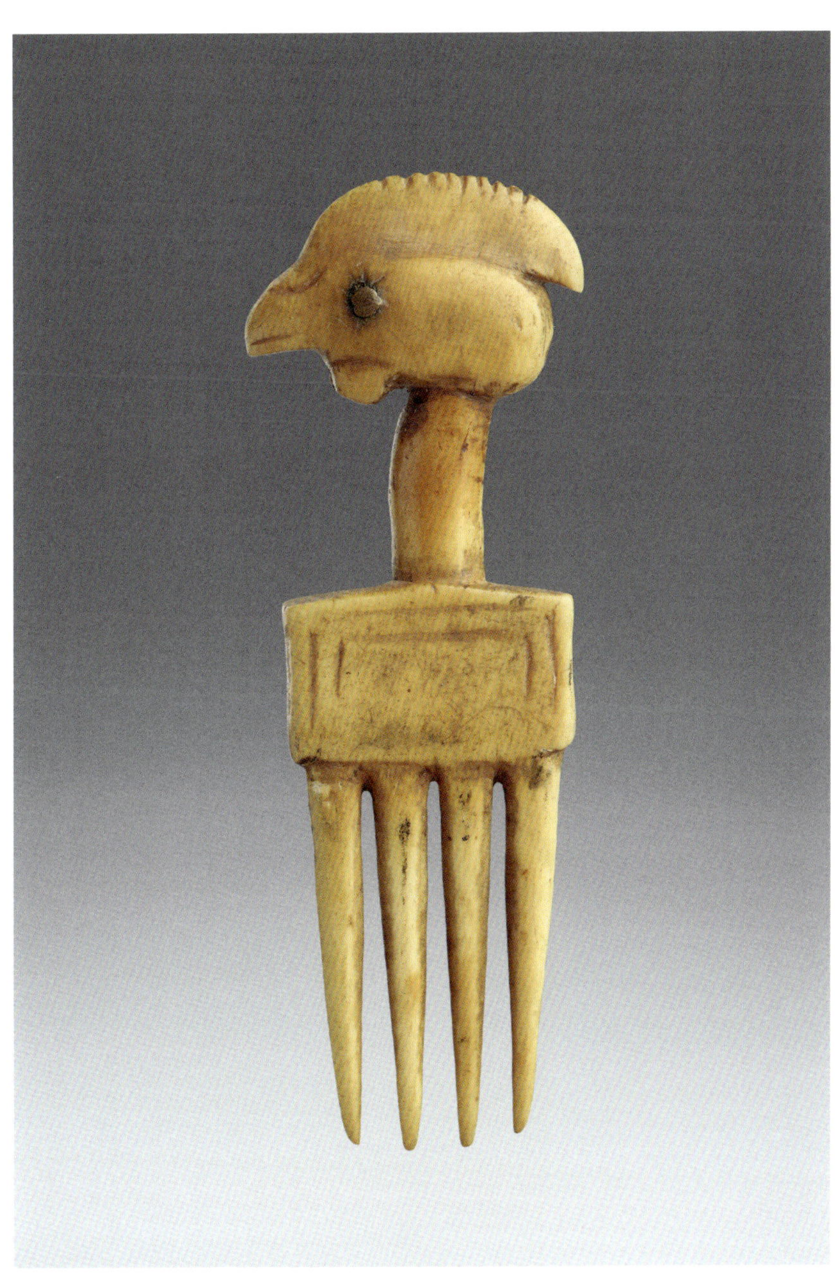

Fig. 87 Peigne | Comb
Attié | Attie, Akan, Côte d'Ivoire | Ivory Coast
Corne ou ivoire | Horn or ivory
7,2 × 3 cm | 7.2 × 3 cm

Provenance
Gaston Diéou

Fig. 88 Peigne | Comb
Attié | Attie, Akan, Côte d'Ivoire | Ivory Coast
Corne ou ivoire | Horn or ivory
7 × 2,3 cm | 7 × 2.3 cm

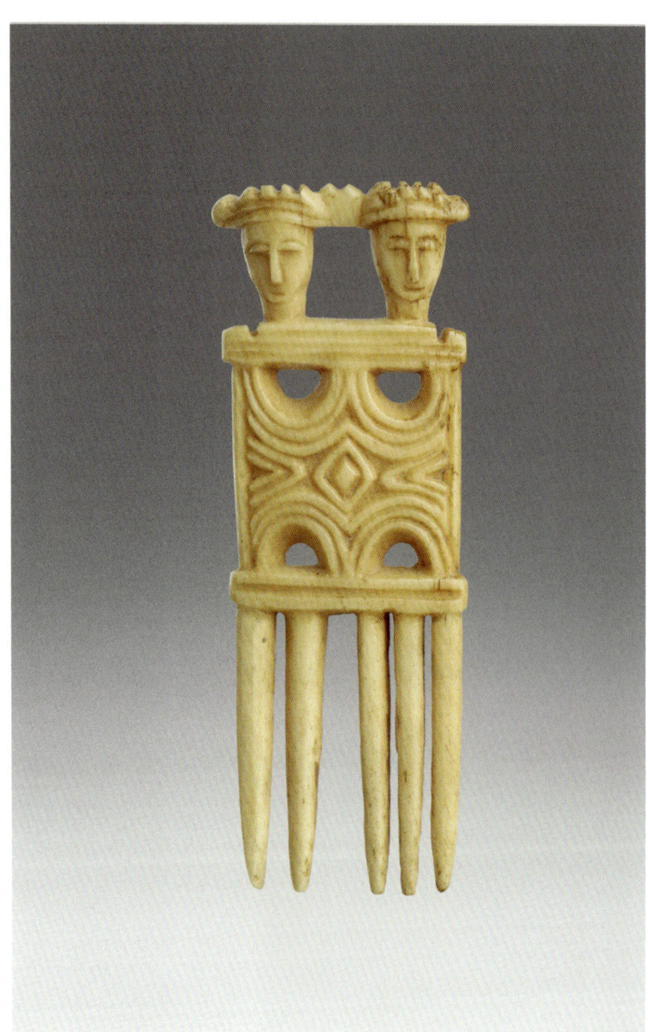

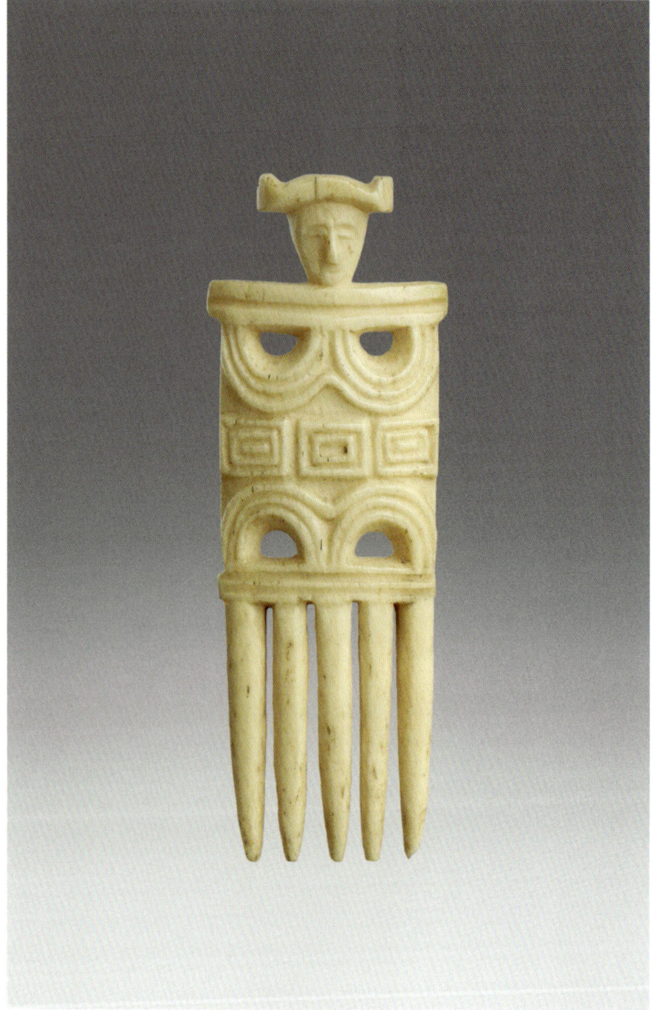

Fig. 89 Peigne | Comb
Attié | Attie, Akan, Côte d'Ivoire | Ivory Coast
Corne | Horn
7 × 3,5 cm | 7 × 3.5 cm

Provenance
Georges Brou

Fig. 90 Peigne | Comb
Attié, Akan, Côte d'Ivoire | Ivory Coast
Corne | Horn
11,5 × 7 cm | 11.5 × 7 cm

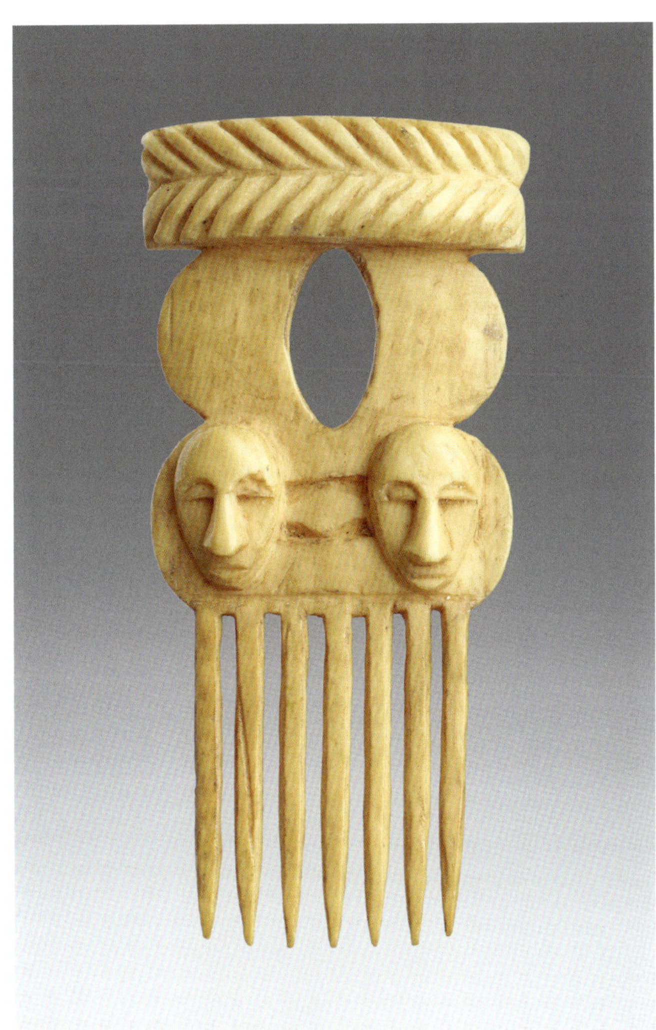

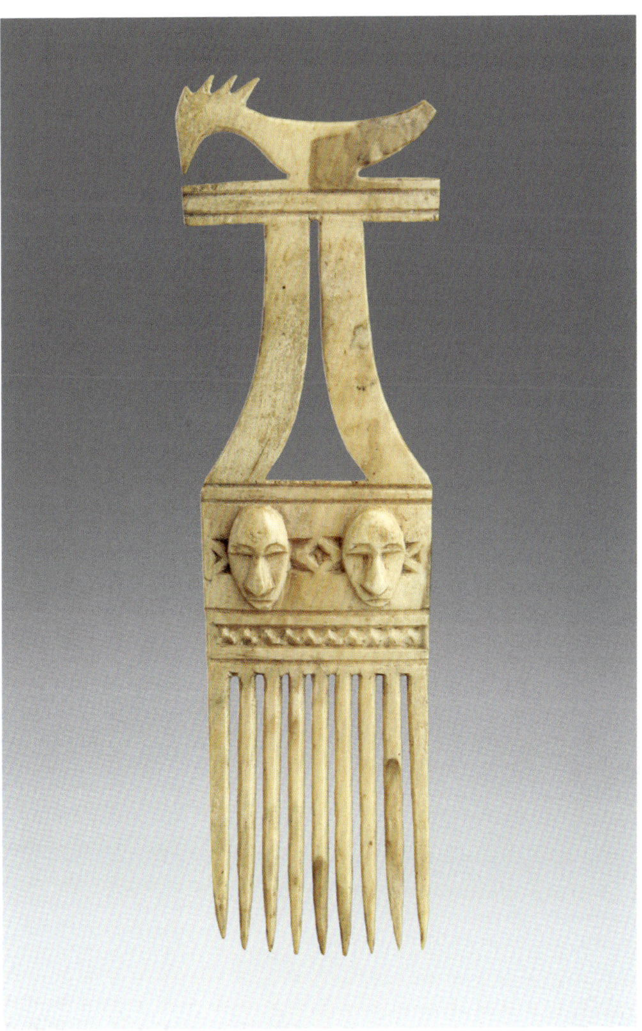

Fig. 91 Peigne | Comb
Attié | Attie, Akan, Côte d'Ivoire | Ivory Coast
Corne | Horn
12 × 2 cm

Fig. 92 Peigne | Comb
Attié | Attie, Akan, Côte d'Ivoire | Ivory Coast
Corne | Horn
8,5 × 3,5 cm | 8.5 × 3.5 cm

Fig. 93 Peigne | Comb
Attié | Attie, Akan, Côte d'Ivoire | Ivory Coast
Corne | Horn
9,5 × 3 cm | 9.5 × 3 cm

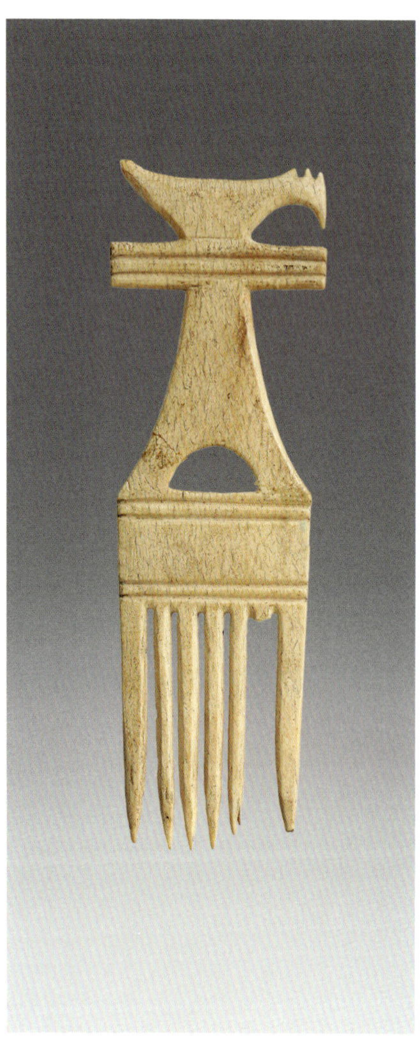

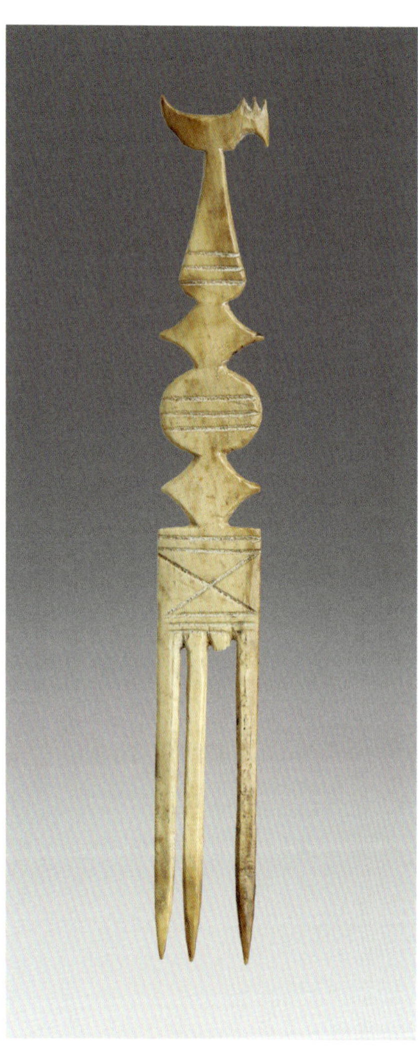

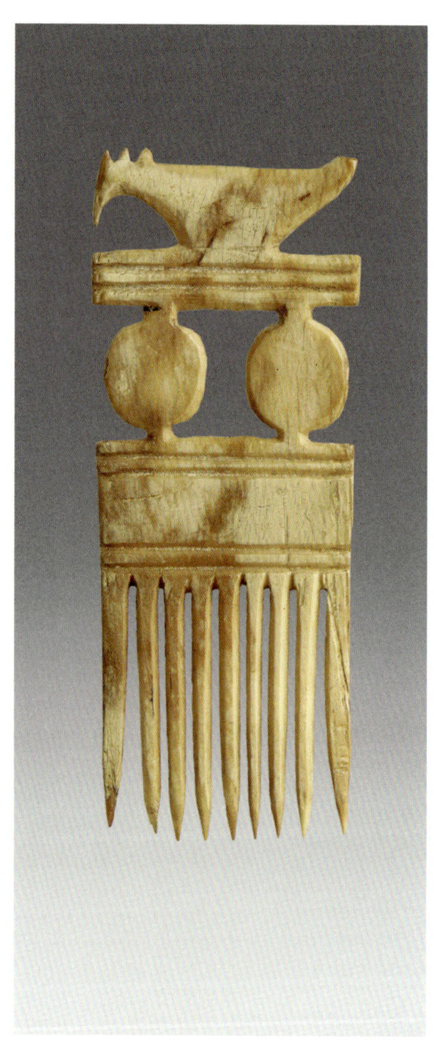

Fig. 94 Peigne | Comb
Attié | Attie, Akan, Côte d'Ivoire | Ivory Coast
Corne | Horn
9 × 5,5 cm | 9 × 5.5 cm

Fig. 95 Peigne | Comb
Attié | Attie, Akan, Côte d'Ivoire | Ivory Coast
Corne | Horn
10 × 3,5 cm | 10 × 3.5 cm

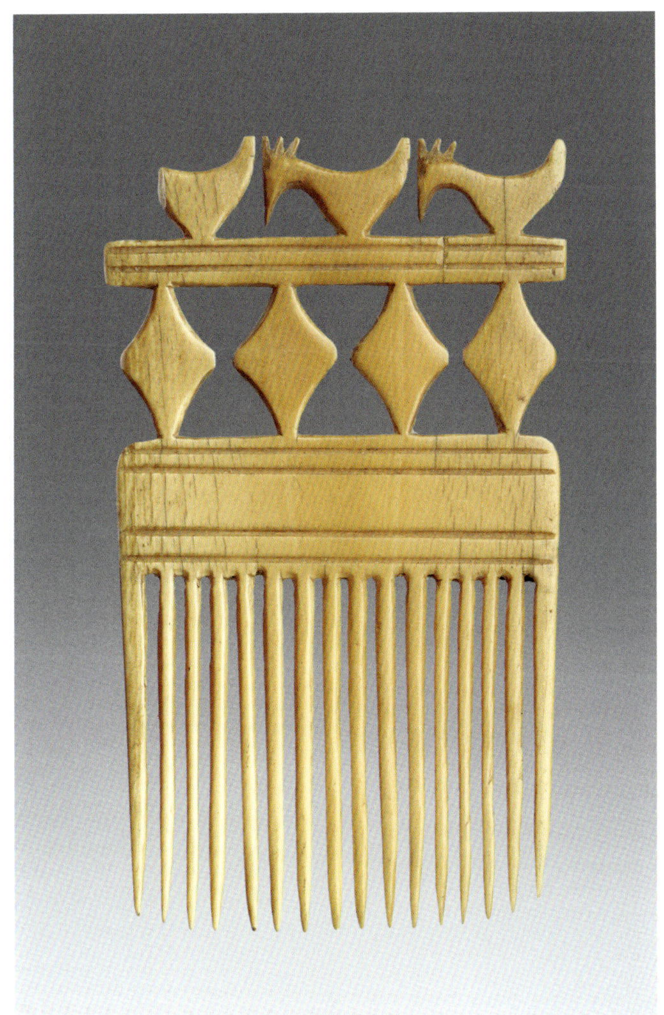

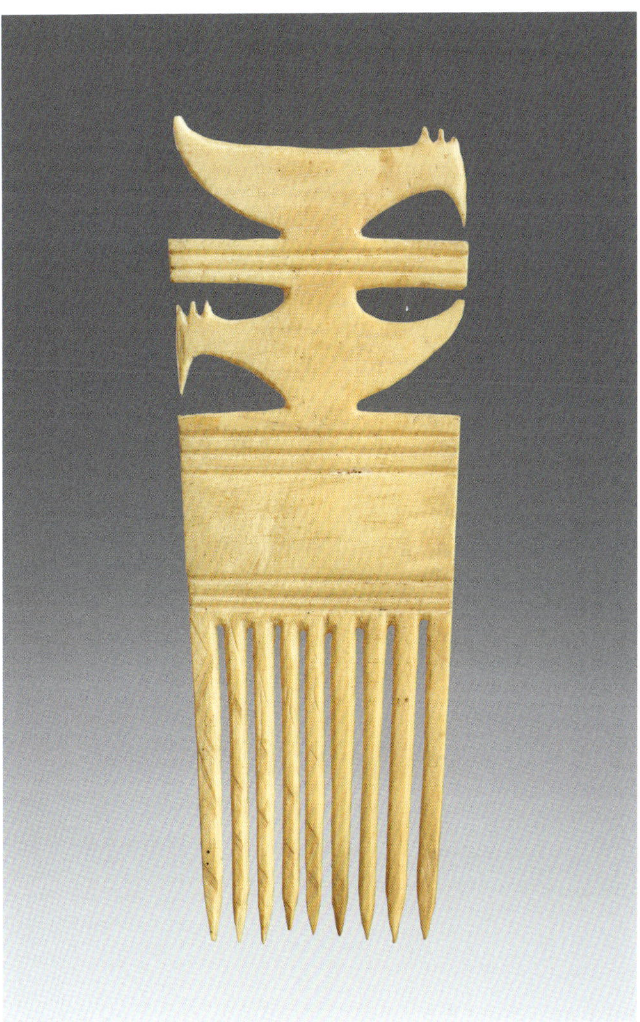

Fig. 96 Peigne | Comb
Baoulé | Baule, Akan, Côte d'Ivoire | Ivory Coast
Ivoire | Ivory
13,2 × 2,5 cm | 13.2 × 2.5 cm

Fig. 97 Peigne | Comb
Baoulé | Baule, Akan, Côte d'Ivoire | Ivory Coast
Ivoire | Ivory
10,6 × 3,6 cm | 10.6 × 3.6 cm

Provenance
Jean-Pierre Laprugne

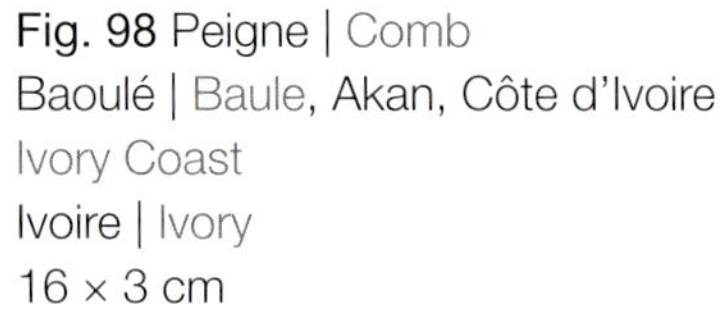

Fig. 98 Peigne | Comb
Baoulé | Baule, Akan, Côte d'Ivoire | Ivory Coast
Ivoire | Ivory
16 × 3 cm

Provenance
Jean-Pierre Laprugne

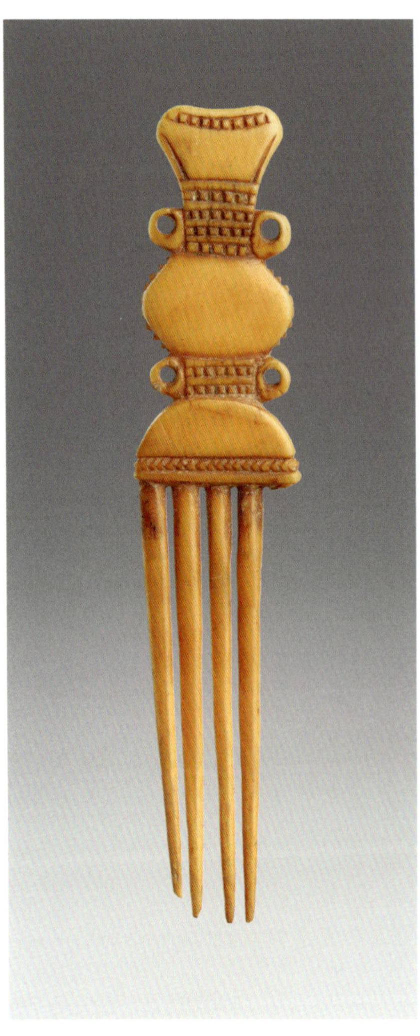

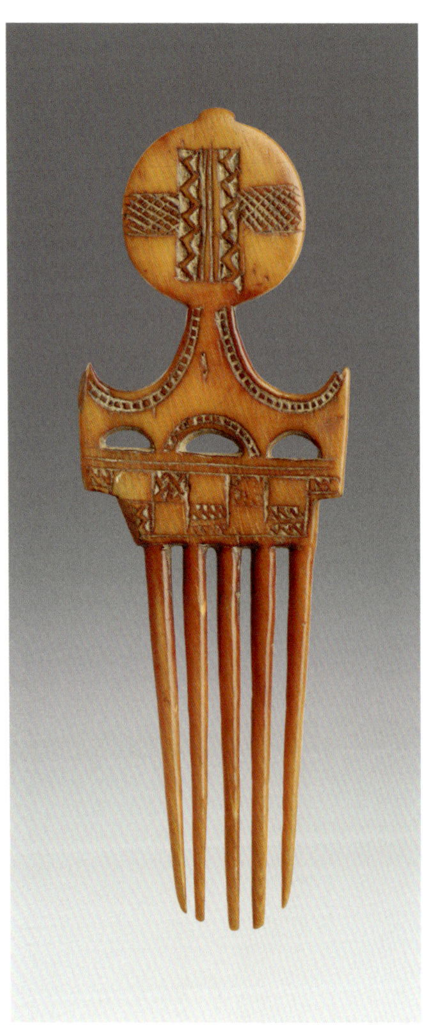

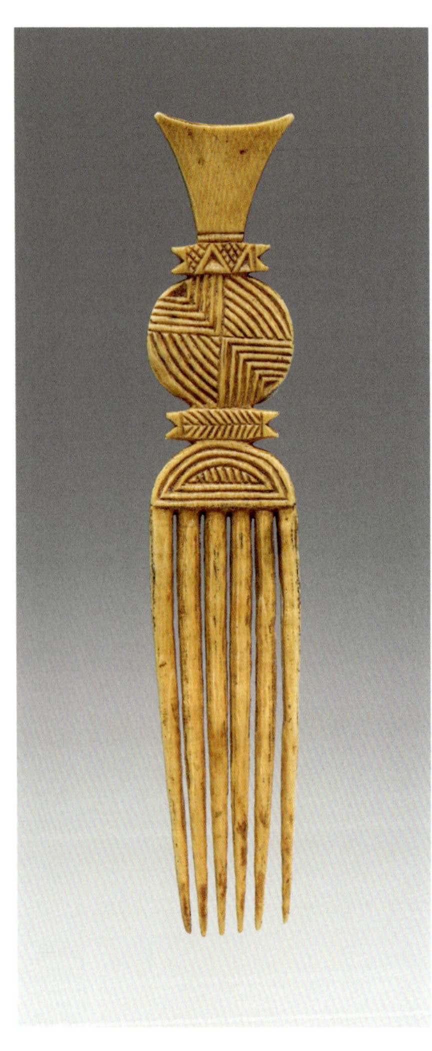

Fig. 99 Peigne | Comb
Baoulé | Baule, Akan, Côte d'Ivoire | Ivory Coast
Ivoire | Ivory
11 × 6,7 cm | 11 × 6.7 cm

Fig. 100 Peigne | Comb
Baoulé | Baule, Akan, Côte d'Ivoire | Ivory Coast
Ivoire | Ivory
7,5 × 4 cm | 7.5 × 4 cm

Fig. 101 Peigne | Comb
Baoulé | Baule, Akan, Côte d'Ivoire | Ivory Coast
Ivoire | Ivory
9,5 × 4,5 cm | 9.5 × 4.5 cm

Provenance
André Blandin

Fig. 102 Peigne | Comb
Baoulé | Baule, Akan, Côte d'Ivoire | Ivory Coast
Ivoire | Ivory
11,3 × 5,3 cm | 11.3 × 5.3 cm

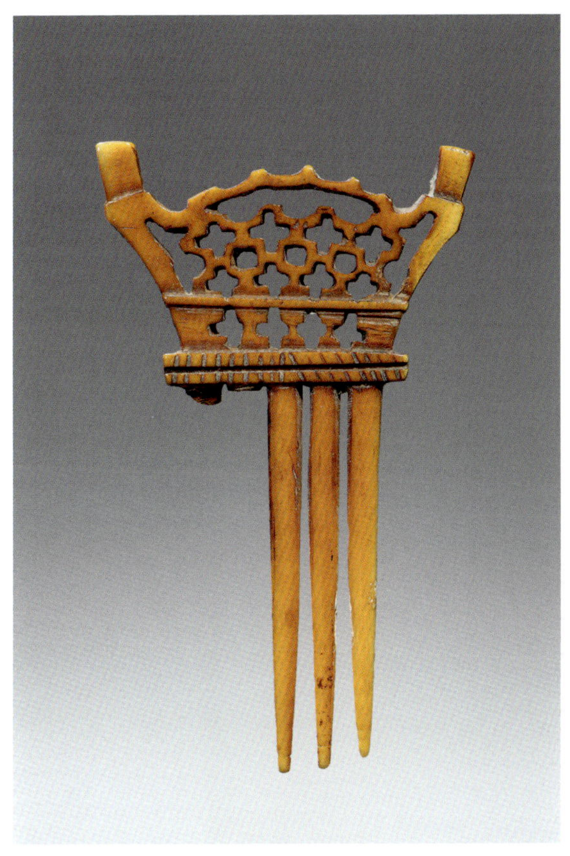
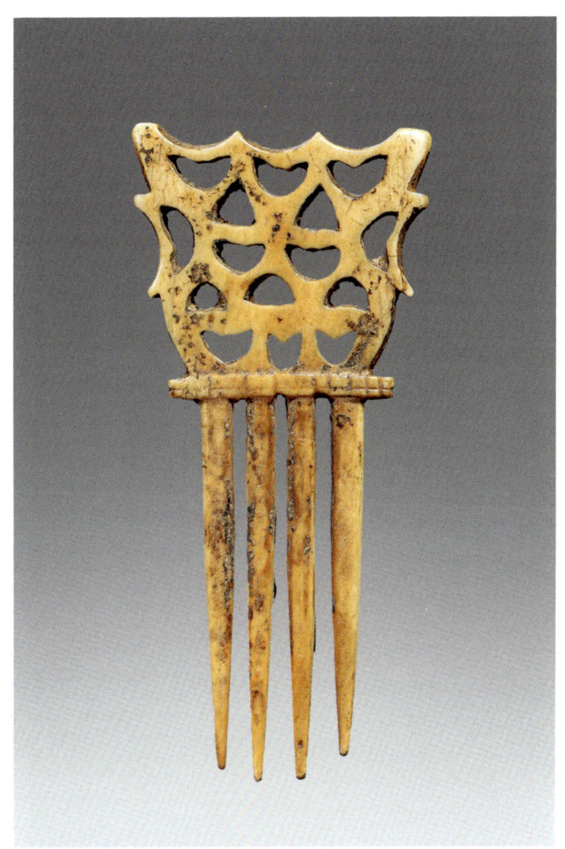
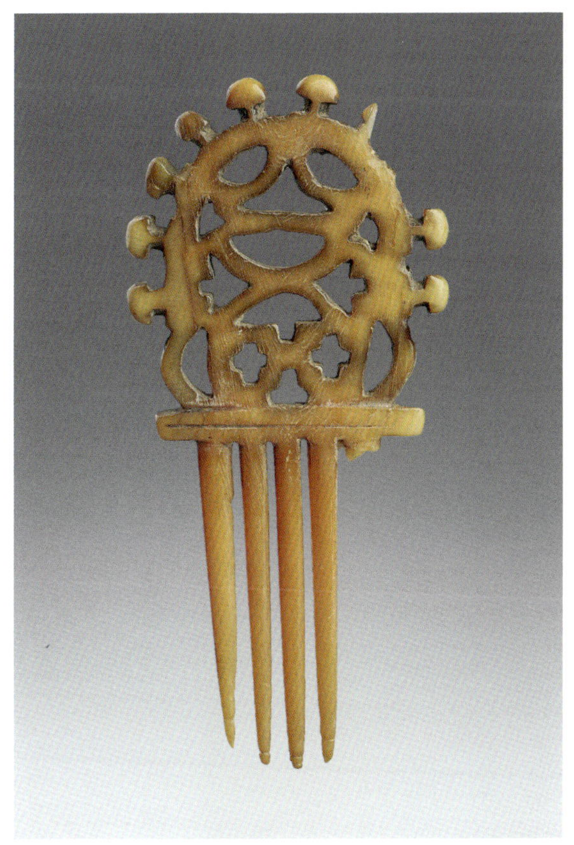
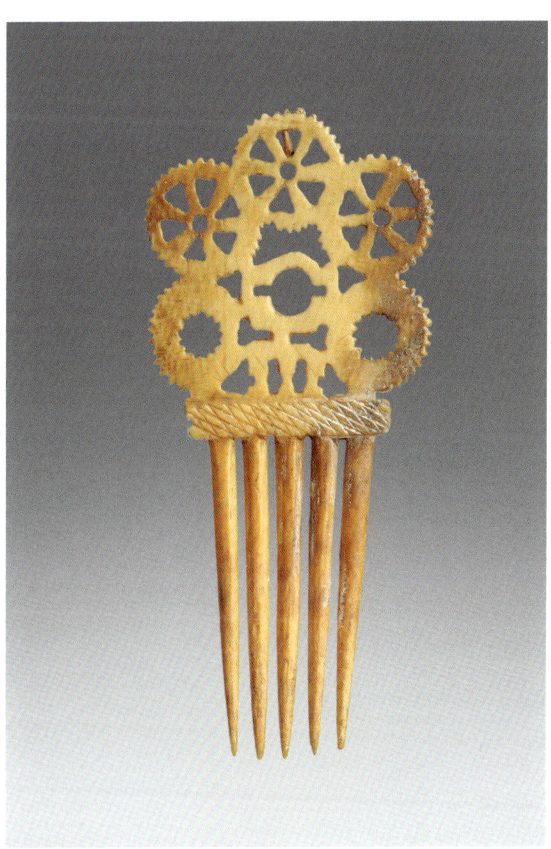

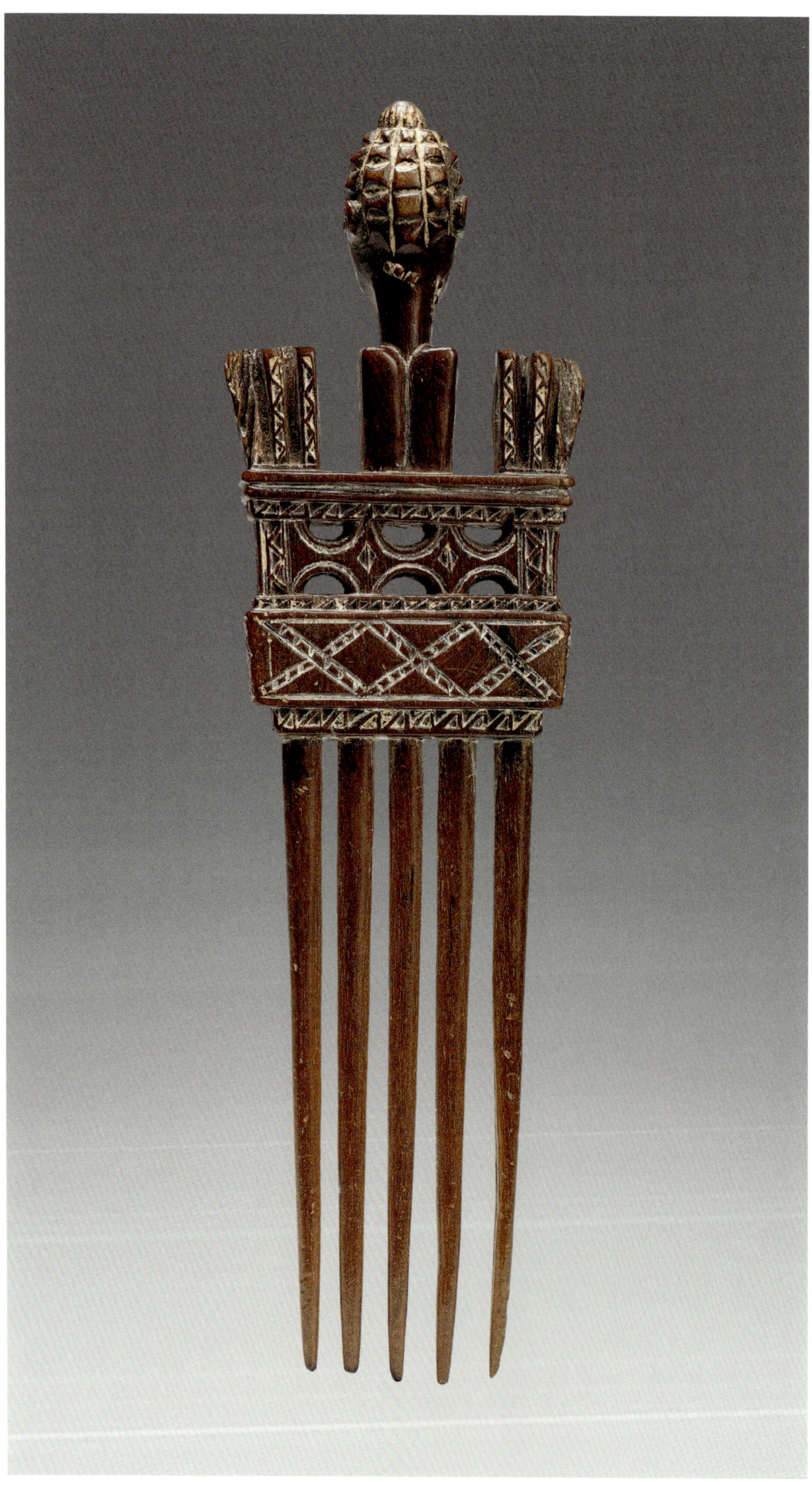

Fig. 103 Peigne | Comb
Abron, Akan, Côte d'Ivoire | Ivory Coast
Bois | Wood
17 × 5 cm

Provenance
Georges Stocklin

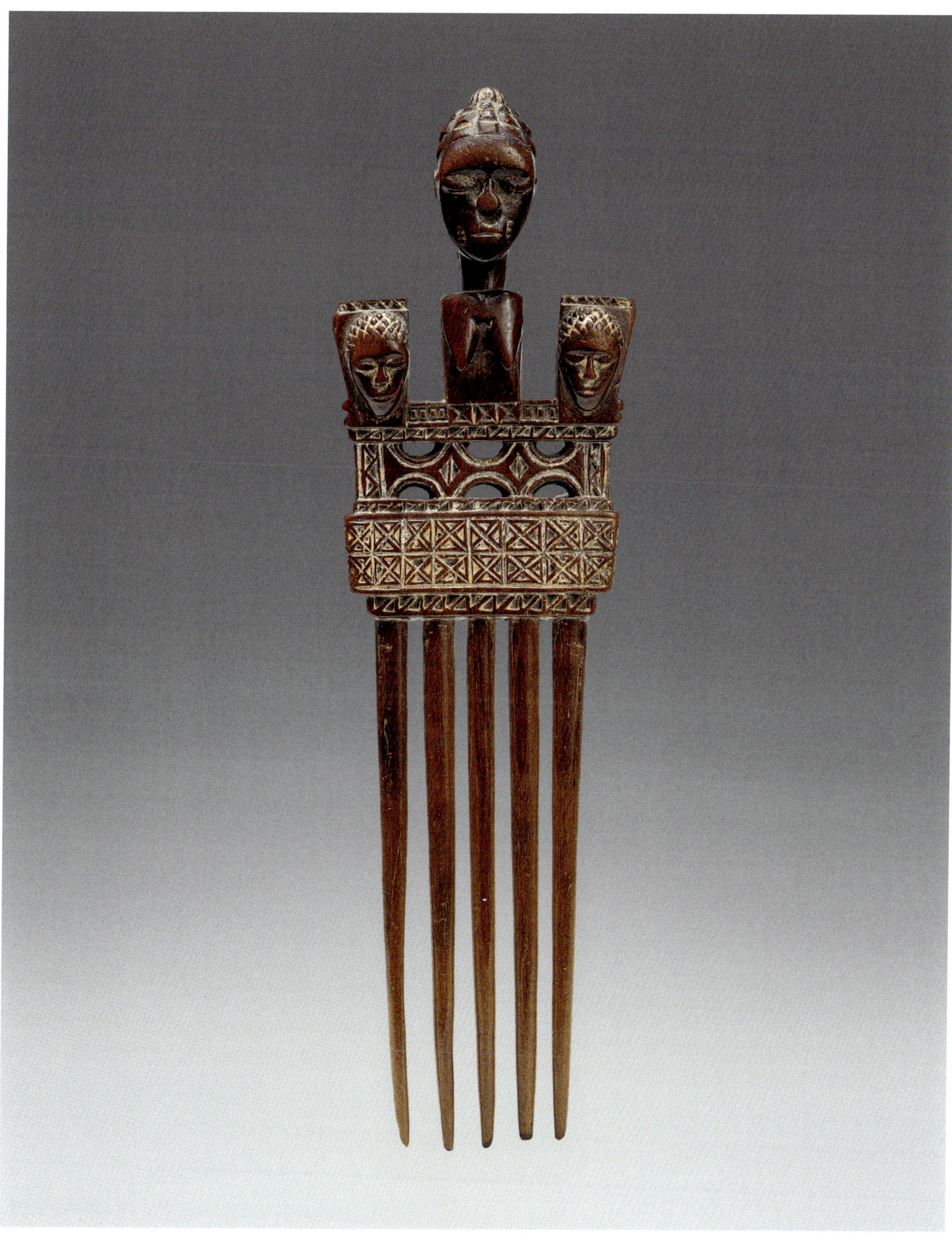

Fig. 104 Peigne | Comb
Koulango, Gur, Côte d'Ivoire | Ivory Coast
Bois | Wood
11 × 4,5 cm | 11 × 4.5 cm

Provenance
Robert Duperrier

Publications
Jean-Yves Augel, Valentine Plisnier, *Coiffures africaines en majesté*, Sainte-Foy-lès-Lyon, Galerie Vallois, 2024, fig. 2, p. 119 ; Hélène Joubert, Jean-Paul Chazal, *Visions d'Afrique*, Taiwan, National Museum of History, 2003, fig. 108, p. 158

Expositions | Exhibitions
Sainte-Foy-lès-Lyon, Espace culturel Jean Salles, *Coiffures africaines en majesté*, 6 – 21 avril | 6 – 21 April 2024 ; Taïwan | Taiwan, *Visions d'Afrique*, National Museum of History, 6 décembre 2003 – 22 février 2004 | 6 December 2003 – 22 February 2004

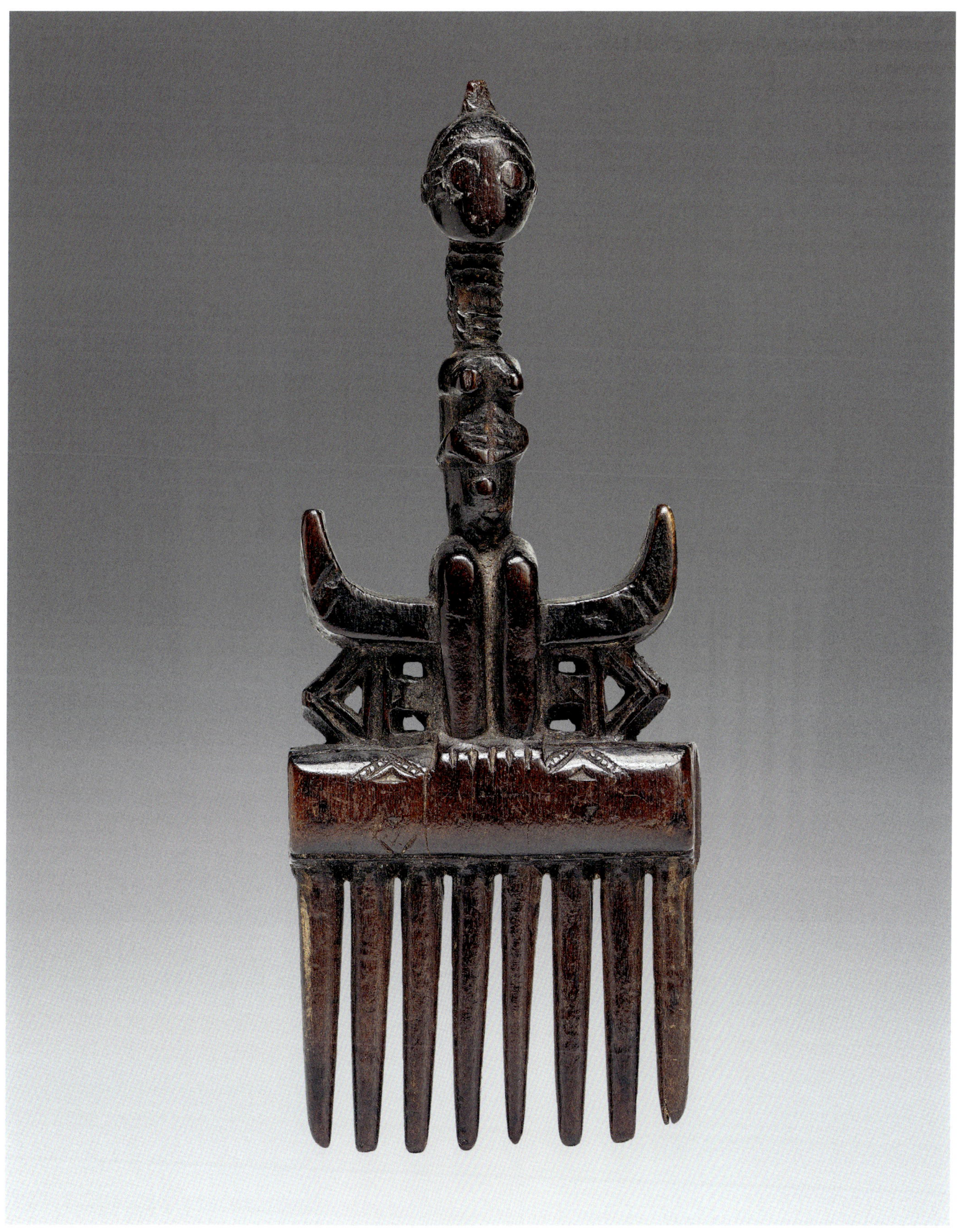

Fig. 105 Peigne | Comb
Baoulé/Attié | Baule/Attie, Akan, Côte d'Ivoire | Ivory Coast
Bois | Wood
18,5 × 7,5 cm | 18.5 × 7.5 cm

Provenance
Saramory Diabaté

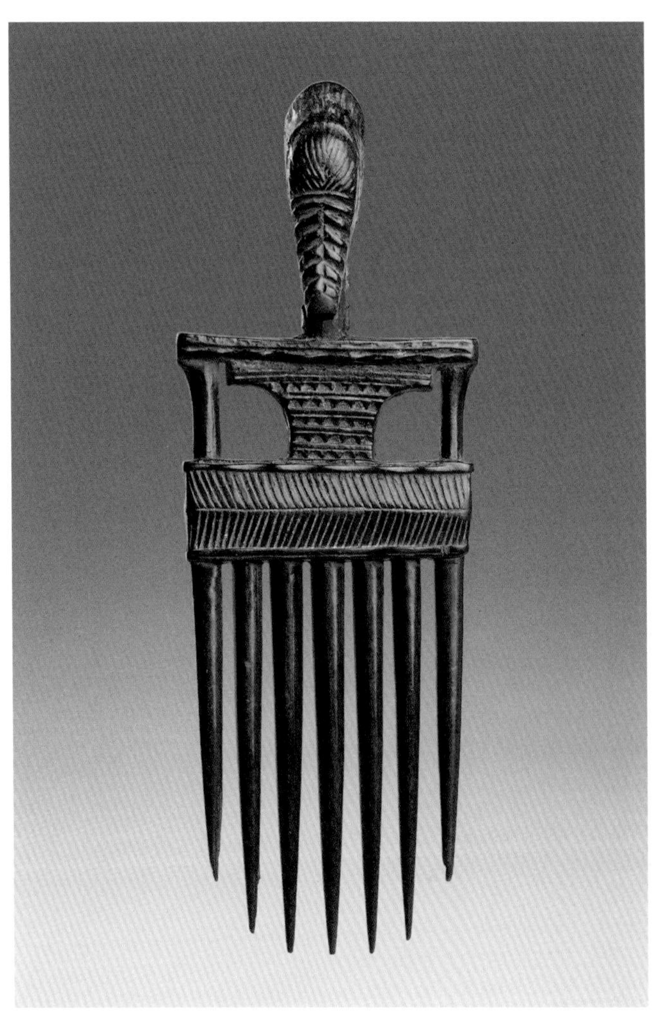

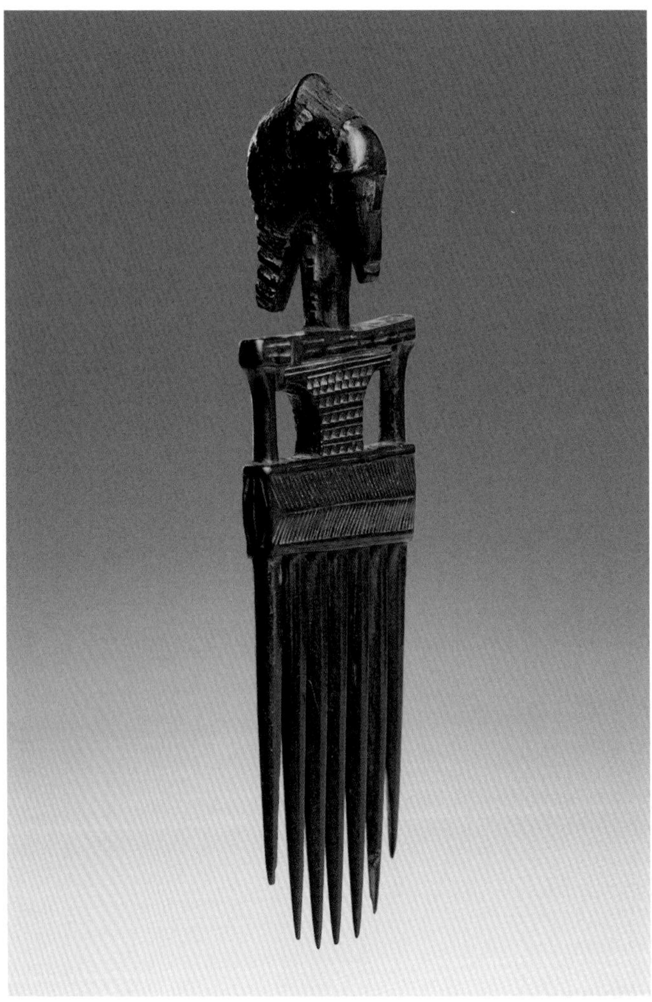

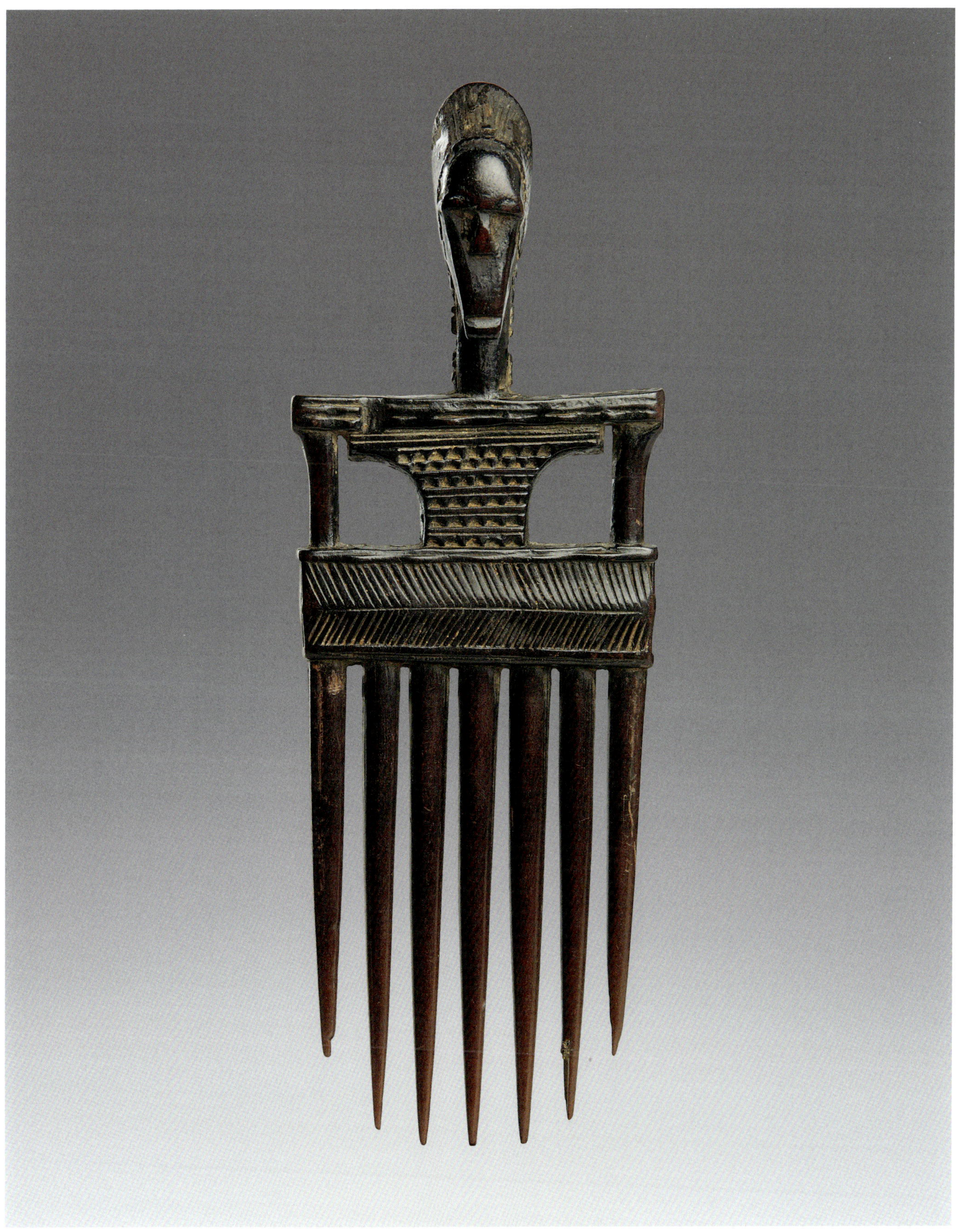

Fig. 106 Peigne | Comb
Baoulé/Attié | Baule/Attie, Akan, Côte d'Ivoire | Ivory Coast
Bois | Wood
20,6 × 6,5 cm | 20.6 × 6.5 cm

Provenance
Jean Kouamé

Publication
Jean-Yves Augel, Valentine Plisnier, *Coiffures africaines en majesté*, Sainte-Foy-lès-Lyon, Galerie Vallois, 2024, fig. 5, p. 119

Exposition | Exhibition
Sainte-Foy-lès-Lyon, Espace culturel Jean Salles, *Coiffures africaines en majesté*, 6 – 21 avril | 6 – 21 April 2024

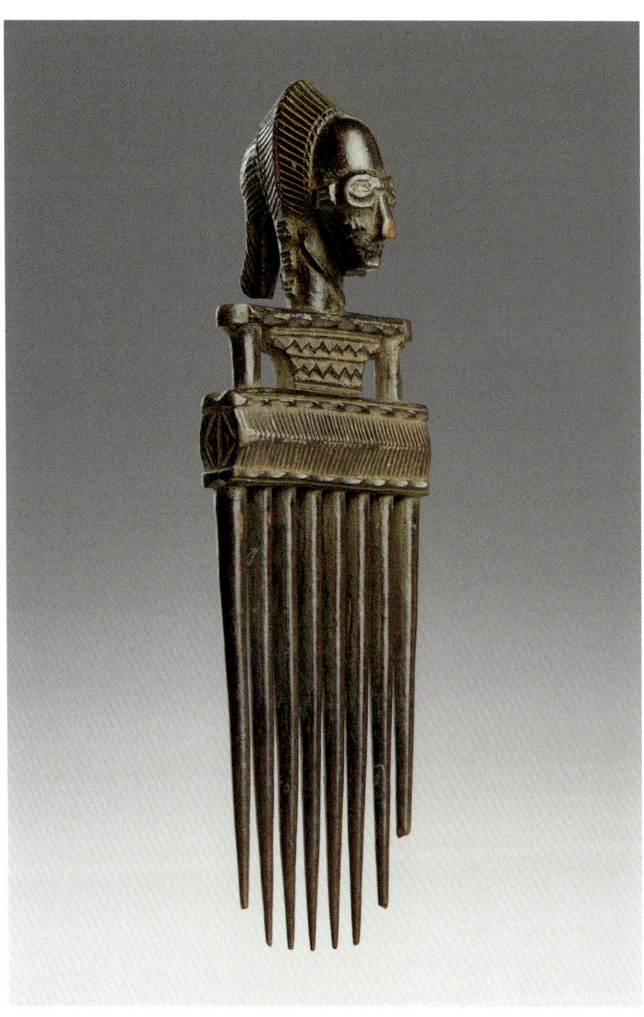

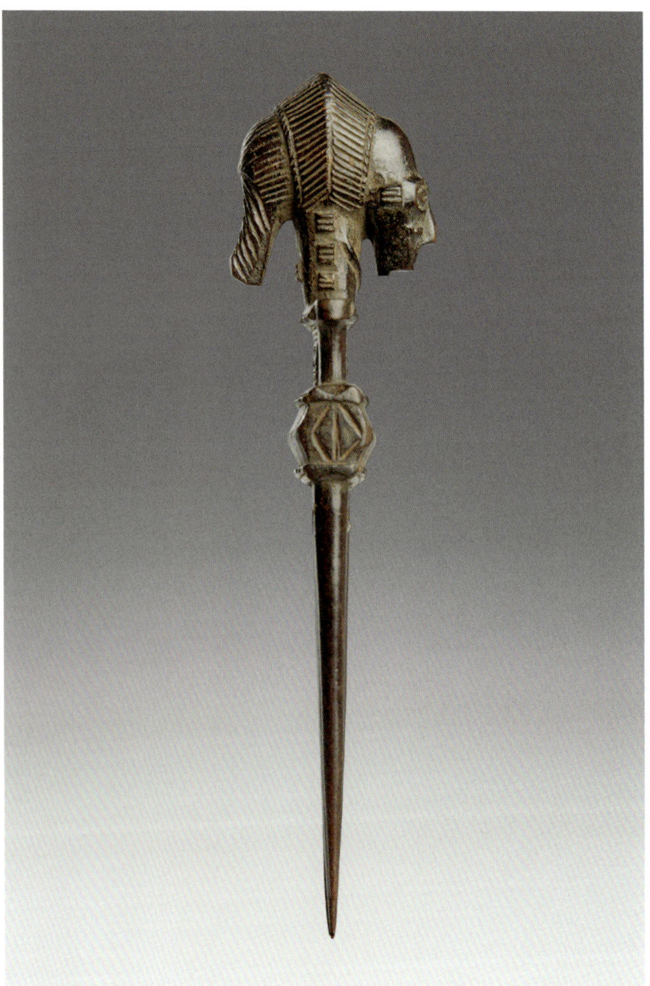

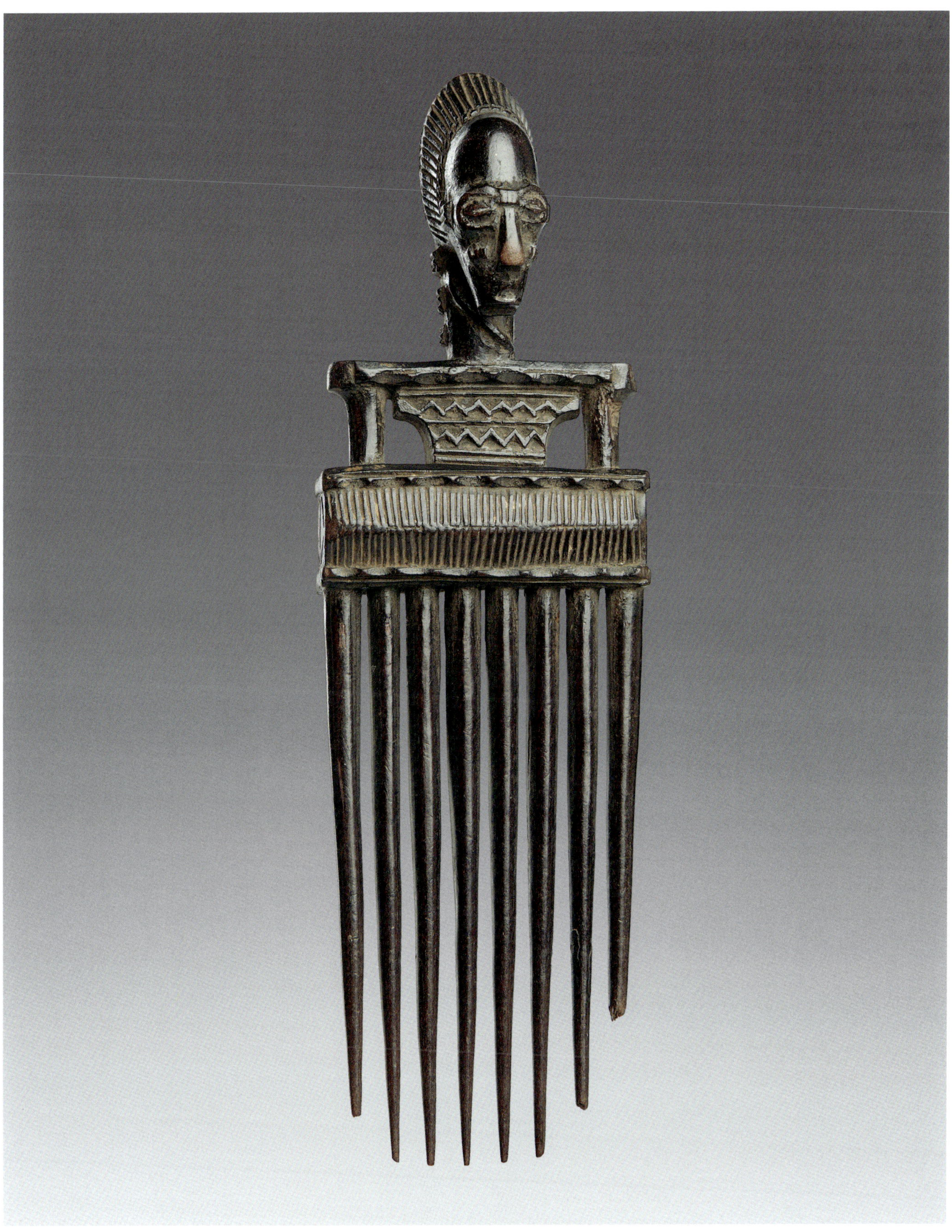

Fig. 107 Peigne | Comb
Attié | Attie, Akan, Côte d'Ivoire | Ivory Coast
Bois, or | Wood, gold
16,2 × 5 cm | 16.2 × 5 cm

Provenance
Jean-Paul Delcourt

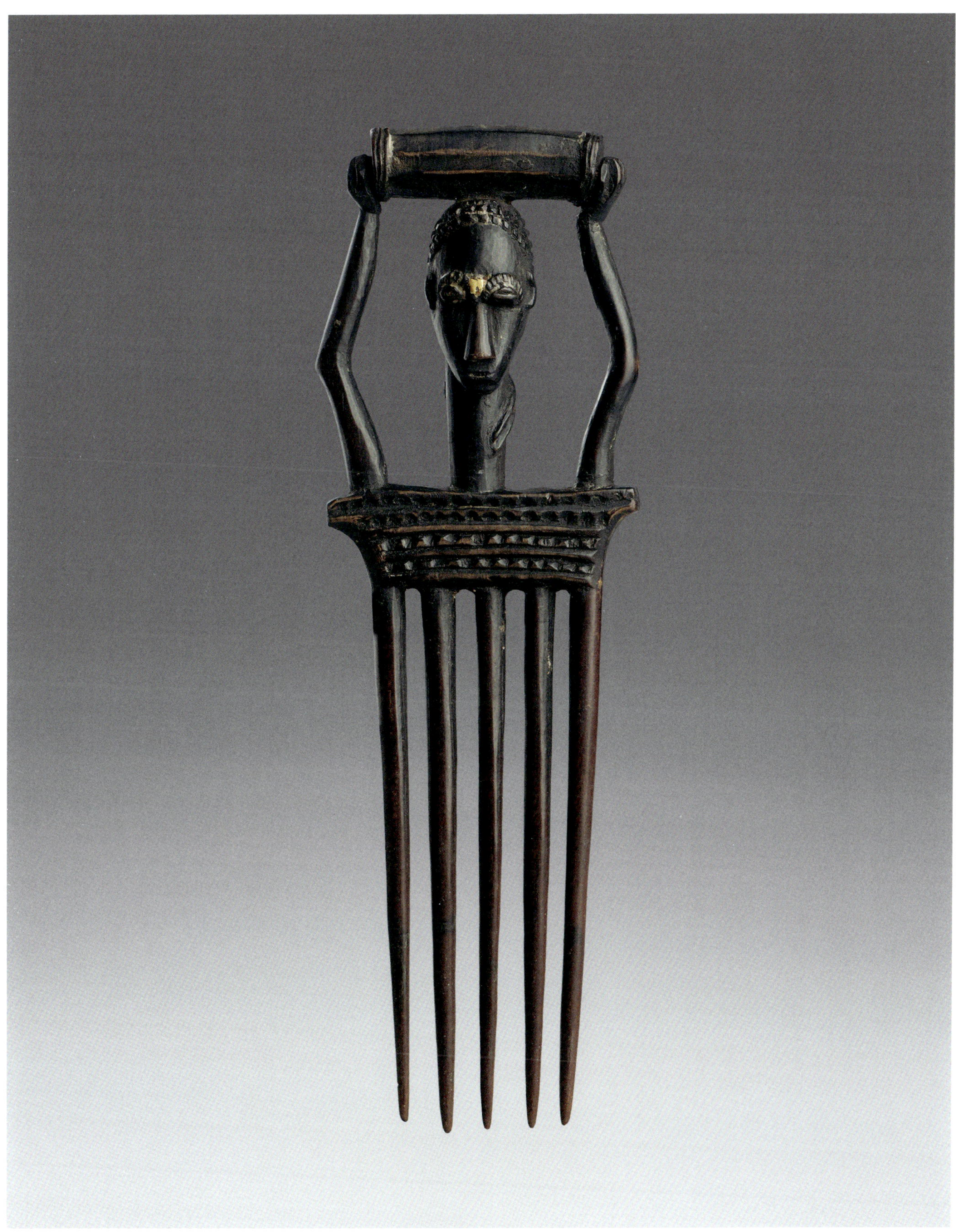

Fig. 108 Peigne | Comb
Baoulé | Baule, Akan, Côte d'Ivoire | Ivory Coast
Bois | Wood
9,5 × 2 cm | 9.5 × 2 cm

Fig. 109 Peigne | Comb
Beté | Bete, Kru, Côte d'Ivoire | Ivory Coast
Bois | Wood
32,2 × 7,4 cm | 32.2 × 7.4 cm

Provenance
Yao Yao

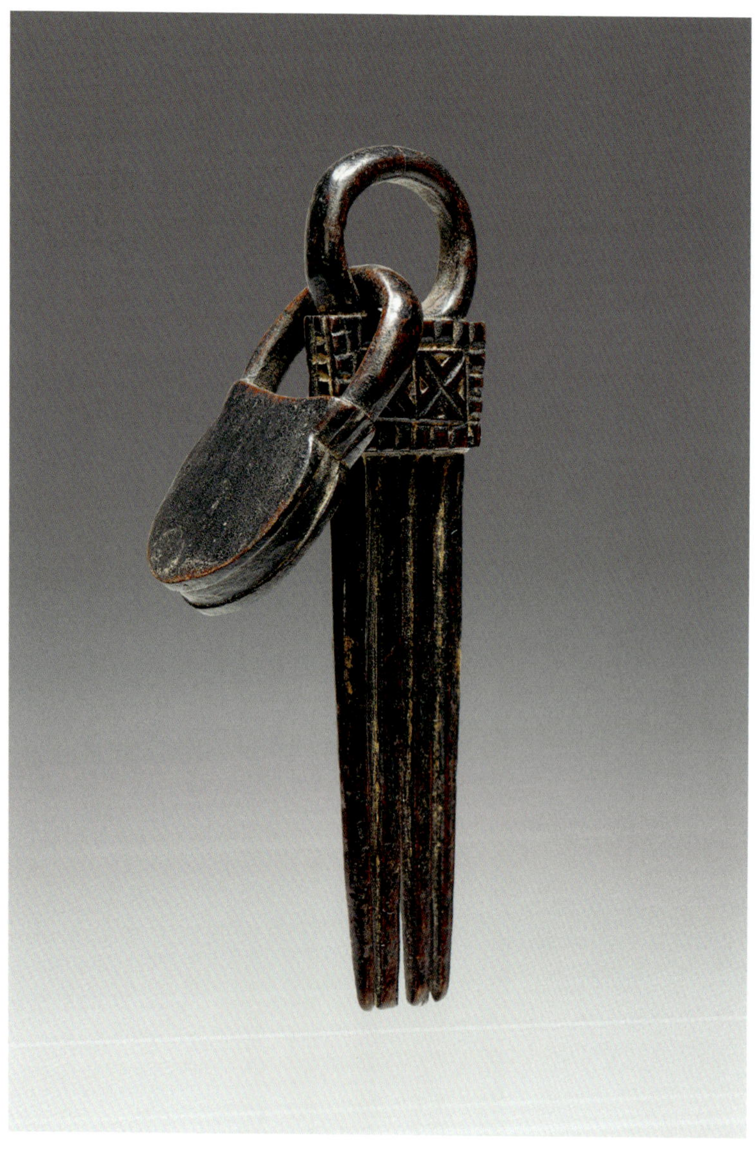

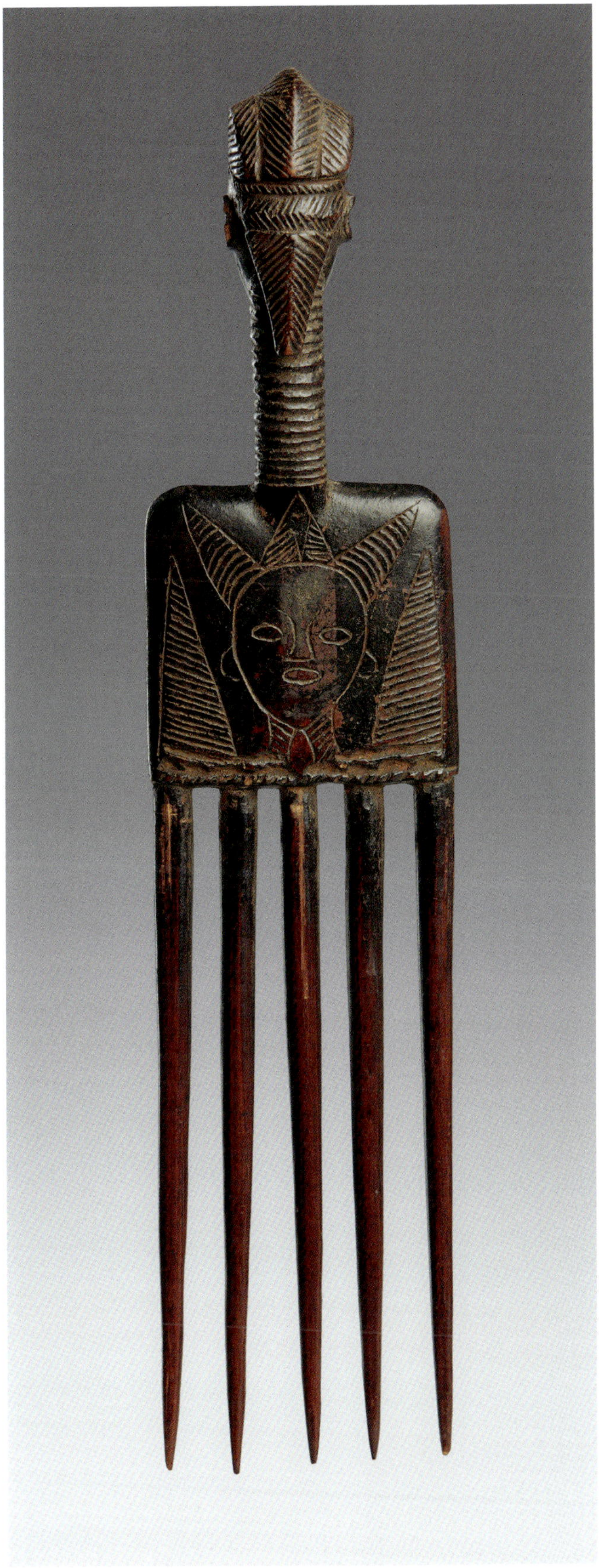

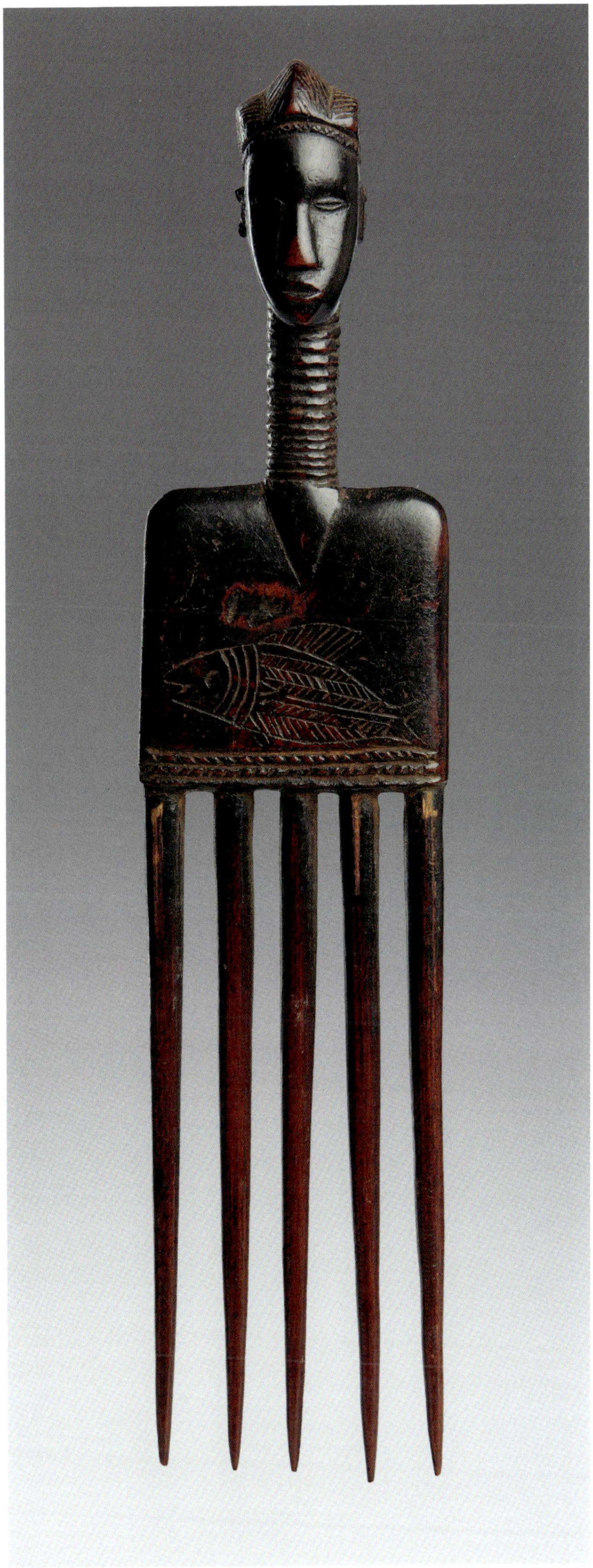

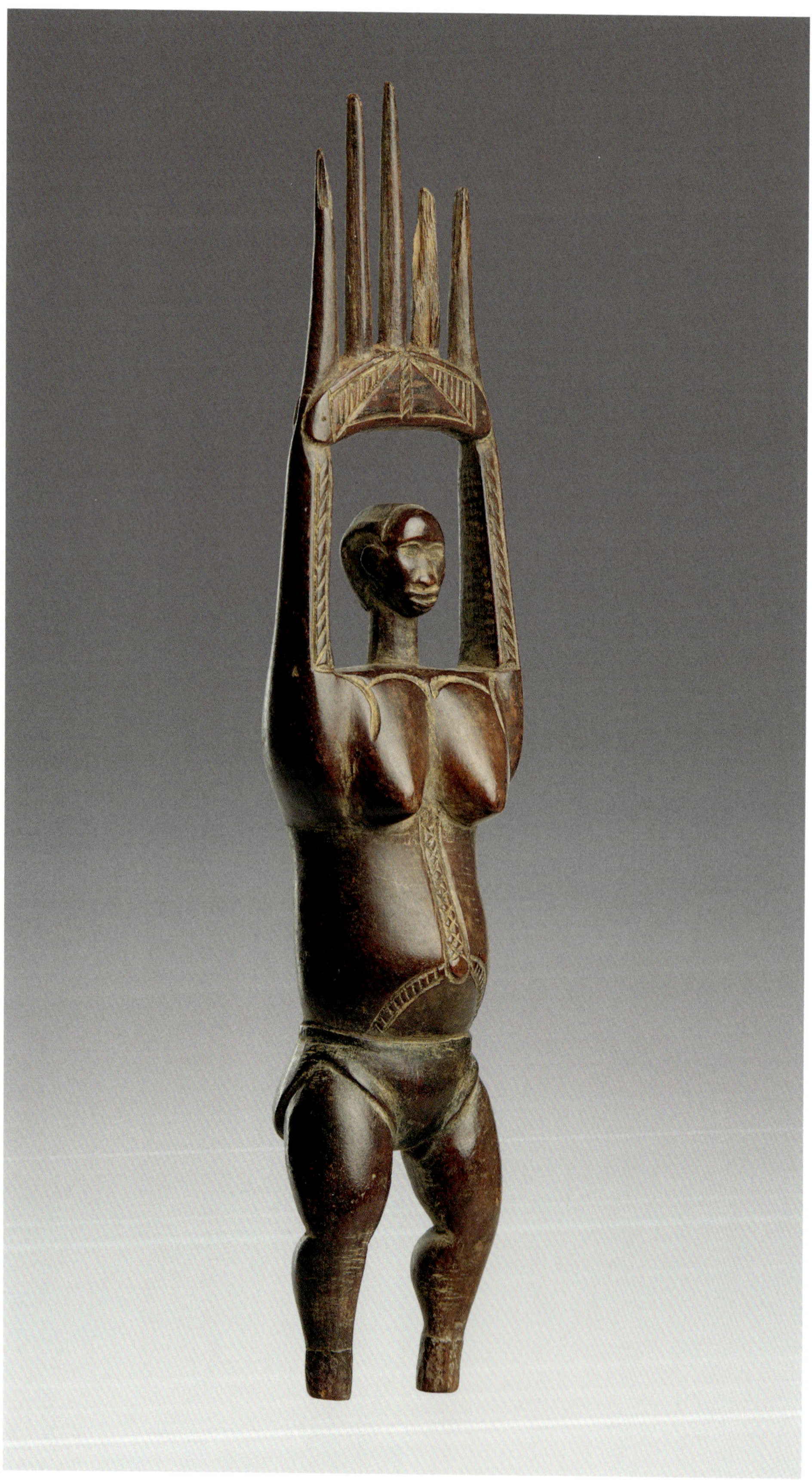

Fig. 110 Peigne | Comb
Dan, Mandé | Mande, Côte d'Ivoire | Ivory Coast
Bois | Wood
35,3 × 8 cm | 35.3 × 8 cm

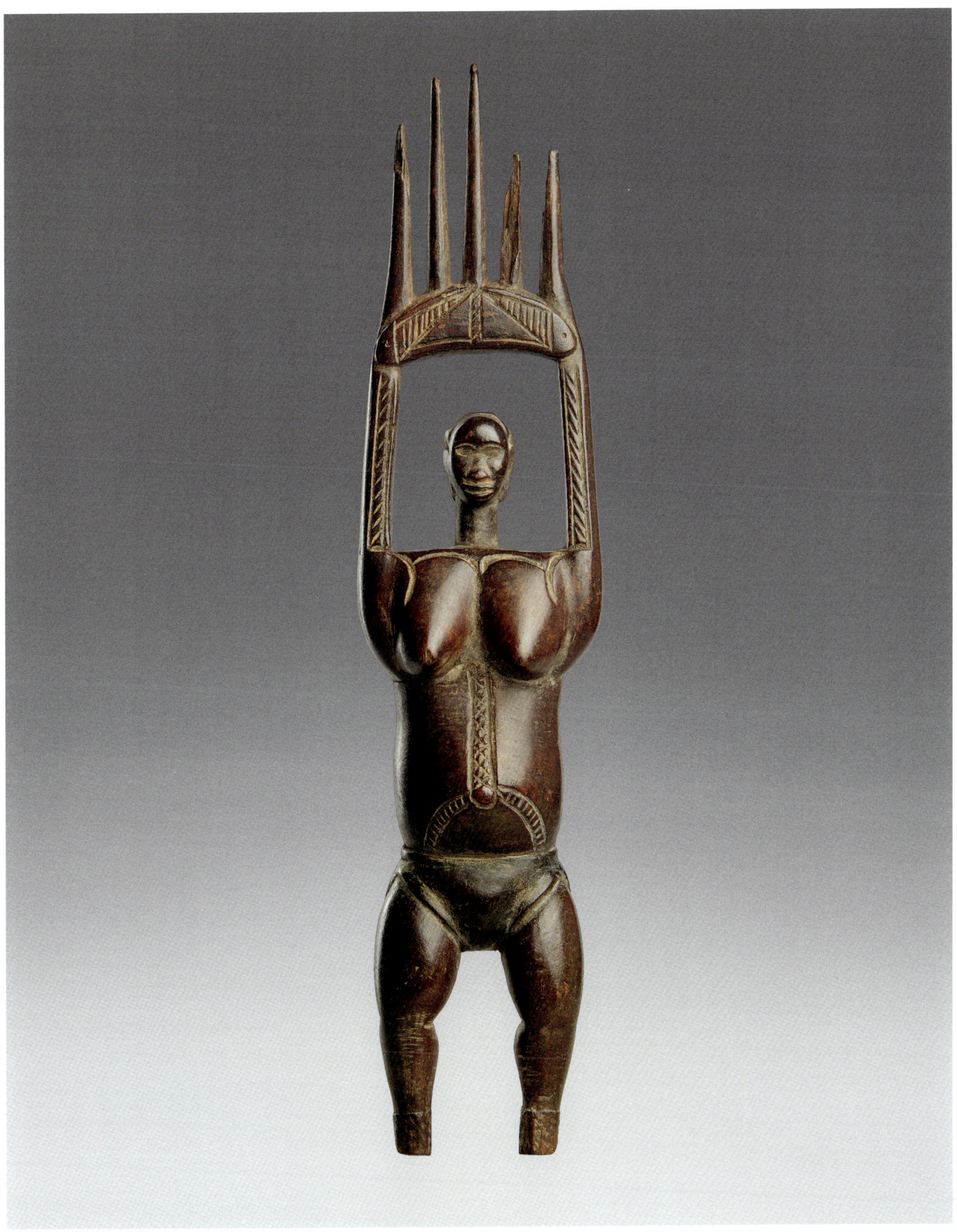

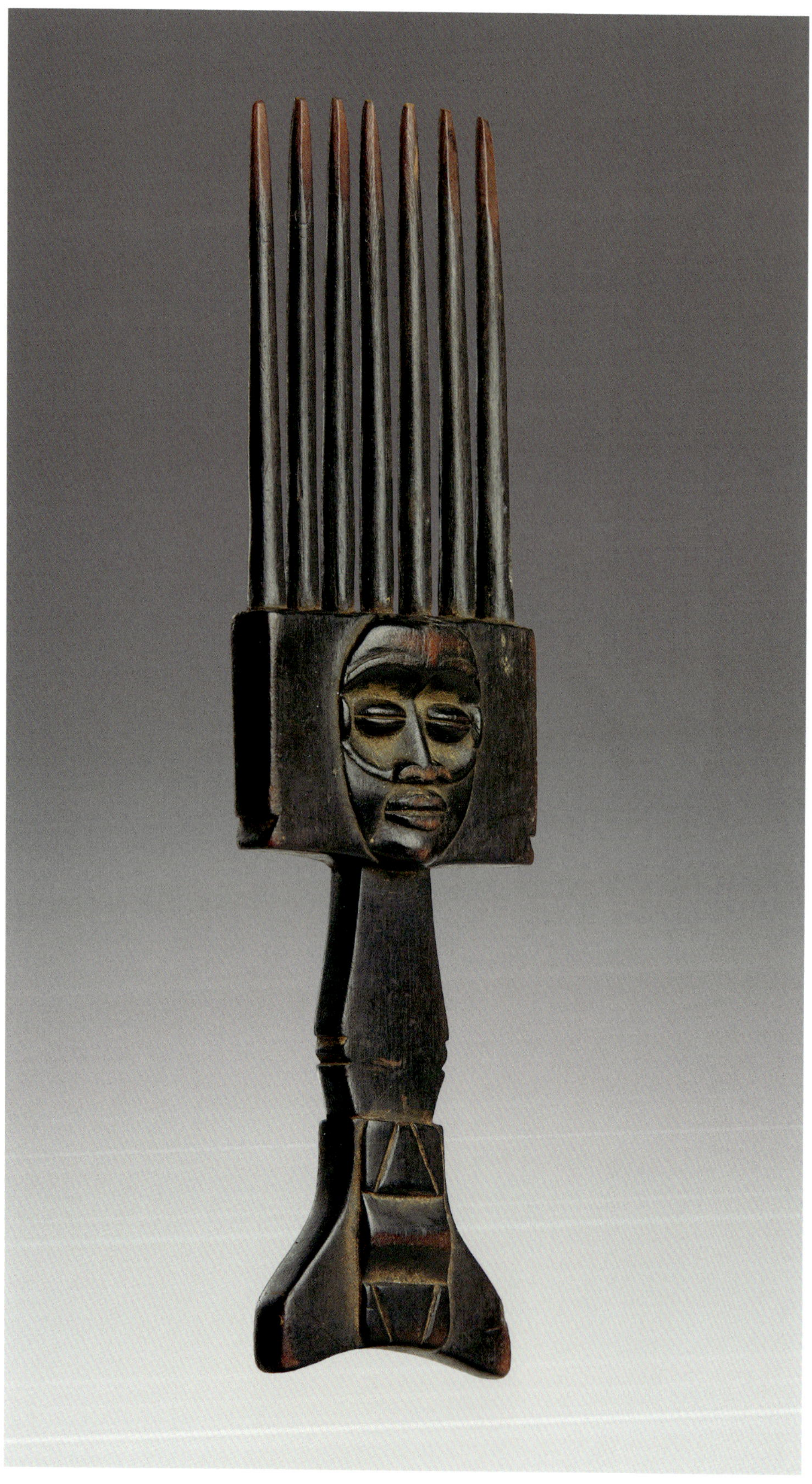

Fig. 111 Peigne | Comb
Dan, Mandé | Mande, Côte d'Ivoire | Ivory Coast
Bois | Wood
22 × 6,5 cm | 22 × 6.5 cm

Provenance
Émile Capeu

Fig. 112 Peigne | Comb
Dan, Mandé | Mande, Côte d'Ivoire | Ivory Coast
Bois | Wood
31 × 5,5 cm | 31 × 5.5 cm

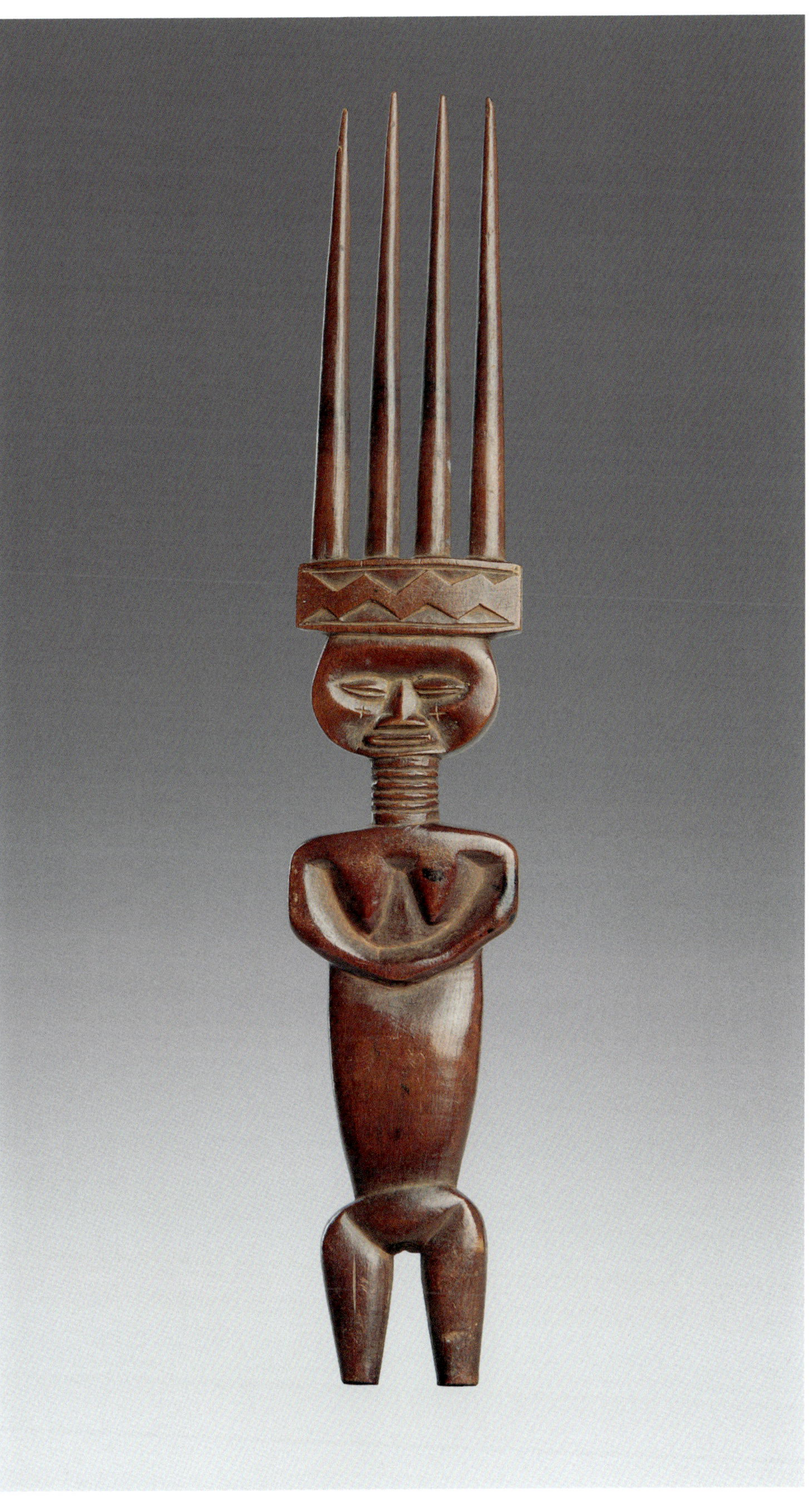

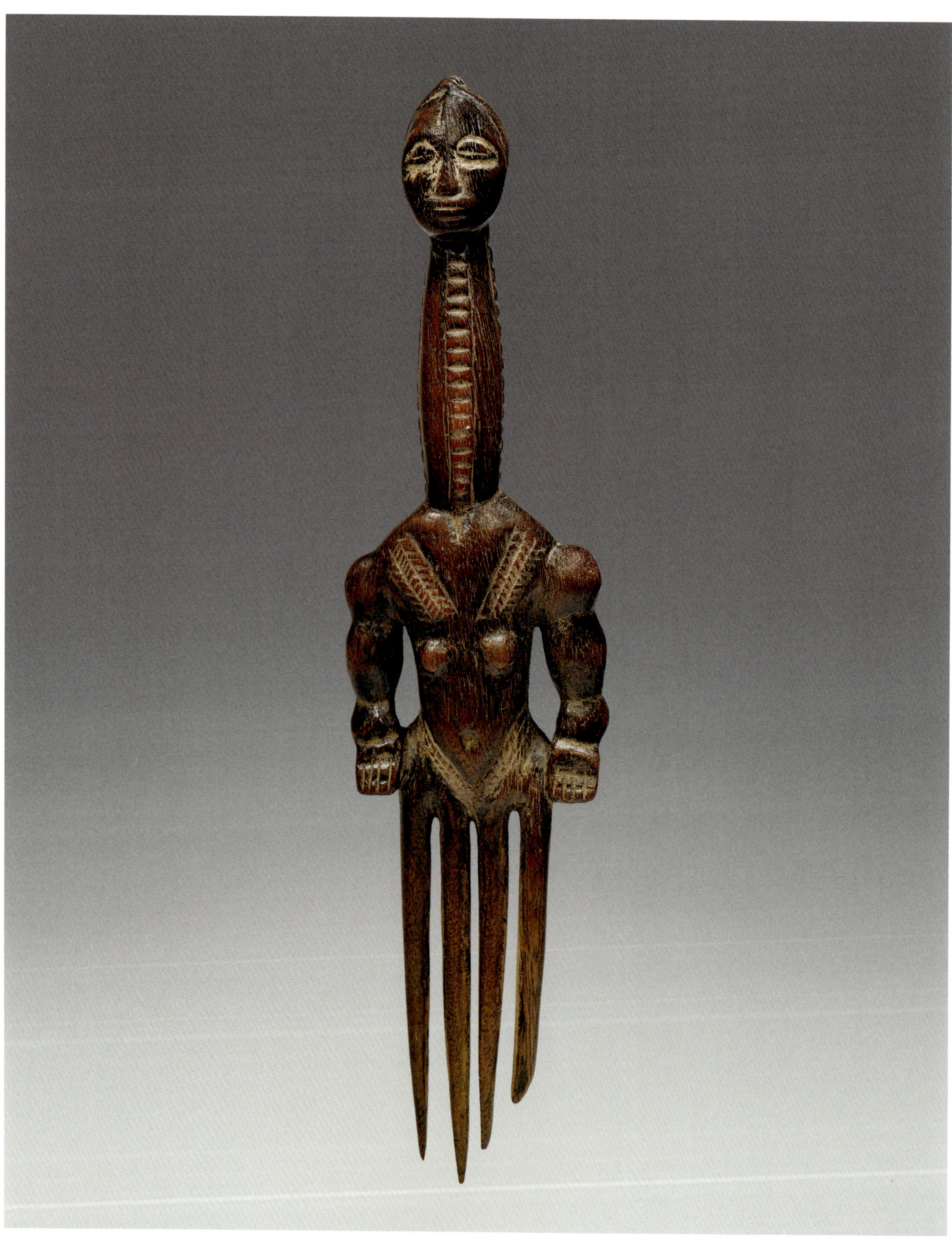

Fig. 113 Peigne | Comb
Beté | Bete, Kru, Côte d'Ivoire | Ivory Coast
Bois | Wood
26 × 6 cm

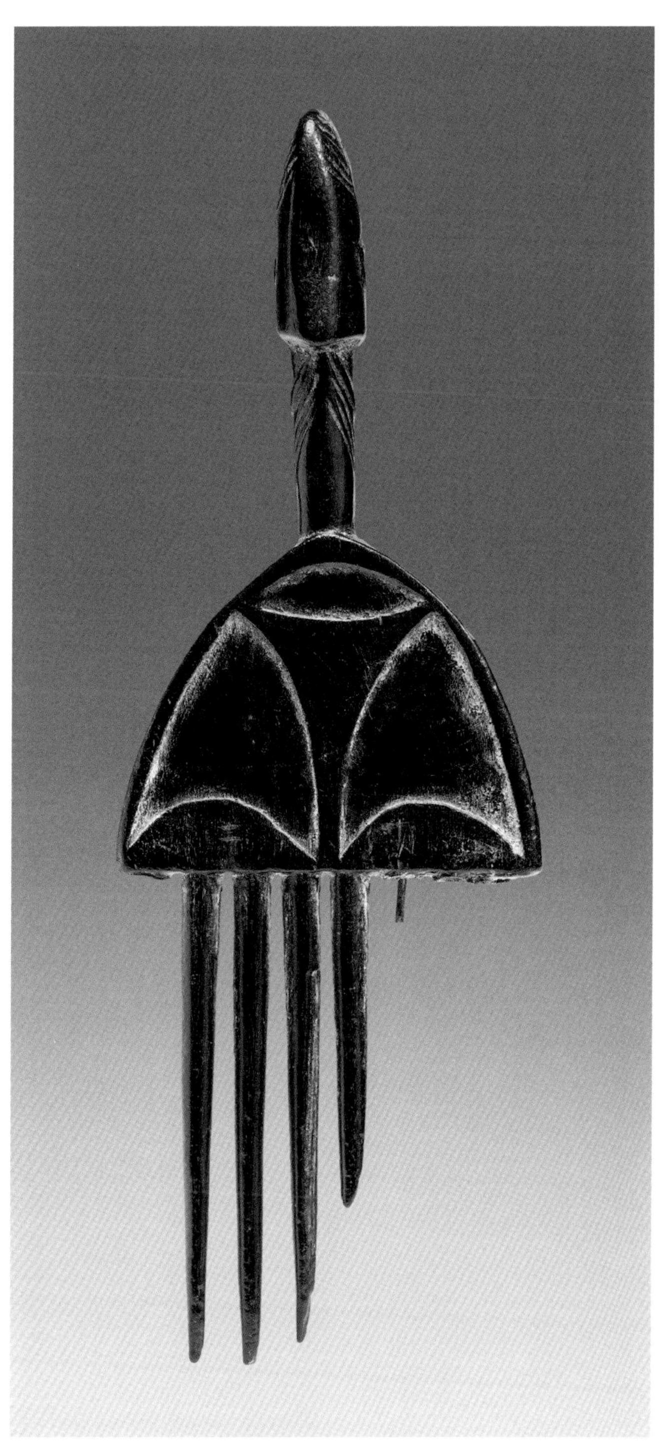

Fig. 114 Peigne | Comb
Beté | Bete, Kru, Côte d'Ivoire | Ivory Coast
Bois | Wood
15 × 5,3 cm

Provenance
Merton Simpson

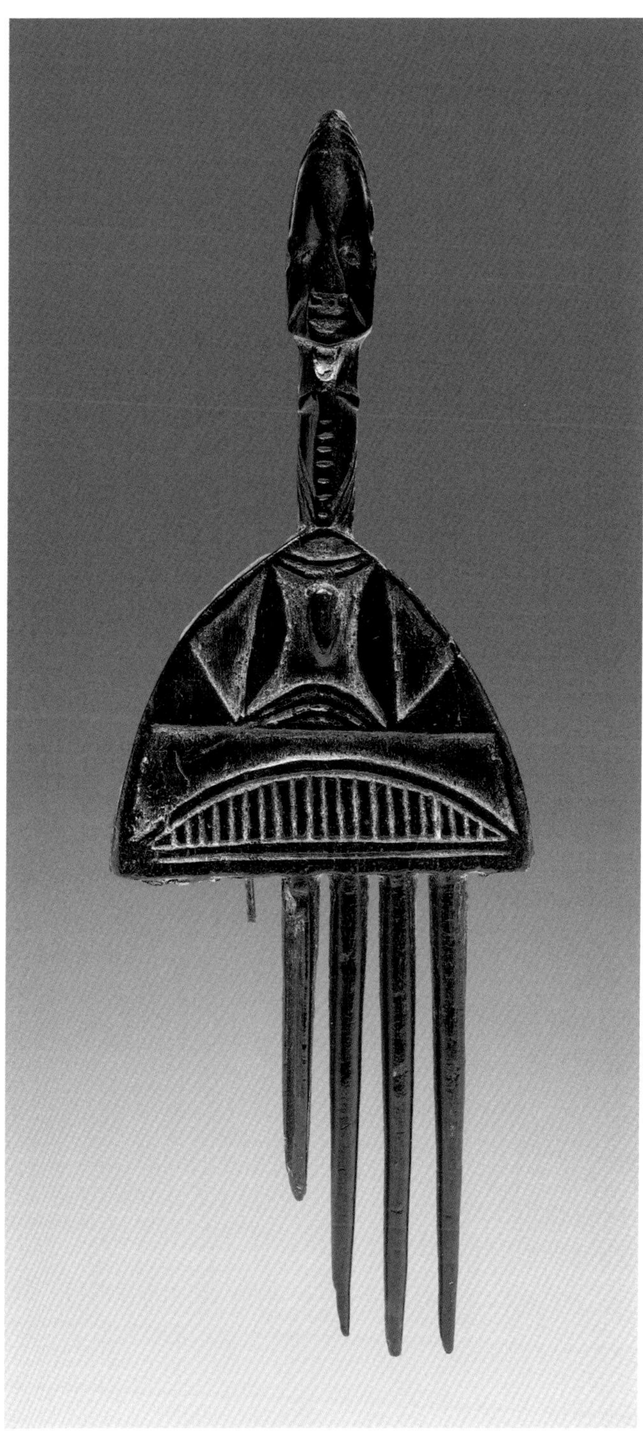

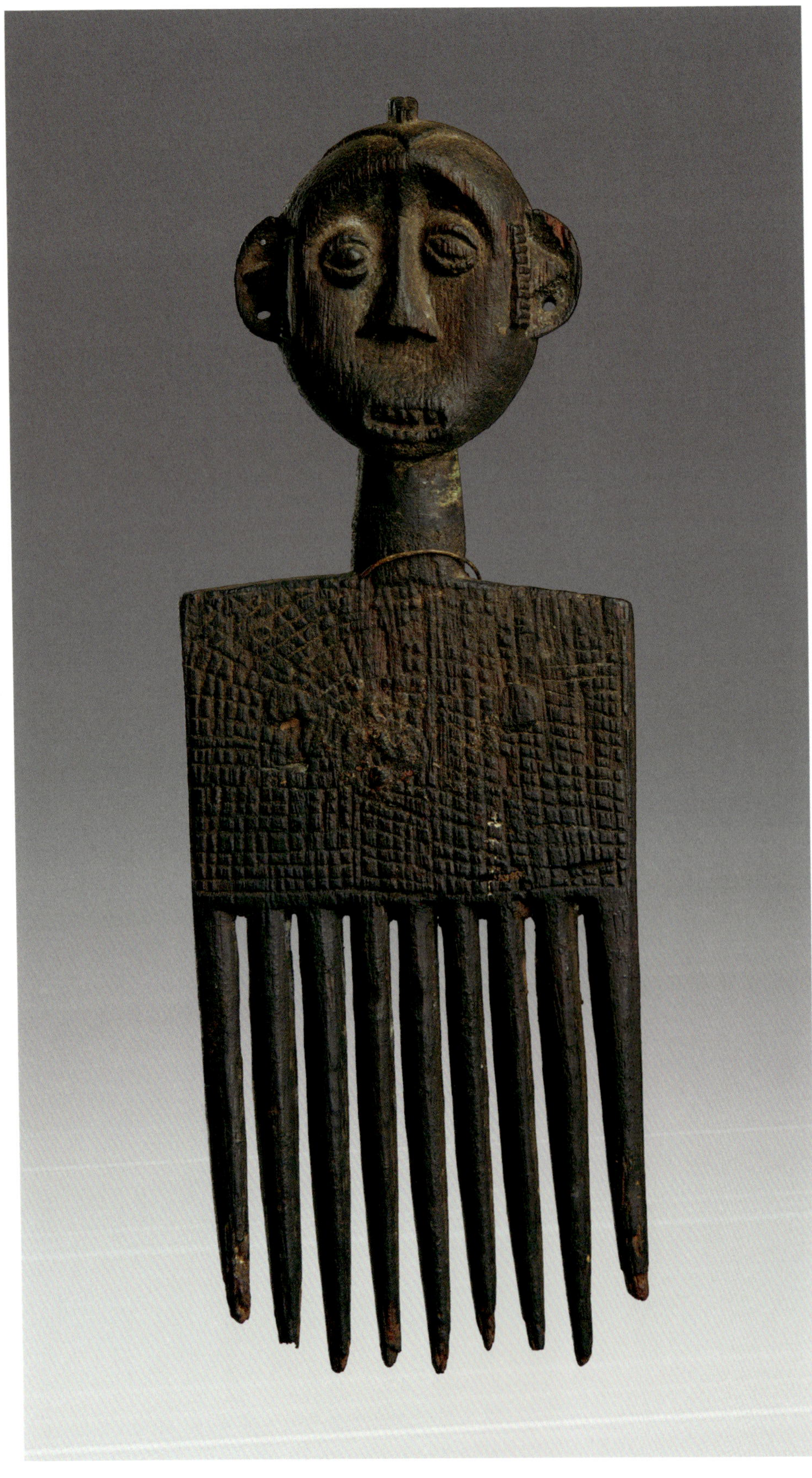

Fig. 115 Peigne | Comb
Idoma, Nigeria
Bois | Wood
23,5 × 7,8 cm | 23.5 × 7.8 cm

Provenance
El Hadj Ibrahim

Fig. 116 Peigne | Comb
Yoruba, Nigeria
Bois | Wood
24 × 10 cm

Provenance
El Hadj Ibrahim

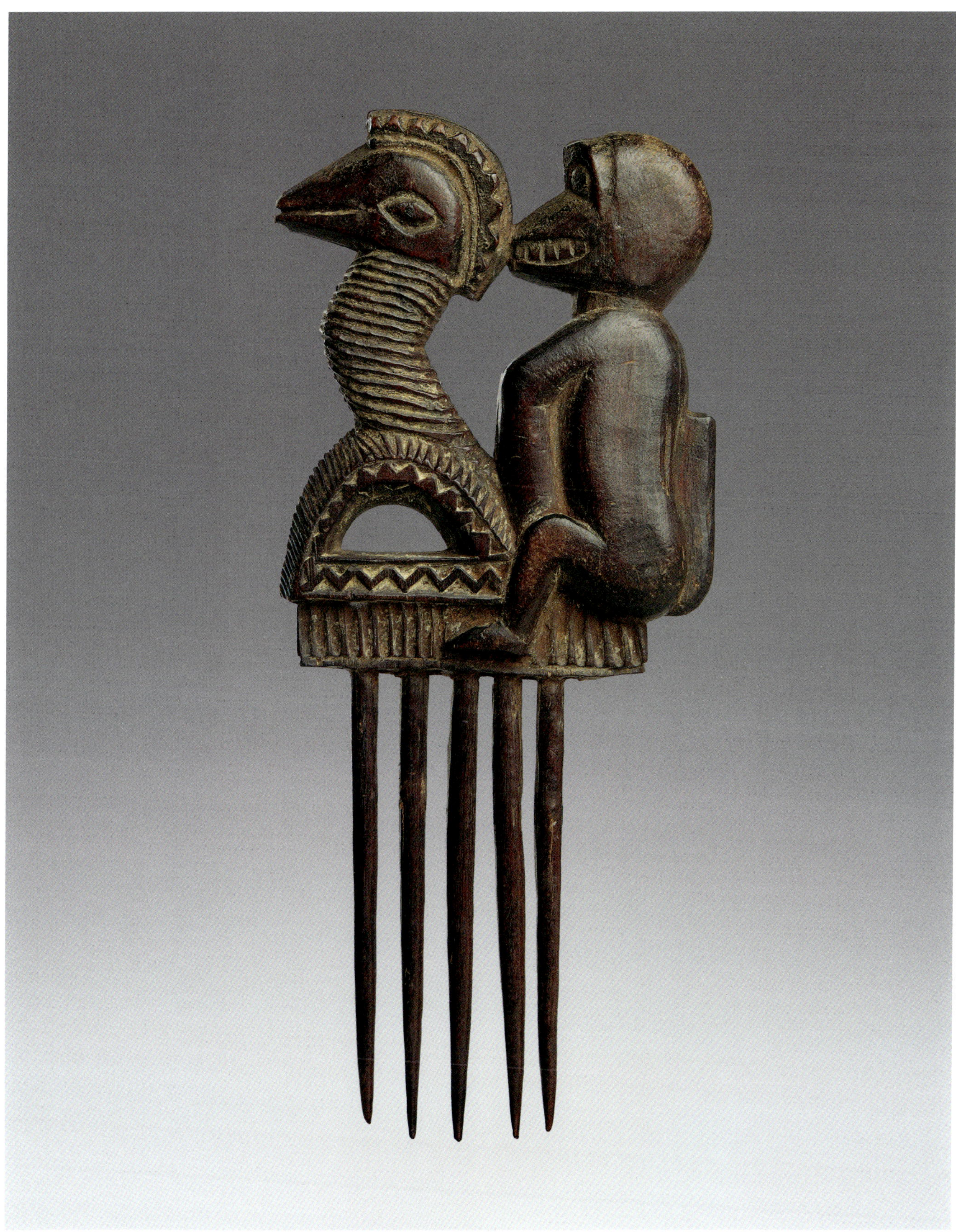

Fig. 117 Peigne | Comb
Idoma, Nigeria
Ivoire | Ivory
20 × 8,5 cm | 20 × 8.5 cm

Provenance
Amadou Yacine Thiam

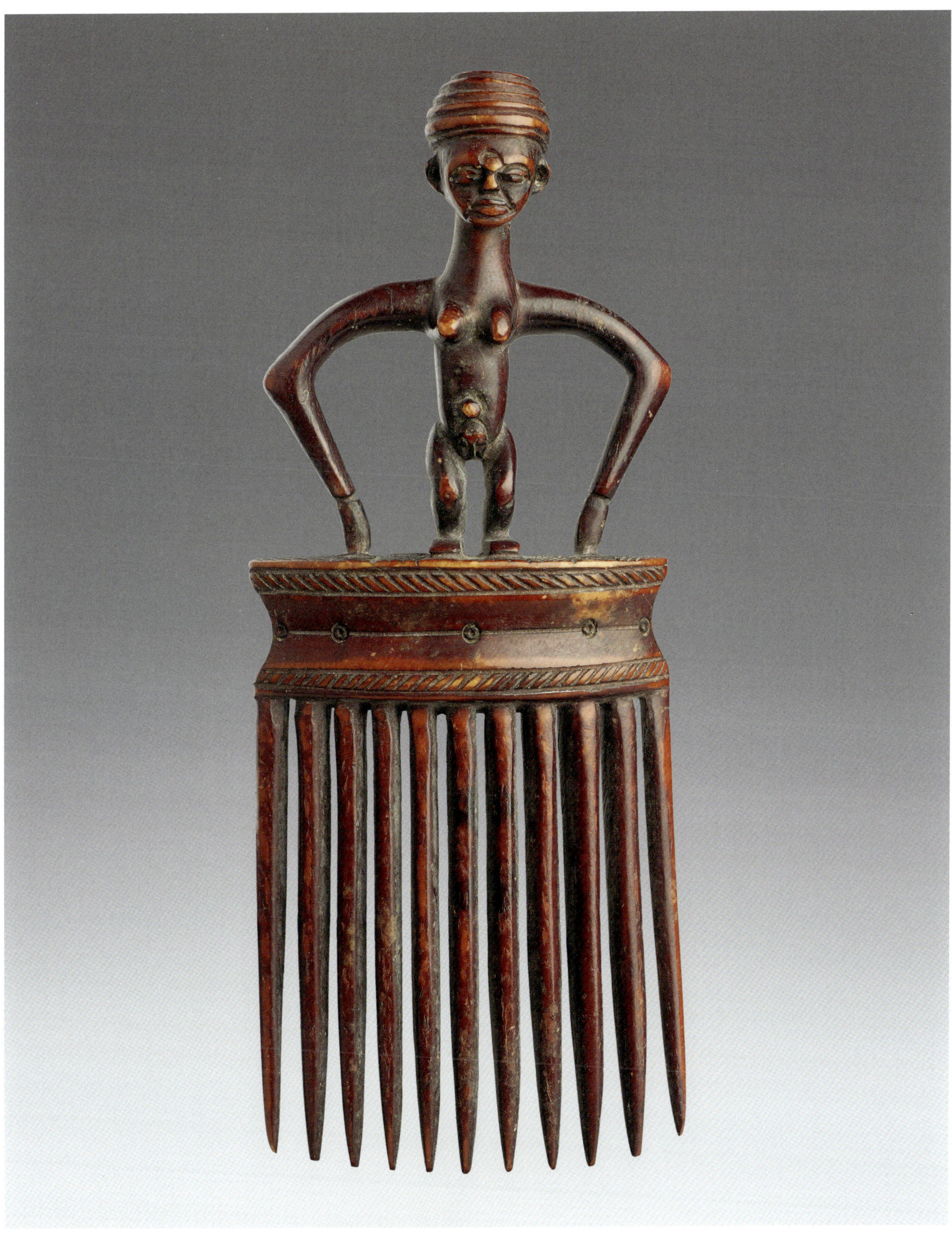

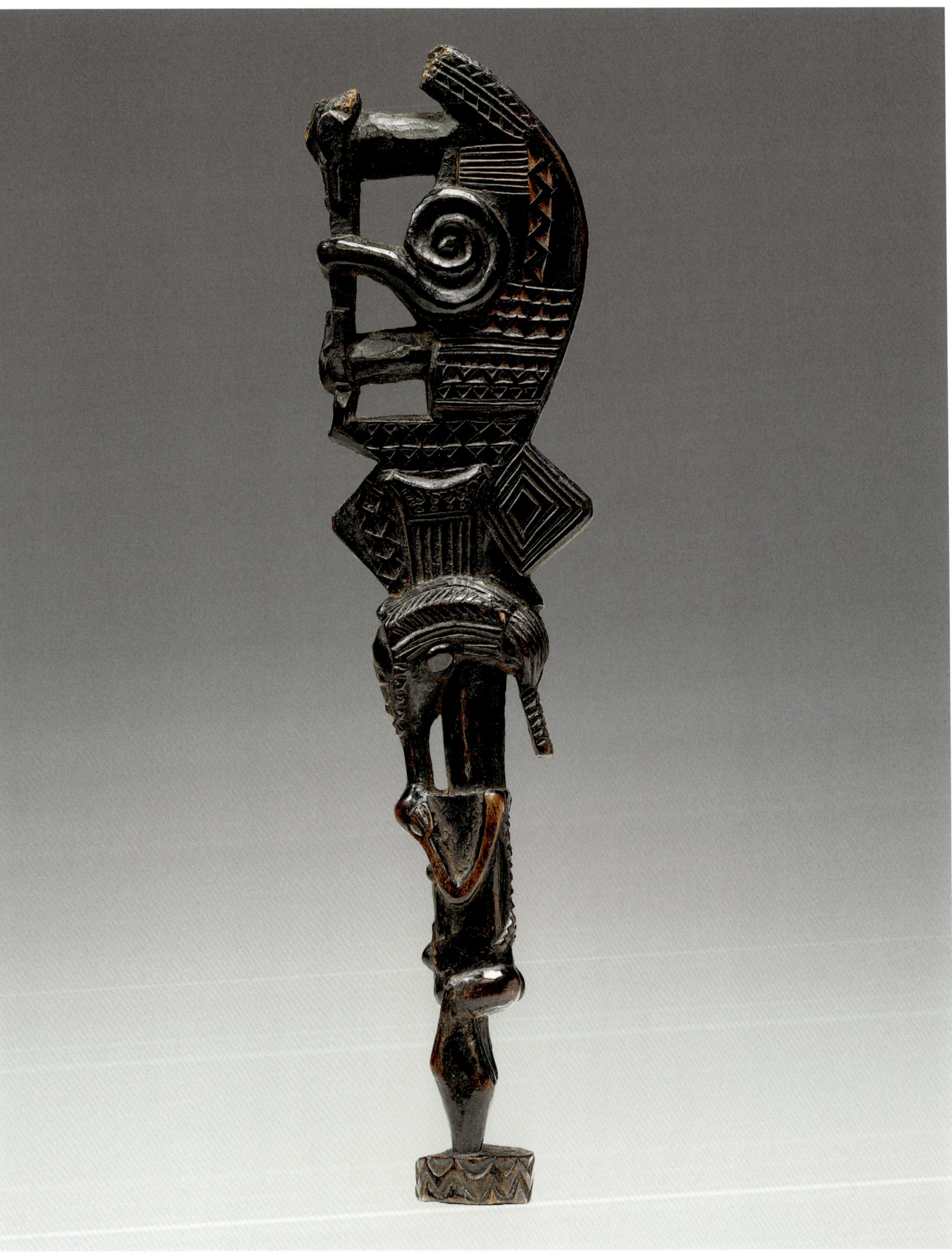

The Iconography of the Comb as a Social Marker: A Baule Music Hammer

Sarah Boukamel and Najwa Borro

A music hammer depicting a man with a comb
Baule, Akan, Ivory Coast
Wood
24 × 6 cm

Provenance
Vente Loudmer-Poulain, Paris, *Arts Primitifs*, 22 novembre 1979

Music hammers (*lawle, lawre*, or *ndawli*) were part of the sacred paraphernalia used by Baule diviner-healers as they performed their activities designed to solve personal or collective problems. The diviner (*komyen, komyen fwè*, or *ngoïmanfwê*) would use this type of hammer to beat a regular rhythm on a small metal gong to encourage the spirits of nature (*asie usu*) to manifest themselves and to induce or prolong a state of trance. Possessed by one or more spirits, the diviner would turn into an *awèfwè*, a 'frontiersman', enabling him to act as the spirits' mouthpiece as he made his highly theatrical predictions.

The object's effectiveness is also influenced by its aesthetic appeal. The *lawle* was one of the rare artefacts belonging to the *komyen* to be made taking such care over aesthetic considerations. The way it was carved and its decoration thus constituted a powerful statement, reflecting its owner's status and the skill of the person who made it: the greater the *komyen*'s renown, the greater the power wielded by these sacred objects made by a talented sculptor. All the object's different aspects – the painstaking attention to detail in the conformation, the judicious choice of decoration (most clearly seen in older specimens), and the choice of iconography – combine to underline the power of its owner. The male figure that makes up the hammer's handle holds in his hands his long, round-tipped plaited beard coated with shea oil, which is a sign of age and a privilege of dignitaries. In Baule iconography, the image of a man pensively stroking his beard suggests respectability and authority, as well as wisdom and introspection. The care taken in reproducing the elaborate coiffure, such as the pigtail hanging over the nape of the neck (*kplolè*), an example of the hairstyles of the past, emphasises his imposing dignity, as do the scars scattered over his face and body, esteemed marks of beauty.

A seven-toothed comb, a highly symbolic object among the Akan, stands upright on the top of the figure's head, completing the ornamentation of the coiffure. Although the fine lines of its seven tapering teeth stand out boldly, the comb is only visible on one side, which is not to say that the object is merely accidental. Like the representation of a coiled snake, which is a common symbol in Baule art, a comb depicted on an object also serves to highlight that object's enigmatic qualities, revealing only a few details of its iconography at a time to the viewer, who has to look at it from different angles to see the others. This head ornament set on a complex male hairstyle thus acts as a declaration of its owner's personal identity and social standing.

Lastly, the top of the *lawle* is decorated with two buffalo-head mask-helmets shown facing each other. They are probably *bonu amuin* incantation masks that summon fearsome supernatural beings. These sacred masks belonging to male associations had a preventative function and helped society run smoothly, exercising a civilising role that enabled hostile forces to be blocked. This iconographic combination has to do with the need to ensure order is maintained within the group and with the crucial importance of the *komyen*, the only person who is able to operate in the realm of the sacred and make the invisible intelligible.

SELECTED BIBLIOGRAPHY

Barbier Jean-Paul, ed. *Arts de la Côte d'Ivoire dans les collections Barbier-Mueller*. Volumes 1 and 2. Exhibition catalogue. Geneva: Musée Barbier-Mueller, 1993.

Boyer Alain-Michel. 'L'art baoulé'. In Barbier J.-P. *Arts de la Côte d'Ivoire dans les collections Barbier-Mueller*. Volume 1. Geneva: Musée Barbier-Mueller, 1993. 302–67.

Boyer Alain-Michel. *Baule*. Milan: 5 Continents Editions, 2008.

Boyer Alain-Michel. 'L'Afrique et la pérennité de l'immatériel'. *Arts & Cultures* 18 (2017): 115–16.

Fischer Eberhard and Lorenz Homberger. *Les Maîtres de la sculpture de Côte d'Ivoire*. Exhibition catalogue. Paris: Musée du quai Branly/Skira, 2015.

Garrard Timothy. 'Les Baoulé: une introduction'. In Barbier J.-P. *Arts de la Côte d'Ivoire dans les collections Barbier-Mueller*. Volume 1. Geneva: Musée Barbier-Mueller, 1993. 290–301.

Falgayrettes-Leveau ed. *Chefs-d'œuvre d'Afrique dans les collections du musée Dapper*. Paris: musée Dapper, 2015.

LaGamma Alisa. *Art and Oracle: African Art and Rituals of Divination*. Exhibition catalogue. New York: Metropolitan Museum of Art, 2000.

Vogel M. Susan. *Baule: African Art, Western Eyes*. New Haven: Yale University Art Gallery, 1997.

Vogel M. Susan. *L'Art baoulé du visible et de l'invisible*. Paris: Adam Biro, 1999.

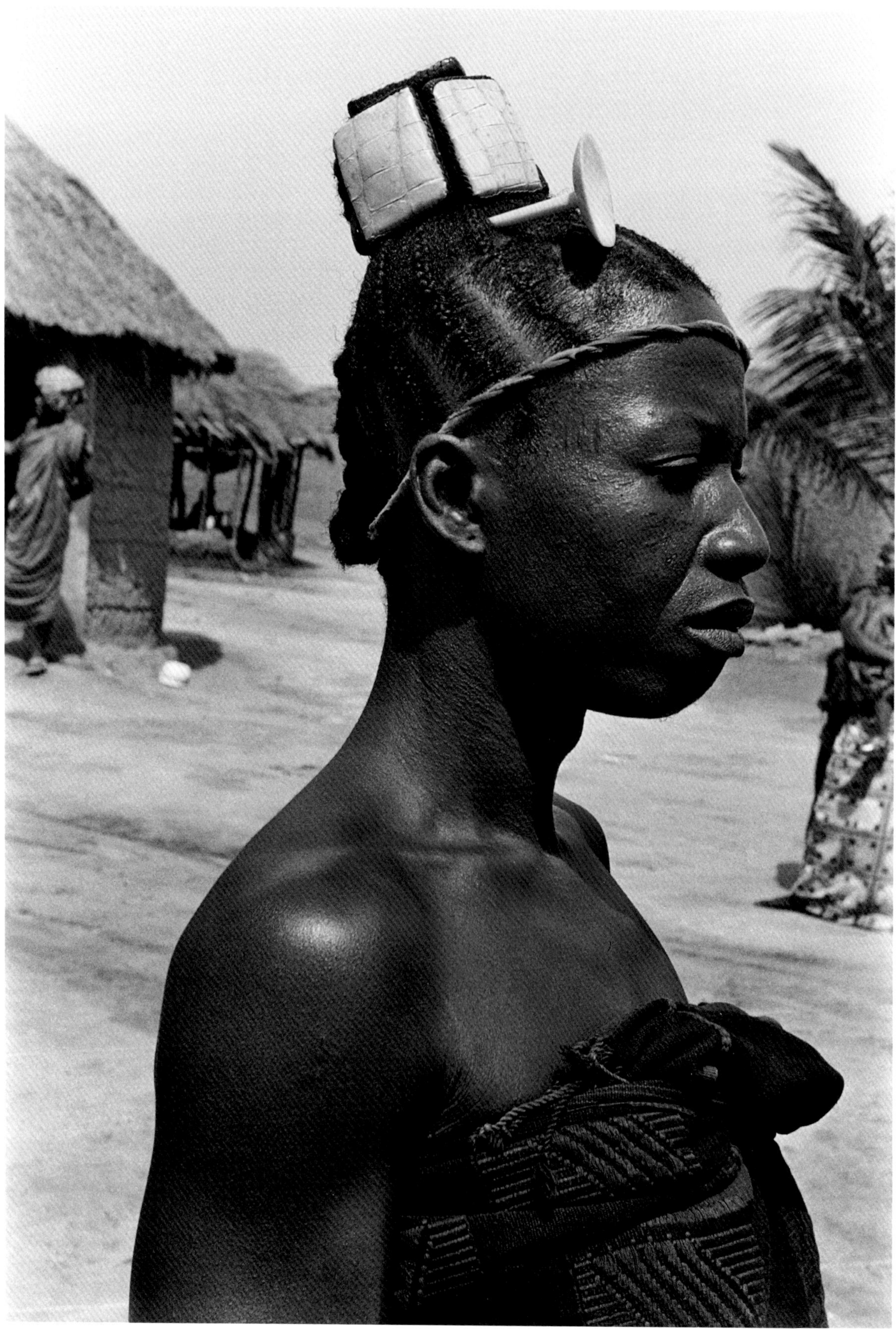

Celebrating Approval: A Guro Mask

Sarah Boukamel and Najwa Borro

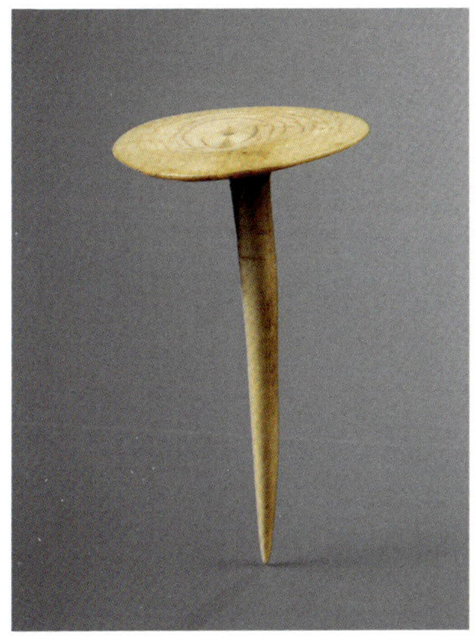

Pin, Guro, Ivory Coast
Ivory
9 × 6 cm

This extraordinarily narrow Guro mask, looking miniaturised like an ornament, is thought to be an example of the kind of mask worn during celebrations and, as such, visible to all. The dancer would appear standing on stilts clad in a spectacular costume made of plant fibres, making a great visual impact.[1] Fallen into disuse in the early 1930s, it is believed to have been replaced by the Flali mask a few decades later.[2] Eberhard Fischer has identified six types[3] of Zuhu mask, in his view all originally from the northern Guro lands.

A masterly example of distilled subtlety, this mask consists of a base section depicting a face, topped by a superstructure[4] portraying a high-ranking young woman. The face is carved on a tapered oval and surmounted by a standing female figure tightly gripping two carved antelope horns emerging from the forehead, creating the impression she is riding the animal. The fine, almost sharp nasal ridge joins the forehead scarification, which begins very high, where the two horns meet. This medial line follows the rounded movement of the forehead and stretches as far as the tip of the nose, which lacks any evident nostrils and is slightly upturned, creating a profile that is both angular and particularly refined – further accentuated by the dark lacquered patina that is typical of ancient Guro pieces. The mouth is picked out with thin lips under a marked philtrum. Within the mouth can be seen a series of pointed teeth, recalling an ancient aesthetic practice popular among the Guro, as does the hairstyle.[5]

The great care taken in carving the female figure's hairstyle (six plaited buns meeting in an impressive pointed ponytail) underlines the figure's social status. These distinctive features are designed to prompt the onlooker's admiration, and such an intricate coiffure could never have been worn when working in the fields. At the nape of the woman's long, powerful neck are three keloid scars; further lines criss-cross her back, forming a rhombus pattern – all signs pertaining to a leading personage. The highlight of the entire composition is an ivory pin inserted in the coiffure – a practice found essentially among the Guro and Baule and here reproduced on a smaller scale. This startling ornament adds a further focal point and creates a contrast between the dark patina and the bright ivory, making an eye-catching statement and turning its wearer into a highlight. Aside from the ornament's sophistication, the attention paid to all the details and their tiniest features points to an aesthetic that focuses on the small-scale and draws the eye towards another form of monumentality.

The combination of this mask's age, iconography, and style make it an extremely rare object and one of a very restricted body of works.[6] There is very little ethnographic information regarding the origin and use of this mask. Although the assumed place of origin, Gohitafla, and its genre associate it with the northern Guro, the forehead scarification,[7] the scars on the cheeks, and the three incised lines marking the hairline suggest an undeniable Bete influence. Unlike Bete-Guro works, which tend to be much more rugged,

Woman adorned with an ivory pin
Guro village, Ivory Coast, 1968
CC by Hans Himmelheber,
Inv. FHH 343-29, Museum Rietberg, Zürich
www.africa-art-archive.ch

Mask
Guro, Ivory Coast
Wood, ivory (removable pin)
39.5 × 9.5 cm

Provenance
Merton Simpson

Publications
Antoine Ferrari de la Salle, *Le Taureau qui aime les masques d'hommes. Regards sur Samir Borro*, Oser Dire Éditions, Bruxelles, Beyrouth, 2018, p. 69; François Neyt, *Trésors de Côte d'Ivoire*, Fonds Mercator, Anvers, 2014, p. 91, fig. 57

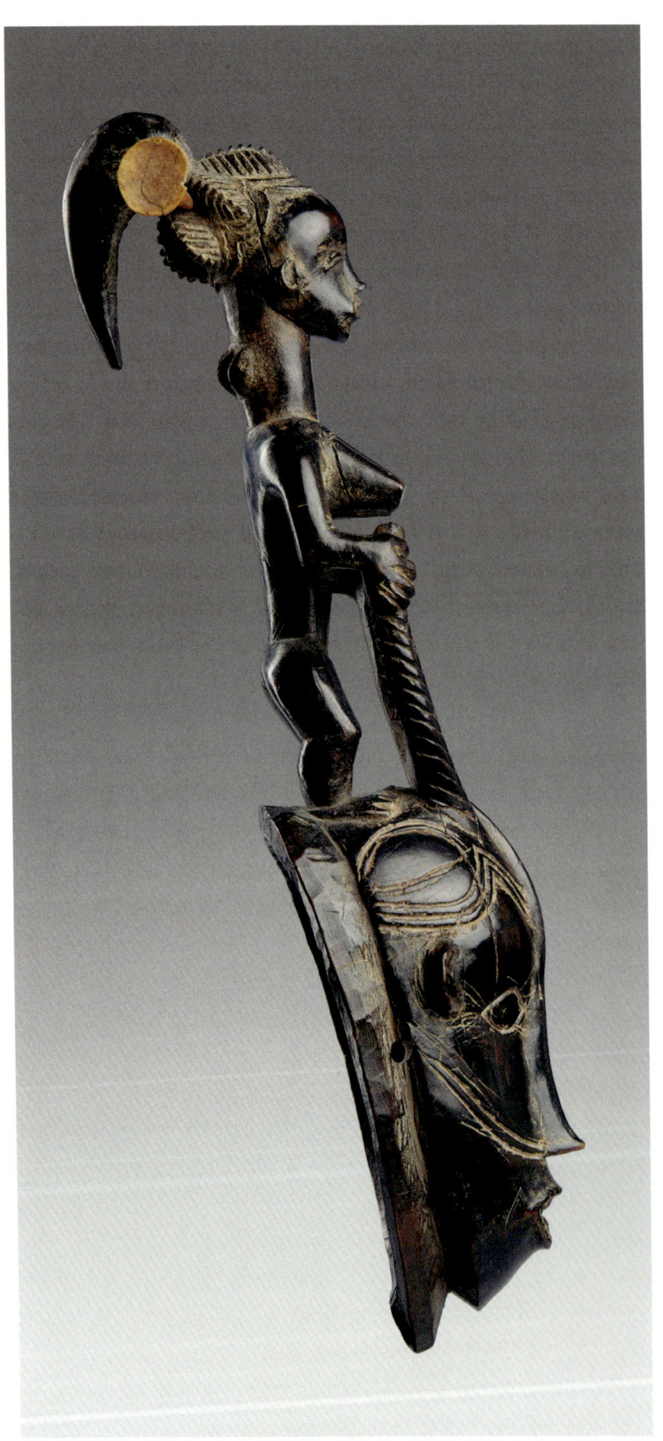

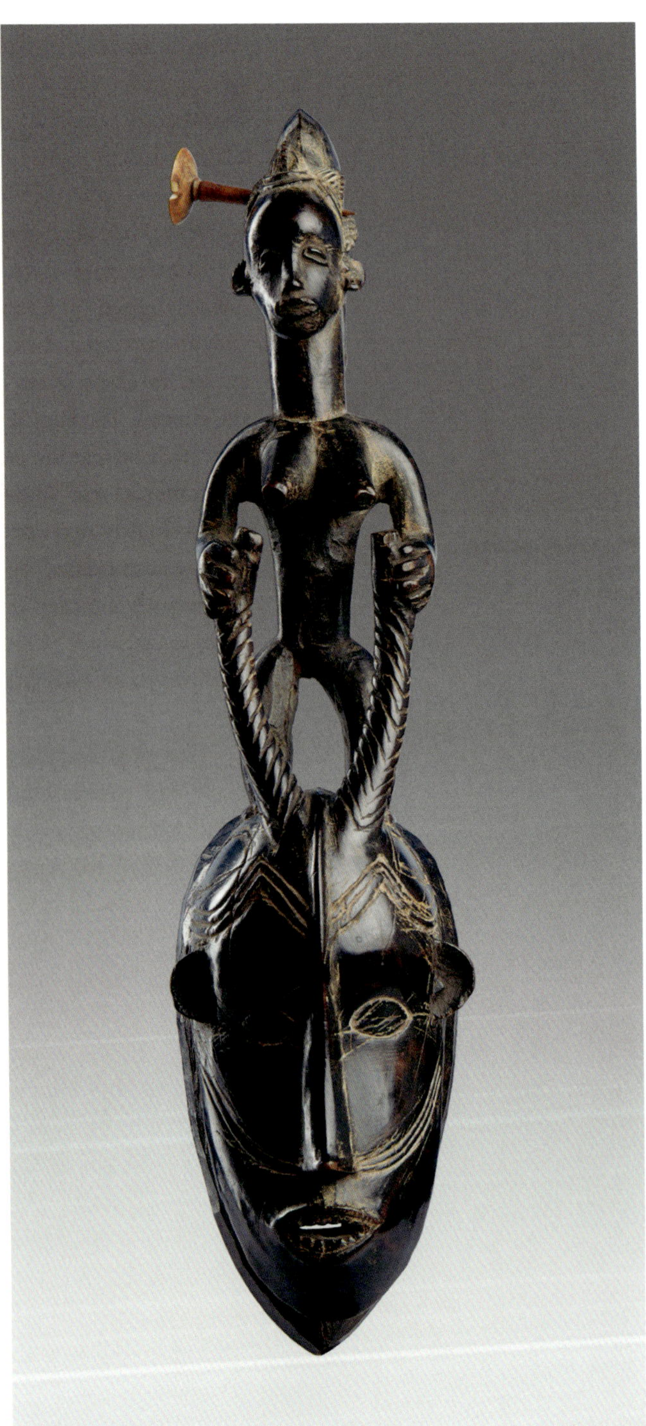

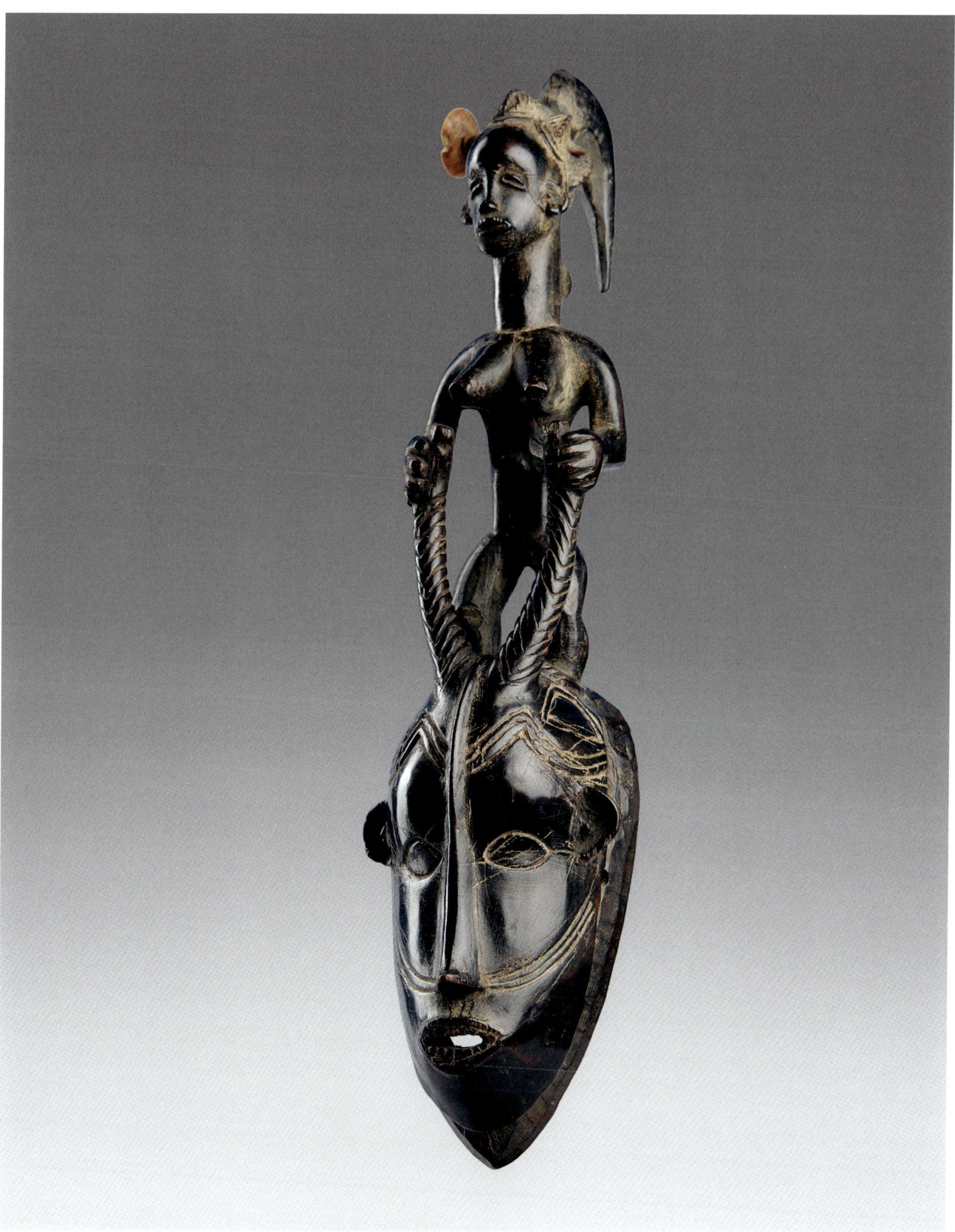

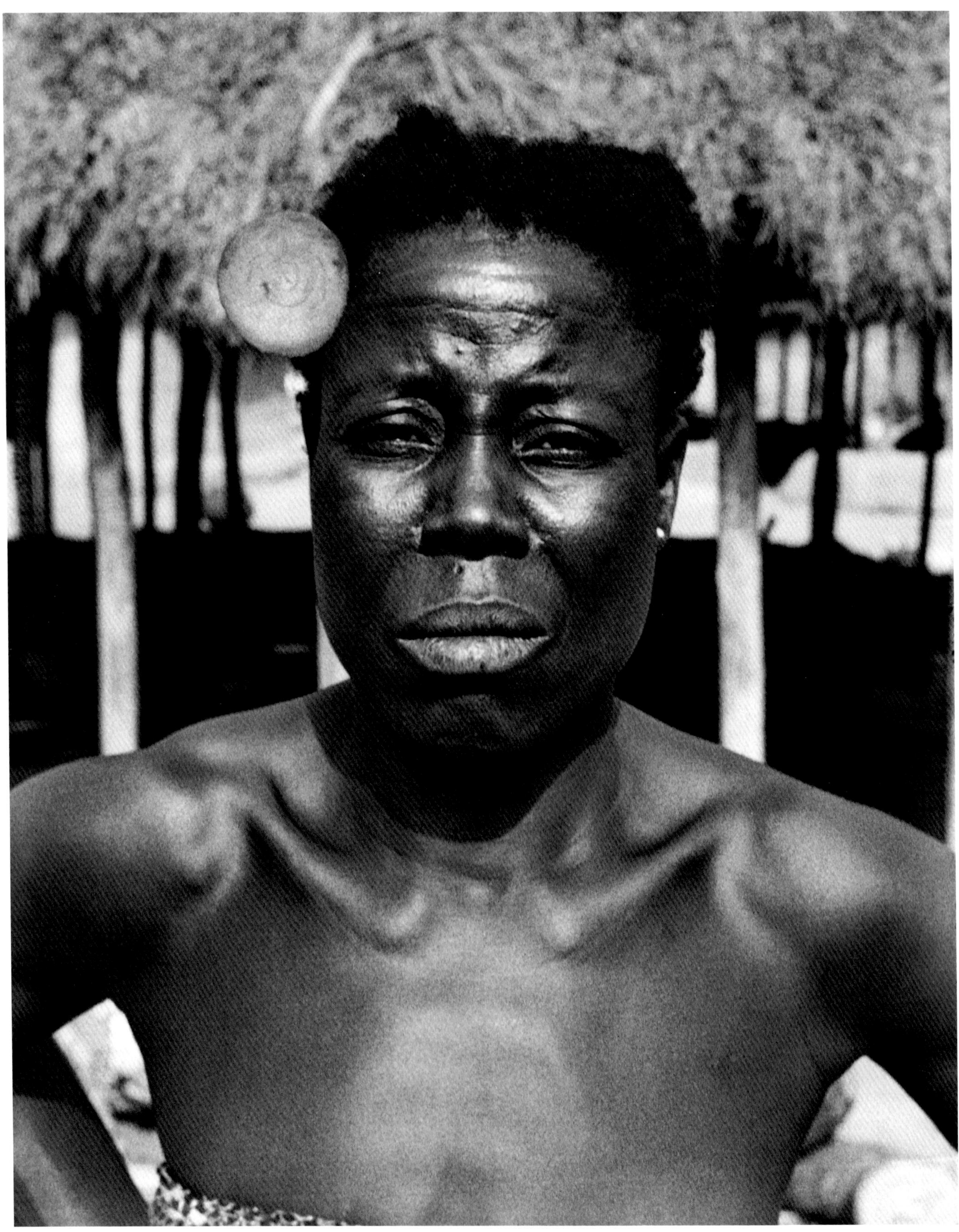

Hairdressing of Betiaba, chief's wife
Guro village, Ivory Coast, 1965
CC by Hans Himmelheber
Inv. FHH 328-27, Museum Rietberg, Zürich
www.africa-art-archive.ch

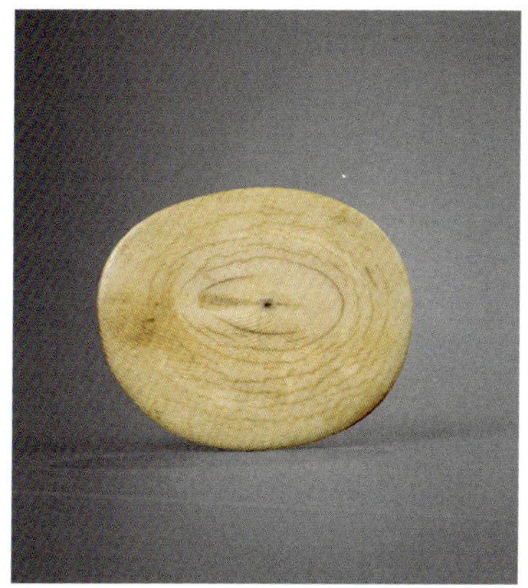

Pin (detail)
Guro, Ivory Coast
Ivory
9 × 6 cm

the extremely graceful profile found on Guro loom pulleys, which are fashioned like jewellery, the delicacy of the composition, and the smoothness of the lines indicate that this is a Guro mask. Its extremely rare style is testament to the lively mutual influence of nearby areas,[8] in this case the close cultural links the Guro had with their neighbours the Bete to the southwest. It illustrates the extraordinary inventiveness of Guro artists, who were able to exploit the infinite pool of forms available to them to inform and renew their plastic work.

SELECTED BIBLIOGRAPHY

Barbier Jean-Paul, ed. *Arts de la Côte d'Ivoire dans les collections Barbier-Mueller.* Volumes I and II. Geneva, 1993.

Bouttiaux Anne-Marie, ed. *La dynamique des masques en Afrique occidentale.* Tervuren: Royal Museum for Central Africa, 2013.

Bouttiaux Anne-Marie. *Guro.* Milan: 5 Continents Editions, 2016.

Fischer Eberhard and Homberger Lorenz. *Die Kunst der Guro, Elfenbeinküste.* Zurich: Rietberg Museum, 1985.

Fischer Eberhard. *Guro: Mask, Performances and Master Cavers in Ivory Coast.* Zurich: Rietberg Museum, 2008.

Fischer Eberhard and Homberger Lorenz. *Les Maîtres de la sculpture de Côte d'Ivoire.* Paris: Musée du quai Branly; Skira, 2015.

Goy Bertrand. In *Binoche et Giquello,* 29 June 2021, p. 50, lot no. 45, p. 31.

Neyt François. *Trésors de Côte d'Ivoire.* Brussels: Fonds Mercator, 2014.

Vogel M. Susan. *Baule: African Art/Western Eyes.* New Haven: Yale Art Gallery, 1997.

1 Bouttiaux 2016, p. 129, pl. 12.
2 Bouttiaux, op. cit., p. 23; Fischer, 2008, p. 267 and 271.
3 Fischer, op. cit., p. 268.
4 See a statue of a standing figure in the former Merton Simpson Collection for a very similar example.
5 Vogel 1997, p. 283.
6 Among the rare examples displaying a similar subject (a superstructure showing a female figure gripping the horns of the base mask, corresponding to Fischer's fifth type of 'emblem') to be found in Western collections, it is worth mentioning two Duonou-Guro masks collected by lieutenant Berthier de Montrigaud between 1911 and 1913 and acquired by Félix Fénéon, a specimen in the Afrika Museum in Berg en Dal, a mask in the former Lucien Van de Velde Collection, and a mask in the former Jay C. Leff Collection, which however portrays a male figure.
7 This medial forehead line is also found on several pieces made by the We and southern Dan.
8 Similarities between the female figures topping the Zuhu masks listed and the very old ones on the Senufo and Dioula *kpélié* or *kodal*, depending on the region, have also been pointed out.

Acknowledgements

To Africa.

To the artists and sculptors from Ivory Coast, Ghana, and Nigeria.

To Alain-Michel Boyer, Jacqueline Boyer, Sarah Boukamel, Faouzi Borro, Valentine Plisnier, François Neyt assisted by Anne Heuse; to Eric Ghysels, publisher of 5 Continents Editions, and to his team, Aldo Carioli, Astrid Cotterli, Lucia Moretti, and Fayçal Zaouli; to the photographers Alfred Weissenegger, Daniel Ilinca, and Valentin Clavairolles; to Françoise Barrier, Alex Arthur, Yves Bernard Debie of *Tribal Art Magazine* for their precious advice; to the archivists Guy, Titus, and Loes Van Rijn; to Claude Henri Pirat; to Lucas and Philippe Ratton and Lucas Ratton gallery; to Didier and Alexandre Claes at Didier Claes gallery.
To Joris Burla at Rietberg Museum in Zurich; to Joëlle Fischer at Basel Mission Archives; to Dr Jocelyn Dudding at Museum of Archaeology & Anthropology, Cambridge University; to Sokhna Fall at l'Institut fondamental d'Afrique noire – Cheikh Anta Diop in Dakar; to Haley Steinhilber, National Museum of African Art, Smithsonian Institution in Washington.

To our unwavering supporters: Séverine Wolters, Michel Assenmaker, Colette Ghysels, Madalena and Isabel Borges Coutinho Casaca, Victoria and Olivier Emsix-Mestreit, Nicolas Roosens, Audrey Guttman, André, Martine and Jacques Rouayroux, Belanna Irizarry.
To our departed friends: Merton Simpson (1928–2013) and Michel Boulanger (1944–2024).

To Mina and Samir and their children Lamya, Nada, Yasmeen, Ali, and Amir Borro in Brussels.
To Issam, Nagela, Najoua, and Faouzi Borro in Abidjan.

And to all those who contributed to this project and wished to remain unnamed.

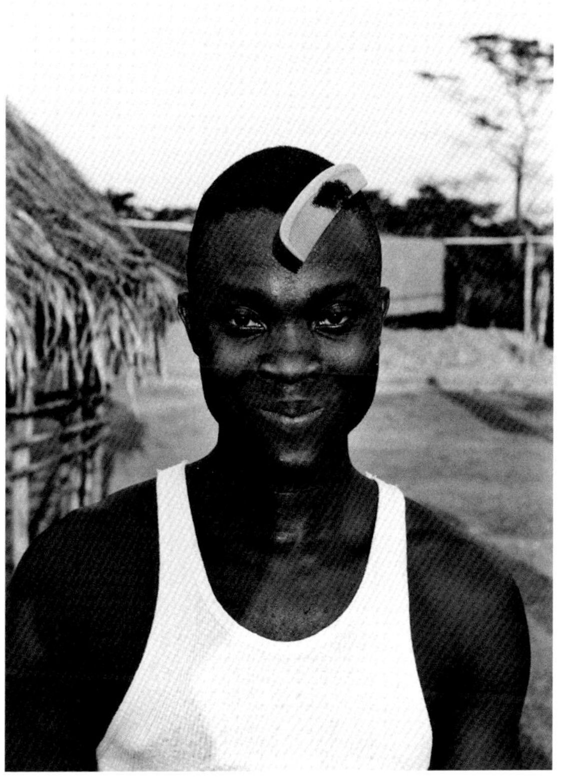

Young man, Liberia, 1952
CC by Hans Himmelheber
Inv. FHH 220-5, Museum Rietberg, Zürich
www.africa-art-archive.ch

5 Continents Editions
Editor-in-Chief
Aldo Carioli

Design and Art Direction
Fayçal Zaouali

Editor
Lucia Moretti

English translation
Julian Comoy

Editing
Charles Gute

Pre-press
Pixel Studio, Bresso, Italy

5 Continents Editions
Piazza Caiazzo 1
20124 Milan, Italy
www.fivecontinentseditions.com

ISBN 978-88-7439-677-1

Distributed by ACC Art Books throughout the world, excluding Italy. Distributed in Italy and Switzerland by Messaggerie Libri S.p.A.

Printed on Sappi Magno Satin 170 gr paper and bound in Italy in July 2025 by Tecnostampa – Pigini Group Printing Division, Loreto – Trevi for 5 Continents Editions S.r.l., Milan

sappi | Magno Satin

Pages 52-53
From a map of West Africa, late 19th – early 20th century, by Gustave-Léon Niox (1840-1921)

Front cover
Comb, Fanti, Akan, Ghana
Wood, 25 × 10.5 cm
(*see pages 72–73*)

Back cover
Comb, Attie, Akan, Ivory Coast
Wood, 16 × 9 cm
(*see page 129*)